YOU ARE BEAUTIFUL AND YOU ARE ALONE

JENNIFER OTTER BICKERDIKE

YOU ARE BEAUTIFUL AND YOU ARE ALONE

THE BIOGRAPHY OF NICO

New York

Hachette Books
Hachette Book Group
1290 Avenue of the Americas
New York, NY 10104
HachetteBooks.com
Twitter.com/HachetteBooks
Instagram.com/HachetteBooks

First U.S. Edition: August 2021

Originally published in the United Kingdom by Faber & Faber Limited in June 2021

Published by Hachette Books, an imprint of Perseus Books, LLC, a subsidiary
of Hachette Book Group, Inc. The Hachette Books name and logo is a
trademark of the Hachette Book Group.

The Hachette Speakers Bureau provides a wide range of authors for speaking events.
To find out more, go to www.hachettespeakersbureau.com or call (866) 376-6591.

The publisher is not responsible for websites (or their content)
that are not owned by the publisher.

Library of Congress Control Number: 2021938268

ISBNs: 978-0-306-92290-9 (hardcover); 978-0-306-92289-3 (ebook)

Printed in the United States of America

LSC-C

Printing 1, 2021

In loving memory of two of the best people ever
Trevor Hart and Hiroshi Narita
I miss you every day

CONTENTS

Introduction   1

  I: Enter   7
 II: Exalted   85
III: Existence   203
IV: End   289

Epilogue   393
Acknowledgments   395
Notes   401

Sources   421
Source notes   447
List of plates   489

YOU ARE BEAUTIFUL AND YOU ARE ALONE

INTRODUCTION

> What I have in common with Nico is the understanding of her
> furious frustration at not being recognized.
>
> Marianne Faithfull

I was very, very late discovering Nico. One night, I was out with
a friend, discussing our personal female rock heroines. I was both
surprised and mortified to find that compared to all of the men in
music that we loved, the list of women we could come up with was
woefully short. Upon getting home, I did a bit of research to see
what fantastic females I had forgotten. I came to Nico. She was in
the Velvet Underground for that one crucial record; she had that
Chelsea Girl album. But what else? I started to look a bit deeper into
her life, my years as a PhD student researching pop culture making
it natural for me to crawl down the rabbit hole of this enigma's history. At the beginning, I assumed I would unearth the usual story
of rock highs, lows, a comeback, and an eventual career playing at
county fairs and heritage gigs. What I found instead was a life and
a myth that became more surreal the further I dug.

Almost every aspect of Nico's life has been haphazardly
recorded, if accurately chronicled at all. The repetition of the same
anecdotes has somehow mutated random incidents specific to
contextualized moments into grand brushstrokes of overarching
truisms. The more I tried to figure out who the "real" Nico was,
the greater the rupture became between the oft-repeated myths,

the few documented facts, and the personal memories of those who knew her best. Any new crumb of information was hard-won and precious, often the result of weeks spent digging in dusty and long-forgotten archives, months of scanning through old microfiche, and countless emails and phone calls, all in the hope of discovering something not previously known. More than a hundred new interviews were carried out in pursuit of establishing a more well-rounded understanding of the icon. What emerged was a didactic example of apathetic misogyny and stereotyping on the part of written history, a narrative that lazily rests upon the familiar, salacious, and utterly predictable realms of sex, drugs, and rock'n'roll excess, without acknowledgment of the unique and often unnerving life circumstances of the singer. At first it seemed too simplistic to blame the quagmire separating the two versions of Nico on nationality, misogyny, and expected cultural expectations. Yet the more I learned about her, the more obvious this explanation became. There were very few women writing about and documenting rock music at the time, and even fewer brave enough to break societal expectations of what or how a female could be as an artist. This meant an often one-sided narrative was created and perpetuated about Nico, as there were no other female voices to challenge it or offer a counterpoint.

From her name to the diametrically opposed personas she inhabited over the span of her life, it is hard to discern who the *real* Nico was. It has not been an easy task to tease apart fiction and folklore from often long-forgotten fact. The majority of Nico's life was spent as a solo artist, with little formal documentation. There are also numerous conflicting claims about her, ranging from when she was born (1938? 1942?) to her political ideas (was she a Nazi? Or a Jew herself?). And though hardship and horror are common threads throughout Nico's story, so are moments of humanity and humor, such as the singer's love for making brown rice and vegetarian soup ("Always have an onion," she once told a friend), or her

2

attempt at seducing a potential partner with a box of Cadbury's Roses chocolates.

Several aspects of Nico's life are certain. Born in Cologne to parents of Spanish and Yugoslavian descent, Christa Päffgen carried with her the guilt and unease of being brought into the world and raised in Germany during World War II. Her father, Willi, was drafted into the *Wehrmacht*; she never saw him again. This would haunt her for the rest of her life. "Nico" was a persona, created one day in 1956, when fashion photographer Herbert Tobias suggested to the then teenage aspiring German model that she should change her name, causing a protective shield between the fragile survivor and the public character to be forged. The *nom de guerre* paid off, as Nico began landing modeling jobs for fashion hard hitters across Europe, including *Vogue* and *Elle*. She moved from modeling to acting, most notably scoring an unforgettable cameo in Federico Fellini's 1960 art house masterpiece *La Dolce Vita*. After being encouraged by a lover to try her hand at singing, Nico eventually found herself at artist Andy Warhol's notorious Factory in New York, a hub for outsiders, creatives and nonconformists. Warhol and his collaborator Paul Morrissey had just decided to work with a then unknown band, the Velvet Underground. The duo agreed to fund the fledgling group, if they let Nico front them as the "visual element."

While the Warhol days boast ample images, anecdotes and interviews, the later, perhaps more "authentic" version of Nico—the *two decades* spent touring the globe as a solo artist—has been virtually lost and rarely discussed. This has created a vacuum, allowing Nico's legacy and impact as a cultural icon to be often solely defined by her supposed superficiality, which sees her cast as a racist junkie who slept with a myriad of famous men. Her fellow Velvets Lou Reed and John Cale are consistently hailed as "American masters," "poets," and "legends," their creativity and talent the main focus for the dispersion of such accolades. When physical appearance, sexual

3

exploits, political leanings, and substance abuse issues are woven into the overall tapestry of their stories, it is often as part of the expected journey for any "real" artist. Yet Nico's genius contributions to rock culture are often overlooked, her value to contemporary music trivialized to her simply being a beautiful mannequin for the Velvet Underground.

Nico's five albums post-*Girl*—many of which are now considered undervalued treasures by critics—showcase a polluted, heroin-addicted, henna-haired singer with a repertoire of songs that are focused on the morbid and the dark. It is the demise of her legendary appearance, not the music, that is often remembered. Though her otherworldly beauty granted Nico access and opportunity, she also saw it as a hugely problematic attribute that prevented her from being taken as a serious artist—not just a female performer with a pretty face. Her apparent need to destroy this valued asset was not lost on those around her. As the years went by, the few press write-ups Nico received often hastened to note that, along with her deteriorating fan base, increasing age and fifteen-year opiate addiction, she had "lost" her fresh-faced youth. Even her former benefactor Warhol called her old and fat in 1980. People rarely saw or acknowledged the woman who could speak seven different languages fluently, read classic literature voraciously and finish the *New York Times* crossword puzzle in near record time.

Nico's continued determination to make music, seemingly against all odds—whether fueled by artistic ambition or a need to fund her drug abuse—along with the empty concert halls, abusive fans and the uncertain and often perilous reality of being an aging artist and addict, have often been cast aside in our cultural memory. This makes her story a chilling modern narrative on the fetishism of beauty, ageism and the romanticization of death, at the cost of a talented, lonely and eccentric musician's life. As a solo artist, Nico created mesmerizing and thoroughly unique projects that inspired a generation of artists, including Henry Rollins, Morrissey, and Marc

Almond. She was a true bohemian who deserves proper recognition for her brave, ballsy, often weird, and always deeply personal albums, which created a template for the modern genres of rock, punk and goth.

Her untimely death in Ibiza in 1988—not from a drug overdose, but instead the result of a bizarre bicycle accident resulting in a severe cerebral hemorrhage—has elevated Nico in the context of popular culture from junkie/hanger-on/has-been to legend. In 1966, Warhol proclaimed her a "Superstar" simply for being "Nico," yet it is Nico's determination to be an artist in her own right, regardless of commercial success, pop accessibility or societal norms, that has made her posthumous legacy authentically iconic. The *real* story of Nico is one of determination, self-destruction and belief in one's artistic vision, at any cost.

I: ENTER

1

Margarete "Grete" Berta Schulz was born on January 10, 1910, in Hardenberg, an area of Germany that is now part of Poland. She was the third of eight children, small in stature, with the same high cheekbones and sultry lips that would bring her daughter global fame. Grete met Hermann Wilhelm "Willi" Päffgen in Berlin. They fell in love. From the very tall Willi Nico would inherit her height, wide-set gray eyes, and distinctive bone structure. But there were some major problems: Willi was the rebellious son of a well-heeled, well-known Catholic family, prominent for owning a major brewery in Cologne; Grete was a Protestant from a humble background—and married.

Grete's first husband was painter Rodolf Paul Emil Schulz. Rodolf treated Grete very well, and the two seemed happy. However, upon meeting Willi, Grete became completely besotted. Following her heart instead of rationality, she left her devoted spouse in order to run away with Willi to his hometown of Cologne.

The mystery of Nico's actual date and place of birth has been woven into her myth, as if to prove the consistency of inconsistency, even from the womb, of a life patchworked with half-truths and fabrications. It has been purported that she was born in Cologne in 1938 or 1942, Budapest in 1943 or 1944, Berlin in 1943, Cologne in 1942 or Poland in 1938. Not only the date but also the surname are inconsistent across various texts, noted as being "18 October," "15 March," "...Pafgens, or maybe Pfaffen." By actually tracking down the formal German documents Nico's true origins have now been clearly established.

From as early as 1880, German citizens had to fill out a *Meldekarte*, a personal registration card documenting a variety of events, including marriage, death, changes of address, and divorce. It also records individual characteristics, such as religion and occupation, and includes the name of the head of the household. The birth certificate—or *Geburtsurkunde*—is always based on the information that is written on the *Meldekarten* of the parents. The personnel in the registry office look at the *Personenstandregister*—birth registrations from the *Meldekarten*—and then write the certificate. While there have been numerous birth dates and places given in various press pieces, this registry provides an incontestable document showing when and where Nico arrived. The third entry on Margarete Berta Schulz's card states: "Born on October 16 1938 at 17.30h in Köln-Lindenthal, Kerpenerstraße 32 a girl. The child was given the name Christa." Kerpenerstrasse, in Köln-Lindenthal, is in Cologne.

The registry documents contain a wealth of information about Nico's family during her early years. Nico being born out of wedlock has been a long-standing part of her "history," her illegitimacy perpetuated by repeated retellings across various biographies. However, this is not entirely accurate. As of October 8, 1937, Grete is listed on her *Meldekarte* as being legally divorced from her first husband, Rodolf. The form marks a difference between children born in and out of wedlock. If the parents are married, the date of their wedding is included on the form. If the mother is without a spouse at the time of the child's arrival, only her date of birth is included. On Nico's birth certificate Grete's nuptials with Rodolf are listed as "the marriage of the parents on May 17, 1933 in Berlin, registry office B lin XIII B (or 13), Nr. 437"—though he is not her birth father. Thus, Nico formally started life as Christa Schulz. Further down the *Meldekarte*, however, this line is crossed out—most likely a reference to the dissolved Schulz/Schulz union. There is no further mention of Christa in relation to Rodolf Schulz.

Another addendum on the birth certificate from April 1939

clearly substantiates Nico's place on the Päffgen family tree. It states that Margarete Berta Schulz married the clerk Hermann Wilhelm Päffgen on December 30, 1938. Due to an order of a local court in Cologne, from March 1939, the child was now considered *ehelich*, meaning "born within the marriage." Thanks to this declaration, Nico became officially, *legitimately* Päffgen. Grete's younger sister Helma Wolff remembers that this news was not welcomed by Willi's family. They were horrified by the young man's nuptials, even more so when they heard of the arrival of an infant daughter. Else Päffgen, Willi's sister (Christa's aunt), insisted that the newborn was not her brother's. The Päffgen coterie pressured the new groom to annul the marriage, arguing that Grete was surely only interested in getting her hands on the family's money. Grete and Willi's divorce is listed on legal documents as going through on May 21, 1941.

Despite the Päffgens' attempts to distance themselves from Nico, she was, according to the formal German documents, legally Willi's daughter. However, the idea of displacement and rejection was very real for Nico, her trajectory of "*ohne feste Adresse*"—"without a fixed address," be that place, family ties or nationality—seeming to have been set in motion from the earliest moments of her life.

The guilt, shame, and disgust associated with her heritage were a constant in Nico's life, an unsettling commonality for many descendants of the Nazi era. She was arguably attempting to separate her personal beliefs from those imposed upon her as an impressionable child, as social currents changed post World War II. However, no matter how valiant her desire to break from her origins may have been, the ramifications of the violence witnessed by Nico in early life cannot be forgotten.

The brutality and genocide of the Nazi regime began less than a month after Nico's birth. On November 9, 1938, forty-eight hours of horrific attacks began on Jews throughout areas of Germany where the Nazis had already installed strongholds. The event is now remembered as Kristallnacht, or the Night of Broken Glass—a reference to the shattered windows and large shards of glass strewn across the streets after many Jewish-owned establishments were destroyed during the two days of carnage. Bloodthirsty rioters attacked Jewish homes, hospitals, and school buildings with sledgehammers, destroying 267 places of worship throughout Germany, Austria, and the Sudetenland—including the synagogue in Cologne.

Located just a hundred meters away from Meister Gerhard Strasse, where the infant Nico and her mother were living at the time, the holy building was burned to the ground like others of its ilk that appalling night. In total, over seven thousand Jewish businesses were either wrecked or damaged. The official death toll from the first night alone was estimated to be ninety-one Jews, with many historians placing the figure much higher. By the end of the atrocity, more than thirty thousand Jewish men had been arrested and sent to the newly constructed concentration camps. In retrospect, the Night of Broken Glass marked the very public beginning of Nazi Germany's overarching racial policies and was the start of Hitler's Final Solution and the Holocaust.

While the Jewish community tried to come to terms with the devastation, Cologne kicked off its annual carnival. The Närrische Jahreszeit—which translates as the foolish, crazy or fifth season—commences every November 11 at 11:11 a.m. 1938 was no exception. Carnival was celebrated by bars suspending their closing time for the duration of the festival, while a massive parade caroused through the streets of the city, featuring people dressed up in colorful costumes. Though families, homes, and livelihoods had just been destroyed and innocents taken to the death camps, that year Nazi Germany reveled in its annual shenanigans, partying drunkenly into the early hours of the morning.

The young Päffgen family spent the first eighteen months of Christa's life living at Luxemburger Strasse 26, in Cologne. The onset of World War II forced Willi—barely twenty years old himself—to join the German army, or *Wehrmacht*. Nico recalled her mother receiving a package of fancy underwear and dates from Willi in 1942. The next communication was far grimmer, bringing the macabre news of Willi's fate. According to Grete's sister Helma Wolff, née Schulz, "My sister was notified by the *Wehrmacht* that he [Willi] was killed in action. But he wasn't dead. He was injured, but alive."

In the summer of 2000, Helma was interviewed by Christian Biadacz, who kindly agreed to share with me these previously unpublished recollections. Her memories provide crucial insights into the lives of both her sister and her niece. Before her own death in 2015, at 101 years of age, Helma never clarified how she knew that Willi was not killed instantly on the battlefield. His actual fate has never been confirmed, the void of uncertainty allowing for various renditions of his demise to be circulated. One story speculated that Willi was shot to death by his commanding officer in 1942 after a bullet from the gun of a French sniper entered his brain, while another vaguely claims he suffered head injuries that proved fatal. Helma went on to say, "We assume they [the Nazis] killed him. That was common practice under Hitler, wasn't it? Any man who wasn't fit to serve was useless."

Nico often repeated these family anecdotes, still enraged almost half a century later at the death of her "dear father" at the hands of the "German Pigs." She firmly believed—or at least *needed* to believe—that her father was a victim of, not a participant in, the Nazi regime. In her personal notes, Nico continuously had Willi as a sympathizer, a heroic rescuer—not a murderer—of those persecuted during World War II. Though never given the opportunity to know her father as anything more than a ghost, Nico wrote that she felt they were "very much alike." Helma confirms this, saying, "He was an adventurer. He had no roots. Sometimes I see him in Christa. She looks like her father."

With Willi removed from their life, Grete found herself a single parent to young Christa. According to her *Meldekarte*, she had Christa placed at the Kinderheim Sülz orphanage for seven months, starting on May 15, 1940, and ending shortly before Christmas, on December 7. A likely reason for her doing so could have been the dire financial circumstances the young mother surely found herself in. In its own brochure, the institution, founded in 1917, sounds like a cross between an Aryan finishing school and an idyllic country club, with its 40,000 square meters of facilities, including an eight-room school, a gymnasium, a swimming pool, a garden, and a pigsty. For the boys, the educational goal was to learn a "respectable" trade; for the girls, it was to acquire domestic skills in order to prepare them for the profession of domestic helper and their later inevitable role of housewife.

When Nico was there, Kinderheim Sülz was the biggest orphanage in Europe, housing up to a thousand children at once. The orphanage's director, Friedrich Tillmann, was a deeply Catholic member of the National Socialist German Workers' Party and attempted to instill his pious values into all of his charges. He had an apartment on the orphanage's premises and was an office manager for the Zentraldienststelle T4 in Berlin. This was a Nazi cover organization that organized and registered the systematic killing of approximately 216,000 people they considered "unworthy of life." This included prisoners, "degenerates," dissidents, and people with congenital, cognitive, and physical disabilities. As manager of the group, Tillmann's duties included inspecting the *Vergasungsanstalten*—gas chambers—used in the concentration camps.

Photographs taken of Kinderheim Sülz during the years that Nico was there showcase Nazi pride. One image features a large group of boys, ranging from toddlers to teenagers, all proudly standing straight in their well-pressed Nazi uniforms. Another black and white frame captures young kids, again in military apparel, standing at attention and looking to the left at an out-of-shot authority figure. A panoramic portrait of the entire grand complex prominently features two large Third Reich flags.

The orphanage was destroyed by bombs in 1944, several years after Nico left. Though it was later rebuilt, the facility was permanently closed in 2009, under a dark shadow of the documented, systematic mistreatment of its vulnerable residents, stretching back to Nico's time there. An investigation into the establishment included interviews with 150 former inhabitants. A shocking 120 of them recalled horrifying instances of abuse, rape, and violence committed by the priests and nuns upon the children housed at the orphanage.

The only other acknowledgment of her time there is in a line Nico included in her diary. She writes: "My mother came to see me every Sunday, when she was not at the factory making weapons."

In an interview, Graham Dowdall, who played in Nico's band the Faction in the 1980s, remembered her saying "something about a factory in Berlin"—corroboration of the line in the diary. The company Nico was referring to could be Deutz AG, an engine manufacturer based not far from Kinderheim Sülz in Porz, Cologne.[1] During World War II, it was ordered by the Nazis to produce artillery, making it a likely place for Grete to work during the months she was separated from her child, as she attempted to eke out a living, impossible though it may have seemed at the time.[2]

3

Before she was even two years old, Christa had lost her father in World War II, been excommunicated from the Päffgen family, and been separated from her mother and forced to live in a violent orphanage. Yet, once reunited with Grete, the brutality did not end, as the war became more intense. Nico later recalled hiding in the family bathtub as explosives rained down around the small apartment where they lived in Cologne.

Helma Wolff was already in Berlin with her son (Nico's cousin) Ulrich, or "Ulli" for short. Like Grete, Helma had lost her husband in the war, and she found herself bringing up Ulli alone. However, she had managed to enroll her son in a school, find a job at a nearby military base as a secretary, and move into an apartment she described as being comprised of "one and a half rooms." It was 1940 when Grete appeared at Helma's door, seeking refuge for herself and Christa. For a short time, the two sisters shared the cramped space with their children, who were just six months apart in age. It was not long, however, until they received a letter from their father, beseeching them to leave the city and return to their home in the comparatively rural German town of Lübbenau.

Fifty years later, Helma recalled the daily terror and near brushes with death during those last days in Berlin, as the Germans struggled to remain in control. "The air attacks grew stronger," she said. "One night I had to run through an inferno of flames with my son in my arms. The strength of the flames lifted us up in the air. I had the sensation we were already burning. Later, my workplace was destroyed." According to Grete's *Meldekarte*, she and Christa fled the capital for the family abode on December 7, 1940. Helma and Ulli followed six months later.

Though only an hour's drive from Berlin, Lübbenau, at first glance, seemed worlds apart from the war-torn city. Leafy, green and lush, the town is located within the Spreewald forest. Nico described No. 4 Güterbahnhofstrasse—her grandparents' house— as a massive four-story brick building with a large outdoor garden, situated alongside the local freight railway line. As an adult, she would often comment to friends that passing trains reminded her of childhood.

At the time of their arrival, Albert, Nico and Ulli's grandfather, or "Opa,"[3] as they called him, was a railroad switchman for his town. His job was to check the tail lights of the trains as they lumbered by his assigned station. Albert's southern position controlled a vital intersection during the war, with one line taking trains from Berlin to Görlitz and Poland, the other to Dresden and Czechoslovakia. When the Reich invaded Prague, he had to direct trains full of troops and guns, switching the tracks when Germany entered Poland. He saw huge carriages packed with Jews on their way to Silesia,[4] yet felt powerless to do anything: any questioning of authority could jeopardize the safety of his family.

It was mandatory for women to join in the war effort, hence both sisters spent their days away from home in different jobs. Helma continued in her position at the military station, commuting in and out of Berlin, while Grete was taken on by a factory near the house that built flying boats. This left the children in the care of their grandparents—Albert and grandmother Oma (her actual first name is unknown)—each youngster the other's main companion. "We spent a lot of time together, my aunt, Christa, my mother and me," says Ulli. "We [would play] in the courtyard. Christa was always afraid of the geese, which were roaming free. When we played, she was funny, foolish and silly. She liked to be entertained. She was a very giggly girl, but not in a relaxed way." Another favorite memory was of Ulli receiving literal bowl haircuts from Albert, an activity that would endlessly amuse his cousin.

Albert loomed large as both protective patriarch and childhood distraction, telling the children elaborate stories and classic German myths. Ulli recalls, "He was wonderful; the most entertaining part of our day was listening to him. You must bear in mind that there were few books around then, no children's comics, no magazines for us, a boring radio service, and, of course, no television. The cinema was very popular, but not in Lübbenau—we had to wait until we were back in Berlin. So our Opi was a fantastic source of entertainment to set our imaginations racing."

When not with her cousin or grandfather, Christa's favorite place to play was in the Gothic graveyard adjacent to the house. Filled with trees, flowers, and bushes, crumbling memorial statues and spiraling ivy, the tranquil environment provided plenty of stimulation for the young girl's blossoming imagination. "She spent so much time in there, sometimes just wandering around," Ulli remembers. "I can't think what she found to do. I think she enjoyed its quietness. On the other side of the house was all this machinery and movement, but here it was natural, and for children it held a certain mystery."

While the bucolic moments of family life provided some stability for the child, the daily realities of the war's atrocities burned into Christa's mind. Nico wrote about these early years, recalling in her diary:

In 1942, the trains passed our house to take the Jews to Auschwitz, I was only four years old, but my family and neighbors waited by the railroad fences to give them food and water, but the guards whipped them away from our reach. I remember very clearly how many hungry people I saw when the trains came to a halt. Freight trains and barbwire windows, the rail line to the camp has lost its tracks... The ribbon of death. I was sighing to my cousin Ulli and refused to wash with soap made from human bones, the material for clothing had been made from human hair, lampshades from human tattooed skin.

She goes on to vividly describe another macabre scene from her childhood, of "dead bodies lying on the sidewalk in Luebbenau, Berlin, any other small Village in Poland."

———

By the mid-1940s, the family was used to sporadic influxes of people coming into their town. Tourism in the region was spurred on by *Kraft durch Freude* ("Strength through Joy," abbreviated as KdF), an initiative set up by the German Labour Front, a government organization created to promote the ideals of the Nazi party. The notion behind the KdF was to make middle class leisure activities available to a wider swathe of the population. With its landscape of marshes, forests, pine trees, and sand dunes, Spreewald was a popular weekend escape for those taking advantage of the KdF scheme, all desperate for a temporary reprieve from the war. Tourism pamphlets from the time capitalized on the contrast between Berlin's war-torn urban rubble and the natural beauty of Spreewald, describing its inhabitants as "honest peasants" who "held fast to simple certainties in a land where sky and water meet by nature's sandbanks." Though the weekly invasion of KdF participants brought outsiders to the rural town, the war still seemed far removed.

This changed dramatically in 1944, when the Soviets began pushing the Germans back from some of their former strongholds across Europe. Information was slow to trickle into Lübbenau, and the family did not hear of the defeat of the Germans in Poland, France or Belgium, although refugees and lone soldiers began to appear in the town en route to Berlin. Autumn arrived. While the war raged around them, life went on. Ulli and Christa began school. The curriculum focused on indoctrinating children with the racial ideas of the Nazis and having them pledge allegiance to Hitler. Textbooks had been rewritten at the start of the Nazi regime, especially on the topics of history and biology, to reflect and promote Germany's "greatness," Aryan "supremacy," and antisemitism. Course work was separated by sex, similar to the teaching offered by the orphanage Nico had stayed at several years before. Boys were trained to be good soldiers, and they studied eugenics, physical education, and the Nazi rendition of history. From an early age, girls were taught to be good Aryan wives and mothers, with an emphasis on home economics, the omnipresent eugenics, and physical education.

By the start of 1945, the Allies had entered Germany, bringing the Nazi regime to its knees on its home turf. Most of the country was invaded by the Allies, specifically the Soviet troops who conquered the region. On April 30, the capture of the Reichstag—the German parliament building—signaled the defeat of Nazi Germany. Nazi soldiers who had been stationed in and around Spreewald began to leave, warning the townspeople of Lübbenau that the invading Russians would steal, rape, and pillage, thus spreading fear and trepidation throughout the native population. Thankfully, Albert's knowledge of the soldiers' language helped keep the family and their neighbors relatively safe. He would occasionally share stories, alcohol and food with the Russians to keep them on side. Yet Ulli has dark, dangerous memories of this time, saying how it "wasn't so nice. These Russian soldiers were looking for women. It was everywhere the same in those days."

Despite the relatively secure standing provided by Albert in Lübbenau, both Grete and Helma longed to get back to Berlin and left at the first chance they had.

The Päffgens returned to a Berlin that was a dystopian wasteland, the once vibrant city now described as a *Geisterstadt*—a "ghost town." As the target of continuous fighting throughout the duration of the war, more than 70,000 tons of bombs had been dropped on the capital alone. What had once been one of the largest and most modern cities in Europe was now unrecognizable. Every street was filled with rubble and debris, a landscape of crumbled buildings. About a third of the city had been leveled. 600,000 apartments had been destroyed, and only 2.8 million of the original population of 4.5 million occupied the city, most of them the wives, mothers, and children of deceased soldiers. The estimated total number of corpses caused by the air raids alone and left to rot on the streets ranged from 20,000 to 50,000.

The suicide of Adolf Hitler on April 30, 1945, secured the Allies' victory over Nazi Germany, making daily existence even more perilous, the streets filled with refugees and Russian soldiers. Though often historicized now as a moment of rebuilding and camaraderie, diaries from the period reveal a much darker reality for families like the Päffgens.[5] New records are still being found, uncovering the violent sexual assaults committed in Germany by the Allied forces— American, British, and French, as well as Russian—both during and after the war. In one set of notes that have resurfaced, an anonymous female journalist recounts how she and almost every woman she knew were repeatedly raped by the Russian servicemen flooding into the city. Her first assault is shocking, as she recalls being dragged from the basement she and her neighbors had been using as an air raid shelter. After screaming for help, she realized she was entirely on her own, as her familiars had already barricaded the door behind her. However, she writes, "better a Russky on top than a Yank overhead"—rape by the Russians deemed preferable to being blown apart by the American bombs. Such increased savagery was also interlinked with the ever-growing problem of starvation. Food was given first to the Russian troops. All other German residents were placed on a five-tier ration card system, with the highest tier reserved for intellectuals and artists; rubble women and *Schwerarbeiter* (manual workers) received the second-tier card, which was more valuable to them than the 12 Reichsmarks they received for cleaning up a thousand bricks; the lowest card, nicknamed the *Friedhofskarte* (cemetery ticket), was issued to housewives and the elderly. During this period, the average Berliner was around 6 to 9 kg (13 to 20 lb) underweight. Women between the ages of fifteen and fifty-five were ordered to get tested for sexually transmitted diseases, with one survivor recalling, "You needed the medical certificate to get the food stamps, and I remember that all the doctors doing these certificates had waiting rooms full of women."

Nico always claimed that, at the age of thirteen, she was raped by a Black American sergeant, who was charged, court-martialled and hanged; however, no record of the case has been found in the U.S. Army archives. Recent research, as well as newly uncovered personal documents from the period, both support Nico's assertion and provide a clear rationale for the lack of formal reports. At the time, in East Germany a lingering social stigma hung over anyone viewed to be criticizing the Soviet and American heroes who had defeated fascism. Such ideas were frowned upon and considered sacrilegious, leading few to report such crimes, and even fewer who would listen to any condemnation of the foreign saviors. This makes it probable that Nico was indeed a victim of this ghastly attack and likely knew or heard about others suffering similar assaults.

Upon returning to the German capital, Helma miraculously found her one and a half rooms in the neighborhood of Schöneberg intact. Unlike most of Berlin, Schöneberg was governed by the Americans, who ran the best black market in the city. Candy bars, cigarettes, and fruit juices were delicacies, with prices for certain items equivalent to an entire month's wages for many workers. Nico's memory of the time consisted of her first immersions into a foreign language: "I think the first English word I learned was 'Hershey.' Later I went to New York and I was shocked to see so many Hershey bars in rows, like they were nothing."[6]

The realities of post-war Germany were grim for the Päffgens. Helma remembered Grete and her daughter living in Nürnburger Strasse, in an apartment similar to her own. Though they were lucky to have any accommodation, the building was cold, leaky, and miserable, with rain often falling through the roof directly into the flat. For Grete, work was hard to find. Though she qualified for the full allotment of ration cards, food and supplies were tight in the Päffgen household. After procuring a sewing machine from the local black market, Grete began working as a seamstress, utilizing the apartment as her studio. Often spending fifteen-hour days toiling away on limited nourishment, the young mother made a name for herself in the city and began taking on commissions from more affluent neighbors. Christa was the beneficiary of her mother's talents, always turned out in impeccable clothing, which was often cobbled together from leftover scraps and old attire. Her wardrobe provided the young girl with some much-needed confidence, her appearance already being treated as an attribute of value, a currency to be used to best advantage. What Nico remembered from the period, however, was being painfully underweight and eternally hungry, as food production and distribution had been greatly impacted across the Continent by the years of fighting.

The nearby Berlin Opera House turned into a refuge for the girl. Music became an important part of life, as school did not offer any reprieve from her harsh daily existence. As an adult, Nico recalled her time at the Wilmersdorf-Schöneberg school as being a cheerless experience, saying, "In these schools nothing is suppressed. A cruel method of education: one is classified, and every child should stand on the same level. You cannot be different. Some children are peculiar. I was a very sad child—now I'm much happier—but they thought I was stubborn. I cannot explain it, it's all so far back."

Helma described her niece similarly, saying, "Christa was a very strange girl. From childhood. She once had a certain pride. She walked very upright. And she was either shy or conceited. Or both." In her diary, Nico agreed with her aunt's assessment, admitting that she had to "overcome mental hang-ups such as painful shyness, in my case."

The girl's first ambitions to leave Germany began to show fairly early, with Christa seeing a career as a prima ballerina as her ticket out of the country. Helma remembers, "At the age of twelve, she said, 'Mother, I would like to go to ballet, I would like to dance.' And my sister said, 'But you make great demands, my child. That costs a lot of money. How am I supposed to earn that?' But my sister thought, 'Maybe something will come of my daughter, maybe she has a talent,' and sent her to Tatjana Gsovsky, a great ballet dancer in Berlin."[7]

After a close inspection of young Christa, Gsovsky gave the devasting news to the anxious Päffgens: Christa was far too old to achieve her dream of being a prima ballerina. Gsovsky admonished Grete for not starting the girl on lessons sooner, as there was no hope of attaining such greatness unless the child had begun at the age of five. Grete blanched; survival had been the priority during the war, and extraneous activities like ballet had not been considered. But neither Päffgen was deterred, and Grete paid for a series of classes. Though on the back foot because of her late start, Christa tried very hard, often coming home sweaty after her sessions. She showed natural talent, yet attaining the top spot was an impossible idea without years of formative training. Once she realized she would never achieve her goal, Christa stopped attending. "Christa wanted to move on to something she could conquer and excel at," said Helma. "I have set myself the goal of always making the most of something. And if that's not possible, then I just quit," the girl told her aunt.

Gsovsky's devasting verdict left Christa seeking another way out of Germany. Her prima ballerina dream in shreds, she decided to exploit her burgeoning asset of striking good looks to attain financial mobility and freedom.

5

As an adolescent, Christa began working on some of the attributes that would become integral to her later "Nico" persona. Helma Wolff pinpointed the time when the deep, baritone pronunciation, which was synonymous with the singer's work, began. "It started about the age of twelve," she recalled. "She often came to me after school and asked me in her strange pronunciation, 'Aunt Helma, is Ulli also there [said using elongated vowels]?' She always sang like that." Though "as a child she had a dark voice," Aunt Helma still tried to get the pre-teen girl to "talk reasonably, say the words short." Grete also noticed the difference in her daughter, but simply wrote off the odd behavior as a symptom of impending puberty. Nico later reflected on this time, stating, "When I was young in Berlin I was not interested in many boys. Well, I was interested, but nothing more. I was shy. I have always been shy, this has been my difficulty. Some people think I am distant, while I think I am shy."

Though admittedly a bit reticent, the determined and innovative young girl set her sights on trying to connect with the local fashionable set, spending time on the most aspirational streets in Berlin. Filled with shops, fashion houses, hotels, and restaurants, the thoroughfares provided a glimpse into a tantalizing world, far away from the atrocities the young teen had seen and experienced. Christa also began haunting key shopping ports of call religiously, praying and hoping to be noticed by anyone who might be able to help her. Helma recounted, "She took walks on the Kurfürstendamm,[8] she went window-shopping. She had no friends, she just went by herself." Another favorite spot for the teen was Berlin's elite shopping center, the Kaufhaus des Westens (Department Store of the West, or KaDeWe for short). Like its upscale cousins Harrods of London and Bergdorf Goodman of New York, the KaDeWe catered to a well-heeled clientele keen to snap up the latest and greatest fashions. With her tall stature, graceful body, and high cheekbones, Christa attracted a lot of attention, with Helma remembering, "Christa was always noticed by everyone. What a proud child this is. A uniquely beautiful girl . . . You couldn't miss it."

———

Considered one of the foremost German fashion designers of the post-war period, Heinz Oestergaard catered to a wealthy clientele and celebrities. Housed within the KaDeWe was his "salon," where his newest pieces were featured. Instead of immobile plastic dummies, Oestergaard used good-looking young women to model his creations for potential customers, yet still referred to them as "mannequins" or "dummies." However, any job with Oestergaard was highly sought after, and his agents were constantly looking for new talent to inject into the daily fashion shows occurring within the sacred rooms. Christa caught the eye of one agent as he was planning the KaDeWe autumn show of 1953. Finally, her persistence had paid off.

Once she began, Christa soon saw that the realities of the job were less than glamourous. Mannequins were hidden behind a screen in the salon, where they quickly changed outfits, refreshed makeup, brushed out wigs and tried not to appear too sweaty as they modeled the newest styles for the attending glitterati. Nico later described the experience as "an alternative school. I understood why everything had to be just as it was; I could see the effect of a walk, a turn, a position . . . I was the center of attention."

The 1995 documentary *Nico: Icon*, written and directed by

Susanne Ofteringer, provides invaluable interviews with many of the key figures in the artist's life. It is a subjective film, painting Nico as neither a fallen martyr nor an unredeemable mess. Instead, it is one of the only texts that presents Nico as a flawed, interesting, troubled human. Ofteringer's first person, primary interviews with family, friends, and colleagues—many of whom have sadly now passed away—provide a fairly well-rounded narrative of the woman behind the mythology.

This is especially relevant through reflections provided by Nico's Aunt Helma.

"She could move her body and act," Helma remembered. Thanks to her success with Oestergaard, the opportunities began pouring in. Christa excelled, even winning the title of "best mannequin at a parade to show off new items" at one event. Her prize for the triumph was the rings she had modeled. A young photographer named Herbert Tobias was enlisted to snap her studded hands—and that, her aunt Helma recalled, "was the beginning."

Tobias—who always went simply by his last name—was renowned for providing ornate, professional portraits for the fashion media, taking mannequins like Christa and transforming them into cover girls. The two quickly became close. Tobias proved to be both a good friend and a mentor. Fourteen years her senior, the photographer gave the teen her first color spread, for the magazine *Bunte* in January 1955. Though not often credited, further collaborations followed. Tobias's images from these early modeling days reflected the teenager's ability to transform seamlessly in front of the camera.[9]

At one of the many fashion shows Christa had started doing, someone from *Vogue* magazine approached her mother. The offer was beyond tempting. Grete was told that *Vogue* could offer her daughter a fantastic, affluent career in Paris. Yet despite living hand to mouth and with the threat of violence omnipresent, it was a tough decision. "Paris was the center of the fashion world, you could not go higher. Imagine what she would earn! Imagine the fame!"

recalled Helma. But Grete was not as easily convinced. "My sister said, 'I couldn't give my child to a completely foreign world. What's all this about?'" Helma recounted. But the girl was obstinate. "Christa cried and said, 'Mummy, even if you don't want it, I'm going without you!' Then she went directly to Paris."

At the time, Christa was determined to provide a better life for herself and Grete. In 1969, she reflected on that first departure from Germany, telling *Twen*, "At 16, I became a photo model. I simply did what seemed easiest to me; after all, I had to take care of myself and my mother." The teen wanted to pay Grete back for the unconditional love and support she had provided, and saw becoming a professional "dummy" as the easiest way to accomplish this. When later asked if she enjoyed the profession, Nico answered, "No. I have not thought long whether I enjoy it. I did it to feed ourselves." Like it or not, Tobias had plans for his new protégée, viewing her as a vehicle for the rehabilitation of his post-war career.[10] In Christa, Tobias recognized his own grit and determination. Having already tasted success on the Parisian fashion scene, he wanted to position the girl for similar fame. Christa was a willing and eager pupil.

Partnering with Tobias was an early example of her ability to take the initiative. One day in 1956, he prompted Christa to make a life changing decision, as her name was "all wrong" and "not international." "Models have one name, just like photographers and designers have one name," he told the model. She recounted how she got her new moniker, saying, "When Tobias took the first fashion photos of me, my name was Christa Päffgen. Tobias said, 'That's no name for a model. You've got to change your name. I'll name you after a man I once loved in Paris. His name was Nico. That's a nice name for you.'"

Christa's new moniker allowed for an entirely different persona to be born, one without the baggage of family issues, poverty, violence, and patriarchal frameworks. As Nico is usually a name for men, suddenly even the limited opportunities and expectations for a female artist seemed temporarily non-existent. "Nico" allowed Christa to seemingly shed her past and step into an unpolluted simulacrum. In the 1969 *Twen* interview, when asked about her memories of the war, Nico responded, "That was not me, that was another girl...My memory consists of shreds and short flashes, never the whole picture." Though she thought she was at last outwitting her past, Christa never fully became Nico, remarking, "You don't have to be you to be you." It would remain simply a role, an "other" that she was portraying to the outside world while still eternally haunted by her youth. When asked how she dealt with the idiosyncrasies of modeling, she responded, "I was an alien...I did not take it seriously. I could laugh...because I was playing the part of Nico." For the rest of her life, she would maintain the dual personas: Nico, the created, cool ice queen that she showed to the world and her audience expected; and Christa, the brave yet damaged survivor at the core of her being, the tormented casualty of a grim childhood. In the over one hundred interviews for this book, not one person remembered ever referring to the singer by anything else but her Tobias-chosen name. Nico had become so good at playing Nico that she rarely showed anyone her authentic self.

———

The birth of Nico began the decline of Grete. Mother and daughter had been in each other's company almost continuously since Christa's birth, and they were incredibly close. Helma recalled them both sobbing hysterically at the airport when Nico first left Berlin; she hypothesized that this initial detachment was one that neither of them ever really got over. It was the first instance of what would become a lifetime pattern of Nico being completely on her own, alone, a foreigner in a foreign country. At first Grete was worried about where the teen was staying and who was chaperoning her. Christa quelled Grete's concern, calling her and reassuring her that she was "well accommodated." The loss of her daughter "almost broke her heart," Helma remembered, as Grete "started to suffer from the separation…Christa would not have seen that, or even understood it." Christa's mind was focused on being Nico, making money and creating a new life away from her past. Her diary overflowing with assignments and bookings, Christa did not come back to Berlin, as the opportunities lay elsewhere. Though the absence of the girl left Grete bedbound with grief, Nico's star was about to soar.

———

In a Parisian dark room, Tobias met his fellow German Willy Maywald, who was already a famous photographer in his own right. Tobias began helping Maywald retouch images, which led to the established shooter introducing the young artist to crucial contacts at elite magazines. Tobias also set his protégée up with a meeting with his new friend. Soon Maywald would begin booking regular shoots for Nico with the esteemed *Elle* magazine.

Maywald had worked in the Parisian fashion industry since the 1930s, making a name for himself with his black and white portraits. He was also one of the first to take models out of the controlled studio environment and onto the bustling streets of the iconic city, capturing the energy and vibrancy that inspired so much of its famed haute couture. His images were featured regularly on the covers of *Vogue* and *Vanity Fair*, with celebrities lining up to have him snap their pictures.

In his autobiography, published in German after his death in 1985, the photographer recounts the day he first encountered the young model:

I was retouching photographs on a summer afternoon at my big working desk, and the door to my garden was open as always. A sound in the room made me look up. In front of me stood a most beautiful girl with bright eyes. She was tall and well proportioned, and her hair was cut short. She gave me a shy glance and introduced herself to me... I had just had the assignment to shoot some ready-made clothes at the Côte d'Azur. And because Nico was exactly the right look for that, I hired her at once.

The two would go on to collaborate repeatedly, Maywald capturing the fresh-faced blonde with the haunted eyes for top fashion magazines and designers, including *Elle* and Dior. Once Nico was firmly under Maywald's wing, her image gained a more consistent, defined quality. Maywald played a crucial role in helping Nico find her signature look of fair hair and long fringe, while fine-tuning her natural ease in front of the camera. Of her Maywald-influenced look, Nico commented, "You could say I looked the same from 1957 for ten years, until I changed the color of my hair for Jim Morrison. Maybe my hair grew a little longer or shorter depending on the cut, otherwise I never bothered to make a change. Whether it was quite the fashion I didn't care, because I had found my fashion. It gave me a security."

Security was important for the teen, who often felt intimidated by the high-powered, high-glamour social situations she suddenly found herself in. Nico's rapid evolution—moving from Berlin to Paris, unaccompanied by family members—must have been extremely overwhelming for a girl of sixteen, especially as she did not speak the native language, having to learn it at the same time as attempting to acclimatize to her new life. She quickly moved from print-ad model—with campaigns for everything from face cream to washing up liquid—to cover girl, adding the catwalk during fashion season to her accomplishments. Maywald helped the teen navigate the fashion business, tutoring her on how to carry herself and act in various social situations. In a later interview, Nico said, "I could say that I reserved all my energy in Berlin for Paris. I was never so lazy in Paris because Willy Maywald was strict, and he counseled me. But when you are eighteen in Paris, you do not want to be lazy, in case you miss something. I tried to miss nothing, but I understood nothing as well."

Though grateful to her mentor, she was still an outsider, a young woman alone in an unfamiliar country. Nico was acutely conscious of her turbulent childhood and lack of formal education. She would often make up for it simply by being quiet and coming off as aloof. The young model would carry a copy of Nietzsche's *Beyond Good and Evil*, in an attempt to prove herself worthy of the attention she received. Nico's coping mechanism became to simply watch, listen and learn from others, teaching herself how to adapt to various situations. Later, she would say of the time, "I could not admit that I was out of my depth, but anyway I found a way to overcome my shortcomings. You might think it was easy, because the men in any case did not assume you had intelligence. But that was a trap, or do I mean a convention? I didn't want anyone to assume I was a stupid girl, because I don't believe I was. I was uneducated because of the restraining system of the school. I found instead an underground way to learn. You can study most from other people not when they are formal, but when they are relaxed."

Nico's quiet demeanor was often perceived as her being vacant and vapid, instead of it being the only protection available to the damaged girl.

6

When she was still just sixteen, Nico traveled for the first time to the Spanish island of Ibiza. Tobias had previously worked there and booked Nico for some upcoming shoots. The sunny Mediterranean climate, a sparkling ocean and cheap rent made it a magnet for the burgeoning bohemian movement, expats and artists alike. Ibiza's geographic location among the Balearic Islands meant it was still relatively isolated when the model arrived, and this combined with an appealing mix of medieval architecture and alternative ideas. Nico was so enthralled by the place that she decided to relocate to the island. In 1954, she persuaded her mother to join her.

While Nico may have found a location she could finally call home, Grete did not share that feeling. In preparation for the move, the elder Päffgen had sold everything she owned, including all of her dressmaking equipment—her way of making an income. Though not even fifty years old, without her sewing machines Grete was at a loose end, having no career path or hobby to keep her occupied. Nico's work in Paris made her visits to Ibiza few and far between. According to Helma, Nico thought that putting her mother up in a lovely home on the Spanish island "would all be wonderful"; however, "she hadn't thought out the practical problems," like the running costs of the new abode. With Nico away, Grete was left on her own, with few opportunities to create a new network of friends or earn a living. "I think my sister made friends with a German schoolteacher on the island, a woman, but I don't think their friendship lasted," Helma recalled. "There were no men. Not one. My sister became ill, ill in the head. I don't think Nico understood this tragedy. It got worse and worse, and my sister was forced to face it alone."

Though Nico loved Ibiza, France was still the center of the European fashion world, and the main stage for the teen to try on different versions of herself.[11] One thing that provided comfort for the young woman was her discovery of jazz. As opera had afforded her escape and solace during her childhood, so Nico found this new form of music permeating the Parisian streets intoxicating. When she arrived in 1956, the French capital was already a hot spot for the genre, having hosted the first Festival International de Jazz in 1948. At scene hotspot Hotel La Louisiane, Nico tried marijuana. The experience left the model "coughing and coughing until I was dark red. Then I laughed too much, and I do not like to be vulnerable in this way." It is rumored that she tried heroin for the first time during this period, with Chet Baker. When asked during an interview in the 1980s how she came to cover his classic "My Funny Valentine," Nico reminisced about listening to jazz when she was sixteen and in Paris, singing along to various songs she heard, even though she did not know the language. "It was a wild music, against all the conventions that I knew then," she later said.

This landscape of eccentrics and mavericks suited Ernest Hemingway perfectly. The writer had already spent ample time in the French capital during the early 1920s, living in the Latin Quarter with his first wife Hadley and fraternizing with other cultural luminaries, such as James Joyce, Gertrude Stein, Ezra Pound, and Pablo Picasso. During a subsequent visit three decades later, in November 1956, Hemingway made a discovery: he had left several large trunks, packed with writing, notebooks and other documents, at the Hôtel Ritz in 1928. The archive provided the material for what would become Hemingway's memoir, *A Moveable Feast*. It was during this period that Nico met the Nobel Prize winner. It has been written that Nico's diary refers to Hemingway taking her to a party before trying to seduce her, all the while promising to write her into one of his books. However, her personal notes mention the author just twice across their entirety: once only vaguely in passing,[12] and a second time when she describes her room on the Contrescarpe as being "next door" to the "Grand Hotel," where Hemingway stayed and "wrote a Novel, which one I don't know." She makes no other claims referring to any sort of relationship or liaison between the two.

While it is incredibly titillating to contemplate the legendary writer and iconic singer having a brief fling in the opulent capital, it was Coco Chanel, not Hemingway, who, Nico said, "corrupted her," beginning the idea that Nico was bisexual.[13] Chanel was already seventy-three years old when Nico arrived in Paris to start modeling, making it unlikely that the two did have any sort of affair. Though it has been written repeatedly that Nico worked for Chanel, the company has no official records documenting this claim. The teenager did socialize with others who were employed by the designer. "We were like a gang, we young girls," observed Anne-Marie Quazza, a distinguished Chanel model of the era. "Nico would call round, say hello to us girls—'What are you doing tonight? Where shall we go?'" This provided ample access to gossip and for allegations made about the fashion house and its founder to be passed along to the teen.

There were similarities between the designer and Nico, providing a clear illustration of why the older woman may have been a compelling figure for the young model. Chanel biographer Janet Wallach provides a take on the designer that could also be applied to Nico, deducing that "Chanel was simply lonely, and while she may have flirted with her beautiful models, she was desperate for companionship."[14] In a world where her worth was based almost solely on her appearance and, later, her notoriety, Nico may have craved genuine connection wherever she could find it.

Clive Crocker is old-school Ibiza, the owner of the legendary nightclub Domino's and a stalwart of the early bohemian scene on the island. Crocker first had a romance, then a friendship with the singer that lasted from her first trips to the island until her death. Crocker,[15] a British expat who moved to Ibiza in 1958, has rarely talked about his relationship with the icon, but kindly supplied an exclusive interview for this book to help draw a more well-rounded portrait of his former companion. The two were lovers during Nico's early years in Ibiza, and he recalled the model having "this crazy idea that she preferred women."

Nico allegedly confided to having an affair with French actress Jeanne Moreau while she was shooting the François Truffaut film *Jules et Jim*. Referring to studio shots promoting the movie, Nico supposedly suggested, "I wonder if you can tell from the picture that she is happy from the love of a woman, not the men you are meant to believe in?" At the time of the possible affair, Moreau would have been ten years Nico's senior. Awed by the older woman, Nico reflected, "She was not a typical woman, at least...She is beautiful and shadowy. She commands your attention with a look, which is how strong people should be." Friend Carlos de Maldonado-Bostock also recalled Nico telling him about the intrigue with Moreau, saying, "Nico had these romances with women...She had this notion that it was chic to be a lesbian. It was like the idea of her reading Nietzsche; she probably carried the book around because it was a fashion...the fashion of bohemianism. It's a kind of put-on rebellion, and she picked it up from other people."[16]

By 1957, at the age of just nineteen, Nico was making more money than she could have ever hoped for. Her hourly rate varied anywhere from 80 to 250 francs, with a whole day being worth 500 to 800 francs, depending on the client. It was not uncommon for Nico to be netting over 10,000 francs a month. Yet even at the height of her earning power, the model still played down her looks, later saying of her success, "I was tall, I was blonde, and I was dignified. Nothing more is needed to make an effect. It is short people who need technique...I had none."

Though she had more money and access than she could ever have imagined, the constant focus on appearances did not sit well with the teen. This was the start of what would be a lifelong internal battle for Nico. She knew her most valued commodity—her physical features—was what allowed for escape, entry, and security. Yet she hated it being the sole quality that she was judged upon, her own possibilities beyond physicality not even being considered. Nico came to detest being called "pretty," as she viewed it as "ornamental, useless and a nuisance." Nico struggled especially with the constant pressure to stay ultrathin in the competitive fashion industry, later confiding, "It is never easy to eat when you are a model. You are hungry but you are frightened you will lose your figure. For a time I took some pills that suppressed the appetite, but they were not correct for the complexion. In the end, I didn't care and I ate more because I was large anyway and that was a part of my character... I would eat normally or eat nothing. But when I ate, I ate like a sparrow—a big, German sparrow. Sometimes I felt this was the hardest part of my work, either to eat, or not to eat. Is there any other job like that?" Though she felt unfulfilled and frustrated by the limitations of modeling, she knew it was a platform that could launch her into other arenas. What those were, she was not sure of.

Her early habit of silently taking in her surroundings, of learning not just new languages, but attitudes, customs, and characters on the fly, was often perceived as vacant unintelligence, her looks being the only thing, besides the uncommunicative behavior, that others saw. Nico's reticent ways often became problematic. Those jealous of or threatened by her—basically anyone not delving beyond first impressions—were quick to note her closed-off personality. It was a double-edged sword, however: the quieter she was, the more it became an inherent trait, which made for people constantly misunderstanding her, thus returning to the beginning of the cycle, over and over and over again, until, in later years, the singer often seemed completely devoid of emotions. "Nico was like the Kelippot, empty human shells in cabalistic mythology. Many people…say there was nothing beneath her surface: no love, no interests, no cares," wrote one journalist.

David Croland disagrees. Even via a transatlantic phone call, the former model and Factory insider is charismatic and witty, leaving no doubt as to why he captured the attention of former girlfriend Susan Bottomly—otherwise known as the Warhol Superstar International Velvet—and legendary photographer Robert Mapplethorpe. Croland spent a lot of time with Nico around the time she was shooting Warhol's *Chelsea Girls* in the mid-1960s. "She was observant, and people don't get this! She was at heart a poetess. Your looks do get in the way of your progress if you're that beautiful, there's no doubt about it. People become *instantly* attracted to you and *instantly* jealous at the same time. She's not the best news for any woman if she walks into a room, the way she looked. What I liked most about her, after the initial shock of her extraordinary beauty, was her reserve, her quietness, and her way of observing people who were observing her," says Croland. "She was very, very curious and very quiet. She didn't spin around; people spun around Nico because of her beauty and her mystery. She was sweet. I liked her shyness. I did not find her aloof, I found her shy."

————

It was in the summer of 1958 that the opportunity to expand her repertoire arose. While in Rome for a photo shoot, Nico stayed with Italian actress Silvana Mangano.[17] It is likely that it was during this visit Nico scored her first role on the big screen in *La Tempesta*, starring Mangano; Nico has an uncredited part as a blonde girl at a large festival scene. This role was quickly followed by an appearance in Mario Lanza's final film, *For the First Time*. Though her character is only on camera briefly, she does get a few lines as the "Leader of Admirers in Capri," who ask Lanza to sing them a song in a village square. Nico's last uncredited part came at the end of 1958, in Willy Maywald's German documentary *Montparnasse*. The ten-minute film focuses on the Parisian district of the same name and features a short-haired Nico in another non-speaking role as a Swedish art student. She is shown sipping coffee in a café for about a minute, before wandering off to a drawing workshop. She is on screen for less than five minutes across all three movies, but it was enough for a new path to emerge.

Though these first films gave Nico a taste for acting, modeling was still the source of her main revenue stream. Throughout 1958, she appeared in a variety of ads and magazine spreads across the continent, under a myriad of different names.[18] The inconsistent moniker reflects a teenager still not entirely sure of her personal or professional identity, even though her images were now being featured across Europe. It also illustrates a young woman wanting to get as far away from her German roots as possible.

In 1959, three years after taking on Tobias's suggestion of changing her name, Nico met someone whom she thought was her namesake. One night at a dinner in Paris, the model leaned over to a handsome dark-haired man sitting next to her and asked his name. Decades later, in an invaluable interview included in *Nico: Icon*, Nico Papatakis remembered the conversation:

"Your name is Nico?"
"Yes, my name is Nico."
"You lived in Paris before?
"Yes."
"Do you know a photographer named [Herbert] Tobias?"

Papatakis did not know Tobias. By the time he and Nico met, he was established as a successful club owner in his adopted country of France, where he ran the famed club La Rose Rouge. With his mixed Greek/Ethiopian heritage, the then forty-two-year-old Papatakis cut a dashing figure. He and Nico struck up a romance. "From that moment, we were never separated. For two years we chose to live together, Nico and Nico," Papatakis said. He recalled Nico once again trying to distance herself from her origins, even when it came to her name. "I liked the name Christa," Papatakis commented. "Isn't it a beautiful name? She hated it. She would always say, 'No! It's too...it's so German!'"

In the young woman, Papatakis saw a talent that she had yet to consider. "I had spent a lot of time listening to singers, and talking to them, because of La Rose Rouge," he later said. "I got to the point where I could recognize by their speech if someone could sing. Nico had this deep tone." While visiting Manhattan together in 1961, Papatakis asked his girlfriend if she had ever considered singing. "She hadn't thought about it," he remembered. "So, I took her to a voice teacher in New York."

Here the timeline of events becomes blurry. Nico said in various interviews that she arrived in New York in 1959, "modeling for [Eileen] Ford."[19] However, Ford Models do not have official documentation available to corroborate the claim that the agency represented Nico. Nico also said that she had been in the "same class" as actress Marilyn Monroe at Lee Strasberg's famous Actors Studio.[20] Already a household name through mega cinema hits such as *Gentlemen Prefer Blondes*, *How to Marry a Millionaire* and *The Seven Year Itch*, Monroe was tired of being closely associated with "dumb blonde roles" and wanted to be considered for more serious dramatic opportunities. She enrolled at the prestigious New York institution in 1955, moving from her native Los Angeles to the East Coast to receive private tuition. This was four years before Nico came to New York to (perhaps) work with Ford. It is possible that both of Nico's claims are true, and that records and dates have been lost over the passage of time; it is also conceivable that she thought positioning herself with both of these iconic entities would help bolster her own reputation.

La Dolce Vita is Federico Fellini's most renowned work. One of the director's first inspirations for the film was the "Hollywood on the Tiber" phenomenon that swept Rome in the 1950s and '60s. During this period, Tinseltown studios set up camp in the Italian capital, using the cheap labor and gorgeous locations afforded by the city. As celebrities emerged from Cinecittà Studios,[21] they would be snapped by waiting photojournalists. This became the foundation of the film's plot, which centers around seven days and nights in the life of gossip journalist Marcello Rubini (played by screen idol Marcello Mastroianni). It was a large-scale satire, a not-so-tongue-in-cheek critique of the soulless celebrity worship emerging in culture. Broken into seven different sequences depicting Rubini's various activities, the movie contains clear references to Dante Alighieri's *Inferno*, as well as T. S. Eliot's *The Waste Land*. It also provided a virtual panorama of Roman life, at the very moment when the capital was evolving from its rural past into a cosmopolitan city, fueling a tourist tsunami that continues to this day. The film went on to become a worldwide sensation. Nominated for four Academy Awards and winning the Palme d'Or at the 1960 Cannes Film Festival and the New York Film Critics Circle Award for Best Foreign Film, *La Dolce Vita*[22] made almost $20 million, crushing the record for the highest box office takings of any foreign film.[23]

Nico's best-known cinematic turn occurred by happenstance. While staying with friends in Rome, the model accompanied them to the studio where *La Dolce Vita* was being made. Fellini was looking to shoot an orgy scene for the film, yet no one was able to give him advice on how best to stage it. Seeing an opportunity to get in front of the camera once again, Nico offered to guide him. Recalling her first meeting with the famed director, she recounted, "I was with my friends and there were some props on a table. I picked up a candlestick with a false light on it, and I was just holding it up. No, it was a candelabra. And Fellini saw me and ran over to me and said, 'I have dreamt of you. I recognize your face. You will look wonderful with candlelight. You must be a star in *La Dolce Vita*.'"

Nico could not have hoped for a better springboard to the higher echelons of cultured society. Fellini was immediately captivated by the blonde bombshell, and quickly elevated the walk-on role he originally conceived for her into a full speaking part, with Nico appearing across various scenes. When the young woman expressed apprehension toward taking on a role that was so much more substantial than her previous on-camera experiences, Fellini instructed her to play a model named Nico.

The years of already "playing" Nico paid off, both on and off screen. Though she does not appear until more than two hours into the film, her character is memorable, an effervescent spark in the scenes she is featured in. Referred to as Swedish in the movie, and credited as Nico Otzak, her time on camera perfectly encapsulates the idea of a role within a role, of Christa playing the part of Nico, who in turn is playing the part of Nico in the film. Whether she is chatting in the back of a convertible on the way to her fictional fiancé's castle, dissecting a coat of arms or biting her onscreen beau's thumb, the script, as well as the action, seemed to echo the frustrations and complications felt by the young actress. One line seemed like an onscreen confession: "I finished modeling a year ago. Enough's enough."

Ignited by her turn in *La Dolce Vita*, Nico became more determined than ever to leave modeling forever and pursue her acting career full time. Twenty-one years old, and on a high after the success of the Fellini film, she landed a lead role in a highly anticipated new project. The film, *Plein soleil*, or *Purple Noon*, was a French adaptation of the best-selling Patricia Highsmith novel, with most scenes shot on a yacht off the coast of the Italian island of Ischia. With René Clément on board to direct, the movie was set to be the hit it became even before the first frame was in the can.[24] *Purple Noon* seemed to be the step Nico needed to take in order to fully escape the fashion world and become completely ensconced in acting.

Yet despite it being the chance she had been waiting for, Nico somehow forgot the date when filming for *Purple Noon* was set to start. Shooting began, and Nico, in the main female role, was nowhere to be found. Frustrated by the setback caused by the missing ingénue, Clément gave the role to French actress Marie Laforêt. By the time Nico arrived in Ischia, the production was well under way, her opportunity gone. The only apparent bright spot was meeting the male star of the film: a handsome French parachutist turned actor named Alain Delon.

Already hailed as the James Dean of France, Delon quickly made her forget about *Purple Noon*, sweeping Nico off her feet in a whirlwind affair and taking her around the island for a few days, during which she admitted to falling in love with the actor. Nico later referred to him as "the most dangerous man I ever met," an idea that was bolstered by Delon bragging that he had connections to dangerous underworld gangs. "He was like a gypsy," she claimed, "with strong eyes and dark hair, and I wanted him for myself. I had never felt so possessive before. It was a very emotional feeling whenever I saw him. I could not control it." But the romance was short-lived: unbeknownst to the besotted Nico, Delon was already involved in another relationship with his *Purple Noon* companion Romy Schneider. Once filming was wrapped up, the actor returned to Rome to be with Schneider. Though still hung up on Delon, and with her acting dreams temporarily destroyed, Nico retreated once again to Papatakis and modeling.

Back in New York, Nico dovetailed taking singing and acting lessons with embarking on a new round of modeling assignments: on magazine covers, in ads for a myriad of products and the ubiquitous fashion spreads.[25] Though she wanted to move away from modeling, she liked the financial security it offered. Friend and fellow model Anne-Sophie Monet spoke highly of Nico, saying that she was "a good model, very professional, though it was obvious... that she didn't take it at all seriously. I think she just wanted to earn the money and do something else...I think she took a lot of jobs on, whatever was on offer—she was always in work. She earned an awful lot of money." This would explain the seeming lack of consistency in the brands she would work for, as having cash seemed to be the priority, regardless of the opportunity on offer.[26]

Toward the end of 1961, Nico found out that Alain Delon was in New York, staying at the St. Regis Hotel. With little hesitation, she rang him up. The two had a night on the town, driving around in a Maserati, before getting stopped by the police. They then made their way to the Blue Angel club, before heading back to Nico's place. Delon stayed the night, leaving in the early hours of the morning.

At the time of the liaison, Delon was engaged to Romy Schneider. "Although she [Nico] knew that he belonged to Romy, she put up with it too. Delon took advantage of it. He has children all over the world, I think, whom he doesn't know," Helma Wolff claimed. "It couldn't have been a great love. Rather an encounter," she concluded. Friend Carlos de Maldonado-Bostock recalled Nico's enthrallment with the actor: "I was just leaving for Paris...when Nico came round, very happy and excited: 'I've just slept with Alain Delon!' It was like Snow White had met her prince. She was obsessed with this ghastly man for some reason."

For several weeks after the one-night stand, Nico felt extremely ill, throwing up almost daily and complaining of nausea. More than eight weeks after her night of fervor with Delon, a doctor's appointment revealed the cause: Nico was almost through her first trimester of pregnancy.

Almost forty years later, Helma still vividly remembered how Grete found out she was to become a grandmother. "[Nico] had rented a very nice house for her mother on Ibiza, right on the beach, and came to her mother: 'Mother, I am pregnant. I'm having a child,' she said. 'The father is Alain Delon.' My sister didn't even know who that was then. 'I'm really happy,' Christa said. My sister suggested an abortion to her, saying that 'You are constantly on the move in the world. How do you want to be a mother to the child?' 'Don't worry,' Christa said, 'I won't let it drift away. This child should be my own. I also want to have a person for me.'"

Though pregnant, Nico did not stop trying to further her acting career. She was considered for the lead in the French–Italian film *L'Année dernière à Marienbad* (*Last Year at Marienbad*).[27] The role eventually went to French actress Delphine Seyrig, freeing Nico up to take on other offers, including a photo shoot for *Harper's Bazaar* in the Bahamas, and to contemplate another seemingly juicy role: the main character in French film director/actor Jacques Poitrenaud's new project, *Strip-Tease* (or *Sweet Skin*, as it was alternatively called, depending on the country). So keen was Poitrenaud to get Nico to sign the contract for his movie that he flew to the tropical location of the *Harper's* shoot to deliver it. After agreeing to the role, Nico informed a most likely startled Poitrenaud that she was pregnant, but would be ready by the time filming was supposed to start in November—just over two months after she was due to give birth.

Model Anne-Marie Quazza recalls encountering a giddy Nico turning up during the spring Chanel shows of 1962. Fresh from the shoot in the Bahamas, she announced to Quazza and the other models, "I am the most happy girl in the world. I have found the most beautiful boy in the world. I wanted a baby and now I am going to have one by him!" Quazza recounted everyone looking at Nico and asking who the father was. When Nico exclaimed, "Alain Delon!" as Quazza said, "You can imagine the silence." Quazza reminded Nico that Delon was not her "boyfriend," calling her "crazy" for getting herself into this predicament. Nico replied, "I didn't want anything from him. I didn't ask for it. I just want now a baby of my own." "It was like a fairy tale to her," Quazza concluded.

Though neither Helma nor Quazza thought Nico wanted to carry

49

on a relationship, let alone get married to Delon, others remember her being deeply infatuated with the French actor and very much looking for a betrothal. Nico Papatakis, her long-time partner, was working on a film in Paris[28] and was the last to know of the impending arrival. He recalled, "One day she called me from New York and said, 'I'm having an affair. I'm expecting a baby. Alain Delon is the father. I want to keep it. He has accepted paternity.' 'Are you sure?' I asked. 'Yes,' she said, 'and I'll marry him.' 'Well, good luck,' I said." In another interview, Papatakis is quoted differently, saying that from the start of the phone call, Nico was acting "very strange," before she broke the news. "We had to separate because of what she had said," he recounted. "I warned her, I really warned her: 'This man has had many affairs, and he couldn't care less. Please don't try any blackmail on Delon. Don't blackmail him.' The whole thing to her was not like something in reality, but like something in a film."

Delon, however, did not share Nico's joy, denying paternity and ignoring any correspondence from the model and her friends.

Throughout the early months of 1962, Nico continued taking modeling jobs.[29] By June, she was ensconced back in Ibiza, where Grete still had the house outside the old town. Though living in a beautiful setting, the elder Päffgen was not well. Friend Anne-Sophie Monet accompanied Nico to Spain. "It was frightening to see her mother, because she was so obviously ill," Monet said. "She was developing Parkinson's disease but there was also something mentally wrong. To put it simply, she was paranoid—everyone was against her, trying to poison her. There was a kind of reversal in the relationship between the two of them; the mother had become the child of the daughter." Carlos de Maldonado-Bostock further embellished the situation, saying, "[M]entally the mother relied entirely on Nico, because she was absolutely lonely otherwise."

Nico's unsettled relationship with her own nationality may have been what pushed her to have Ari in France, thinking that her son would automatically receive citizenship in the country of his birth. Now heavily pregnant, the only available transport from Ibiza involved various trains and boats. Grete insisted upon coming, wanting to be on hand when her grandchild was born. Monet accompanied the Päffgens on the harrowing journey, which included a night spent in Barcelona. "The mother started to howl," she remembered. "She became hysterical, thinking that strangers were after her, frightening hallucinations...[she] was unpredictable the entire time. Then we had the train journey, and this was nerve-racking, because the mother would react in an unstable way that drew attention and could not be controlled."

Monet said in an interview that she had a small apartment on the rue Jacob in Paris, which she allowed Nico and Grete to stay in before the birth. It is likely that Nico Papatakis accompanied Nico to the Clinic Emmailloté, located in the western Paris suburb of Neuilly-sur-Seine, where she was admitted on August 9, 1962. Having nowhere to stay at the hospital, Papatakis was forced to leave Nico on her own. For the next two days, he waited anxiously by the phone for any update on what was happening. On August 11, the hospital called with the news that Nico had delivered a baby by Cesarean section. De Maldonado-Bostock recalls Papatakis being "beside himself with fury" after hearing the news, slamming the phone down and immediately going to the hospital. "I was angry with this arrogance of the surgeon," Papatakis said. "These kinds of men always want to open people up! He had no right to assume this with Nico, who was in no condition to argue."

Papatakis signed the witness document for the baby boy, Christian Aaron, writing down "Päffgen" for the last name. Instead of using his formal name, Nico decided to call her son "Ari," meaning "little lion," Leo being Ari's zodiac sign. Her naivety with regard to formal documentation later led to Ari being "stateless" when he came of age (at fourteen) in France. "[Taking French nationality] was not possible under the law because there was no father, nothing registered in the name of a father, nor of anyone French," Alain Delon's half-sister Pauledith Soubrier later said in an interview. "As a German citizen, she should properly have gone to the German Consulate for the purpose of registering Ari. So he was not German, he was not French, he was not anything."

Despite Nico very publicly naming Delon as the father of her child, the actor—"the most famous man in France"—refused to accept that Ari was his, even though the resemblance between the two was indisputable. At the time, some people questioned Nico's claim of Delon's paternity. Nico had been openly captivated by the Frenchman since the two met on the set of *Plein soleil.* Maybe she had made the entire affair up. It could be Papatakis, not Delon, who was the child's dad. Nico was, after all, living sporadically with Papatakis when she got pregnant. And Papatakis was the only person there to witness the birth documents (though, as Ari points out, "No declared father…at this empty place," referring to the line where paternity would be normally be listed). Ari also had a Mediterranean skin tone, similar to that of Papatakis.

Yet as Ari got older, the striking likeness between Delon and him became ever more uncanny. Though Papatakis and Nico had lived together for two years, de Maldonado-Bostock said that the relationship was "a romantic liaison with very little physical intimacy." Papatakis did seem to genuinely care about Nico. Unlike Delon, he did not want to leave the new mother alone, with only the sickly Grete for support. As soon as he could, he picked Nico and the infant Ari up from the clinic, collected Grete and brought the trio to the studio he had rented for them in the Marais. "Papatakis was a decent chap. He had integrity in the matter," de Maldonado-Bostock recalled. "I think he only wanted to see that Nico was treated right… He was simply being honorable, unlike Delon."

———

When Ari was six weeks old, he, Nico and Grete returned to Ibiza. This time renting a small set of rooms near the harbor, Nico set about learning her lines for her upcoming star turn in *Strip-Tease*. Grete made a convenient babysitter, living just up the hill. It was during this period that Nico first met Mancunian jazz musician and self-proclaimed bohemian Victor Brox. Still playing shows and making music today, Brox has a hearty laugh and a beguiling storytelling style that is apparent even over the phone. Though at the time he had heard about Nico and seen her from afar, they had not been formally introduced. Having bought the latest in technology—an audio recorder—to help her memorize her script, Nico soon found herself taping the flugelhorn player who lived above her. When his errant football fell onto her balcony, a flustered Brox had to knock on the model's door. "She was simply breathtaking to look at... but she was very shy," he recalls.

Nico was ravenous for information about music and soaked up any crumb of knowledge provided by Brox. "She wanted to know everything about jazz and blues, absolutely everything. She started to come upstairs, and I'd talk her through the history of the forms, the styles, the key musicians, the singers, like Bessie Smith—just everything I could tell her and play her. She just sat there and listened intently, though I had no way of knowing how much she took in," he notes. These salad days in Ibiza built on Nico's aborted singing lessons in New York, as she found herself surrounded by artists, gaining entry to Brox's group of like-minded jazz players. Eventually, she joined in with the locals' improvisation sessions. "There was a rule for entry: you had to bring an instrument," states Brox. "Nico brought her tape recorder." A romantic affair lasting a couple of weeks followed.[30]

Though having found romance and a freewheeling set of friends in her beloved Ibiza, Nico had a film to make. Flying to Paris with baby Ari in tow, she prepared to start work on *Strip-Tease*, where she was billed as "Krista Nico" for tax purposes. Upon landing, her old mentor and trusted friend Willy Maywald surprised the model/ actress with a trip to his studio. There he shot a color portrait of the new mother and her infant son.[31] Nico looks much older than twenty-four, her hair ratted and teased into a sweeping, chin length bouffant. She is wearing a bright-pink blouse, with a gold and pearl-studded pendant necklace. In her arms, she proudly clutches Ari, who is swaddled in a white, fluffy, cloud-like blanket. In all of the various images of Nico throughout her life, it is one of the only ones in which not only is she smiling, but she looks truly, authentically happy and hopeful.

10

Once your chance goes by, that's it.
Nico as Ariane in *Strip-Tease*

Paris plays a commanding role in *Strip-Tease*, the movie which finally gave Nico her turn as female lead. Director Jacques Poitrenaud captures the boozy, swinging nightlife of the time, the clubs filled with socialites looking for danger and kicks, drowning in equal parts cash, boredom, and sadness. The plot revolves around a dancer, Ariane (Nico), and supplies a haunting foreshadowing of many very real events and themes in Nico's own life. Having been unfairly cut from starring in a traditional dance troupe, Ariane must somehow find a way to pay her mounting bills. Enter her old pal Dodo, whose husband Paul runs an upmarket burlesque club called Le Crazy. Though hesitant at first, for financial purposes Ariane eventually does acquiesce to appearing at the venue, her routine accompanied by a wooden marionette in her likeness that mirrors her moves on stage.

As a stripper, Ariane becomes the toast of the town, finally getting the fame and recognition she craved before with the formal dance company. She catches the eye of playboy Jean-Loup, played by an extremely handsome Jean Sobieski. He attempts to woo her with gifts, flowers, and nights out, all of which Ariane refuses, though in one scene a friend of Jean-Loup's points out that "Everything is for sale, even a halo." Dodo and Paul do not understand why Ariane is rebuffing the eligible bachelor's overtures, saying she is a "complicated girl," to which Ariane responds, "Sometimes I need to feel alone...No one gets away scot-free."

Ariane eventually accedes to her suitor and allows herself to be swept up in the romance. Her spartan existence is suddenly injected with lavish gifts, furs, and jewels. As a rapid succession of glamorous nights and days out flashes across the screen, she confides in voice-over that "It was good at last to feel you were someone. It was good after being a nobody to be recognized. Then eventually you stopped remembering why. Days, nights, all merged into one." After a substantial amount of time together, Jean-Loup takes Ariane to meet his family at their massive estate. In front of all the dowagers, he reveals to Ariane that he is completely broke and has run through all of the money that his trust fund had afforded him. He tells the gathered elders that he is going to marry Ariane. He then throws down on a table a handful of her promotional postcards, all which feature her in various states of undress. Realizing that he had only been using her to blackmail his family the entire time, a devasted Ariane silently cries as the men escort Jean-Loup away.

The next sequence shows Dodo with Ariane in her dressing room. Jean-Loup has sent an exquisite diamond necklace, which Dodo gushes over. Dodo is surprised by Ariane's lack of excitement over the opulent gift, to which Ariane responds, "It's not a present, it's just my salary check." The music starts, and the camera pans to a packed Le Crazy. Jean-Loup is in pride of place at the front of the stage, surrounded by a rabid pack of his catty, vapid friends. The curtains open to reveal a fully clothed Ariane, wrapped not in her skimpy stage clothes but in the mink that Jean-Loup gave her. She opens up the coat, revealing a bevy of jewel-encrusted accessories. One by one, she takes them off, starting with the earrings, and drops each piece into the lap of a shocked Jean-Loup. The final bauble Ariane removes is the first gift she accepted from Jean-Loup: a flowered diamond brooch. She looks down at it sadly, fingering it in her hand. Seeing the piece, another member of Jean-Loup's group comments, "He gave Dora exactly the same piece." As Ariane drops the last trinket into Jean-Loup's hands, a woman turns to him and says, "She humiliated you...for all Paris to see," while a muffled male voice concurs, "You're a laughing stock now."

Strip-Tease's portrayal of a strong young woman chasing her dreams against the odds is not new; it is Ariane's journey and evolution that make it an incredibly compelling and unique film. Though in other works the allure of money and societal elitism are almost without exception placed as the most important goals, in *Strip-Tease* those ideas are turned on their head. Here it is Ariane's rejection of materialism and the normative symbols of success—for example, the mink, the jewels—that is celebrated.

Strip-Tease is shocking in many ways. Most astounding are the incredibly modern ideas of the independent woman and racial equality. Ariane never needs to be saved by anyone—especially a man. The movie ends with her walking away—entirely by herself—into the unknown, throwing away all security in pursuit of her authentic self. The only male that Ariane trusts is Sam, played by American rock'n'roll legend "Big Joe" Turner. He is the African American owner of the Blue Note jazz club, and the one person who sees, appreciates, and nurtures the "real" Ariane, never being taken in by fame and wealth.

Yet none of this is mentioned by critics. It is Nico's appearance that is recalled and remembered, the film itself all but forgotten. Reviewers focused solely on the same outer shell the movie critiques, with one saying, "One should certainly raise objections to the foreign accent of the principal actress, Miss Krista Nico. Her diction is dreadfully labored, the accent a touch crude. But, nevertheless, there is the compensation of Miss Krista Nico's glamourous physique, not only the beauty of her big eyes, but also the sculptural allure of her body." A film review from Catholic watchdog journal *Les Fiches du cinéma* sums up the overwhelming negativity thrown at the movie: "The road to hell is paved with good intentions. We thought our interest would be held by this—alas!—banal story of a young girl who strays into the arms of dubious types. But, frankly, it's nothing more than a pretext to present a spectacle that does not respect human dignity. This is why we reject this film finally as empty and degrading."

———

Strip-Tease made its debut in Italy in May 1963. Clive Crocker was Nico's date, and he recalls the night clearly: "We went to see the premiere. We had dark glasses on and put our collars up and sat in the back because we didn't want to be recognized. Suddenly, the nude scene came on, and she started giggling! She didn't have much of a figure—in fact, she was flat-chested. She kept laughing, so we had to leave the cinema."

The presence of alcohol plays heavily in Crocker's memories from the time. This is not surprising, as the average adult in 1960s France drank 250 ml of wine a day. Nico seemed to be no exception, as evidenced by her flat in Paris ("It was in Le Roux or in Benoit, something like that. I'd know it on the map," says Crocker of the abode's location). "This apartment was filled with bottles of Dom Perignon—empty. They were all over the place. She must have nearly drunk herself to death when she lived there," Crocker remembers. "Another time, we were at a grand hotel. Lying in bed at four in the morning, and she'd shake me. 'What's the matter?' I'd say. 'Come on, we've got to have a brandy,' she'd reply. A waiter, an elderly guy, would come in with two brandies on a silver plate."

———

When in Ibiza, Crocker's nightclub—the Domino—was Nico's "favorite place to spend time on the island," he remembers. "We would always sit in the back. She would smoke cigarettes. She didn't take any drugs. She sometimes smoked marijuana. I never smoked ever in my life. I used to have to clean the ashtrays in the morning, and it was a disgusting job. She'd do things like dare me that she could put a cigarette out on the back of my hand, burn me. I would say, 'You better bloody not dare!' She thought it was funny. One time, she decided she wanted to bite my arm. I smacked her in the face to get her away. 'You silly bitch!' I said. It wasn't huge, though I do have a little scar on my ancient arm. She burst into tears and ran out. The next day I came down to open the bar. It was absolutely full of flowers. She'd gone to the florist and she'd bought the whole lot. The tables and the bar, everything was covered in flowers. It was wonderful."

Crocker tells a story of Nico possibly acknowledging that she may not have been in an ideal situation to raise a small child. "She brought this young kid, this tiny kid, to her mother in this little house on Platja d'en Bossa [in Ibiza]. That's how we were able to have an affair, because the kid was with the mother [Grete]. Then she decided to find a proper parent for the kid. She wanted to go to Paris. She had a car, a convertible. The kid wasn't a year old, and we went to Barcelona in this car full of stuff. The mother took the kid and the plane to Barcelona, stayed in a hotel. It had great rooms. We took the kid to England because we had this vague idea that my ex-wife, who had a house in Maidenhead, would adopt him, but it was impossible. You can't adopt just like that."

It was during another trip to the UK that Nico revealed to Crocker her dream of being an artist. "I remember being in England with her. It was quite funny. I went to Chelsea art school when I was twenty-one years old, a young guy. I knew the area and had a few friends. We'd drink red wine and go to restaurants. She'd just disappear one day and come back the next day. She had these crazy ideas about being a singer."

11

Upon meeting Danny Fields, it is obvious how he has charmed some of the most important culture shapers of the twentieth century. On a walk around London, his enthusiasm for everything—from random street graffiti to a pigeon in flight—is contagious and addictive. Though completely humble and unassuming, he is one of the most influential figures in punk rock, signing and managing Iggy Pop and the Stooges, the MC5 and the Ramones, as well as working with Jim Morrison, the Velvet Underground, and the Modern Lovers. However, in 1963, the eventually legendary rock manager and record label executive was a journalist, going between attending classes at Harvard Law School and running with the emerging underground circle that frequented Andy Warhol's Factory and Max's Kansas City.

Fields and his friends were listening to the radio in New York on November 22 when they heard the news: President John F. Kennedy had been assassinated. "I was paralyzed," Fields recalls. Though shaken by the events, he decided to go ahead with a party that he had already planned for Thanksgiving, to be held at his loft, located at 7 West 20th Street, where future Warhol Superstar Edie Sedgwick crashed for a few weeks in 1963. He recalls, "Everyone was down from Harvard. Then I thought of calling it off, then I thought I really should have it, because everybody needs a party when something so horrible happens. There were people there from the Warhol Factory, there were people that I only knew from the Village. People were dancing to the Ronettes and sitting around." The beverage served still sticks in Fields's mind almost fifty years later. "The only thing we had to drink was vodka and grapefruit juice, which is just wonderful, 'cause it's cheap and it's potent and no one knows what the proportions are. You can turn them up or turn them down. No one on earth can tell, until you see the effects. It's like silent, tasteless poison," Fields laughs, remembering the gigantic booze-heavy punch bowl.

Then the door opened. "In the middle of the evening, Nico came in, dressed in tattered Levi's and a tattered Levi's jacket. She came in with two men, one of whom was a Chilean count [really just a playboy from Chile], and the other who was an English dandy [Dennis Deegan]. And the room of beautiful people just turned," he recalls. "And, of course, I knew her at once. 'My God, this is the person from *La Dolce Vita*. Oh my God. That's the woman walking up the staircase!'" he exclaims. Not bothering to get a cup, the actress walked over to the table, "threw her head back" and "poured a perfect vodka-fall into her lips. And that was amazing. Showstopper. I wanted to go 'Bravo!,' but she seemed terrifying," says Fields. Even in a room of fabulous, smart attendees, a ripple of interest started immediately. "People stood back. They made this ten-foot circle and asked, 'Who is this woman?' Then it started to get around that she was the person in *La Dolce Vita*. She was very scary."

Though intimidated, Fields struck up an instant rapport with the new arrival, bonding over a shared interest: cute guys. Almost immediately, Nico had her eye on a friend of Fields, "a lovely, beautiful, nineteen-year-old Jewish twink from Brooklyn named Seymour Avigdor, who went on to play Divine's lawyer in *Female Trouble*." Undeterred, Nico "shrugged her shoulders as if to say, 'So what?'" says Fields. He told Avigdor, "Now Nico there wants to fuck you," to which the frightened man replied, "'I don't know how to do it with a girl. What am I gonna do?' I said, 'I don't know, but she looks unstoppable. She's a movie star.' She got him. The first night I met her, she took my boyfriend. Hello?! So what am I supposed to say? Yeah, she really had good taste," Fields laughs. Throughout their friendship, he remembers men being scared off by Nico's appearance. "She was so impressive to look at that boys feared her, mainly. Men, boys," says Fields. "But, of course, she liked cute boys too. So while they were being afraid of her not liking them, she was probably getting a crush on them. We've seen this happen so many times: 'Oh, no, I can't talk to her.' And then a few weeks later, they'd be, you know, lovers."

A letter from Fields's personal archive, written on December 6, 1963, reveals the impact she had on the young writer (as well as his secret "punch" recipe). Though surrounded by fabulous people, it is Nico (or "Nikko," as he types here) that is the standout personality from the party:

> Our party was held in due course one week ago tonight. The apartment looked lovely; the kitchen finally was painted Euripides; much furniture was thrown out or left in my car, we set up a big table with a huge crystal punch bowl and punch cups, into which, before the thing was over, went 24 quarts of vodka and 24 quarts of grapefruit juice. We had been contemplating the most elaborate recipes, and were to have had a bartender, but he didn't show up at the last minute, and I was not ready to spend the evening measuring out herbs and spices. There were about 100 people, including many girls, many marvelous girls, I should say. My celebrity was something called Nikko, a very tall, very beautiful German girl who played the fiancée of one of the sons of the manor in the ghost hunting scene in LA DV [*La Dolce Vita*]. Do you remember her? Also she's the mother of Alain Delon's son. She's now hung up on Seymour, do you believe it, and is trying to seduce him or something—they spend a great deal of time together.

———

Not long after attending what would later be referred to as Fields's "Assassination Party," Nico scored her first public performance as a singer. The Blue Angel, located in midtown Manhattan at 152 East 55th Street, made the actress audition for the gig. She later told people that she fainted with nerves right after the trial, waking up to find that she had been booked. An invitation card clearly states that Thursday, December 19, 1963, was the opening night, featuring "the intimate songs of Nico during cocktail hour from 5–8 p.m. and all drinks 85 cents; no minimum, no cover."

At the start of 1964, Nico was still shuttling baby Ari around, either taking him with her to the various locations that modeling demanded or leaving him with an ever-worsening Grete in Ibiza. The added pressure of being a surrogate mother to her grandchild was taking a toll on the elder Päffgen. Years later, Ari recognized the layers of guilt, love, illness and isolation experienced by himself, his mother and his grandmother: "Parkinson's disease and solitude seized [Grete's] reason. The terrible situation was doubly desperate for my mother, but she had no choice but to leave me in [Grete's] company to pursue her career." Nico needed to earn money for both Ari's and Grete's care, even though the situation was far from ideal for all. Grete was in no state to be on her own, without help, let alone looking after a baby. Nico would come back to Ibiza to find that Ari had been left to look after himself for hours on end, while Grete rattled with Parkinson's disease, the house rancid with the stench of feces and vomit. In his memoir, Ari describes in detail the perilous times he lived through in Ibiza with the severely ill Grete, whom he called "Omi": "We were alone, Omi and me. I had to suffer the mental degradation, the aberrations and the paranoid phobias of my dear Omi, who became famous on the island for the scandals she provoked in front of the Montesol Hotel—she thought that everyone wanted to kill her...One day she shut me up in a room and threw away the key...I was terrorized."

During one of Nico's stints away from the island for work, Willy Maywald had been given the message from the island doctor that Grete needed to be admitted to a hospital immediately for treatment. Nico despaired as to who would look after her son while she earned money for the family. Maywald encouraged Nico to contact Alain Delon's family and see if they would be willing to help with the child. From here it is unclear how exactly Ari's paternal family members got involved in his life.

Delon's mother, Edith Boulogne—she remarried after her husband, Alain's father, passed away—has said in several interviews that she first found out about Ari's existence through the media. In his book, Ari shares a letter that Edith wrote to her lawyers "eighteen years later," in regard to what he calls "paternity proceedings":

> I learned of Ari's existence through the press. At that time, he was two years old and lived in Ibiza with his maternal grandmother... [Nico] went to get Ari from Ibiza and took him back to Paris to one of her friends, Monsieur Maywald, where I had to meet him. I went with my husband, Paul Boulogne, and Ari immediately snuggled in his arms. By instinct and by his physical resemblance to my son, even in his tics, his expressions and his very little child's morphology, I always felt that Ari was my grandson. I wrote it in the many letters that I sent to my son. He never answered unless it was through a lawyer, telling me not to take the child. This child was unbalanced, his mother had no life, and most of the time he lived with his maternal grandmother who had an incurable disease.

Another version of how the initial connection was forged between Ari and the Delon family is that Maywald rang Boulogne and arranged for the parties to meet up. Maywald always wanted to protect and help the Päffgens and was one of the few sources of consistency and support for both Nico and Ari. "At Maywald's, we were with my family, my mother and I, for he was, for us both, to different degrees, a father," Ari writes. "After protecting and advising my mother at the age of sixteen, he did the same for me from birth to death." In yet another take on the story, it is Pauledith Soubrier—Delon's half-sister, whom Ari refers to as "Aunt Didi"— who is tasked with retrieving Ari from the ill Grete in Ibiza: "I arrived and I was shocked," Soubrier recalled. "The boy was kept in a room, quite dark, and he was afraid, crouching like an animal. That's what I remember most, that he was more like a little frightened animal than an eighteen-month child. Nico's mother would not let him go. She wouldn't give me his entry papers, so I couldn't take him. I had eventually to fly back to Paris empty-handed. My mother decided she must go there and take charge. I have to add that this was not easy for us, because we had to pay for our own travel. Nico never paid a penny."

Though her son was one of the top actors in France, Edith had not received any of the spoils of his success. Maywald, upon first reaching out to Edith, was shocked that she "still worked for a living, at a little souvenir shop in the staid southern suburb of Bourg-la-Reine, near the Château de Sceaux." While her finances may not have been in the best of health, Boulogne was determined to provide Ari with a stable home. Perturbed at Didi's aborted attempt to pick up Ari, she got in touch with Nico directly, somehow getting her to send the appropriate paperwork regarding Ari over to her:

With these papers, I went to the French Consul in Ibiza to explain what I was doing. Then I saw the doctor, to get a note that the grandmother [Grete] was not a fit guardian, as she was in hospital with Parkinson's disease. I got another letter to enter France with Ari. What I did was kidnapping, lawful kidnapping!

My grandchild was so wonderful. Suddenly Nico turned up and asked to "borrow" Ari so she could take him to London. Well, she was the mother. They flew to London. But three days later Nico phoned me, "Please come and take Ari back." Now I had to go to London to collect him. She never asked me if I had enough money for these journeys. I went to London, stayed a couple of days and brought him back to Paris—for the last time, I hoped. But there's never a last time where Nico's concerned.

Ari recalls a different scenario: having a German passport, he had to hide in the air dock toilets to avoid detection by customs officials. "The adventure was all about a kidnapping," Ari writes. He never saw Grete, his Omi, again.[32]

So began the back and forth Ari would experience between Nico and Edith Boulogne. Nico would come and take Ari on work assignments with her, then drop him back off for long periods in Paris with the Boulognes. Even his name was in flux, Aunt Helma noting that "He was christened Ari, but later Delon's mother had that changed. She said, 'What is that name—Ari?' Then his name was Christian Aaron."

"Before we took him, she [Nico] dragged him around everywhere. He ate nothing but French fries, in train stations, hotels, airports... they lived like bohemians," Edith recalled. In the interview with *Twen*, it seemed that Nico had finally put Ari's well-being above her own desire to have him when it was convenient for her, accepting that a home with Edith may be best for her son.

Edith "truly believed" that her son would accept Ari. "She took over the kid. She wanted to adopt him. She believed it was her son, Alain Delon, that it's his kid," Crocker recounts. Aunt Helma confirmed this but added that if Nico allowed the adoption to go through, she would not be able to see Ari: "She [Edith] said to Christa, 'I will adopt your son and you will not have access to your child.'" Delon wanted nothing to do with Ari or, in fact, his own mother, if she continued to be involved with the young child's life. "When he heard about it, two years after we had taken the baby, he had his agent tell me by telephone that I had to choose between the baby and my son," Boulogne said. "My husband said, 'Your son can feed himself, but Ari can't raise himself.' So we kept him. Think about it, he was so little."

On January 13, 1964, Bob Dylan released his third studio album, *The Times They Are a-Changin'*. In support of the record, Dylan found himself on a tour of Europe in the spring. He hit London in May, making TV, radio and press appearances, before playing a sold-out show at the Royal Festival Hall. The gig was a surprise success, and the record went on to reach no. 4 in the UK charts. After the show, Dylan decided to go to Paris.[33] It was during a stroll around the city that he bumped into Nico and another acquaintance. "I was traveling with one of his friends, and we happened to meet him on the street," Nico recalled to *Twen* of her first meeting with Dylan.[34] The folk star recognized Nico almost immediately as the girl from *La Dolce Vita*. Legend has it that Nico invited the folkie up to her apartment, where they stayed for "an evening and a week." "His music fascinated me, and we became good friends," Nico told *Twen*. She found Dylan "magnetic...[with] heavenly blue eyes! He should not wear sunglasses. His whole personality is in the eyes. At first he is not easy to judge." Dylan lectured her on the politics of Germany, without having a clear grasp of issues that were intimate to Nico. In Richard Witts's biography of Nico, she confides, "As I was from Berlin, he [Dylan] asked me if I knew the playwright Brecht. I told him that Brecht had run a theater in Berlin, but we were forbidden to go there because it was in the Soviet sector. He said, 'You see? That would never happen in America. At least we are free to see things.' I said, 'But it's the Americans who are stopping us walking through.' For a man who was preaching about politics he did not know his history too well. Anyway, what about William Burroughs? Wasn't his book banned in his own country? I could buy it in Berlin."

However, Nico was able to put the singer's naivety, possible sexism, and bloated gravitas aside, saying, "He was so charming. I had not quite met someone like him—assertive and delightful—and young." The two headed to Greece for a short vacation in a small village near Athens, bringing Ari along. Dylan looked after the child while Nico did modeling work. It was here that he wrote most of what would become his fourth album, *Another Side of Bob Dylan*. He also penned "I'll Keep It with Mine,"[35] which Nico claimed was written "about me and my little baby," and that Dylan "sent [me] the acetate [of his version] because he had promised [me] a song for singing."

Connecting with Dylan was a turnstile moment for Nico. Before spending time with him, she believed her only singing opportunities would come from following in the footsteps of her countrywoman, Marlene Dietrich, and performing jazzy swing songs. Feeling pigeonholed by her nationality, and deflated by her other lackluster attempts at performing and the failure of her recording of *Strip-Tease*'s title song to be released, Nico credited Dylan with opening her eyes to the possibilities, saying in the Witts book that "he...changed the idea that I had that I should only sing torch songs, you know, love songs." Though setting her firmly on course for her next career move, Dylan was not necessarily a fan of Nico's voice. She remarked in a later interview that "[Dylan] didn't like it when I tried to sing along with him. I thought he was being chauvinistic and a little annoyed that I could sing properly—at least in tune—so he made me more determined to sing to other people."[36]

Dylan suggested to Nico that she revisit the idea of playing live, specifically to give the Blue Angel nightclub another try. When a modeling job brought her back to the East Coast, she got booked to sing there for a couple of nights. Billed as "That Girl from *La Dolce Vita!*" Nico once again found herself in front of a crowd at the venue named after the Dietrich movie. Despite her newfound chutzpah, the same issues that Nico found challenging during her previous Blue Angel engagement began repeating themselves. Nico would come in late and forget lyrics and she found the behavior of drunk patrons degrading. Once again striking out on her aspirations for a singing career, Nico went back to Paris to do some modeling and visit Ari.[37]

At the start of 1965, Nico was twenty-six years old, ancient by industry standards. Still parlaying her part from *La Dolce Vita* into credibility, she found work in the burgeoning Swinging London scene. However, there were some challenges: though still looking young enough to score assignments, Nico's appearance was not in line with the emerging gamine styles popularized by current It girls like Twiggy, Jean Shrimpton, and Pattie Boyd. An inch shy of six foot tall, she towered over the petite, doe-like models popular with photographers and fashion houses alike. Designers such as miniskirt inventor Mary Quant were creating lines for the "everygirl" to wear in her everyday life, not high-end couture to be donned by untouchable glamazons like Nico.

Nico's weight was another issue. During the height of her modeling years, Nico and many of her fashion contemporaries were expected to adhere to a steady diet of amphetamines to keep their waistlines tiny and appetites in check. Now off the stimulants, the pounds began piling on. "To be a model in that period, you had to be seriously skinny," recalled iconic photographer David Bailey. "But she was fat—well, plumper than the others, I mean. Weight was obviously a problem for her. It wasn't under control." However, Nico's drive to make money was evident to Bailey, who described her as "a bit of a hustler." Yet despite her graft, she did not have the right look for the UK market. "You felt she was trying to prolong her career. I did some shots of her for *Vogue*, but I don't think they were used. She wasn't very commercial; she was unusual, stunning but unusual," Bailey concluded.

Despite the obstacles, Nico still managed to find print-ad work, most notably in a campaign for London Fog trench coats. Shot on a blustery day in March near Trafalgar Square, Nico is shown in profile, looking at the ground, long hair somewhat obscuring her face, the text attempting to capitalize on the manic energy of the bustling city. Any opportunity for income was welcomed: Nico needed to make money to post back to Ibiza for a fading Grete.

———

In January 1966, Nico sent £200 to her aunt Helma Wolff, encouraging her to use it to visit Grete in Ibiza. It had been six years since Helma had last seen her sister, and the change in Grete's health was dramatic and "terrifying." Her hands shook almost constantly. She had acquired a drinking problem, having rum throughout the day to take the edge off both her mental anguish and her physical disability. Helma found herself doing basic tasks like cooking and shopping, as Grete lay in bed most of the day. She was mortified by the crippling circumstances—not only financially, but emotionally—that her sister was existing under. "She had nothing to do... Nowhere to go... She was a prisoner there, drunk and in need of a doctor," Helma later stated. With appropriate medical care a reprieve from the impending paralysis and trembling limbs caused by Parkinson's could be had, yet without any sort of health insurance these were beyond Grete's reach. Nico had failed of late to send any money back to her mother to provide for such aid, and she was even defaulting on the payments for Grete's home.

———

While her mother's health was getting increasingly perilous, Nico was busy trying to forge a new romantic—and career—path. It was at a party thrown by their record label in celebration of their second LP that Nico met the Rolling Stones. The entire band—Mick, Keith, Brian, Bill, and Charlie—were in attendance, as was their manager, Andrew Loog Oldham. Oldham had been a major catalyst for the Stones' meteoric rise, including positioning them as the dangerous bad boys, in contrast to the Beatles' clean-cut image. He was as commanding and charismatic as the band he looked after, donning Mod suits and sunglasses indoors and exuding sexy self-confidence. Oldham was not the only one in the Stones' camp whose interest may have been piqued that night; guitarist and well-known ladies' man Brian Jones was also reportedly giving Nico the eye throughout the evening.

In April, Nico found herself in Paris on a modeling assignment, on the same night as the Stones were playing a concert. Her friend, fellow model Zouzou,[38] was with Jones at the show and shuffled Nico backstage. It is thought that this is when Nico and the Stones' co-founder first connected romantically. At the tender age of just twenty-two, Jones was already notorious for his sexual conquests, having fathered four children by four different women before hitting twenty.

None of this put Nico off. Asked later about what attracted her to the guitarist, she said, "It's really very simple...He was sexy. He seduced girls. He was charming, until he locked the door." It was then that Jones's sadistic tendencies came to the surface, often aided by his copious drug use. "Brian was the kind of man who would take anything you gave him. Offer him a handful of pills, uppers and downers, acid, whatever, and he'd just swallow them all," poet Brion Gysin wrote of Jones's insatiable appetite for illegal substances. Yet the very drugs he voraciously consumed caused him to have a myriad of physical problems, ranging from debilitating asthma to more dire conditions demanding immediate medical attention. The illicit substances also hampered his sexual performance, making him impotent and violent. Nico later spoke about various occasions when Jones became almost frenzied in his rage, on one occasion hitting and punching her hard enough to leave a bruise. Another time, while tripping on acid, Jones cut her labia during an attempt to skewer them with a brooch. Sex acts would often include various objects, with Jones using both candles and a gun as dildos, inserting them roughly into Nico's vagina. He dripped hot wax onto his nipples and the sensitive skin of Nico's vulva. In a later account Nico revealed that Jones anally penetrated her without using any lubricant, causing pain and copious bleeding.

Despite all these tales of abusive behavior, Nico would still say, years after her time with Jones, that "It was fascinating and frightening...But Brian gave the best sex, when he could. He took too many drugs. He was like my little brother, and I had to stop him sometimes from destroying everything, including himself." "Best sex," though, was not enough for Nico. She often tried to strike up conversations about poetry or music with Jones, but found that "he was really too stoned to talk about anything, and often so was I... but he was gifted and could have made some original music. I kept saying that, but he called me a nag."[39]

Model Zouzou contended years later, though, that it was actually Nico who held the upper hand in the relationship, if for no other reason than the difference in height between the two. Standing at barely five foot five, Jones was significantly shorter than the German model. "He was scared of her and frightened of confrontations with her. We would be at parties and if Nico came into the room Brian would say, 'Oh no, you'd better disappear for a bit.' She was a big, threatening woman."

Andy Warhol was in Paris for his May 1965 exhibition.[40] Nico was visiting Willy Maywald and was out at a nightclub when she first encountered the Factory entourage. In his memoir, Maywald, recalling the evening, writes, "One evening we were together in the nightclub Castel when she made herself known to a group of Americans. One of them was the young American artist Andy Warhol." The Factory was the name of Warhol's art studio, which doubled as a clubhouse for a chosen set of artists, weirdos, and eccentrics deemed cool enough to gain entrance. Spotting her friend, actor Denis Deegan, with the New York contingent, Nico made her way over to where Warhol was holding court with Factory insiders Gerard Malanga and Edie Sedgwick and introduced herself.[41]

Warhol already knew of the model from her turn in *La Dolce Vita* and had cut out and saved the London Fog ad for his scrapbook. The model immediately began regaling the group with her personal résumé, starting with Fellini and sprinkling in new additions Dylan and the Rolling Stones for good measure. The New Yorkers were impressed. Nico later recalled this first interaction, saying, "Gerard Malanga told me about the studio where they worked in New York. It was called the Factory. He said I would be welcome to visit when I was next in New York." However, the trip had to wait, as Nico had already been promised a shot at working with Andrew Loog Oldham.

Having already launched the Stones, Oldham was in the process of starting his own label, Immediate, with Tony Calder, the producer behind Marianne Faithfull's success. Nico was keen to produce a single through the new endeavor and thought the track Bob Dylan had given her would be perfect to entice Oldham to sign her.[42] Oldham had other plans, however, deciding to have Nico cover the Gordon Lightfoot song "I'm Not Sayin'" instead of using the Dylan original.

Time has not mitigated the magnetic aura of the legendary manager. Our interview took place over a cup of tea in the London neighborhood of Soho. Oldham separated misconstrued stories from the facts of his time working with Nico. Though it has been written previously that Brian Jones promised to both coach Nico and play on her debut, Oldham vehemently denies either occurred. "Pundits seem to have it Brian played on the A-side. Impossible! [The Musicians'] Union would not have let him on [the studio] floor," he declared.

Oldham had instated a new head of A&R at Immediate, a young man named Jimmy Page.[43] He believes that it was Page who recorded and demoed the model, with two acoustic guitars, at Regent Sounds, a recording studio in the British capital. "I obviously heard the result of that [session], and then I made the most awful record with her, the A-side 'I'm Not Sayin','" Oldham recalls. Not happy with the way the Lightfoot song was turning out, Oldham quickly penned some lyrics for a new cut, "The Last Mile." He then gave the words to Page, who wrote the music for the track, which became the single's B-side. "He [Page] didn't have anything to do with the first one ['I'm Not Sayin']. He might have been playing on it, but he was just reading parts. One way or the other, I wrote the lyrics [for 'The Last Mile'], and he put the music to it. Either way, I just gave him the fucking poetry, and she sang it. Looking back at it, the B-side is better than the A-side."[44]

An appearance on British TV's Friday-night hipster show *Ready, Steady, Go!* to promote the single proved to be equally problematic, with Nico rushing through the performance, leading to an abrupt and premature end, her lip-syncing concluding long before the backing track had finished. She later brushed these early disasters off, saying in the Witts biography, "I was acting a role that I had to do...It was like being back with [Lee] Strasberg [at the Actors Studio]. It was fun, really. But I was not acting a role on a stage or on a record. I was acting for contracts. I was too shy to be me, and it's easier to play someone else, isn't it?"

What Nico did excel at was winning over the people she met during an Immediate promotional tour. An entourage consisting of Oldham, Nico, a driver, and a person hired to be the designated "joint-roller" made its way to a record label sales conference and then up to Manchester to introduce themselves at the Philips Records plant. "We were all so wonderfully stoned on hash, and we had a great laugh. But everybody loved her because...she was funny, and she enjoyed herself...When the single didn't go, I don't think I saw her again...I didn't socialize with her, and the next thing you knew she turned up in New York with Warhol," said Oldham, adding, "She wasn't aloof at that point." Though the song did not prove to be the breakthrough hit he was hoping for, he still praised the singer later, saying, "She was one of a new breed of woman, like Anita Pallenberg and Yoko Ono, who could have been a man. She was no doormat. Far better that than the silly little English teacups around at that time."

The video for the song, shot by the London docks, showcases an incredibly skinny Nico miming to the camera. Clothed in a long-sleeved black blouse, below-the-knee print skirt, and high boots, and with long hair and an eyelash-skimming fringe, the singer looks chic—but out of step with the 1960s fashion of microminis and asymmetrical Vidal Sassoon hairstyles. A set of negatives, taken from the video shoot, show Nico vamping and, in some images, even smiling. An unknown young man with long brown hair is her companion in some of the proofs.

A scene from the 2007 Bob Dylan documentary *65 Revisited* not only provides a glimpse into Nico's hopes and dreams during that time period, but shows her naive vulnerability, masked by a rigid determination.[45] Directed by D. A. Pennebaker, the film is composed of footage from his original Dylan movie, 1967's *Don't Look Back*, as well as outtakes not included in that version. The feature, shot in 1965, follows Dylan and his entourage during their tour of the UK that year. The Nico clip opens with an image of a newspaper, the Beatles and Dylan splashed across the front cover. It then cuts to Nico, wearing a long dress and what looks like leggings, sitting in front of a window in what appears to be a living room. She is talking to Dylan's manager, the much older, stout Albert Grossman. The camera quickly zooms in on her face, as the two discuss another entertainer—most likely Marianne Faithfull:

> Grossman: Last time I saw her she had a little yellow bow in her hair, and she looked like a [*gets interrupted*] . . . grammar-school girl.
>
> Nico (*over top of Grossman saying "grammar-school girl," smiling*): You think that would suit me?
>
> Grossman: No! You'd have to find your own thing.
>
> *Camera zooms in on Nico's face, looking away from Grossman and smirking.*
>
> Grossman: But she takes full advantage of the fact that she can put on her yellow hair ribbon and go talk to the head of Paramount Pictures.
>
> *Nico's face becomes serious.*
>
> Nico: And she hasn't been [*gets interrupted*] . . .

Grossman: And she's concentrating on what she has to do, and he's looking at the hair ribbon.

Nico looks at Grossman.

Nico: She never thought of herself looking like a fool?

Grossman: She doesn't look like a fool!

Nico (*smiling*): No?

Grossman: Not at all.

Nico smiles incredulously and laughs.

Grossman: What, you think that would be the worst thing, would be to look like a fool?

Nico (*frowning*): Yes.

Grossman: Yeah?

Nico nods.

Camera pans across the room to a man on a sofa.

Nico: Like [a flower?]

Grossman: Oh, yeah really? Your heart is in the right place. (*Camera cuts to close-up of Grossman's face.*) You have good instincts, right?

Camera pans to Nico. She smiles at Grossman's question.

Nico: Yes.

Grossman: So you're just talking about style.

Nico (*smiling and laughing*): That's about all!

Grossman: You're just talking about style.

Nico may have been hoping for Grossman to take her on and help her become established in U.S. music circles. This film snippet illustrates the reality that Nico had nothing and nobody to fall back on; she had only herself. While it may be easy to accuse her of being a name-dropper, it is by associating herself with others that she wisely maneuvered and wiggled her way through society. Friends later commented that she always felt inadequate and uneducated compared to her contemporaries, who had either been to college or dropped out of one, like Dylan. That makes it a much more poignant and heartbreaking scene when Grossman says to Nico that she has "good instincts" and her "heart is in the right place," and she responds with a sad, melancholic smile. Though he never officially managed her, Grossman did give Nico the idea of returning to New York.

———

With the failure of her Immediate single, Nico once again boomeranged to New York, swinging by Paris to pick up Ari from where he was staying with his grandmother Edith. With no clear plan, modeling work provided much-needed income. As per usual, Nico was not snobby about what product to promote, as long as it paid.[46] She remembered her invitation from Gerard Malanga to come to the Factory and decided to take him up on his offer. "She called us from a Mexican restaurant and we [Warhol and Paul Morrissey] went right over to meet her," Warhol wrote in his book *POPism*. "She was sitting at a table with a pitcher in front of her, dipping her long beautiful fingers into the sangría, lifting out slices of wine-soaked oranges." On spotting Morrissey and Warhol enter the premises, Nico "tilted her head to the side and brushed her hair back with her other hand and said very slowly, 'I only like the fooood that flooooats in the wiiine.'" Over dinner, she proceeded to tell the duo about Dylan writing a song for her, her appearance on *Ready, Steady, Go!* and the promises made by Dylan's manager Albert Grossman to look after her if she came to the U.S. She carried on, telling the impressed Warhol and Morrissey about her fling with Alain Delon, *La Dolce Vita* and the Immediate record she had cut with Oldham. By the time dinner was finished, Warhol recalled, "Paul said that we should use Nico in the movies and find a rock group to play for her. He was raving that she was 'the most beautiful creature that ever lived.'"

The return to the East Coast also brought Nico back in touch with her former flame Brian Jones. Jones suggested that they go to the Factory and visit Warhol at East 47th Street. Nico brought a copy of "I'm Not Sayin'" along with her. "I first heard of Nico, one day, an afternoon, at the Factory," recalled Billy Name. Born William Linich, Name was a Factory insider, collaborator, and archivist for Warhol. "Andy was at his worktable doing silk screening. I was either helping him or doing something else. Gerard Malanga came up the elevator into the Factory and said, 'Hey Everybody! I want you to hear this record I have. It's by this new friend I have in Europe. Her name is Nico.' He put this little 45" on our stereo system and it played in."

Just to have the confidence to breach the Factory walls was an accomplishment for the non-initiated, according to Name. "It was perilous to be there. A lot of people couldn't even come there. They wouldn't come there because of what they heard about it. Or if they did come, they left immediately. The aura was so intense. High-powered people. Andy was a magician. A wizard. The specialty at the Factory was a synthetic aura where anyone who came into it who did have skills or talent was accepted by Andy and the rest of the group there as another player in the play and could interact."

Nico, however, was an entirely different kind of person than previous Warhol intimates. "Most people at The Factory were very loquacious and verbose and would easily talk or tell you something. Nico... rarely spoke. And only when someone spoke to her," remembered Name. "She was totally nonflamboyant, nonpretentious, but absolutely magnetically controlling. She didn't wear all the hippie flowers, she just wore these black pantsuits, or white pantsuits—a real Nordic beauty. She was too much, really, let me tell you, so anything we could think of to have her play a role in our scene, that's what we were gonna do."

Paul Morrissey agreed. Morrissey managed all of Warhol's business affairs, as well as directing films with the artist.[47] Possessing the talent to turn art into commerce, he spotted an opportunity with Nico that differed from what was offered by those already inhabiting Factory circles. "Nico was spectacular," he said. "She had a definite charisma. She was interesting. She was distinctive. She had a magnificent deep voice. She was extraordinary-looking. She was tall. She was somebody."

Warhol, too, was taken by the new arrival, and immediately brought her over to a pre-existing "set" within the Factory: a chair set against a plywood background, with lighting and a camera. Here Nico undertook the right of passage experienced by everyone, from Dylan to Allen Ginsberg, who entered the Factory: the Warhol screen test.[48] Four and a half minutes later, Gerard Malanga, who was operating the camera, declared that they had enough material and started shooting a second piece with the model. He was also enthralled by the tall blonde.[49] While the first test had captured the icy, detached Nico, with barely a smile, the next one showcased the fun side of the singer, as she flipped her hair around before rolling a magazine into a tube and peering down it into the camera. Several days later, Warhol cast her in what would be their first collaboration, the sixty-six-minute-long film *The Closet*.

Shot in November 1965 at Panna Grady's[50] apartment in the Dakota building on Central Park West and 72nd Street, the stunningly attractive Nico and a young, gay college student, Randy Borscheidt, find themselves in a closet.[51] She tries to coax him to literally come out of the closet—to no avail. There was no script that the actors followed; everything was ad-libbed on the spot.

Photographer and friend Peter Sahula accompanied Nico to some of the first shoots for the film and was not impressed by what he saw. "The way they did movies was very, very bizarre," he later recalled, adding, "It was like they spent all day doing nothing. I can't imagine how anybody really could have done a movie. There was just a lot of people milling around, and nobody knew what they were doing. Nico was supposed to be in the movie, but she wasn't doing anything, and everybody was just talking. It was crazy. I said, Get me out of here."

The film was rarely seen;[52] however, it did grant Nico an entrée into the Factory's inner circle, providing her with a proverbial foot in Malanga, Morrissey, and Warhol's door. *The Closet* was the first of the nine movies she would make with Warhol. These early notable interactions with the Warhol gang provided a strong foundation for what was to come, as meeting the pop artist would change the entire trajectory of Nico's life.

II: EXALTED

14

In the autumn of 1965, Andy Warhol made a bold statement: he was going to leave painting behind altogether and concentrate on other projects. This decision would ultimately allow the artist to become a multimedia provocateur across various platforms. It was also a shrewd business move. "He withdrew from the art world for a number of years to put his price up and make the earlier stuff more collectable," said Paul Morrissey. Already bringing in thousands of dollars a week from his past successes, Warhol did not want to be burdened with any additional tax, so, using the excess money, he financed the making of short films. He had just completed a successful run of eight movies featuring his newest Superstar, Edie Sedgwick. "An hour's worth of developed 16 mm black and white film cost $200. Well, for $200 we weren't exactly going to compete with Hollywood," Paul Morrissey confided. "These films were truly experimental, no one in their right mind thought there'd be an audience." Warhol's films were unconventional, "quickie underground movies, shot in shaky black and white with a single handheld camera; the action on the screen takes as long as the action in real life." It was at this pivotal moment that Morrissey came into his own as an integral member of the Warhol machine. "I really became his manager in the sense that I did all the talking," he recounted.

The Cinematheque was the weekly Monday-night event held by young filmmaker Jonas Mekas at an off-Broadway theater. Mekas offered Warhol a venue to show his movies, including putting on a retrospective starring Sedgwick. From an upper crust New England family, Edith Minturn Sedgwick, known simply as "Edie," was the seventh of eight children. Though having wealth and access, at just thirteen she started exhibiting various eating disorders, descending into anorexia, which eventually led to her being institutionalized at a private psychiatric clinic in Connecticut. Upon release, she moved to Cambridge, Massachusetts, looking to study sculpture alongside her cousin. On turning twenty-one in 1964, Edie received her $80,000 trust fund,[53] provided by her maternal grandmother, and moved to Manhattan. It was there that she met Warhol.

For Warhol, "Superstar" was a mantle bestowed upon the newest face *du jour* who caught his fancy. The title was "handed down," says Factory insider David Croland. "Our crowd was photographed a lot; the pictures went to the highest order: American *Vogue* and the *New York Times*. You can't get better publicity than the *New York Times* worldwide. It's like you didn't have to do anything because of the way you looked, you were just photographed all the time." Warhol's assistant Vincent Fremont concurs, pointing out how an association with the artist provided anyone in his orbit with a global stage. "Andy was very good at launching people or giving them opportunities to launch themselves. Whether they could handle it or not was their problem."

But it was not an endless gravy train of fame. The reigning Superstar would escort Warhol to parties and dinners and often be the focus of his current film or project—only to be unceremoniously discarded once they no longer intrigued him, another, new, fresh face taking their place. "He liked to possess them," said friend and photographer Jerry Schatzberg of Warhol's attitude toward his "creations." The vulnerable, rich, and stunning Edie—with her emaciated frame and huge, innocent eyes—was the perfect candidate for the title. After all, as Warhol once said, "A girl always looks more beautiful and fragile when she's about to have a nervous breakdown."

Edie became a fixture at Warhol's side, snapped constantly by the press at various functions and public outings. She often picked up the tab for meals for the entire Factory entourage, and had herself and Warhol chauffeured around New York in a Mercedes. Her saucy smile and model-perfect poses made her a press darling and saw her dubbed an "It Girl" and "Youthquaker" by both paparazzi and magazines alike. Her signature look of leotards, oversized, shoulder-dusting earrings and Mod makeup—heavy liquid eyeliner, fake eyelashes to accentuate her already large eyes—made her the perfect companion for Warhol. She even colored her naturally brown hair silver blonde, cutting it to mimic Warhol's trademark wigs. He later said of Edie, "I could see that she had more problems than anybody I'd ever met."

Around the same time, the pop artist received a new proposition. Always on the prowl for a means of bringing cash and visibility to the Factory, Warhol and Morrissey were intrigued when they were approached by theater producer Michael Myerberg. Myerberg was opening a seventeen-thousand-square-foot club in Queens and wanted the glow of übercool that Warhol and the Factory provided. He suggested calling the venture Andy Warhol's Discotheque. Warhol countered with Andy Warhol's Up. Morrissey quickly realized that to both make it financially viable for the Factory and get people to trek out to an outer borough of New York, there would have to be some added elements besides just hearing records being played. He proposed that they use the films they had already shot as moving backdrops at the event. He also suggested that Warhol add a house band to his repertoire, to which the artist replied, "Ooh, that's great." Now Morrissey had to find a group to complete the bill. Gerard Malanga had recently been to a Velvet Underground show and suggested that Morrissey go check the band out.

Recalling his initial encounter with the Velvet Underground, Morrissey later said, "The first thing that registered to me, and I think to Andy later, was the drummer Maureen, because you could not tell whether she was a boy or a girl. This was a first within rock'n'roll because The Beatles all looked like little girls but you knew they were boys. You had no idea what Maureen's gender was. The second thing was John Cale's electric viola. And the third thing was they sang a song called 'Heroin.'"

Morrissey felt he had found the band to feature at the Warhol event, and wanted to officially sign up the Velvets for his proposition. There was one issue, though, that made him hesitate: frontman Lou Reed. "The first thing I realized about the Velvet Underground was that they had no lead singer, because Lou Reed was just such an uncomfortable performer," he revealed in the legendary book *Please Kill Me: The Uncensored Oral History of Punk*. "The singing was done by Lou Reed, and he just seemed not a very good singer. Not a good personality. There was something too seedy about him. He was not an actual performer."

Having existed only for a matter of days before their meeting with Morrissey, the newly formed band were still working out their kinks at the residency their then manager Al Aronowitz had booked for them at the beatnik hangout Café Bizarre. Despite any misgivings, Morrissey took Warhol and part of the Factory entourage— including Malanga and Sedgwick—to see the Velvets. There were no more than a dozen people that Thursday evening at the club; a distinct separation was still apparent between the art and music scenes, and the Warhol crowd went unnoticed upon arrival.

During the Velvets' set, Warhol became animated. As they sat watching the band, he asked Sedgwick what she thought of the idea of the group playing while her movies were shown as a backdrop at the upcoming Cinematheque retrospective. The Superstar was hesitant about the proposition as the band would take away interest from her movies. Though they left after the first set, for the rest of the evening Warhol reportedly kept saying, "We have to think of something to do with the Velvets. What can we do? What could it be? WE HAVE TO THINK OF SOMETHING!"

Illustrating her seemingly infallible ability to be in the right place at the right time, Nico was also in attendance at Café Bizarre that evening, an event she later referred to as "the most beautiful moment of my life." Aronowitz takes credit for bringing her to see the band, proclaiming in *Please Kill Me*, "Nico never had any taste and she had the immediate hots for Lou Reed—because she had visions of being a pop star herself."[54] Nico later recorded seeing the group in her diary, though it is her melancholy about not receiving love from either Dylan or Delon that reverberates in her passage:

> One night we went to the Café Bizarre to see a new group, the
> Velvet Underground, who played there last night...people
> couldn't dance to their music, and they had to go. I had
> told Bob Dylan about them too, but he was busy...I was
> probably getting on his Nerves, being in Love with him the
> way I was. In my heart, I still loved Alain but he did not even
> think about me now.

Malanga introduced Morrissey and Nico to each other before the Warhol entourage set off. While Nico may not have fixated on the Velvets that night, Morrissey had. He needed that interesting element to prop up what he saw as a bland Lou Reed. He immediately identified his solution in Nico. In Victor Bockris's *Lou Reed: The Biography*, Morrissey recalled, "I felt that the one thing the Velvets didn't have was a solo singer, because I just didn't think that Lou had the personality to stand in front of the group and sing. The group needed something beautiful to counteract the kind of screeching ugliness they were trying to sell, and the combination of a really beautiful girl standing in front of all this decadence was what was needed. That very night, right away I said, 'Nico, you're a singer. You need somebody to play in back of you. You can maybe sing with this group, if they want to work with us and go in this club and be managed.'"

Like Morrissey, Warhol saw potential in Nico, whom he described as looking "like she could have made the trip over right at the front of a Viking ship, she had that kind of face and body." Her aesthetic made her stand out from the other women on the Factory scene, her "very mod and spiffy white wool pants, double-breasted blazers, beige cashmere turtlenecks, and those pilgrim-looking shoes with the big buckles on them" creating an immediate impression on the pop artist. "She had straight shoulder-length blond hair with bangs, blue eyes, full lips, wide cheekbones—the works," Warhol later wrote in *POPism*. But it was Nico's unique voice that completed the package for him: "She had this very strange way of speaking. People described her voice as everything from eerie, to bland and smooth, to slow and hollow, to a 'wind in a drainpipe,' to an 'IBM computer with a Garbo accent.' She sounded the same strange way when she sang, too."

Warhol and Morrissey both saw Nico as the missing element to complete the Velvets, and they would not move forward without her as part of the band. "Andy always liked to have beautiful women around, even though he wasn't interested in them in a physical way—it was just the whole look of presenting yourself," recalled Fremont. "Andy's persona—there was a public and private side—but his physical look was part of his art, so he was always adjusting what he looked like, so he understood that in other people...and going out with a beautiful woman made sense because he loved glamour. She was part of that."

Nico was ready to use her appearance to get her further into the Warhol universe, and to take Morrissey up on his offer. She was tired of modeling and "only wanted to be with the underground people." Her timing was flawless. Seeing the past few years as a succession of missed opportunities, Nico viewed Warhol as the solution at last to her quest for stardom. "I have always been in the wrong place at the wrong time," she said. "But when I was with Andy Warhol, I seemed to have got it right."

Just days after meeting Warhol, the Velvets were fired from Café Bizarre. The artist suddenly became an attractive—and also their only—option. Morrissey was eager to make things official with the band. "After we met them, they came to the Factory and right away I proposed that we would sign a contract with them, we'd manage them and give them a place to play. They said yes. Andy immediately bought them some new amplifiers and they started rehearsing at the Factory," Morrissey says in *Uptight: The Velvet Underground Story*. Morrissey was also determined to bring Nico into the mix. "We wanted her to have a starring role in what we were doing and since she was a chanteuse, we thought it would be great to have her sing with the band. Which of course was the totally most wrong thing you could say to them at that point in their development, when they are going to be the stars!" remembers Billy Name. "They're supposed to work this other person into their musical arrangements and setups? It was like, hey, what more wrong thing could you say to a group? But because they were new and fresh in the scene too, it just squeezed together and worked out, and turned out to be sort of magic."

Time was not wasted getting the Velvets and Nico together in a legal sense. Contracts were signed, with management duties officially handed to the Warvel Corporation—the name a mash-up of "Warhol" and "Velvet." The company directors were Warhol and Morrissey, who were set to get 25 percent of both the Velvets' and Nico's earnings from the work the corporation got them. Band practice began promptly on January 3, 1966, and was captured in the seventy-minute film *The Velvet Underground and Nico: A Symphony of Sound*, shot at the Factory by Warhol. Featuring casual chatter, nonchalant playing around on instruments and unstructured jamming, the tapes have Reed teaching Nico the lyrics to "Venus in Furs," while the rest of the group strums away in the background. There is also an attempt at a full song, "There She Goes Again," with the chanteuse on lead vocals. Other highlights of the movie include the New York Police Department interrupting the jam session at one point, citing a noise complaint.

Nico is visible in one scene slapping a single maraca against a tambourine, while another shows her playing Cale's Fender Precision Bass. The reels were originally shot for posterity, with a view to possibly using them as background visuals for performances or during band setup and tuning.[55] Critiques of the Nico-led rendition of "There She Goes Again" have seemed to ignore the fact that English is not her native language, that she is just learning the words and melodies for the first time—in contrast to Reed, who has not only written the tunes, but has been playing them regularly. One review sums it up, saying, "She doesn't do too bad a job with the song, especially when you consider that she's probably barely familiar with it, but her rendition throws up an immediate red flag to whatever plan Warhol and Morrissey might have in mind." It was easier for many reviewers to stay with the theme that Nico was a poor singer and frame her as a simpleton, as another writer claims: "They [the Velvet Underground] try several times to find a key that suits Nico's voice," and the band "even seems to try it with both Nico and Reed singing it together, although it could be that Reed is guiding her along as she learns the words." According to another write-up, "Nico tries many times to vocalize lyrics that prove to be too fast for her broken English to master." But regardless of the realities facing the new band member, "the simple fact is that the song sounds far more convincing and confident when sung by Reed," writes one author. While this may be one opinion, it was not held by everyone. Morrissey, for example, was pleased with his addition to the group. "Most of the songs were sung by Lou, who had no personality, and I thought that could be remedied," he later said. "She [Nico] could actually sing in a beautiful deep German voice."

Morrissey's early support of Nico raises the possibility of the negative reviews being a product of her heritage—tinged with a bit of misogyny—not a lack of talent. "She got her share of ridicule from the press with her deep Germanic voice, which I always tried to get her not to sing with," the Velvets' guitarist Sterling Morrison said in retrospect. "She could sing high and sweet if she wanted to. But Nico could sing, she could sing the songs that we had her do and sing them well." What cannot be ignored watching Nico on film is that the camera loved her. Just as Warhol and Morrissey had envisioned, she provided a stark contrast—tall, blonde, and almost noble—to the black-clad Velvets, with one writer saying, "She did not steal the limelight so much as absorb it."

Besides possible issues with the songs themselves, another problem was already apparent, in the shape of a disgruntled—and displaced—Reed. "I realized from the start that Lou didn't like it one bit. He made that obvious," Morrissey concluded. In the documentary *Lou Reed: Rock & Roll Heart*, the singer confirms his initial dismay, saying, "We didn't really feel we had a choice. I mean, we could have just walked away from it, or we had a chanteuse. So we had a group meeting and said, 'All right, we'll have a chanteuse, and Lou will write a song or two for her, and then we'll still be the Velvet Underground.' You know, why not?" In the same film, John Cale notes, "When Nico was introduced as sort of the great headline-maker, that was when I started thinking about Andy as the media manipulator, the master of all that." Nico's appearance, once again, was a quality to be exploited—not only as a part of the fledgling group, but as integral to maintaining Warhol's glamourous image in his ever-revolving PR machine. "Her appearance was spectacular, tall and very feminine, very elegant, and she didn't jump up and down and wave her hips...[she could] also be the girl that can replace Edie for Andy's photo opportunities. It was a perfect idea," Morrissey recalled.

From the start, there seemed to be a miscommunication of what exactly Nico's role within the Velvets would be. Early on, Morrissey thought that he and Warhol would "put her in the band because the Velvets need somebody who can sing or who can command attention when they stand in front of a microphone, so she can be the lead singer, and the Velvets can still do their thing." Though Warhol offered the money, space, potential fame and associations that the Velvets—and Nico—were looking for, there were immediate clashes of personalities, taste, and expectations. Nico interpreted the offer as her chance to front a group and become an integral part of the Warhol/Factory scene. She wanted the Velvets essentially to be her backing band and for her to sing all of their songs. This, however, was not an option for the multi-instrumentalists and composers. In *Nico: Icon*, John Cale remembers, "The idea of having her in the band in the first place was really offensive...especially to Lou and I...It was a very good publicity move from Andy. And no one could understand the value...of having a beautiful blond lady standing there doing not much more than playing tambourine for the show."

The other Velvets felt similarly. "Andy suggested we use Nico as a vocalist," recounted Sterling Morrison. "We said fine, she looks great, and just gradually tried to work her in." But "there were problems from the very beginning," he said, "because there were only so many songs that were appropriate for Nico, and she wanted to sing them all—'I'm Waiting for the Man,' 'Heroin,' all of them. We said, 'No, no!' She wasn't very egotistical; I always explained it by saying she's not very good at English."

Drummer Maureen "Moe" Tucker also had issues with the new addition, proclaiming that Nico "was a schmuck, from the first. She was this beautiful person who had traveled through Europe being a semi-star. Her ego had grown very large. I kept to myself until she wanted to sing 'Heroin.' But then I had to speak my piece."

Lou Reed "was hostile to Nico from the start," said Morrissey. He was especially upset about the reasoning behind the Warhol/Morrissey proposition. "Of course, Lou Reed almost gagged when I said we need a girl singing with the group so we could get extra publicity," Morrissey said. The singer did not want to fold Nico into the Velvet Underground, so the annexation of the Velvet Underground & Nico was created. "I didn't want to say they needed somebody who had some sort of talent, but that's what I meant," Morrissey concluded. "Lou was very reluctant to go with Nico, but I think John Cale prevailed on him to accept that as part of the deal."

"Andy Warhol persuaded Lou Reed to have her in the front as a singer. It is such an extraordinary thing to do, it is hard to believe you could do that to Lou Reed. Andy had the power," said Victor Bockris, who has penned several biographies on Reed and Warhol.

Nico seemed completely alien to the Velvets, an appendage rather than an addition, from the start. "No one knew what to make of her, but we were far too self-concerned to either argue or refuse. Here was this formidable woman, the world's first supermodel. We were awed by her style," recalled Cale. "She was quintessentially the person that Andy used to make us aware of another dimension to music: publicity and image making."

Nico's own talent and her drive to make the arrangement work are rarely discussed. Despite the hostility around her, Cale claimed that she did want to be a part of the band. "She was much more ready to adopt new ideas," he said. "She had a thirst for it. I don't think particularly that she and I got along any better than anybody else in the band. They all thought that she was a little bit of a fly in the ointment."

Regardless of her desire to contribute to the project, the bottom line, at the end of 1965, was that Nico was already well established in certain arty circles, while the Velvets were virtually unknown. "Nico was sort of the bigger of the two," said Morrissey. "She had had one record released in England, and she was in *La Dolce Vita*, and she was a famous model. Nico was somebody, they were nobody." Even *Playboy* magazine waxed poetic over Nico, calling her "the most ethereal and lovely of Warhol's superstars; seeing her in her floor-length cloak and listening to her musical, remote talk, one gets the impression of a medieval German Madonna glimpsed in a dream full of images of spring and sunlight."

———

Though initially unconvinced about Nico's presence in his band, Reed quickly changed his mind. He was not immune to her allure, and found himself falling in love with her, confiding to his friend Richard Miskin, "Nico's the kind of person that you meet and you're not quite the same afterward. She has an amazing mind." Miskin also claimed that "Lou loved the fact that Nico was big."[56] Reed spoke publicly of the undeniable appeal of the model to journalist Vernon Gibbs, saying, "If you get into Nico, there's always the danger that you don't want to leave." In describing the dynamic between the two, he seemed almost to worship Nico for a time, considering her far out of his league: "I was this poor little rock and roller...and here was this goddess." However, Sterling Morrison saw the emerging relationship as a sly maneuver by Nico to gain status and control within the band. "You could say that Lou was in love with her, but Lou Reed in love is a kind of abstract concept," Morrison later said. "She would try and do little sexual politics things in the band." He continued, "Whoever seemed to be having undue influence on the course of events, you'd find Nico close to them."

As a woman with little education, even less family mobility and living in the context of the pre-1960s women's movement, Nico's sexuality would have been one, if not the only, tool she knew she could use to find a place in the world, outside of the expected homemaker matriarch that she often played in print ads. Within this framework, it seems unfair and arguably misogynist simply to cast her as either a femme fatale or a woman looking for a man to define her. Nico's remarks about her relationship with Reed could be seen to back this up, as they are fairly innocuous, suggesting almost a brotherly love rather than a rabid affair on her part. She described Reed as "very sweet and lovely. Not offensive at all. You could just cuddle him like a sweet person when I first met him, and he always stayed that way. I used to make pancakes for him. Everybody loved him around the Factory; he was rather cute, you know, and he said funny things." She also admitted that "I fell in love with him. He was so beautiful," describing him in words that were often applied to her, saying he was "very tough. Tough like a statue." Yet she confessed that the two "quarreled a lot," and he made her cry. But Nico was willing to take the crumbs of affection offered by the frontman, saying, "But he could be nice to me."

At the end of 1965, Reed, Morrison and Cale all moved into an apartment at 450 Grand Street in the Lower East Side. However, Reed started being noticeably absent, instead choosing to spend the night at the apartment Nico was subletting on Jane Street in Greenwich Village.[57] It was here that Lou wrote a song for the tall blonde. "One night Nico came up to me and said, 'Oh Lou, I'll be your mirror,'" he recalled. "A close friend of mine always said that I bring out the idiocy in people, but I can also bring out something in them which is the best they've ever done. It's like with Nico and John Cale. They were fantastic with the Velvet Underground. They helped produce a great sound then. When I gave Nico a song of mine to sing, I knew she would totally understand what was being said and perform it from that standpoint." Gerard Malanga stresses the importance of the relationship for Reed, saying of "Mirror" in *Uptight*, "Lou must have been in love with Nico when he wrote this beautiful, tender love song." Warhol encouraged Reed to write more songs specifically for Nico to sing. "Andy said I should write a song about Edie Sedgwick. I said, 'Like what?' and he said, 'Oh, don't you think she's a femme fatale, Lou?' So I wrote 'Femme Fatale' and we gave it to Nico."[58]

It is very likely that Nico experimented with drugs during her time with Reed, though manager Paul Morrissey actively tried to persuade her not to. Victor Bockris believes that it was the uppers popular with the Factory crowd that were most likely passed around recreationally. "Nico has a little time living with Lou, then a little time living with John. Both those guys are drug users. When you are living with someone, you get high together. She obviously took drugs with Lou Reed. She obviously took drugs with John

Cale. I don't think these drugs were heroin. I can't say for a fact they weren't, but I think it is more likely they were amphetamines," Bockris tells me. "It's a rock world thing, in those days. Andy was famous for the amphetamine rapture sensibility that went into a lot of his work at the Factory, from 1964 onwards. It was pretty much fueled by that. That is true." Bruno Blum recalled a much different vibe, noting a distinct change in his friend Nico once she entered the Factory orbit. "I have a couple of interviews of Nico in the Factory in the '60s, and the way she's speaking shows evidence that she's completely spaced out, that she was on drugs," he claimed. "The way she speaks is very hazy and she doesn't really know what she's doing there...She's completely on a cloud, and that's the impression I always got with her...she was always on this cloud looking at the world and she's not part of it." Either way, the drugs cannot have helped the budding *amore* between her and Reed, and the camaraderie provided by the pair's romantic infatuation quickly crumbled.

Cale labeled the duo's affair as "both consummated and constipated," Reed's odes for Nico being "psychological love songs." "It was very much a love–hate relationship," Cale says in *Nico: Icon*. "Lou's affection for Nico quickly faded." Nico's warm, almost maternal love for Reed also turned cold, with her later claiming that "Lou liked to manipulate women, you know, like program them. He wanted to do that with me. He told me so. Like computerize me." Tension between Nico and the band also revolved around her vocal delivery—or what they saw as the lack thereof. "I don't think anyone was impressed with her musical ability," said Cale. "Singing in tune was the first objection that was brought up. But then we didn't play in tune."

The Nico/Reed breakup during a band rehearsal at the Factory was very public. Nico's ability to deliver one-liners was perfectly illustrated when she decided to call it quits officially with Reed. "Nico came in late, as usual," Cale recalled. "Lou said hello to her in a rather cold way. Nico simply stood there. You could see she was waiting to reply, in her own time. Ages later, out of the blue, came her first words: 'I cannot make love to Jews anymore.'" According to Cale, Lou was "absolutely torn up about it all" and did not take the breakup well. Nico's antisemitic comment, however, did not faze the frontman, as racy and edgy quips were de rigueur with the Factory crowd. Cale points out that Reed was not the most pleasant person to be around at the time, recalling that "Lou wanted to be the queen bitch and spit out the sharpest rebukes of anyone around." In an interview with *The Times*, he highlights this, saying of the comment, "All the revisionist speculation about her [Nico] being a racist is ridiculous. She told a joke, at least partially at the expense of her own national stereotype, and people chuckled and got on with their chores." Nico was simply trying to assert some control within the parameters of a band that she had been foisted upon and get the upper hand within the often catty environment of the Factory.

On February 6, 1966, the Delmonico Hotel was hosting the annual dinner for the New York Society for Clinical Psychiatry. In an attempt to add a hipness factor to the proceedings, Dr. Robert Campbell, the chairman of the dinner and director of the psychiatric unit at St. Vincent's Hospital, invited Andy Warhol to speak after the meal. In *POPism*, Warhol explained how the historic event came to fruition: "I told him I'd be glad to "speak," if I could do it through movies, that I'd show *Harlot*[59] and *Henry Geldzahler*,[60] and he said fine. Then when I met the Velvets I decided that I wanted to "speak" with them instead, and he said fine to that, too."

The dinner was not meant to be a serious undertaking or premiere. It was more a dry run, to see how far the freaky Factory entourage could push the proverbial envelope before an audience of "straights." "The psych convention started out as a con," remembered Billy Name. "We were mingling with them as they arrived, but it was more as if Edie Sedgwick's aunt had thrown a big party. We would naturally talk to everybody, but not like they were guests, more like they were Edie's relatives." Little did the attendees anticipate the mayhem that broke out the second their main course was set in front of them: this was the Factory entourage's signal to begin the real entertainment.

Like most things in her life, Nico's live debut with the Velvets was unusual. As soon as the dinner plates had been set down, "The Velvets started to blast, and Nico started to wail . . . Over roast beef," reported Superstar Ultra Violet, going on to say that "the doctors are bombarded by the decibels of three fire engines and blinded by stun gun lights...Four Freudians and one Jungian walk out needing first aid for their eyes and ears. One Fifth Avenue practitioner regurgitates his roast beef, and several analysts are hard making appointments with each other for the next day." Not to be left out, Gerard Malanga and Edie Sedgwick joined in the cacophony, jumping up on the stage, Malanga swinging his whip and Sedgwick shaking her butt. Behind the band, a film was being shown—a high contrast black and white movie of a man tied to a chair being tortured. Just as the bewildered doctors were coming to their senses, Factory member Barbara Rubin and director Jonas Mekas crashed through the banquet doors. Armed with bright lights and cameras, the two young cinematographers rushed over to the startled psychiatrists, screaming in their faces, "What does her vagina feel like?" "Is his penis big enough?" "Do you eat her out? Why are you getting embarrassed? You're a psychiatrist; you're not supposed to get embarrassed!"[61] The unsuspecting audience had mixed reactions to the stunning exhibition. Maureen Tucker remembered, "Those people were flabbergasted. I just sort of sat back and said, 'What the hell are we doing here?' Then I realized that maybe the shrinks thought they'd take notes or something...two hundred psychiatrists and us, these freaks from the Factory."

If the objective for the event was to create more publicity for the Factory, Warhol, and the new group, it was a success. "The press played it like it was ironic confrontation, which it wasn't at all," Billy Name later claimed. "We didn't shock anybody. Psychiatrists may be stiff, but they all have a sense of humor, and they're all intelligent." The following day, there were long write-ups about the banquet in both the *Herald Tribune* and the *New York Times*, the headlines declaring, "Shock Treatment for Psychiatrists" and "Syndromes Pop at Delmonico's."

The Delmonico gig marked not only a coming-out for Nico as the new focal point of the Velvet Underground, but the ejection of former Warhol muse Edie Sedgwick from the Factory's inner sanctum. At the psychiatrists' convention, Sedgwick's attempt to sing along to the Velvets was less than exceptional. "It was obvious she didn't have a voice," Malanga later told Warhol. Though Warhol claimed that "Gerard had noticed how lost Edie looked at that psychiatrists' banquet," he himself did not, later commenting, "I can't really say that I noticed." In his mind, Edie was the old. The Velvets—in particular, Nico—were the new.

In Nico, Warhol saw possibility. He immediately christened her his latest Superstar and placed upon her the title of Miss Pop 1966. She was quickly positioned as the front person of the group, becoming, according to Warhol, the "Mick Jagger of the Velvet Underground, while Lou took the humbler Keith Richards role," though the German obviously displayed a reserved restraint not familiar to the Rolling Stones' singer. These accolades were well deserved, Warhol believed, for Nico represented the next era of not only the Factory, but culture in general. "She was a new type of female superstar," said the artist. "Edie [was] outgoing, American, social, bright, excited, chatty—whereas Nico was weird and untalkative. You'd ask her something and she'd maybe answer you five minutes later. When people described her, they used words like memento mori and macabre. She wasn't the type to get up on a table and dance, the way Edie might; in fact, she'd rather hide under the table than dance on top of it. She was mysterious and European, a real moon goddess type."

There was a certain kind of person who seemed to be attracted to the Warhol dazzle. And no matter how fast one ascended into his inner circle, the descent was almost always as instant and as devastating, because, as biographer Steve Watson wrote, "in Warhol's version of stardom, beauty and glamour were inextricably linked with its demise." The year before, former Superstar Ondine had summed up the Warhol phenomenon perfectly, commenting, "Divinity, star, what's the next category? After a star is what. Has-been."

———

Performance artist and filmmaker Barbara Rubin had originally come up with the concept and name of Andy Warhol, Up-Tight, the idea being that the actions of the Factory crew at events made people feel incredibly uncomfortable—or uptight. Soon after being christened with the updated name, the Warhol group was on the lookout for a space to showcase the venture. Mekas's Cinematheque was a small movie house, specializing in experimental films, making it an ideal venue for Andy Warhol, Up-Tight's public debut.

The evening kicked off with a screening of *Lupe*, the second-to-last project that Warhol and Sedgwick worked on together.[62] The Velvet Underground and Nico followed, walking onto the stage and tuning their instruments in the dark. Behind them, *Lupe* was replaced with *Vinyl*, Warhol's version of *A Clockwork Orange*. Close-ups of Nico singing her Bob Dylan track, "I'll Keep It with Mine," were superimposed over the top. Her own image flickering behind her, Nico picked up the song from her screen image, and the rest of the group joined in. She was dressed in a white pantsuit, which contrasted with the head-to-toe black attire of the other musicians on stage. As the band launched into "Venus in Furs," Malanga and Sedgwick hopped onto the stage and began free-form dancing. The Nico movies were replaced by reels shot the previous month at the Factory, titled *The Velvet Underground and Nico: A Symphony of Sound*. With the two films—*Vinyl* and *A Symphony of Sound*—playing side by side as a visual backdrop for the stage, photographer Nat Finkelstein roamed through the audience, snapping images of unsuspecting people. Meanwhile, Rubin repeated her abrasive confrontations with the gathered fans, rushing up to them as she had at the psychiatrists' convention, screaming into startled faces. As the band's set progressed, the dancing, the unsettling visuals, and other jarring elements continued. It came to a crescendo when Malanga, using a lead pencil, mimed injecting heroin.

The next day, Warhol and the Velvets were featured in a segment on the New York public television station WNET, in which they invited the public at large to come and experience the spectacle. Announcing his new venture, the artist proclaimed, "We're sponsoring a new band. It's called the Velvet Underground...since I don't really believe in painting anymore. We have this chance to combine music and art and films all together. We're sort of working on that. The whole thing's being auditioned tomorrow at nine o'clock. If it works out, it might be very glamourous."

Andy Warhol, Up-Tight ran from February 8 to 13, 1966, at the Cinematheque. Everyone involved was pleased with it, except Nico. Given only two songs to sing, she was relegated to simply standing on stage, shaking a tambourine and looking off into a distant horizon. This turn of events did not sit well with her. Hoping to at last be fronting a group, she felt like she had barely changed roles from the fashion world she wanted to leave behind. In some ways, the part of chanteuse was just another modeling job, her contributions valued only for their visual, not creative, content, her performance as posed and inorganic as any fashion spread.

Further insult was heaped on an already distraught Nico when she saw the advertisement for the gigs. Hoping to be at the top of the listing, instead she found herself near the bottom of what was essentially a Factory roll call, lower down even than the band she believed she was to be fronting:

ANDY WARHOL, UP-TIGHT
presents live
THE VELVET UNDERGROUND
EDIE SEDGWICK
GERARD MALANGA

DONALD LYONS
BARBARA RUBIN
BOB NEUWIRTH
PAUL MORRISSEY
NICO
DANIEL WILLIAMS
BILLY LINICH

"My name was somewhere near the bottom, I remember, and I cried," Nico said. This was not helped by the continued sticking point of her wanting to include the Dylan song in the set, an idea the other band members found abhorrent. They wanted no possibility of any comparison between themselves and the folk star. "When Nico kept insisting that we work up 'I'll Keep It with Mine,' for a long time we simply refused," remembered Sterling Morrison. "Then we took a long time to learn it (as long as we could take). After that, even though we knew the song, we insisted that we were unable to play it. When we finally did have a go at it on stage, it was performed poorly. We never got any better at it either, for some reason." Instead of the Velvets performing the song with her, Nico was forced to use the vinyl copy of the cut as her backing track. "They played the record of Bob Dylan's song 'I'll Keep It with Mine' because I didn't have enough to sing otherwise," she said. "Lou wanted to sing everything. I had to stand there and sing along with it. I had to do this every night for a week." Feeling deflated, she called the shows "the most stupid concert[s] I have ever done."

Attempting to placate his newest Superstar, Andy instructed Nico "not to care" about the perceived shortcomings of the new situation as it was "only a rehearsal." He told the singer that there were bigger things coming up in the near future, an opportunity at last for Nico's vocal abilities to be showcased without her looks distracting from the music.

However, another member of the Factory inner sanctum was also disgruntled by the Cinematheque run. Thinking that the week was going to be a celebration of her film collaborations with Warhol, Edie Sedgwick was sorely disappointed to be just one small portion of a larger exhibition. Contributing musically to the Velvets was unsuccessful for her, with Nico noting that "Edie Sedgwick tried to sing along, but she couldn't do it." Edie, like Nico, was also disappointed and unclear as to how she fit into the Velvet Underground's actual stage show. "Edie began asking Andy, 'What's my place with the Velvets? I'm broke. I have no money. Why am I not getting paid?'" said Malanga. "And he said, 'You gotta be patient.' Edie said, 'I can't be patient. I just have nothing to live on.'"

Edie's displeasure at her demoted status was immediately evident. After the mention of working with Dylan's manager, Albert Grossman, and what she felt was a slight at the Cinematheque shows, Edie began to distance herself further from Warhol. "She told Andy that she had signed a contract with Bob Dylan's[63] manager Albert Grossman and he'd said she shouldn't see Andy so much because the publicity that came out of it wasn't good and she didn't want him to show her films anymore," Malanga remembered. However, Edie's hopes in Grossman for professional advancement and the folk star for romantic stability were quickly crushed. The same day that she revealed her plans to him, Warhol heard that Dylan had been secretly married for months to Sara Lownds. "Andy couldn't resist asking, 'Did you know, Edie, that Bob Dylan has gotten married?'" remembered Malanga. Edie's reaction was immediate. "She was trembling. They realized that she really thought of herself as entering a relationship with Dylan, that maybe he hadn't been truthful," concluded Malanga. After receiving this devastating news, Sedgwick excused herself and made a call—most likely to Dylan. Upon returning to the group, she announced that she was leaving the Factory for good. "She left and everybody was kind of quiet. It was stormy and dramatic. Edie disappeared and that was the end of it. She never came back," said Malanga.[64] Nico, reflecting on the shows, added, "It was Edie's farewell and my premiere at the same time."

16

At the start of March 1966, Andy Warhol found himself taking up an invitation from the Rutgers College Film Society to screen some of his movies. Seeing it as an opportunity to take his touring troupe on the road, the artist loaded up three cars with the Velvets, Nico, Gerard Malanga, Paul Morrissey, Barbara Rubin, and assorted others to make the trip down the freeway to the university campus. Upon arrival, the entourage found that only fifty-two tickets out of the thousand available had been purchased, and that a majority of the two dozen posters advertising the event had been ripped down.

This did not deter the Factory gang. In his book *POPism*, Warhol recounts the pandemonium their arrival provoked among the undergraduates, particularly in the cafeteria, where the Manhattanites had been directed to eat before the show. "The students couldn't take their eyes off Nico, she was so beautiful it was unreal," he remembered. However, the angelic presence of the chanteuse was quickly forgotten as Rubin began filming unwitting students, while Malanga yelled at security guards. Everyone in their party got kicked out, providing the perfect publicity to boost their underperforming ticket sales. "We did two shows for 650 people," Warhol writes. He clearly saw Nico as being the star and main draw of the performance. In a "datebook" now housed in the Warhol archive, Nico is listed as receiving $100 for this show, the same amount the other four Velvets had to split between themselves.

———

Fresh from the glow of their Rutgers triumph, the eleven-strong Warhol troupe piled into a van—complete with a toilet that did not work—to undertake the 1,500-mile round trip to their next booking at the University of Michigan. The most notable part of the show was actually the travel leading up to it, for at the wheel was none other than Nico. Adorned in a black leather jacket, long blonde hair flowing over her shoulders, the singer was literally taking control of the trip and the group's destiny. "Nico drove, and that was an experience," Warhol wrote. "I still don't know if she had a license. She'd only been in this country a little while and she'd keep forgetting and drive on the British side of the road. She was shooting across sidewalks and over people's lawns." For Nico, it was a way to contribute to the overall tour effort, even if it provoked fear in her companions. "I still had my American license and I was the only one who could drive," she said of her duties after the tour. "Edie used to be their chauffeur, or I mean, her chauffeur was their chauffeur. Now I was their chauffeur and chanteuse." Nico claimed that Warhol was not overtly frightened of her high-speed maneuvers at the wheel. "Oh my God! He was the only one who wasn't scared," she said. "He just couldn't care less. He figured that if I could take charge of 15 people on the bus, I have to be a good driver not to land in a ditch."

Of the shows, Warhol commented, "Ann Arbor [home to the University of Michigan] went crazy. At last the Velvets were a smash. I'd sit on the steps in the lobby during intermissions and people from the local papers and school papers would interview me, ask about my movies, what we were trying to do. 'If they can take it for ten minutes, then we play it for fifteen,' I'd explain. That's our policy. Always leave them wanting less." Nico was singled out as the highlight of the night by local reviewer Ellen Goodman of the *Detroit Free Press*: "While a beautiful blond girl sang, her image was projected on three separate 'screens,' including her own white jacket. The result was a vision of something simultaneously larger and smaller than life-size."

With two mini tours under their belts, the Velvets and Nico returned to New York, this time set to perform at a store named Paraphernalia, located on Madison Avenue. The establishment featured designs by Syracuse University graduate Betsey Johnson (who had been in the same class as Lou Reed). She was already familiar with the Velvets, having been taken on to create attire for Warhol's newest prodigies. In the audience was Nico's former flame, Brian Jones. Also present was an eighteen-year-old David Croland. "I walked into that store looking for jewelry at the time. I tried to leave the store and I heard someone say, 'Get that boy!' I was used to hearing that because I was a model and people thought I looked good…which I did! But I didn't turn around. Someone put their hand on my shoulder; it was Rene Ricard.[65] He said, 'That man over there and that girl want to meet you.' I said, 'I'll meet the girl—but who's the old man?' The old man was Andy Warhol! Keep in mind that I was eighteen, and Andy was thirty-one or something! The girl was Susan Bottomly [who Warhol later renamed International Velvet]. She'd just come to the Factory as the new Superstar. Gerard Malanga, Paul Morrissey, and Nico were also sitting amongst the crowd."

——

Located on St. Mark's Place in Greenwich Village, the Dom was originally a part of the Polish National Home. As artists of various ilk began to move into the neighborhood, the space was used as a restaurant, before being transformed by Warhol and Morrissey into a nightclub. The duo decided to place an ad in the March 31, 1966, edition of the *Village Voice* promoting the updated version of Andy Warhol, Up-Tight, which would premiere at the Dom in April. The paper used the troupe's new name, imploring readers to "come blow [their] mind[s]. The silver dream factory presents the first Erupting

Plastic Inevitable with Andy Warhol, the Velvet Underground, and Nico."

At noon on April 1, 1966, the name Andy Warhol, Up-Tight was swapped for the Exploding Plastic Inevitable (EPI), the original idea of "erupting" now replaced with "exploding." As Paul Morrissey signed the contracts, agreeing to rent the Dom for a month of shows, equipment for the multimedia event began to be hauled in. Ink not even dry, Gerard Malanga frantically painted a wall of the venue black, creating an impromptu blank screen for movies to be projected onto. Morrissey planned on using five film projectors and five slide projectors to create the visual effects for the nights. He had also found a disco ball to bounce lights off. It was set to be a spectacle, if not spectacular.

The installation of the EPI transformed the former Polish National Home into a de facto ground zero for the Velvet Underground. "When we opened the Dom, a nice setting in a spacious hall in St. Mark's Place, people didn't talk yet about the East Village," recalled Sterling Morrison. "When we started moving around, things changed. Never again did we have a place like that. We needed a base of operations, and the Dom was ideal." People were particularly intrigued as the Dom brought all of the various elements and interests of Warhol's Factory into a single space, making it a one-stop experience for all things edgy and underground. Biographer Victor Bockris described the revelers as "a cross-section of straights and gays, art tramps and artists... the thrill-seeking rich, the drugged and the desperate, beautiful girls in miniskirts and beautiful boys." Superstar Ultra Violet's memory of the venue echoes that of Bockris. In her autobiography, she reminisces, "When you go to the Dom on St. Mark's Place in the Village, you step into a magical cave. Long lines of limousines form outside. If you don't have a limo, you may as well skip it. Everybody mixes together: art people, society people, film people, drag queens, druggies, voyeurs, tourists, rock freaks, kids, kids, kids—a potpourri, which in French means rotten pot."

From the start of the EPI's time at the Dom, there was anticipation and a feeling that something meaningful was about to happen. Those running the bar had been uncertain as to whether it should open on the first night, fearing a lack of business. Instead, it was slammed by ten thirty, with customers lining up for drinks (beer 75 cents, cokes 50 cents) and food (fifty-cent sandwiches, with a choice of salami, bologna or Swiss cheese) in preparation for the evening's events. Warhol himself was impressed by the turnout of stylish youngsters wanting to immerse themselves in his circus.[66]

The EPI's success illustrated Warhol's uncanny ability to pull various disparate elements together and create something new and unexpected. "The amazing thing is that while Andy doesn't seem to be doing much more than hanging out, somehow he assembles all these people, figures out what they should be doing, pushes them to perform beyond their normal ability, devises new ways to augment the sound, intensify the visual impact, and heighten the frenzy," Ultra Violet later reflected.

———

The Dom show was choreographed to highlight Nico. During the month-long run at the club, she ascended to be the star of the event. Though Reed sang most of the Velvets' material, Nico was the focus, lit up at the front, literally glowing in spotless white pantsuits. Her command of the stage was aided by her height advantage, standing more than an inch above John Cale. Though she had openly despised her former profession, the time spent in front of the camera as a model had provided her with the ability to captivate any room. David Croland describes her performance at the Dom as "incredible...It was like Marilyn Monroe, she was lit from within. She had that thing, and it's not just because they were both blondes. She was a beacon of light, because of her looks and the way the light hit her face and her extremely pale hair. It was the visual of seeing her on a black stage and everybody dressed in black, and she was the only platinum blonde up there."

The Dom shows proved to be a financial success. In the first week, the event earned a cool $18,000, which was stored in paper bags. Though the takings were stowed unconventionally, the money paid to the performers was carefully accounted for, said Sterling Morrison. "Our actual salary from Paul Morrissey, who handled the business side for Andy, was five dollars a day, for cheese or beer at the Blarney Stone," chuckled Morrison. "He had a ledger that listed everything, including drug purchases—'$5 for heroin.' When the accountant saw it, he said, 'What the hell is this?'" The Warhol contingent all together in one place made it *the* hip place to be in town, with everyone from Allen Ginsberg to Salvador Dalí to Jackie Kennedy to TV news anchor Walter Cronkite dropping in to check out what the buzz was about. "We played music surrounded by people who were in every respect more glamourous than we were," commented Morrison. "A lot of people would come to see any kind of Warhol endeavor. The first time we played 'Heroin,' two people fainted. I didn't know if they'd OD'd or fainted. So that was our real debut—playing in Manhattan."

Press coverage of the EPI was surprisingly light. Notably, the pieces that did come out mentioned the Velvet Underground, although their focus was firmly on Nico. In the *East Village Other*, editor John Wilcock wrote, "And with the Velvets come the blonde, bland, beautiful Nico, another cooler Dietrich for another cooler generation...Art has come to the discotheque and it will never be the same again." The EPI does appear in the *New York Times*, but was shoved into the women's section, focusing more on fashion than any sort of serious revolution. The Velvets were not even referred to by name, noted as simply a "four-piece band" that appeared behind their chanteuse, who is "a fashion model, answering only to the name of Nico." Nico was the only person interviewed or singled out in the article—much to Lou Reed's annoyance. There was an accompanying picture of Nico, who was quoted saying, "Modeling is such a dull job. I don't care to get $60 an hour anymore." She received an unflattering review in the *Columbia Daily Spectator*, the Columbia University newspaper: "Nico sings terribly—she has a flat, dull voice—but the sincerity of her attempt evokes true sympathy from the audience, who accord her light applause. She smiles slightly and sings more songs, the contents of which defy interpretation, and she exits unceremoniously." Though none of the press offers kudos to Nico's vocal ability, it is the attention she received as the focal point—the very element that Warhol signed her up for—that irked Reed. As the weeks passed, more and more people came to the event, propelling Nico that much more as the breakout talent of the EPI. "Everybody in the Velvet Underground was so egomaniac," Nico later said. "Everybody wanted to be the star. I mean like Lou wanted to be the star—of course he always was—but all the newspapers came to me all the time."

Tension between Reed and Nico began to become evident during the performances. "Nico took an age in the dressing room, and then we had to wait while she'd light this candle," remembered Cale. "It was for her own good luck or something—and she held up the band, held up the gig. Lou had very little time for women and their accoutrements, and this ritual would really irritate him. The comic thing was, she'd do all this to help her performances, and then she'd start off singing on the wrong beat! Where she started in the song was a real focal point of the night! Lou would look across the stage and say, 'We know what we're doing, Nico.'"

Morrissey saw Nico as the true talent in the band. "Lou was always ill at ease as a performer," he commented. In contrast, "Nico walked out with this gorgeous face and voice and stood absolutely motionless. Oh, such class and dignity." Such appraisals did not sit well with Reed. He took out his frustration on the most vulnerable target in the entourage—the chanteuse. This treatment was not missed by others who witnessed his behavior. "He was mean to

Nico," said Malanga. "Lou could not stand to be around somebody who has a light equal to his or who shines more intensely." Hope Ruff was a musician who worked with Reed and witnessed firsthand the abuse laid upon Nico by the disgruntled Reed. "He had a reputation for being mean to women... He was wild to Nico. I remember Lou talking to Nico like she was a pile of trash. Put it this way, he was caustic with anybody who was weaker than he was."

———

After just a few weeks at the Dom, Warhol realized that he needed to cut a record of the Velvet Underground and Nico. Though he would use some of the cash from the recent EPI gigs, Warhol did not want to foot the entire budget for the project and brought in a seemingly unlikely investor in the form of Norm Dolph. Dolph was an account representative for Columbia Records, and moonlighted by running a mobile disco. He agreed to put up the rest of the cash needed to cut the record, asking to be paid by Warhol in art. Dolph used his connections to secure what seemed like a good deal: three nights—enough time to lay down an album—at the Cameo-Parkway Studios on Broadway, for the rock-bottom price of $2,500. However, the facilities proved to be less than glamourous, as they were in the midst of construction. "The floorboards were torn up, the walls were out, there were four mikes working," described Cale. But this did not stop the group. "We set up the drums where there was enough floor, turned it all up, and went from there."[67] Most of what appeared on the first acetate copies of *The Velvet Underground & Nico* was laid down during these initial sessions.

Though partially footing the bill, Warhol was not present for most of the recording.[68] It was not his physical presence but his artistic license and support that was most crucial for the Velvets. Cale and Reed both said later that it was the pop artist who insisted that the band remain faithful to their vision and not bow to commercial pressures. In the documentary *Transformer*, Reed delves further into this idea, pointing out, "What he did do is he made it all possible... One by his backing. And two, before we went in the studio he said, 'You've got to make sure—use all the dirty words. And don't let them clean things.' And so, when he was there, they—you know—they didn't dare try to say, 'Hey, why don't you do that over?' or any one of all the other things they would normally have done never happened."

Though they were having some creative breakthroughs, the usual tensions between the chanteuse and the original four Velvets haunted the band. Reed did not want Nico on the record at all, while she wanted to sing more than the paltry handful of songs that her ex-lover had reluctantly thrown her way. Morrissey was keen to see the German be the lead on most, if not all, of the tracks. "Lou didn't want Nico to sing at all," he later confided. "I'd say, 'But Nico sings that song on stage,' and he'd reply, 'Well, it's my song,' like it was his family. He was so petty." Gerard Malanga shares a similar view: "All I remember is suddenly Nico had no material to sing," he says in his book *Uptight*. "Lou didn't want her on the album. Lou was always jealous of Nico and he only let her sing little songs on the album and then he wrote a song for her called 'Sunday Morning' and wouldn't let her sing it." Various accounts of the sessions mentioned Nico being brought to tears after receiving criticism from her bandmates, anecdotes that could very well be true, based on what Warhol recounts in *POPism*: "The whole time the album was being made," he wrote, "nobody seemed happy with it."

17

In May 1966, a young record executive by the name of Tom Wilson announced a big move in *Billboard* magazine, the bible of the recording industry. He would be swapping his former home of Columbia Records, where he had worked to make the first electric recordings of folk heroes Bob Dylan and Simon & Garfunkel, for Verve, a subsidiary of MGM. At the time, Wilson was quoted as saying his mission was to "build up an LP operation and establish artists with consistent LP value" at his new place of work. He was already producing the Mothers of Invention's debut and saw the Velvets as perfect for the unconventional roster he was trying to assemble. According to Sterling Morrison, Wilson offered the Velvets the freedom that had been lacking at other possible record companies. "[Wilson] told us to wait and come and sign with him when he moved to Verve [because he swore] that at Verve we could do anything we wanted," Morrison said. "And he was right."

Paul Morrissey, however, offered up another view on why the band signed to the label: it was their only choice. "I sent it [the demo] to all the record companies, they all said no," he said. "Finally this guy from Verve contacted me, Tom Wilson. He was a very nice guy, Harvard-educated." But it was not the band as a whole that enticed Wilson; it was their beguiling blonde. "He said, 'I'm interested in recording them, I went to see them. I can't put any of this on the radio.'" However, this did not dissuade the Verve employee. "That girl is fantastic," Wilson told Morrissey. "She could be a big star, and I'll sign the whole group just to have Nico."

This was not the news that Reed wanted to receive, and it did nothing to ease the already palpable tension between the foursome and the German addition. "When I went back, I made the mistake of telling that to Lou, and he really froze," said Morrissey. "The last thing in the world that he wanted to hear was this album was only being taken on because of beautiful Nico with the beautiful voice, and that Tom Wilson really wanted her, not them."

———

On the last day of April 1966, the fourteen-strong Exploding Plastic Inevitable flew to California. On May 2, just two days after touching down in Los Angeles, all four members of the Velvet Underground and Nico signed two contracts with MGM Records.[69] The band would receive a grand advance of $3,000 to split between them and a royalty payment of 7 percent of the suggested retail price of every album sold.

Besides signing a record deal, a series of shows had been planned. The first was a residency at Los Angeles venue the Trip, scheduled to last from May 3 to 18. Before that, the entourage checked in at the Castle, a large medieval-style mansion. Popular with the rock set, the entire party was housed there, atop the Hollywood Hills, at a cost of $500 a week. Lou Reed and Nico got the best rooms in the dilapidated abode and used any down time to rehearse on a third-floor balcony. Mary Woronov was part of the cast of the EPI and had traveled with the rest of the act to Los Angeles. In her biography, she illustrates the lack of any sort of support system for Nico, underscoring how lonely and judged the singer must have felt: "On tour, Nico was the one I had to avoid. She was so beautiful she expected everyone to want to fuck her, even the furniture, which groaned out loud when she walked into the room. I had seen chairs creep across the carpet in the hopes that she might sit down on them. Naturally I treated her like the plague, bunking instead with Maureen, the drummer, who was so frightened of me she wore her entire wardrobe to bed every night."

Warhol, however, was excited about showing off his newest project to the sunny West Coast, proclaiming, "I love LA. I love Hollywood. They're beautiful. Everybody's plastic but I love plastic. I want to be plastic." He was especially looking forward to debuting his new Superstar and felt that she would be an immediate hit in Tinseltown, saying, "Nico could probably make it here tomorrow. She has that ability to be 5 and 50 at the same time." Despite the artist's optimism, things started to fall apart almost immediately after touchdown in the City of Angels. John Cale later said, "From the moment we landed in Los Angeles...we sensed something was wrong." The psychedelic free love movement had taken root and was evident everywhere, from the radio waves being filled with dreamy bands like the Mamas and the Papas to the drugs of choice being LSD and marijuana. Everything seemed upbeat and hopeful, in contrast to the Velvets' jaded, speed-influenced minimalism.

With tickets selling at $3, the Trip was set to be close to capacity on opening night. The crowd was packed auspiciously with various members of Laurel Canyon royalty, including several of the Byrds and Mama Cass. Hollywood elite in the form of Ryan O'Neal, as well as Sonny and Cher Bono, rounded out the star-studded audience. Also among the attendees was a young film student from UCLA named Jim Morrison.[70] Though he would later play a big part in Nico's life, the two did not formally meet on this occasion, the aspiring frontman just one punter in a sea of many.

Things quickly went downhill. The first blow was when the Velvets found out that the opening act was their soon-to-be Verve labelmates the Mothers of Invention. The hometown crowd of hippies and peaceniks cheered the Frank Zappa-led band and booed the slick, black-clad Velvets. This immediately caused a rivalry between the East and West Coast rock acts, a face-off between flower power free love and amphetamine-fueled energy.

Reed took an instant dislike to Zappa, referring to him as "probably the single most untalented person I've heard in my life." Cher was equally unimpressed with the New Yorkers, telling the press that the EPI "depressed" her and that it "will replace nothing, except maybe suicide." Warhol picked up the quote and began using it for the group's own ads. The second night at the Trip proved equally problematic. At the end of their set, the frustrated Velvets turned all of their amplifiers to full power and placed their instruments on them, creating loud, abrasive feedback, then walked off the stage, making them even more unpopular with the club owner.

Any news outlet brave enough to contend with the East Coasters had differing opinions of the entire troupe, but they almost universally singled Nico out, giving her mixed reviews. *Los Angeles Times* journalist Kevin Thomas described the singer as "the long-haired, deep-voiced German model [who] sing[s] songs as beautifully banal as herself," and the Velvets as "a rock group that goes beyond rock... It was like a searing sound from another planet." An equally provocative description was supplied by the *Los Angeles Free Press*, reporter Paul Jay Robbins writing, "Nico, the chanteuse, mitigates the impending collapse of sanity primarily because of her ineptitude as a singer. Her heavy and diffident voice seems to suggest that perhaps this is all a put-on—and by the time you realize it isn't, you've grown accustomed to the mace."

The most damning critique came from the weekly magazine *Hitline*, which was put out by local radio station KFBW. "It's nice that the Trip wanted to try something new, but this is a tasteless, vulgar review that should never have opened," an author going by the singular handle of Burton wrote. "The show consisted of questionable 'underground movies' shown on four screens plus music by the Velvet Underground (very uninteresting) and singing by Nico (fantastic beauty, but no voice)." In another Los Angeles newspaper, the EPI was accused of offering "neither art nor order but contempt, contempt, which is death by negation," with Nico singled out as "a blonde Nordic standing like a three-way lamp, turned on dim."

Any fear that the negative reviews would scare people from coming to the rest of the EPI's month-long residency was quelled when, on the third night, the club was suddenly shut down by the Los Angeles County Sheriff's Department. Decades later, Maureen Tucker spoke of the ill-fated gigs, commenting, "The audience was fine, but the critics and the club owners and music people didn't like us at all." Reed echoed this sentiment, reflecting, "They saw this as this terrible, terrible influence of the virus and disease of New York City into the beautiful new counterculture of the West Coast."

Though feeling like *personae non gratae*, the Factory group could not leave Los Angeles immediately. In order to fulfill the rules of their Musicians' Union contract and collect their $3,000 performance fee, the entire troupe had to stay in town, regardless of whether the Trip reopened or not. The unexpected down time was used to record the debut album, with Tom Wilson producing.[71] The process was very hard for the chanteuse, who was aware of her various difficulties in providing the performances that the band expected of her. "We used to tape our rehearsals, to check. Nico was very vulnerable to this," remembered Cale. "We'd listen and hear her go off-key or hit the wrong pitch at the start. We would sit there and snigger, 'There she goes again!,' which might seem a little cruel now... This made for interesting times. Every now and again she went 'weeergh' and lost control of the pitch; she was very sensitive to all this and when I produced her albums later on I would have her sing and the musicians play in separate sessions."

Throughout the recording, Wilson pushed for Nico to be included on more tracks. "Listen. The only thing I don't like about the record is, there's not enough Nico," Paul Morrissey recalled the Verve executive saying. "You've got to get another song from Nico. And there's nothing here we can use on the radio, so why don't we get Nico to sing another song that would be right for radio play?" The result is the Reed-penned "Sunday Morning," a track that Morrissey described as "terribly insipid" and "dopey," although first run-throughs of the cut "sounded all right," he said, because Nico "brought something weird to everything."

However, upon hearing that the song was a possible radio single, Reed insisted at the last minute on recording himself on lead vocals. As Morrissey recalled, "He sang it! The little creep. He said, 'I wanna sing it 'cause it's gonna be the single.' Tom Wilson couldn't deal with Lou, he just took what came. Then later, he got Nico back into the studio and gave her a verse or put her with Lou's voice or something, I can't quite remember. Tom Wilson had to force Nico to take this option, you can imagine. We were always fighting tooth and nail to get poor Nico on. She didn't fight this sort of thing herself, she was very shy and self-effacing. She would make a little remark. Or then she would giggle a lot. She'd giggle like a girl."

Still clinging on to the hope that some positivity might result from their trip out west, the EPI headed up to San Francisco. Prior to the gigs scheduled to take place at the Fillmore Auditorium from May 27 to 29, Warhol, Malanga, and Nico did a flurry of interviews, including one filmed press conference for public television station KQED. All of the questions fired at Warhol were instead answered by the other two Superstars. Nico's presence at the various junkets underscores the continued effort to position her as the star of the show.

However, similar to their experience down south, the Velvets found themselves out of step with their northern Californian contemporaries. The two big psychedelic bands coming up at the time were the Grateful Dead and Jefferson Airplane, whose beards, beads, and bohemianism did not gel with the Velvets' aesthetic. There was also an almost immediate animosity between promoter Bill Graham and the Factory contingent, the two parties clashing on everything from light shows to drugs, with the Velvets' show coming to an abrupt end. Writer Bruno Blum summed up the conflict between the two coasts, claiming, "Everyone [from New York] was on drugs. Nico was on amphetamines, she wasn't going to sleep for 25 hours... simple as that. They got kicked out of the Fillmore because they had a giant plastic cock on the stage and the sheriff saw it and closed down the club."

———

Though having issues with her bandmates in the Velvet Underground throughout the first months of their union, Nico was still held in high regard by other members of the Factory's inner circle. In his book *Uptight*, Gerard Malanga shares a recorded chat with his fellow Superstar Ingrid, as well as his own essay, originally written for a magazine in early 1967. By this time, both Ingrid and Malanga had been on the road with Nico as part of the EPI. Yet in both pieces, Nico seems two-dimensional: it is her appearance, once again, which is fundamentally the basis of their admiration, not her personality. When her singing is mentioned, it is not very complimentary, the one area she is trying to become known for being negatively critiqued and brushed aside. Ingrid describes Nico's voice as "very bland and low and smooth... some people mistake it for a boy's voice. And she sings sort of like in one tone mostly. She doesn't have too much modulation." Malanga is equally unsympathetic, likening her voice to "the sound of an amplified moose."

Her appearance, however, is "impeccable," writes Malanga. "If there exists a beauty so universal as to be unquestionable, Nico possessed it," he gushes. And though Nico is twenty-seven years old at the time of the recording, Ingrid refers to her as "just a very, very beautiful girl—a cool Dietrich for a cool generation." Any interest in engaging with the singer as anything but the most vapid simulacrum is dashed, the essay going on to argue that "Nico would be most effectively represented in sculpture"—making her mute as well as impassive.

The emphasis on her lifelessness is repeated throughout numerous press pieces and reviews. An article in the June edition of *ArtNews* substantiates this theme of Nico being present but absent, a specter of sorts on the stage. Writer David Antin portrays her as "perfect as a cadaver" and having a "macabre face," as well as a "marvelous death-like voice." While these details may evoke the stage persona of the singer, they also dehumanize her. The more the trope of wooden, unemotional performances was repeated, both among friends and in the press, the more it seemed acceptable, normal, and correct to categorize Nico in these incredibly simplistic of terms, without bothering to look beyond them.

David Croland offers a completely different portrait of Nico, one that points to the public and personal sides of the singer—the latter one that she rarely revealed, and then only to those she trusted. "Nico was not a phoney," he asserts. "If she didn't like somebody, she wouldn't go out and say something nasty; she just didn't respond. If she liked someone, she very quietly let you know she liked you or even loved you."

———

Warhol's support for Nico continued into June. Having left for Ibiza, she did not appear at the Velvet Underground's week-long residency at Poor Richard's in Chicago. However, the posters none-theless advertised "the new sound of the Velvet Underground and Nico—Pop girl of '66." Warhol also set her up to feature as a host-ess in a series he consulted for on local station WNAC-TV.[72] In August, Warhol and Nico did a photo shoot for *Esquire* magazine, dressed as Batman and Robin. The text called for "an end to the sixties," begging that "the next four years be a vacation." In *POPism*, Warhol asserts this is because "everyone was feeling the acceleration" of events around them—or else it was simply the omnipresent uppers. "Amphetamine was the big drug in New York in the sixties because there was so much to do that everybody was living double-time or they'd miss half of what was going on," he later reflected. "There was never a minute around the clock where you couldn't be at some kind of a party. It's amazing how little you want to sleep when there's something to do."

———

July 1966 marked six months since Nico had officially become a part of the Velvet Underground, at least on stage. However, various relationship issues, jealousies, and pettiness within both the band and the Factory as a whole were beginning to frustrate her. She found that the reality of her daily circumstances did not match up to what she read about herself and the EPI in the media. Needing a break away from Warhol and New York, Nico once again escaped to Ibiza. On the way back, she decided to swing by Paris and pick up Ari. He was about to celebrate his fourth birthday and was staying with Pauledith Soubrier—his aunt Didi. Nico made her presence known by "knocking unannounced" at Didi's house. "Even the way she arrived at the house was exceptional," Soubrier remembered. "She would just turn up, hello, as though you had seen her last one hour before. There was never a warning, an arrangement. She arrived, and after she had exhausted your hospitality, she left."

However, Nico's love for Ari and disappointment in the non-existent bond with Delon were evident to many who met her. "She was a Francophile and the only time I ever saw her show a little bit of some vulnerability was when she mentioned Alain Delon in her song. You could see a little twinge of it there," recounted Iggy Pop, who first saw Nico at the Velvet Underground show in Ann Arbor. Though she was by no means a traditional mother, Pop remembered seeing "pride that she'd had a son...That was important to her, even though I don't think she was a peanut butter and jelly sandwich type. She was not one to say, 'Hey kids! How was school today?'"

18

Now with Ari in tow, Nico returned to New York. Almost immediately upon arrival, she found herself once again involved with a Warhol project. Andy had already begun shooting his new film the month before and would continue to complete one thirty-three-minute reel a week on average for almost four months. His primary set was dingy bohemian dive the Chelsea Hotel. At the end of the process, Warhol found himself with too much footage, some black and white, some color, some with sound. In an ingenious stroke of creativity, the artist decided to show two films side by side on a split screen. Composed of twelve separate episodes featuring Warhol's assembled cast of Factory intimates and Superstars, the finished product was, according to critics, "beautiful," "impactful" and "schizophrenic," especially when the same person was shown on both reels, exhibiting different actions or parts of their personalities. Created more as an experiment than a serious cinematic release, *Chelsea Girls* became a surprise hit. Made for less than $1,500, it grossed over $500,000, setting a precedent for underground films.

There were no scripts and barely any direction from Warhol, leaving the Factory regulars who featured to make up their own sketches and scenes on the spot. Warhol's few instructions would be along the lines of "Tell the story of your life, and somewhere along the line take off your pants." Echoing her time in *La Dolce Vita*, where she felt she was "already playing the role of Nico," the singer found herself a bit confused about how to once again inhabit an additional role on top of the persona she was already channeling. As Nico later recalled, this was reflected in the scenes in which she featured that eventually made it into the finished movie: "For my scenes, Paul and Andy could not think of a situation for me...I was already Nico. So, for one scene I was nothing but Nico and they put lights on my face. In the other, we were in this white kitchen. I think they wanted somewhere white, isn't that it? A white girl with blonde hair in a white room. Ari was there, and I think they wanted to keep Ari in control...Then Andy said I must do something. But they wanted me in close-up for the whole reel. I could make a meal in the kitchen, but no, this was too busy...There were some scissors, and maybe Paul said, 'Cut your hair.' I didn't want to. But it was something I could do that was in shot of the camera. The bastards made me cut my hair."

———

Though he had been tasked with writing the theme song for the film, Lou Reed had not delivered, illustrating what biographer Victor Bockris told me was "a passive-aggressive signal of how he felt about any further collaborations with Warhol and Nico." His behavior toward her became even more nasty. He was openly critical of her in front of other people. The various issues with the release of *The Velvet Underground & Nico*, ranging from technical problems with Warhol's peelable banana on the LP cover art to West Coast rivals the Mothers of Invention's record coming out first, only added to near catastrophic tension.[73]

Chelsea Girls being a hit did not sit well with Reed, either. As the movie's popularity grew, so did Nico's profile and status, making her known beyond the underworld art house crowd. Soon she was more famous than Cale—whom she now was sleeping with—or Reed, who was openly jealous of her rising fame. Seeing Nico's ascent, Morrissey encouraged Warhol to continue his support of the chanteuse, as he thought she was a much more marketable star than Reed. To further her blossoming singing career, Morrissey booked Nico to play some dates in October 1966 at Stanley's, "a hip place where Harlem met bohemia." The arrangement seemed mutually beneficial for Nico and the proprietor, Stanley Tolkin, who also opened the Dom at St. Marks Place. Nico had Ari to support and was anxious to start performing properly as a solo act. Tolkin saw her as a way to rid the venue of the "almost 100 percent black clientele" that he currently had coming in, because they didn't drink much and lowered the bar take. Tolkin wanted to "get some white people in" and thought that "black people [would] hate Nico's music."[74] A suggestion that the Velvets perform as her backing band—what Nico thought she was signing up for in the first place when she agreed to work with the Velvets—was vehemently opposed by an irate Reed. He did not want any of his bandmates participating either, finally suggesting that they make a tape to accompany her. Warhol vividly remembered Nico "trying to work a little cassette recorder" at the Stanley's shows. However, he despaired at the overall effect, as "it was pathetic to see this big, beautiful woman singing to music coming out of this cheap little cassette, and in between acts the tears would roll down her face because she just couldn't remember how the buttons worked."

There has never been a definitive date or incident that points to Nico either officially quitting or being fired from the Velvets. In *Nico: Icon*, Sterling Morrison makes it seem like a mutual drifting apart, commenting that "she sort of spun off out of the band, just as she spun into it." Warhol's account of the final fallout between the dueling divas (Reed and Nico) suggested it was more heated, and he hints that the main issue that dogged the fivesome from the start revolved around who was the band leader—a factor that often goes unacknowledged. In *POPism*, he writes, "Nico and Lou had a fight. ('I've had it with the dramatic bullshit,' he said. 'Yeah, she looks great in high contrast black and white photographs, but I've had it.') He said he wouldn't let her sing with them anymore and, moreover, that he was never going to play for her again, either. (That was actually the big problem right there—was she singing with them, or were they playing for her?)"

Nico's interview in *Twen* matches Warhol's memories. As she recalled, "They threw me out because I wanted too much. I wanted to sing more songs and they could have given me more songs... The farewell was unpleasant; they did not even give me the opportunity to say goodbye." In subsequent interviews, she was less transparent, simply saying, "Too many scenes of jealousy," when remarking on the reason for the parting of ways. Illustrating Nico's point, drummer Moe Tucker later said of the split, "I was glad to see Nico go. To me she was just a pain in the ass."

Though being on the receiving end of such comments once she left the group, and having been bullied to the point of tears when she was working with the Velvets, Nico rarely ever uttered a disparaging remark about the band, even saying that they were "a very good group." One exception is recorded in *Twen*, when she asserts, "They do not like women at all, except John Cale. They are misogynists." Later interviews saw Nico trying to spin her departure into a scenario where it was her choice, thus casting her as the decision-maker, while also desperately trying to shift the conversation from the Velvets back to her own work. Glimpses of her true feelings about her time in the Velvets are far and few between, though she did confide in another 1974 piece that she did not "regret a minute of it!" especially because the band "were 20 years ahead" of their time.

By November, the Velvets had stopped practicing at the Factory. Nico finished her residency at Stanley's and was living with John Cale, having just ended a short liaison with her *Chelsea Girls* co-star and Factory regular Eric Emerson. Still deeply entrenched in the Warhol cohort, she appeared in a promotion with the artist at the Abraham & Straus department store in Brooklyn. The event was held to highlight a $2, one-wear, disposable dress, available in "whitest white twill of Kaycel R," that came with a do-it-yourself paint set, the idea being that each woman could customize her own apparel. Donning one of the white paper outfits, Nico lay prone in front of silver foiled screens, which were meant to resemble a portable Factory. One hundred spectators crowded into the shop and spilled out onto the streets, waiting to see the artist in action.

In pictures taken of the event, Ari can be seen seated at his mother's feet. He added his own touch to the ensemble, spraying green paint over Nico's stockinged legs. According to Ultra Violet, Nico then performed "All Tomorrow's Parties," which was "barely audible against the amplified guitars and male voices." Just discernible above the din, Warhol proclaimed to the baffled spectators, "Nico is the first psychedelic singer with the Velvet Underground. They do two hours of songs with only buzzing from a burglar alarm in between."

Nico was featured in three more Warhol short movies before the year was out. The first, simply called *Nico/Antoine*, features Nico and French singer-songwriter Antoine Muraccioli. The singer and Muraccioli are sitting under a huge banana poster, much like the image that would become the cover for *The Velvet Underground & Nico*. In the color film, the pair are eating the fruit and smirking at the camera. Muraccioli also appears in several images with Nico that have been recovered during research for this book. This is not surprising, as according to a February 1967 datebook, he was invited to New York by Warhol and Nico in October 1966 for a brief twenty-four-hour visit. Nico met him at the airport (she is noted as his "escort" in the datebook) with a large bunch of bananas.

The second Warhol short is called *Ari and Mario*. Three-year-old Ari is the star in this color film. The premise has Nico hiring drag queen Mario Montez to watch the young child. Hilarity ensues, as Montez, adorned with heavy makeup, loads of costume jewelry and light-blue lounging pajamas, tries to entertain a lively Ari. The third video, informally titled *Mod Wedding*, is a silent black-and-white piece with a two-minute running time that features Nico almost exclusively. It documents a wedding that took place on November 20, 1966, as the concluding event of a three-day festival in Detroit called the Carnaby Street Fun Festival, which was sponsored by a supermarket at the Michigan State Fairgrounds. The Velvet Underground performed, alongside appearances by other luminaries including the Yardbirds and Dick Clark. Tickets cost $2.10— or $1.10 if purchased in advance. The happy couple, Gary Norris and Randi Rossi, an "artist" and "unemployed go-go dancer," according to Warhol in *POPism*, had volunteered to be married in order to score a prize package that included a three-day honeymoon in New York City and a screen test with Warhol. In front of an audience of approximately 4,500 people, the bride, wearing "a white minidress and high white satin boots," was escorted down the aisle by the pop artist as her parents looked on. Nico, clad in a lavender pantsuit, warbled a rendition of "Here Comes the Bride," while a local DJ stood in as best man.[75] While the footage mainly showcases Nico, there are glimpses of the other Velvets performing on stage under a strobe light. The bride's mother provides the understatement of the year to United Press International, commenting, "This is not exactly the wedding I had planned for my daughter."

By February 1967, Nico had started another residency at the Dom. This one lasted until April. She was still performing sporadically in the random shows the Velvets did and was no longer modeling.[76] Though her burgeoning solo career was her only means of support, Nico was not particularly keen on playing live, telling an interviewer, "I do not like to perform in nightclubs. I do not like bars at all, not even to listen to other singers there. I feel out of place even to listen to other singers there." Regardless, the Dom offered a regular income and the chance to develop her own career away from the Velvets.

David Croland remembers four-year-old Ari's presence at the Dom. "He was one of the most beautiful children I've ever seen in my entire life," says Croland, "and I've seen many gorgeous people. This kid was so beautiful and so sweet; he was like a male version of Nico. He was very quiet; he was very shy. He only liked certain people—he had a radar even as a child—but what an incredible little boy he was. She would bring Ari to her gigs. He used to sit on my lap when Nico would be singing. Me or Susan [Bottomly] would take him, because Nico didn't want to leave him in places with some stranger. We're talking late at night! Sometimes he would crawl off of our laps and go under the table, you know how kids like to make houses under tables and stuff... He was very loved in our group. The way she used to dress him, he looked like a little rock star, little boots and black clothes... I never saw a child dressed in black in those days. I mean, 'Where did you even find these things, Nico?' He was a little rock star even then."

All through the Dom shows and the random EPI dates, Ari rarely left his mother's side. The late nights and living according to the schedule of his artist mother was not healthy for the child. He remembers going around the Dom, drinking leftover alcohol from glasses, confessing that he "swallowed anything—that is, everything in my path. Remnants of vodka, whisky, orange-flavored vitamin pills in my mother's bag..." It has been written, but not confirmed, that Nico allegedly smeared heroin on the young child's gums to calm him down. "For a little boy of four and a half, it was too much," and Ari came down with what he calls a "major hepatic crisis."

Unsure of what to do, Nico called Alain Delon's mother, Edith Boulogne, for help. Boulogne agreed to once again take Ari back to France with her, but only if Nico promised that he would be able to stay, adopt a proper schedule and be put into school. Realizing it was the best thing for her son, due to her own uncertain career, the singer agreed.

David Croland remembers when the child left with his paternal grandmother. "That was one of the saddest things I've ever seen, because Ari loved all of us. He loved Andy, he loved me—we were like his family," Croland says. "He adored Nico, and Nico adored him, but we were dropping him off so that he could spend the summer and get to know his grandparents in France. He was crying and crying. I'm sure he got over it, and the grandparents were really sweet...but that was sad."

Even at his young age, Ari realized that this was going to be a more permanent separation from his mother than previously. "It was only on the plane that I felt that the separation, this time, was more serious," he writes. Upon arrival in France, Ari found himself surrounded and haunted by constant reminders and mementos of the man who publicly denied his paternity. "I slept in the bed where Alain Delon had been conceived and where he had slept before me. All my childhood, and well beyond, until the death of my grand-parents, and still beyond, Alain Delon—the eternal absent whose history and glory were shaking the spirits of this family." However, the physical absence of his father did not stop the young boy from being curious to know more about the missing figure. "The TV seemed to have been invented only to show the films of Alain Delon...I devoured my father's eyes, immersing myself in each of his pockets, in each of his tics."

In *Nico: Icon*, Boulogne reveals the struggles and challenges she faced in taking on the role of matron to her grandchild and talks about Nico's absence and lack of attention to her son. "She came to see him once in three years," Boulogne recalled. "Packages I had sent came back. Moved, address unknown."

Nico's aunt Helma has a slightly different version of the events of 1967, which may further explain how little Nico saw Ari once he moved in with the Boulognes. "He was christened Ari, but later Delon's mother had that changed. She said, 'What is that name— Ari?' Then his name was Christian Aaron. She said to Christa, 'I will adopt your son and you will not have access to your child,'" Helma claims. She also says that Grete desperately wanted to take Ari on herself but was far too ill. Though only fifty-seven years old, Grete's Parkinson's disease had progressed to the point where she could barely even form a complete sentence, let alone look after a small child. "She couldn't take care of herself anymore and had to return to Berlin," says Helma. All of the furniture from the Ibiza house was sold for pennies, while Ulrich, Nico's cousin and Helma's son, paid for his aunt Grete to be put into residential care. Nico was now truly alone, without the anchor of her mother or the companionship of her son.

For the rest of Nico's life, Delon continued to deny paternity of Ari, a situation which "she was angry about...most of the time, because he wasn't recognizing his responsibility," according to Nico's friend and former lover Robert King. King was the lead singer of Scars, a post-punk band from Edinburgh, Scotland. He had a romantic relationship with Nico in the 1980s, which led him to become close to other members of her extended family. During his relationship with Nico, King once found himself at the same event as Delon. "It was at a record company party, you just had to be polite." He recalls that Delon did not acknowledge Nico throughout the event, though King went on the verbal attack, "slagging off" the actor. "I was calling him a cunt—'So you're that cunt'—and he was looking at me as if he couldn't understand me. It was pretty bizarre, because he then got two guys to come over and protect him…It was really funny. The Scottish use of that word is particularly potent."

Though Nico originally had to embark on her solo shows accompanied by a tape, at the urging of Paul Morrissey her former bandmates eventually took turns backing her up, though none of them was overly thrilled to help out, seeing it more as an obligation than anything else. To alleviate the problem, Morrissey began to bring in a revolving cast of other performers to play with her. The first was a young singer named Tim Buckley.

Some biographers say Buckley was introduced to Nico by Jackson Browne, while Browne himself has said in interviews that Buckley brought him into Nico's fold. Morrissey, acting as Nico's manager, claims it was none other than Danny Fields who suggested pairing Buckley and Nico together. "Tim would back up Nico and play a set of his own and not take it very seriously," recalled Browne in 2014's *Follow the Music: The Life and High Times of Elektra Records in the Great Years of American Pop Culture*. "He didn't like this place or any of the people in it. He would sing a lot of Johnny Cash songs or whatever he felt like doing, and after a week...he was out of there." After just two shows, Buckley left, passing his opening slot on to Browne.

On a whim, the eighteen-year-old Browne, from Orange County, California, had driven with two other friends to New York at the start of 1967. The singer-songwriter was already beginning to make a name for himself, having signed a publishing deal with Elektra Records, when Buckley got him the gig playing with Nico. "He was doing this gig with Nico," Browne recalled. "The night I went, Sterling

Morrison of the Velvets was playing guitar and accompanying her. And another night, it would be Lou Reed... But she needed her own accompanist. And they were all trying to get her squared away so she could have her own career, because she wasn't going to stay in the Velvets. Tim called me a couple of days after I saw the show and said, 'Do you think you would want a job as an accompanist?'... I had just gotten to New York and everybody knew I was out of money. I mean, we spent my 50 bucks getting there. I was just living on Mrs. Paul's fish cakes and mooching off my friends... there was snow on the ground, and I was wearing penny loafers—I'm from Orange County! So I started being her accompanist. And it was really an interesting thing, for the first time, to try to make up an arrangement in a key and to figure out how best to represent a song for somebody else who didn't play an instrument."

Part of the deal with Browne backing Nico included him switching from his acoustic guitar to an electric one, as Morrissey was worried that the former would see the singer classed as a folk act. Not owning the desired equipment, Browne had to borrow the appropriate instrument from a friend in Long Island. "We didn't play every night. They'd put this sign up saying, 'Andy Warhol's Mod Dom' (apparently he liked the name Dom because it was Mod backward). I went in there one night when we weren't on and it was a different place entirely, just ordinary people drinking, old songs on a jukebox. But on Nico's nights, it was kind of like a freak show," Browne recalled. This was even more apparent on the occasional nights when Warhol would show up at the Dom and provide visual accompaniment. "On the nights that Andy had the bar, there were these films being projected," Browne said. "There were loops. So there was a skydiver that was just sort of falling through the air eternally. I mean, if you looked really carefully, you could see where the loop jumped. Another loop was a loop of Lou Reed sort of glowering at the camera, eating a candy bar... Playing these sets was for people who were in there sort of to observe that scene. They were sort of voyeuristic…it would be a bunch of people from uptown, hoping to catch a glimpse of Andy Warhol and his wild entourage of freaks. You know, a bunch of lawyers or society people or whatever."

Though it was a hangout for those wanting to catch a glimpse of the Factory crowd, the Dom may not have been the most nurturing environment for Nico to launch her solo career. Rock writer Richard Meltzer claimed in a 1971 article for *Screw Magazine* that Nico "never noticed the crowd at the Dom…all those cats sitting around at ringside drawing unflattering pictures of her on their napkins in ballpoint. Pictures of Nico with a bony face with tears streaming down her face and fragile wings at her shoulders. And spiders crawling across her forehead and they used to pass the drawings around and giggle. But she never noticed, because the people talking at other tables were even louder than the laughter. Nobody ever used to listen but once in a while they used to yell out requests. 'Ruby Tuesday' and 'The Ballad of Ira Hayes' and stuff like that… once somebody even asked for some raga-rock. Jackson usually protected her from such swill and he once said, "We know it but we're not gonna do it."

Jonathan Talbot played on the same nights as Nico, and described a similarly unfriendly atmosphere at the Dom, saying it was "smoky [and] noisy, [with] the bar to the immediate left of the stage from the performer's point of view. This was not a house that particularly respected art…the Dom was a hard house to work. You just didn't expect much attention, and you didn't get it. I don't think she was playing for the people there. She was just doing her thing and leaving." Regardless of the challenging circumstances, Nico, Talbot said, "certainly got more attention than I did. And I believe she got more attention than Jackson Browne did. It varied from night to night. I think sometimes they paid good attention and they liked her, and sometimes she couldn't get that audience's attention for anything. It was real hard with all the audiovisuals going on around."

But it wasn't just the special effects that were off-putting to Talbot and other audience members not entrenched in the Factory scene; there was not much of a musical community at the venue, which was obvious to anyone not already established in the peculiar social hierarchy of the Warhol crowd. "The camaraderie which had been part of many different musical situations for me did not exist at the Dom," said Talbot. "I found Nico to be standoffish... The Warhol scene and the scene that surrounded Nico... from my experience there, a lot of it was built on pretension, or on posturing, or something like that. It didn't make for a whole bunch of interchange."

The lack of authentic artistic collaboration was not lost on Nico, who was finding the expectations of Morrissey and Warhol limiting. She felt their ideas were not positioning her to be taken seriously as a credible artist in her own right. "They originally wanted Nico to sing inside a plexiglass box," said Browne. "She flatly refused; she often grumbled about this novelty stuff they tried to make her do. We would sit up on the bar and play the same set twice nightly. She would do the Lou Reed songs, which sounded so hypnotic the way she sang them, a Tim Hardin song, a Bob Dylan song—all of them unreleased; it was an exceptional repertoire to hear, basically the songs we later recorded on *Chelsea Girl*. They were all simple songs to play, and none of us guitarists saw it as demanding work."

———

One Nico convert was a young writer who first stumbled upon Nico at the EPI shows and who religiously attended her solo gigs. Warhol noticed his constant presence, writing in *POPism*, "Leonard Cohen the Canadian poet was there [at the Dom] quite a few nights in the audience down at the bar, just staring at her [Nico]." Cohen recounted his first meeting with the vocalist, saying, "I didn't know any of these people. I saw this girl singing behind the bar. She was a sight to behold. I suppose the most beautiful woman I'd ever seen up to that moment. I just walked up and stood in front of her until people pushed me aside. I started writing songs for her then." Cohen was besotted from the moment he met Nico, though he reflected, "[W]ithin five minutes of our conversation, she told me to forget it, because she was only interested in young men. But she said, I'd love to be a friend of yours—and we became friends."

This did not stop the thirty-three-year-old from pursuing the intimidating blonde. "I was madly in love with her. I was light-ing candles and praying and performing incantations and wearing amulets, anything to have her fall in love with me, but she never did…" Cohen confessed ruefully. "The years went by and we became quite tender with each other, but nothing romantic ever came of it." Nico, however, was less than bowled over by the singer's attentions, saying of their initial meeting, "He came to see me at La Dom every night. And we both ate the same kind of food—well, he turned me on to that kind of food at the time, macrobiotic things."[77]

Cohen was not the only one lusting after the tall, stunning blonde. "She was physically like a goddess," Browne said. "There were men sitting there utterly infatuated with her. At the time there were these twenty-foot-high posters of Nico all over Manhattan, I forget quite why. It was impossible to work around the Village and not see these gigantic images of her. She didn't exploit it herself. At the Dom she sat on a straight-backed chair and crossed her long legs… She did not tout her sexuality. She didn't need to trade on it. She was dignified in her seduction. I had this gigantic crush on her, too."

Despite the ten-year age difference, romance quickly blossomed between the ex-model and the West Coast transplant, with Browne telling a friend, "Gee, I'm barely eighteen and here I am sleeping with the most beautiful girl in the world." He would often stay over at Nico's, the two artists drinking wine and watching Ari together. "She had a very childish laugh and she smiled a lot. She could be icy and distant with certain people—this is a woman bringing up a kid, you know? Of course, in real life she had her defenses…I did notice that she was always friendly with people who supported her, like doormen and the personnel who'd help her get cabs and folk like that; she was very sweet to them and I think they adored Nico in return."

Sadly, the romance was short-lived, but the Dom partnership lasted for over a month, even though Browne began bad-mouthing Nico privately. Meanwhile, Nico had begun to make her scorn for him public, during one performance accusing Browne of being the creep who was harassing her with obscene calls. Their relationship had been deteriorating, but this final blow made him so upset that he walked off mid-performance, to be replaced by a Bob Dylan associate, a willing Bobby Neuwirth, who just happened to be sitting right at the front.

Before his departure, Browne had played Nico some of his songs, several of which she began to include in her repertoire. She was the first to sing "These Days" and "The Fairest of the Seasons," which he'd written with Greg Copeland, as well as another tune called "Somewhere There's a Feather." As he left New York, Browne wrote a last song about Nico. He never gave it to anyone, and she never saw it.

———

In the midst of Nico's residency at the Dom, the long-awaited full-length *The Velvet Underground & Nico* LP was finally released. The exact date it arrived on the streets is uncertain, with various biographies placing it sometime between January 28 and March 4, 1967.[78] While initial sales were disappointing, the cover art was striking. The front featured a bright-yellow-and-black-outlined banana against a stark white background. The silk-screened image, illustrated by Warhol, includes the instruction to "Peel Slowly and See" in tiny letters. When peeled back, the fluorescent pink flesh of the fruit is revealed. Warhol's signature is prominently scribbled across the bottom right-hand side, making each copy a piece of art in itself. Flipping over the album, the back features a large photograph, captured by Paul Morrissey, of the band playing live, accompanied by smaller head shots of each member of the group.

The particular image Morrissey selected as his contribution to the LP shows the Velvet Underground performing at an EPI gig at the Chrysler Art Museum in Provincetown, Massachusetts, with a still from Warhol's *Chelsea Girls* projected behind them. The still is an upside-down image of Eric Emerson, Nico's co-star in the film. Morrissey had picked the image and produced the cover art without obtaining the actor's permission to include his likeness. Emerson, though having no malice toward the Velvets or his Factory cohort, was broke and thought that asking the band's label Verve for a fee for using the picture would result in a painless payout. He asked for an exorbitant $500,000 for the supposed distress the inclusion of his picture had caused him. "It wasn't done in any kind of malicious way. It was to get money out of the record company, basically, from my understanding of it," Factory intimate Gregg Barrios later said. Sterling Morrison, however, claimed that Emerson needed the dosh to fight an acid-possession charge, while artist Ronnie Cutrone said the actor wanted it in order to go to the UK. Whatever the reason, Verve/MGM immediately pulled all copies of *The Velvet Underground & Nico* until Emerson could be blurred out of the cover.

Emerson also asked Warhol for a further $750,000, claiming he was never asked if his likeness could be featured in *Chelsea Girls*. The entire circus resulted in the album losing any momentum or excitement that the year of touring and press had generated. The updated sleeves were free of Emerson but had either a strange, smudgy spot where his face once was or a black-and-white sticker slapped over the offending image.[79] It was not the record release anyone involved had hoped for, and it did nothing other than underscore the feeling shared by Warhol, Morrissey, and Verve label man Tom Wilson that it was Nico, not the Velvets, who was destined to be a star.

Despite the setbacks with the LP, the Velvets soldiered on, still trying to drum up support for their live show and sustain any momentum they had from the previous year. Several gigs were booked on the East Coast. Nico did not appear at many of them, though she was still advertised as the star attraction, her name featuring in a larger, bolder, more predominant typeface than that of the Velvets. Her absence was felt by those attending the non-Nico shows. A gig in New York at the start of April featured Warhol visuals of a John Cale screen test, but the tall blonde "focal point" was nowhere to be seen. One audience member recalled the Nico-less performance was "much to my and many other people's disappointment. Even those who'd never heard the band were familiar with her iconic beauty."

She was billed as the "unbelievable Nico" in the advertisement for the show that appeared in the *Michigan Daily*, as the Exploding Plastic Inevitable returned, almost a year to the day, to Ann Arbor, Michigan. In another attempt to provide visibility for the group, a residency of several nights was booked at the Gymnasium on East 71st Street in New York. Again, adverts for the shows completely omitted the band:

A NEW HAPPENING DISCOTHEQUE THE GYMNASIUM

NATIONAL SWINGER'S NITE with ANDY, NICO, LIVE
BAND and FREAK OUT LIGHTS
making the wildest swing-in
the EAST SIDE'S ever seen.
SUNDAY, APRIL 30, at 6 P.M.

20

Nico now had several months of solo performances under her belt and a well-practiced repertoire of songs ready to go. Verve record producer Tom Wilson and manager Paul Morrissey decided it was time to cut her debut album. Though performing several times a week, Nico's set list was made up entirely of other people's songs. The idea of writing her own had not even crossed her mind, as it seemed far beyond anything she could possibly do. Regardless of any inner doubts, she was still receiving a lot of press attention, from both the sporadic Velvets/EPI shows and the continued interest in *Chelsea Girls*. Wilson may have wanted to take this visibility and mold Nico into his label's very own Judy Collins. Collins was riding high on a fleeting trend referred to in the press as "baroque folk"—a mishmash of folk music combined with classical arrangements. This may be why he later added various woodwind instruments to the final mix of Nico's debut record. However, such intentions were not made clear to any of the musicians during the sessions. "I didn't go for the arrangements on that album too much, all the strings and all that. I didn't think they were particularly tasteful. I played guitar on two or three tracks, but none of us had any say about anything," Lou Reed later confided. Though relations with her fellow Velvets were tenuous at best, Reed, Sterling Morrison, and John Cale all contributed to the record, even gifting Nico several songs they had written but which were deemed unsuitable for the next Velvets release. These included "Little Sister," "Winter Song," "It Was a Pleasure Then," "Chelsea Girls" and

"Wrap Your Troubles in Dreams." Jackson Browne also provided three songs for the album: "These Days,"[80] "Fairest of the Season" and "Somewhere There's a Feather." Nico finally got to include her coveted Bob Dylan song, "I'll Keep It with Mine," as well as Tim Hardin's "Eulogy for Lenny Bruce." In *Jackson Browne: The Story of a Hold Out*, Browne is quoted as saying that the album was "loosely put together," claiming that Tom Wilson "seemed to be on the phone most of the time. I don't think he was too interested in that particular project…he was off on a lark…he didn't take it too seriously. Nico didn't like the album much."

The entire recording process took place at breakneck speed. In a 2005 interview, Browne recalled, "This record was basically made [in]…probably two sessions…The day I went in and played the songs of mine that she sang, Lou Reed also came in and accompanied her on the songs that he had written." In another article, Browne said that it could have taken no more than three days in total for the backing tracks for the entire album to be completed. Even though the process was so short, frustrations still ran high within the studio. "None of us had any patience so it was very sloppy. We didn't have anybody telling us how to do things," John Cale claimed in a 2002 interview. Reed also bemoaned the final product, saying, "If they'd just have allowed Cale to arrange it and let me do more stuff on it."

Though possibly still smarting from the *Chelsea Girl* sessions, in May Nico had something to look forward to. Warhol had decided to bring his top Superstars with him to the Cannes Film Festival, where a screening of *Chelsea Girls* was planned in order to launch the film into the international market. However, upon landing in Saint-Tropez, the entourage was disappointed to discover that the movie would not be shown at the prestigious event, having been deemed too risqué. Things did not get better for Warhol when he returned to New York. Upon arrival, he found Reed waiting to break the news: the Velvets were leaving the pop artist. Nico, meanwhile, had made a quick trip to see Ari in Paris.

Album recorded, residency done, film premiere aborted, Nico was unsure about what to do next. Since childhood, when she had lived in freezing conditions, she had been dealing with a perforated eardrum. It was getting worse, and the singer was experiencing increased deafness. With time on her hands, she decided to go to London to seek medical attention. However, she needed a place to stay. According to one claim, the singer originally had her sights set on staying with renowned celebrity photographer David Bailey. She showed up, bags in tow, at Bailey's Regent's Park residence. "She just turned up on the doorstep with her suitcases," Bailey supposedly said. "She wanted to move in with me. I got a bit panicky—I was having too good a time to cope with Nico as well. I think I said, 'I'm very fond of you, Nico, but not that fond.'" He suggested that Paul McCartney might be willing to house the singer. With this in mind, Nico swiftly adjourned to the Beatle's house. McCartney's girlfriend at the time, actress Jane Asher, was conveniently away in the U.S. However, his new crush, photographer Linda Eastman, had just arrived in London and wanted to spend some time with the bass player. McCartney didn't know what to do.

After several weeks with Nico ensconced in his house, McCartney was starting to worry, wondering how to possibly juggle the various women. Before any drama could ensue, Warhol and Morrissey arrived in London, looking to have a meeting with McCartney and Beatles manager Brian Epstein. Epstein was familiar with the Velvet Underground, and Warhol was hoping he might be able to take on some management duties and arrange a European tour for the group.[81] Most likely to the relief of McCartney, Warhol and Morrissey took Nico back to the East Coast with them, telling her there was a Velvets show scheduled in Boston that she had to perform at.

However, the homecoming gig proved to be disastrous for Nico. The May 26 and 27 shows were billed as "Andy Warhol's Nico & the Velvet Underground." However, upon arriving at the gig, Warhol was surprised to find himself replaced by club owner Steve Sesnick, who refused to let Nico join the rest of the group on stage. The press later tried to spin it that Nico's "arrival on short notice from London didn't give her enough time to ready herself." However, the message was loud and clear: the band was done working with Warhol, and over trying to accommodate Nico. She never sang with them again as an official member.

———

In later interviews, it is clear that the Velvets never, ever considered Nico to be a crucial element nor accepted her as part of the group. "Nico really was never a member of the band, and she didn't consider herself one. It was just something to do for fun on the first album, and because it worked," Maureen Tucker says in the Lou Reed documentary *Lou Reed: Rock & Roll Heart*.[82] Snapping his fingers for emphasis, in a 1968 interview Reed asserts that the songs that Nico performed with the Velvets were dropped "just like that" after her departure. "It was time for her to leave…I mean, it's just obvious. When things are supposed to happen, they always do." In another article, from 1971, Reed further talks down any meaningful contribution by Nico, claiming, "What she was doing was just a part. You could always take a lot of different parts. I think we always knew that she would leave so no one was surprised. It wasn't that major a point, so it didn't matter. It was fun that she was there and it was fun that she wasn't." More than twenty years later, he added, "It was never meant to be an ongoing thing, and it wasn't." Only John Cale seemed to have any regret about things not working out with Nico in the Velvets, while also explaining why the band helped so much with her Dom shows and in the recording of *Chelsea Girl*. In a 2008 *Uncut* interview, he confided, "Her leaving was…tinged by disappointment, we felt we had failed her in some way…She had that ability—to make you feel you had failed her but no matter: she would survive all the stronger for it." Regardless of who left whom, Nico's impact on the band is incontrovertible. Former manager Paul Morrissey commented on her contributions to the Velvets, noting, "Nico set the tone for the group with her elegance and her presence. She stood on stage and nobody could take their eyes off her, no matter what the song was. Unfortunately, this didn't make Lou Reed very happy. He didn't like the attention that Nico got. He seemed to be jealous."

It would have been easy, even expected, for Nico to be outwardly bitter and disappointed by the way the relationship with the Velvets had publicly broken down. "I was never totally a part of the group," she confided in a 1971 interview. "I was the contrast, the gentler side. But I admired them because they weren't afraid to be bad. I thought they were very honest, and I wasn't doing anything at the time. So I just thought it'd be a good idea to travel around with them, play colleges and universities. But I never considered myself a member of the group because I never felt close enough to what they were doing."

It is easy to see how she would have found it difficult to feel truly integrated into the band's inner workings, as from the start there were inherent tensions, jealousies, and miscommunications thanks to her being thrust upon the Velvets. After all, it is unlikely that Warhol would have associated himself with the group without the addition of the German model. She made the band noteworthy and helped gain them a vast amount of publicity.

Guitarist and modern rock icon Dave Navarro agrees. He points out how unique Warhol's choice of Nico to front the Velvets was, especially during the 1960s. "At the time there weren't a lot of women doing experimental music on an underground level like that. I would say that had it not been for her presence on that record [*The Velvet Underground & Nico*], it wouldn't be as seminal as it is today. It was absolutely mandatory [to have Nico on the LP]."

Though Nico "was so unhappy" when she "heard the result of that flute taking over," *Chelsea Girl* also ended up becoming an important record for a later audience, influencing an entire new generation of musicians who were too young to appreciate it upon its release, or not even born in 1967. "When I was a teenager, twelve years old... I was pretty young, there was this bookshop in our town where this guy had a lot of records which nobody would have bought had I not found them," says Mark Lanegan. Lanegan is a living legend himself, having fronted grunge band the Screaming Trees before embarking on a very successful solo career that has included collaborations with some of the greatest artists of the twentieth and twenty-first centuries, including Queens of the Stone Age, Kurt Cobain, and Moby. "It was pretty much a redneck town; nobody knew who these bands were. I bought all these records and started listening to them and got really into it. Later, I listened to *Chelsea Girl*, which I think is one of the greatest records of all time."

Navarro also holds *Chelsea Girl* in especially high esteem. He continues, "It's kinda hard to be a fan of Nico and not fall in love with her. You hear this voice and you see her image, the cheekbones, the whole package, it's strong, unapologetic, haunting, melancholy. As soon as I heard that voice I fell in love with her—I'd marry this girl today." Peter Hook, the iconic bass player for groundbreaking bands Joy Division and New Order, calls the LP "my favorite female album of all time... If I'm feeling a bit blue and a bit melancholic and need to wallow—we all need to wallow at times—I'll stick *Chelsea Girl* on and have a proper fucking one."

Nico's subsequent solo albums after *Chelsea Girl* are arguably more avant-garde, weird, and uncommercial than most, if not all, of the Velvet Underground's total output. Paul Morrissey cites *Chelsea Girl* as the pinnacle of Nico's career, publicly declaring his dislike for the records that followed. "The material she sang [after *Chelsea Girl*] was atrocious," he later decried. "She imagined herself a songwriter, and at the same time she just made mournful sounds with her voice and played a child's toy organ to make the sounds even worse. That's what she thought was some sort of art. The real singing, which she did on *Chelsea Girl*...she hadn't the vaguest idea as to how good it was. Performers, they're almost always wrong about what the hell they were doing, and she certainly was. Once she became a drug addict, she never sang a real song again."

The impact and trailblazing of Nico have often been forgotten or omitted from history, placing Reed as an iconic musician and Nico as simply a fringe figure. Una Baines was the keyboardist for the Blue Orchids, who played with Nico during the 1980s. She points out the contrast between the way that history has treated Nico and her male Velvets contemporaries. "People more want to talk about who she slept with and how many drugs she took. All the men around her at the same time were doing exactly the same thing. They were all taking drugs, all sleeping with loads of people, but that doesn't matter if it's Lou Reed or John Cale. Because they're blokes. I think that's the truth. She knew that and I think that must have been the frustration, really. She knew that she would never be treated on the same footing. I think in the future she will be recognized as the tremendous artist that she was." Long-time Nico fan and musician Jonathan Donahue of Mercury Rev agrees, telling me, "That's all she faced in her life it seems—male perspectives. Breaking through the male dominance in the Velvets and breaking through all the producers she had and all the men in her life. She was more than human, even beyond a woman."

———

Having now been officially ousted from the Velvets, Nico needed something to do while she waited for *Chelsea Girl* to be released. A new event in central California, the Monterey Pop Festival, seemed the perfect distraction. She packed her bags and headed west. Once in Monterey, she found herself reconnecting with her past flame Brian Jones, as well as former Stones manager Andrew Loog

Oldham. "I was not in good nick. I came out of a place where I was having shock treatment, and then I went to Monterey," Oldham says. "But the shock treatment was good for me. And then I had to share a house in Monterey with my first wife [Sheila Oldham], Brian Jones, and Nico." In a 2007 interview for *Mojo* magazine, Oldham confided that the festival marked the "last time I saw Brian Jones truly happy, carefree, as free and high as a bird." It was also the last time that he saw Nico. Her attendance at the festival is captured indelibly in a series of images from the event, as well as in a fleeting shot of the singer walking with Jones through the crowds that appeared in a documentary released later to celebrate the festival.[83] Nico is dressed head to toe in black; Jones is resplendent with his fringe, fur, and paisley.

It was at Monterey Pop that Nico first saw Jimi Hendrix perform. Some biographers have claimed that Nico "bragged of her fling with Hendrix," that "her attraction to Hendrix was obvious." While this makes for tantalizing reading, no one interviewed— friend, past lover, family member, or colleague—could ever recall Nico mentioning any sort of liaison with the guitar genius. This is in contrast to her well-documented and oft-repeated tales of relationships with other iconic musicians with whom she crossed paths. It seems unlikely that anything actually happened between Nico and Hendrix. His untimely passing in 1970, just three years after his spectacular performance at Monterey Pop, makes it doubtful that this rumor will ever be properly substantiated or resolved, though Nico having relations with three members of the so-called 27 Club—Jones, Hendrix, and Morrison—conjures up some enticing theories.

There are two different versions of the circumstances that brought Nico and Jim Morrison together. Morrison had already seen the chanteuse perform with the Velvets at their 1966 show at the Trip, though they did not connect properly until the following year. Morrison's Doors bandmate, drummer John Densmore, thought that it was in March 1967 when the duo first met. The band was in New York and, like Jackson Browne, could not help but notice the twenty-foot-high Nico posters pasted up all over Manhattan. Densmore's memory of the first time he observed the German beauty in the company of Morrison is very clear. He recalled, "We were staying at the dumpy Great Northern Hotel on 57th Street. Convenient location, but the place smelled of old people. I was rooming right next to Jim, which turned out to be better than TV. Not that I was the drinking-glass-to-the-wall type, but the racket that was coming from next door one night was hard to miss. Jim brought Nico, the Velvet Underground's famous German vamp, back to his hotel room, and I'd never heard such crashing around. It sounded as if they were beating the shit out of each other. I was worried but never dared to ask what happened. Nico looked okay the next day, so I let it slide."

A similar tale about Nico and Morrison's *amour* came from Aaron Sixx, who would go on to put out Nico's much-disputed *Drama of Exile* LP in 1981: "I once heard a story from Bill Siddons, the Doors' manager. He told me that Nico went back to Jim's place, and they spent the entire night drinking and drugging and probably having sex, and the next morning Jim was just totally flat out, basically dead to the world—and Nico was ready for more... The story this guy told was that the only person who could outdo Morrison was Nico!"[84]

Ray Manzarek, the Doors' keyboard player, gave an incredibly salacious account of his memories of his band's lead singer and the German blonde. He described the relationship between the two icons as Nico going "gaga" for Morrison and knowing how to "push his [Morrison's] buttons," which he claimed she did "at every opportunity, in a deep and Germanic-accented voice." In his memoir, *Light My Fire: My Life with the Doors*, he recounts a very graphic encounter between Morrison and Nico. He portrays Nico as equaling Morrison in excess, egging him on to keep up with her: "'I'm going to take another von. Vhat's the matter, Jeem, are you afraid?' the Valkyrie would say to the California Dionysus, who would always respond to the challenge. 'Afraid? Shit, I'll take two!' 'Jeem, you are crazy. That's why I loff you.' And they would retire to a silver-foiled room for more. More of everything. More drink, more pills, more sex."

The "silver-foiled room" he refers to is Warhol's Factory. Danny Fields, a frequent visitor there, was stunned by the assertion that any kind of sex would have taken place in this space, as described by Manzarek. "It just wasn't that sort of vibe," he told me. Regardless, Manzarek provided a detailed narrative of Nico pleasuring Morrison: "Evidently, she gave great head, understanding the proper use of the tongue on the underside of the penis, especially that supersensitive area at the base of the head where that small crease attaches to the shaft, that crease that when lightly licked and flicked with a moist, soft tongue produces shudders of ecstasy in the male of the species. And she wasn't ashamed to do it. To bring her man to climax and not remove his penis from her mouth. To hold it close and take it in even deeper at his moment of consummation. To not deny him the warmth and moisture of her mouth as he ejaculated. To swallow his semen and wait for his member to soften and recede back into itself. Only then would she take her lips away, look up at Jim, and smile… 'Did that please you, Jeem?' Jim could only nod in pleasure, being speechless at the intensity of his ejaculation."

Besides framing Nico firmly as a sexual object, Manzarek's account (if true) illustrates not only her desire to please, but, by 1967, her desire for obliteration, which became more apparent as the year went on.

The more well-known account of how the two icons first met places the timeline as June or July 1967. The Monterey Pop Festival over, Nico decided to go back to a former haunt: the Castle in Los Angeles. It was here that Danny Fields decided to play cupid. Fields was working at Elektra Records at the time and had been charged with looking after the hot new band on the label's roster: the Doors. The band had released their breakthrough hit, "Light My Fire," in June, and had already been no. 1 on the charts for three weeks, making the band's lead singer, Morrison, an immediate heartthrob. His chiseled cheekbones, tangled mane of brown curls and sinewy body, perfectly showcased in leather pants (perhaps inspired by Gerard Malanga the year before), made him lust-worthy far and wide. He was not averse to taking full advantage of his exalted position, and soon became well known for his voracious sexual appetite. However, it appeared that quantity may have been of more value than quality, as Fields was not impressed with the women he saw flocking around the frontman: "I saw them [the Doors] perform in San Francisco, it was very jolly. I went backstage—I was horrified! There were all these groupie things… dirty girls. Just rags and dirt and things falling off them, and too much eye makeup and a dopey, glazed look. I was concerned that this was bad for his image. What if a photographer got this? They're [rock stars] always supposed to be alone. Alone is sexy. You're never supposed to see them with a girl… I had a little electric lightbulb in my head. I said, 'Say, Jim, I'm staying with Edie Sedgwick and Nico, up in the hills.' I thought I would bring him up there, and then he would fall in love with Nico, and then he would see the error of his ways in letting all these slimy little groupies...and he would never settle for a woman less beautiful or mystical or exotic as Nico. And since there were not too many, then he would never have too many girlfriends, and my plot would be on its way."

Fields did not hold Morrison in the highest esteem, however. "Jim Morrison was a callous asshole, an abusive, mean person...I think Morrison's magic and power went beyond the quality of his versifying. He was bigger than that. He was sexier than his poetry—more mysterious...more difficult, more charismatic as a performer. There has got to be a reason why women like Nico...fell so deeply in love with him, because he was essentially an abusive man to women. But it sure wasn't his poetry. I've got to tell you, it wasn't his poetry. He had a big dick. That was probably it. The ultimate rock star is a child. How can you not be spoiled by everything's that's going to come along? For most rock stars, what's in store for them, realistically, is a lot of spoilage, denting and banging around exploitation, being used up, and ruination."

Fields had also taken up residence at the Castle, the "strange haunted house in the Hollywood Hills, all overgrown, with a mossy pool high on a hilltop...It was this two-story house, owned by some old Hollywood queen who rented it out to rock bands. Everyone had stayed there—Dylan, the Jefferson Airplane, the Velvets. The owner would rent it out to rock & roll bands because it was in such a state of ruin that it didn't really matter what happened to it," he further described in *Please Kill Me*.

Fields recalled what happened when he and Morrison arrived at the Castle: "We finally got up to the house and Nico was standing in the doorway. He just looked at her, and she looked at him, and then they both cast their glances downward. They stared at some imaginary spot on the floor in between them.

"I tried to start a little chataroonie, I saw this was going nowhere.

This was some kind of thing they were acting out. I came back about an hour later; they were still in the exact same positions, they hadn't moved...they hadn't said anything. This was their way of acknowledging, 'You're a beautiful, special person,' I suppose."

Finally, after an indeterminate amount of time, as Fields recounted, "Nico and Edie fled to their bedrooms to hide, giggling and taking drugs. He [Morrison] started taking drugs as well and just downing quarts of vodka. Nico had stolen all my stash of pills, downers and amphetamines, but somehow I had managed to save the pot, the hash, and the acid, so Jim and I sat up and he took all that. I thought, 'Uh-oh, he's going to get so drunk he's going to get in that car and drive off the cliff and I'm going to get fired,' so I snuck down to his car and hid the keys and he kept trying to search me. He didn't find them."

The evening wore on, with Morrison imbibing heavily of Fields's remaining supplies. "We started smoking a lot of hash. I started making a major speech to him about 'I have these things in mind for you, and life is a roller coaster, and stardom is a trip and...' I didn't know what I was doing, I was just sounding like every movie I had ever seen about what's in store and how to play the game," Fields recalled. "He would just open his palm about every five minutes and ask for another drug. Incredible amount of hash. About six hits of orange sunshine...I was scared! I thought he was going to die! I had never seen...! I mean, this was enough drugs for me and everybody I met in two weeks in California! I kept giving stuff to him. He wouldn't answer...'What do you think about that flight of brilliance, Jim?' He would say, 'Got any more acid, man?'"

Fields eventually fell asleep, only to be awoken by the sound of Nico sobbing. Rushing to his window, he saw "Jim and Nico standing there under the full moon in the courtyard. Jim was pulling Nico's hair and she was screaming. He never said anything. He just kept pulling her hair. Suddenly he ran into the house and left Nico weeping in her deep voice. Next thing I know, Morrison is completely naked, walking along the edge of the crenelated roof. Nico came flying into my room crying, 'He's going to kill me!' I said, 'He's not going to kill anyone. Leave me alone, I'm trying to sleep.' The view of the courtyard was like the cover of some Gothic bodice ripper."

Unlike her former beaus, Morrison encouraged Nico to pursue writing her own music, for the first time giving her confidence that she could create her own material. "He said to me one day, 'I give you permission to write your poems and compose your songs!' My soul brother believed I could do it. I had his authority," Nico confided. She must have been shocked that at last she had found a man who valued her intellect as much as her appearance. "He was the first man I was in love with, because he was affectionate to my looks and my mind," Nico later remarked of the frontman. "He told me to write songs. I never thought that I could, because when you come out of the fashion business—I did flimsy sort of writing, not systematical…He really inspired me a lot…It was like looking in a mirror." Nico worried that she was not capable of composing anything with structure. To alleviate this concern, Morrison suggested that Nico begin writing down her dreams and start reading some of his favorite classic works, by the likes of Céline, Blake, and Coleridge. Not long after, Nico composed her first song, "Lawns of Dawns," inspired by that initial night with Morrison at the Castle.[85] "That's what I think started her on the road to writing," John Cale asserted. "Jim Morrison…showed her that poetry and music and all that could really dominate your life. She became single-minded about it…I got the sense that she decided she was going to do it."

Morrison unleashed in Nico a self-possession that allowed her to step into a role that previously she may have been too afraid to even dream of: that of writer and musician. He also introduced her to his own ideals of artistic creativity, cobbled together from his personal obsessions with classic literature, Native American culture, and the spiritual abyss. He and Nico would drive, alone, from

Los Angeles into the outlying desert. Part of this ritual included gathering peyote buttons from cacti. "Peyote was a spiritual drug," said Nico. "We were in the middle of the desert and everything was natural, you know, in the open air, nature all around, not a hotel room or a bar. And the cactus was natural. You did not buy it from somebody on a street corner."

The two ingested the harvested buttons, allowing Nico to experience firsthand visions that Morrison argued were similar to those encountered by some of the literary heroes he had introduced Nico to. "We had visions in the desert," she remembered. "It is like William Blake; he would see visions like Blake did, angels in trees, he would see these, and so would I. And Jim showed me that this is what a poet does. A poet sees visions and records them. He said that there were more poets in Comanches than there were in bookstores. The Comanches took the cactus, too. We were like the Indians who lived in this way for thousands of years, before the Christians and as long as the Jews." It was this, the near democratization of writing and poetry, and the man who was opening this realm of possibility to her—not the actual peyote trip—that allowed Nico to fully embrace her own potential as a writer, making writing something that even those lacking a "traditional" education could pursue and excel at. "Everything was open to us; there were no rules," Nico later remarked in an interview. However, this caused inherent problems within the union. "We had a too-big appetite. But we took too much drink and too many drugs to make it, that was our difficulty." After years of diet pills and spending time in the amphetamine-fueled Factory, Nico was already familiar with drugs, but Morrison used them differently, letting them inform and guide much of his creative process. "You could say that Jim took drugs because he wanted visions for his poetry. It is like people in the office who drink coffee to help them work. It is really the same," she rationalized to a journalist.

There was unquestionably a physical as well as a mental

connection between Morrison and Nico; however, the intellectual reciprocity made the relationship different, more impactful and unique than any others Nico had had. During their desert adventures, they cut their thumbs with a knife, intermingling the blood. For Nico, this symbolized a different, more lasting bond than any before, and was surely a sign that Morrison felt similarly about her. In a 1985 article quoted in the Witts biography, Nico described her time with Morrison in unprecedented detail, saying, "I like my relations to be physical and of the psyche. We hit each other because we were drunk and we enjoyed the sensation. We made love in a gentle way, do you know? I thought of Jim Morrison as my brother, so we would grow together. We still do, because he is my soul brother. We exchanged blood. I carry his blood inside me. We had spiritual journeys together." Of the intimate moments she shared with her famous lovers, Nico coyly told a writer in the 1980s: "Jim Morrison had the best sex I ever had inside me...Jim was more involved in his dreams. He liked to sleep and to find visions, because there were private things he showed me. I think Brian [Jones] was more of a musician than a composer, and Jim was more of a poet."

The two continued their affair throughout the summer of 1967, but though Nico had finally met her match, they slowly drifted apart as the autumn months rolled on, with Morrison eventually returning to his long-time partner, Pamela Courson. Their romantic relationship may have been short-lived, but her time with Morrison had an indelible impact on Nico. Through the frontman, she finally found the courage to write and not be dependent on other people for her lyrics.

Though their torrid romance had ended, the Doors singer's influence over Nico was profound and long-lasting. Warhol Superstar Viva recalled how months, even years later, "She [Nico] was obsessed with Jim Morrison...Carrying around this photograph of Jim Morrison, with a vigil light...A little candle she'd light in front of it, at night before she went to bed. She practically did prayers to Jim

Morrison [even though] he was still alive then." She dyed her hair red, as he had a fetish for redheads, and told writers that she wanted to record the Doors' song "You're Lost Little Girl." For the rest of her life, she would credit Morrison as being the one person who truly knew and understood her.

22

Morrison had persuaded Nico that she could play an instrument; she just needed to find one that suited her. Following his advice, she bought a harmonium in San Francisco, when she went up there from Los Angeles to join Andy Warhol, Paul Morrissey, and Ultra Violet on a promotional junket for *Chelsea Girls*. The instrument was acoustic, portable and, most importantly, allowed Nico to not be reliant on anyone but herself.

This time, San Francisco embraced Nico and the East Coast crew, flocking to see the film and covering all of the quartet's moves. Ultra Violet recounted, "In San Francisco, we're a smash. The students, who are already in an uproar over Vietnam and civil rights, slaps us to their bosom. They can't get enough of *Chelsea Girls* and us. The press, on cue, heats up the furor. When they've written all they can, praising and damning the film, the papers turn to feature stories about the Warhol entourage." One press piece she may be referencing is an article featuring Paul Morrissey, Nico, Warhol, and Ultra Violet that ran in *The Berkeley Barb*. Its content is closer to a stream of consciousness than an insightful profile, the cool New York chic clashing with the laid-back, flower power Bay Area. Ultra Violet later summed up the experience, describing a conversation with Warhol: "I say to Andy, 'You've had publicity, fame, headlines. Now what?' 'More fame.'"

Now singularly focused on mastering her instrument, Nico was making up for what she saw as the many lost years of not being proficient at anything musical. She practiced endlessly, attempting to become not just adequate, but excellent—at playing, composing, and writing lyrics. Needing a place to stay, she moved in with new Factory Superstar Viva. "She would practice it [the harmonium] for hours, simple things, chords—really annoying stuff," the Superstar recalled. "She was very serious about it, dreadfully serious, like a Nazi organist. She'd pull the curtains across and light candles around her and do this funereal singing all day long. It was like I was living in a funeral parlor." Though having "invited herself" to room with Viva at her "garden apartment on 83rd Street, between Madison and Park Avenues," Nico quickly became the dominant personality and rule-maker in the house. Viva recounted how Nico "thought she was the Queen of Sheba. Nico was a spicy combination of arrogance and insecurity. She tried to take over the house, take it over completely, you have no idea how she lorded herself about. She would get very angry if I had any boyfriends round that she didn't like. She would say, 'You can't invite him round anymore.' Can you imagine?! You are in your place and you get a house guest that turns into your mother."

Nico did not care about her new companion's complaints. She had left New York an uncertain chanteuse and returned a focused, serious artist, determined to master her craft. Yet despite having an extensive network of talented musicians around her, she did not trust any of them with her emerging skill, still feeling too unsure of herself to openly display a lack of knowledge. She turned instead to Ornette Coleman, a young and well-respected African American improvisational jazz musician, for guidance and help. Coleman proved imperative in helping Nico master the harmonium. It was he who explained to Nico the convention of the left hand on the keyboard being used as the bass, playing the supporting harmony, while the right hand was the treble, providing the melody. With her low register, Nico flipped the practice around, playing harmony in the treble and melody in the bass.

By October, she felt ready to make a public appearance as a solo artist performing on her own. Seven nights were booked for her at New York club the Scene, a venue she had graced before with the Velvets. *Chelsea Girl* was about to come out, and the *Village Voice* featured ads for the gigs and the new album. A picture of a blonde, glum Nico accompanied the album ad, with the text, "The moon goddess Nico will conduct services nightly at Steve Paul's The Scene leading you in all your splendor with her liturgical chants," and going on to promise "dancing for the body and soul also available before and after the services." The opening act was a folk-rock band from California called Kaleidoscope.

The attendees anxiously awaited Nico's return to the stage. "Chic crowds turned up at Nico's opening, and there was only an organ onstage, and she sat down at it and there was one spotlight on her," Danny Fields recalled. "It was like a child discovering a musical instrument for the first time. She would just press one note and bend her ear toward the keyboard and listen to it, and press it again and again, and then another note, and she'd listen to that. And this was in front of this reverent opening-night audience, which didn't know what to make of it, not at all. She did this for half an hour, then she tried a few combinations of notes and got into that." Yet the moon goddess's noodling around was not appreciated by a majority of the crowd, as "people were starting to file out quietly, except for about twelve of us who were just mesmerized, transfixed by the whole performance. She finally performed two chants and it was over. It was one of the most beautiful things I'd ever seen. Not the kind of thing you could do at the Fillmore East, but there was a quality of magic in it, in everything she did."

Chris Darrow was a member of Kaleidoscope, and he remembered it being a similarly notable debut in the book *The Age of Rock 2*:

Opening night was very crowded and [Frank] Zappa and members of the Mothers of Invention showed up to show their support. Warhol and his minions showed up. Our first set went fine and then it was time for Nico. Nico's delivery of her material was very flat, deadpan, and expressionless, and she played as though all of her songs were dirges. Her icy, Nordic image also added to the detachment of her delivery. She was certainly beautiful—Greta Garbo and Marlene Dietrich certainly come to mind. The audience was on her side, as she was in her element and the Warhol contingent was very prominent that night. However, what happened next is what sticks in my mind the most from that night. In between sets, Frank Zappa got up from his seat and walked up on the stage and sat behind the keyboard of Nico's B-3 organ. He proceeded to place his hands indiscriminately on the keyboard in an atonal fashion and screamed at the top of his lungs, doing a caricature of Nico's set, the one he had just seen. The words to his impromptu song were the names of vegetables like broccoli, cabbage, asparagus…This "song" kept going for about a minute or so and then suddenly stopped. He walked off the stage and the show moved on. It was one of the greatest pieces of rock'n'roll theater that I have ever seen!

While this must have been a sight to behold, it is hard to imagine Zappa pulling the same stunt on Lou Reed, John Cale or one of his other male counterparts.

———

Though back in New York, Nico was now more focused on her music than on her standing in the Factory. Warhol, however, still wanted to work with the singer, proclaiming in *POPism* that he and Morrissey were "always trying to get [Nico] to do a feature-length movie with us." Nico agreed to star in a new Factory vehicle, but only on the condition that Jim Morrison would be cast as her co-star. "She had a big crush on him then. When she asked him, he said sure; he said he knew all about underground movies, that he'd been a film student and all that," Warhol recalled.[86] However, there was a huge issue: instead of Morrison, Nico arrived for the shoot with Tom Baker, Morrison's best friend. Having been convinced by his manager that the Warhol film would be a bad career move, Morrison had talked his friend into taking his place. The main story line of *I, a Man* was, as Warhol summarized, "a series of scenes of this guy, Tom, seeing six different women in one day in New York, having sex with some, talking with some, fighting with some."

——

When *Chelsea Girl* came out in October of 1967, it was a commercial flop,[87] even more so than *The Velvet Underground & Nico*, though Nico mentioned in later interviews that it was the only one of her solo albums to bring her any income. She hated even talking about the record, saying, "Most pop music to me is noise, all right?" When asked about her solo debut by a journalist in 1985, her physical response was as powerful as her actual words in illustrating her distaste for the album: "[*smoking a cigarette, starts playing with her hand and acting disengaged after mention of* Chelsea Girl, *shakes her head, then looks at interviewer and smiles*] Why don't you just leave that out? I can't relate to it at all, so…[*trails off*]. They weren't my own songs and it doesn't interest me to talk about it."

The cover art for the LP is gorgeous. Shot by Paul Morrissey, it features Nico superimposed over herself in one shot. The main image is a black and white portrait of the singer, blonde bangs, heavy eyelashes, looking out forlornly into the distance. The smaller image is in color and is of her looking down. These were the only elements of her solo debut that Nico confirmed approving of. "I like the [cover] picture, even if it looks sad," she told journalist Kurt

Lassen in a November 1967 interview. "Sometimes I'm sad and mostly I like sad songs… when I sing I try to imagine I'm all alone, there's nobody out there listening. I play with the notes, with the feeling. People tell me that the album is good and that it is selling well. I honestly don't think it is the best I can do. That's why I'm working on another one, a better one."

The ads that accompanied the album seemed farcical by comparison to the somber cover art. "You've seen her in Andy Warhol's Exploding Plastic Underground [and] starring in his *Chelsea Girls*," screamed one, while another said, "They call her the Dietrich of the Velvet Underground. Nonsense. She's Nico. And you can hear her making the scene as NICO: CHELSEA GIRL." Nor did other promotional efforts help move Nico in the direction of a serious artist, once again focusing mainly on her looks. On a radio advertisement, sent by MGM/Verve to FM stations (and later included on a promo-only edition of the record), a voice booms, "Nico is beautiful, and in a world where so much can be so easily possessed on a whim, over a promise, she's unpossessable," as "The Fairest of the Seasons" plays in the background.

——

Nico rounded out 1967 with a cameo in yet another Warhol project. Warhol and Morrissey wanted to do a second film, similar in format to *Chelsea Girls*, this one lasting an entire day and to be shown across two screens. The working title they gave the new undertaking was "the 24-hour-movie" then "FUCK," before finally settling on ****, or *Four Star* for simplicity while doing press. *Four Star* was first released on December 15 and 16 as part of a twenty-five-hour marathon showcasing all thirty sections of the film, with the longest part—*The Imitation of Christ*, starring Nico—clocking in at an eye-watering eight hours. A 100-minute version was also eventually cut and released for those who were not as dedicated.[88]

Imitation had been shot as a stand-alone piece in May/June of the same year, before being folded into the full *Four Star* project. In it, Patrick Tilden plays the cross-dressing son of Factory insiders Brigid Berlin and Ondine, sitting with rapt attention as he listens to Nico reading aloud from the fifteenth-century work of the same title by Thomas à Kempis. Other segments of *Four Star* are just as esoteric and reflect the time spent on the West Coast by Warhol and company. One part has Ondine, Nico, and Ultra Violet in San Francisco's notorious Haight-Ashbury district, capturing the hazy, spinning, flower power vibe of the Summer of Love. Another portion features shots of the docks and streets of Sausalito, a town just north of San Francisco. As flickering images play across the screen, Nico provides a dreamy, whimsical narration:

A man is walking on the sea.
The sea is walking.
The sea is after me.
The night grows into the sky.
The light grows back into the earth.

At the time of its production, *Four Star* was just another film being pumped out of the Warhol Factory for fun, art for art's sake. Future films embarked upon by Warhol and Morrissey were geared to make a profit, not simply push the bounds of possibility.

Besides a shift in creative focus, other changes were afoot within the Warhol clique. Just as Nico had replaced Edie Sedgwick, Warhol crowned Viva, Nico's roommate, as the new Superstar to feature in his future endeavors. Nico did not seem to mind or even notice; she had a new focus, a new instrument and a new path ahead. In a 1979 interview with Kristine McKenna, she admitted to her discomfort working with Warhol on his movies, saying, "I've never much cared for [the Warhol films] because I've always been in opposition to his ideas... The way he'd always come around and want to film me, whether I felt like it or not—he was a rapist. Plus, he used so many people in films that they were ultimately quite distracting."[89]

The last event of 1967 to include the Velvet Underground and Nico working in some capacity together dropped just before the end of the year, with the launch party of *Velvet Underground Untitled* or *Index* taking place on Thursday, December 14, at 457 Madison Avenue in New York. The project consisted of an oversized book, packed with irreverent and unexpected formatting, that perfectly showcases Warhol's multimedia aesthetic.[90] Part of the package is an "unrecorded song," comprising almost five minutes of conversation taped at the Factory between Nico, Reed, and others as they look at copies of *Index* while *The Velvet Underground & Nico* plays in the background. One person can be heard asking what will be included on the record that still needs to be added in order to complete *Index*; the gathered crowd is told it will be what they are taping at that moment. Unfazed, the conversation carries on, mostly focused on the various black and white images of the Superstars and Factory events that are featured throughout the publication. Nico can be heard randomly singing the chorus of the Beatles' "Good Morning, Good Morning," indicating *Sgt. Pepper* had already been released when the recording took place. She sounds zoned out and not completely present. This is one of Nico's few documented appearances during December. Though *Chelsea Girl* had been out for only a short time, she was visibly absent during the promotional rounds. An article from the December 2 issue of *Cashbox* magazine declared, "Elektra's Danny Fields is in something of a quandary at the moment as he's been trying to get in touch with Nico and meeting with no success," and adding, "Danny says that she's not at her old castle any longer. Danny's problem is that he's running out of castles."

Nico's spaced-out audio on *Index*, combined with her apparent disappearance, were symptoms of an ever-increasing problem: her dependency on heroin.

23

Nico was no stranger to drugs before joining the Velvet Underground. As a model, she had often used diet pills to curb her appetite and help maintain a svelte figure. "She used to say how there used to be lots of speed, lots of amphetamine to keep them [the models] thin; they were always handing that out," says biographer and musical collaborator James Young.

I met Young in Oxford, where he greeted me at the train station. With his trim frame and sparkling eyes, it was easy to see why Nico wrote in her diary that he "looked good." "They'd pretend, these agencies, that they don't do such things," he tells me. "But she said, 'I really got into drugs then. I got into drugs without realizing I was getting into drugs.' You just thought that's part of what you did. Like you take vitamin pills—that's what keeps you thin. It didn't have the stigma that getting into heroin would have, but nevertheless it's an addictive thing."

Lou Reed knew of this affinity and, according to some, used it to gain power over a singer whom he felt threatened by. "Nico was into drugs way back into the 1960s," Victor Bockris tells me. "Lou knew that she really liked amphetamine, so he would just play with her. It was his way of controlling and reducing her."

Drugs allowed for a sense of release, and in the 1960s the long-term impact of using them was not well known by many. "Most people self-medicate," Vincent Fremont says. "Lou was on drugs at one point and cleaned up. John Cale was taking a lot of coke; it was considered a recreational drug until we saw what damage it did." Nico's friend and co-star Tina Aumont stresses this in *Nico: Icon*, saying, "Show me one person who doesn't have problems with alcohol or with drugs and is happy and creative. That's very rare."

Legions of examples illustrate the unquestionable mythology of drugs and art, one that goes well beyond Nico. "I guess artists have always had an affinity for substances which could alter the way they thought or responded. I suppose it has a valid creative context. Some drugs provide energy when it is needed to people who are working extremely hard and long hours," said Danny Fields in a 1974 interview. "Some drugs provide a sedative effect on people who are in the public eye, constantly nervous and may or may not be insecure in the first place." Yet Fields also points out that the music industry is really a reflection of culture as a whole, noting, "As there is in our society, there is in this industry."

"Some of the most well-known jazz musicians were well known to be heroin addicts. At the time, there was a certain romanticizing of heroin use and the whole ritual of scoring, going and buying the heroin, injecting it, and so forth. It was almost like a religious ritual among these people who did that," Bockris told me. "Nico's use of junk was the way many musicians also used it, as a way to keep working through the pain that comes about by being in that profession, which either rewards you ridiculously or punishes you ridiculously if you don't succeed."

Yet the shadow of addiction has been cast over Nico in a manner not often experienced by her contemporaries. The double standard applied by popular culture to male and female drug users cannot be overstated. For many male addicts, substance abuse is simply part of the expected artistic package and can even lend them a level of credibility. A lot of the men Nico surrounded herself with all, at one time or another, either dabbled or were hooked on opiates, yet their music and artistry, not their substance abuse issues, are in the foreground of their mythology. For women, such issues become part and parcel of their overall public persona, in a way not often experienced by their male counterparts. The label of "junkie" sticks to women, whereas it often seems to bounce off men. This may be simple societal misogyny; as Una Baines says, "She [Nico] just fits into those fears that men have of women who are outside of the norm."

Musician and performance artist Cosey Fanni Tutti, best known for her time in the avant-garde group Throbbing Gristle, calls attention to this idea when we connect on the phone. "People tend to look at male musicians or artists when they're drug addicts [and think] that's part of their creative streak, putting them on a bloody pedestal, no matter how shit they are to everyone else," she says. "I don't think they offer that to women in that situation. I think with Nico being a woman amongst all those people back then, there's a tendency to think of her as piggybacking. You know, that old 'Oh, the girlfriend of…' And she's sort of dressing the scenes for Warhol, which she did! He took her in on that. I think she was probably aware of that to some extent, but as a model that's your job. You're decorative. You do as you're told. You join the thing and you are part of it. That would have been just a natural thing for her anyway—a scene that she fitted in completely, rather than the modeling scene."

"Nico's slide into heroin would have come through hanging out with Jim Morrison, Bob Dylan, and all those people that she would have hung out with at the Castle in Los Angeles in '67. She definitely was not into heroin at the Factory," Bockris asserts. Her past lover Robert King disagrees, saying "it was the Velvet Underground" that introduced her to the drug. However it happened, Nico's fall from recreational user into addiction was a "quick turn," according to her long-time friend Clive Crocker. "I remember she used to come back to Europe. She had started on heavy drugs, and I had nothing to do with it. I tried to dissuade her, but she was into heroin…I know who put her onto it. She came back and told me who was the first person, but I can't tell you that name because he's still alive." Many of the criticisms lobbed at Nico post-Velvets, while she was in the throes of addiction, are directly linked to common behavioral changes exhibited in users, not to traits unique to Nico.[91] Yet this is never considered in articles about her. Similarly, it is rare to see such behaviors held against male addicts.

Nico's son Ari thinks there is a correlation between him going to live permanently with the Delon family and his mother's dependency. "She started to take more drugs because of this adoption thing," he says. "That made her very sad. 'Child's thief'—that's how she called my grandmother. It's like her soul had been stabbed."

Nico's contributions to twentieth-century music have often been ignored and overlooked, "obscured for years by the blanket of drug accusations," though "she was a major figure," says Bockris. "Nico was a very generous person," he continues. "It's important to understand that 'junkies' are not necessarily bad people, they are not necessarily fucked-up. People say, 'Oh, she was a junkie,' and that takes care of that. That doesn't take care of that! The fact she is a junkie is secondary. It is not the number-one thing to describe her as. She's an artist, from the time she first emerges."

Heroin may have offered Nico a temporary escape from the expectations of others as well as relief from yet another persona she had created in an attempt to dramatically overhaul her image. Her switch of musical styles, from folky *Chelsea Girl* to creator of her own music, came with an equally dramatic shift in her appearance. Gone were the eyebrow-skimming bangs and the multiple pairs of fake eyelashes adorning heavily lined lids. Her blonde mane was replaced by red locks that progressed to flowing brown hair. Floaty black—always black—capes and robes in weighty fabrics replaced tailored white suits. Heavy boots replaced flimsy knee-high pumps. "It was almost a burden to be so beautiful... She was a very serious person and wanted to be recognized as a poet and songwriter," said Fields. "Everything was turbulent about her, starting with the bombs during her childhood. You can hear it in the words of her songs. It's a mythical thing that I think we are going to be trying to explain for a long time. She was terrifying in her austere beauty, which she didn't want. She really was girlish, in a nice way. She just liked to laugh." In another interview, Fields provides a further illustration of the complicated layers behind the facade: "In her photographs, she looks glacially beautiful but unapproachable. She was really very shy, which can frequently be mistaken for disdain, arrogance, lack of interest or inhumanity. It is one of the consequences of being shy. You don't expect that. There was Nico, the persona, and then there was Christa Päffgen—but nobody called her Christa Päffgen. She was easily hurt, easily wounded, very sensitive."

John Cale underscores this, noting in the 2018 radio documentary *Being Nico*, "Nico arrived in the Factory as a dazzling, blonde beauty. She didn't like what had happened to her or how she'd gotten to *La Dolce Vita* and all that. She just felt that nobody took her seriously as a person and certainly as a woman...She came into the Factory a blonde goddess and left to become a hennaed, dark-haired, dressed-in-black musician/songwriter. This is a lady who really did not end up liking herself very much. There's a lot of fear and loathing, and that comes through. Everything she did was part of this statement that now she was a different person." Whether completely inspired by her liaison with Jim Morrison, revealing a long ignored or untapped aesthetic, or simply playing up to the new moniker of moon goddess, Nico seemed to fully embrace the crepuscular mantle. However, she was in need of somewhere new to stay. The constant organ-playing and candle-lighting had become too much for Viva, who had kicked Nico out after a heated argument. Shelter came via a new face at the Factory: Fred Hughes.

Hughes had become Warhol's business manager, running the art side of Warhol's empire, while Paul Morrissey looked after the filmmaking enterprises. Tired of the catty, drug-infused, silver-walled Factory, the duo closed down the original studio, opening a new Warhol home base on a floor of an office block located at

33 Union Square West. Hughes leased an apartment on East 16th Street, opposite the new Factory. It was here that Nico found sanctuary after the blowup with Viva. It was a mutually beneficial setup, as Hughes provided the perfect environment to encourage the songstress. "Fred doted on eccentrics…And the more peculiarities Nico indulged in, the more fascinated Fred became—to find a woman that beautiful and that eccentric was a fantasy come true for him," said Warhol. One such "peculiarity" was Nico's affinity for the bathtub in Hughes's house. Though she had a lifelong aversion to water, the tub at East 16th Street held a particular allure for the singer, providing her with unprecedented inspiration. Warhol recalled how Nico "liked to lie in the bathtub all night with candles burning around her, composing the songs that would be on her second album, *The Marble Index*, and when Fred came home from Max's [nightclub] really late, she'd still be in the water." Another of Nico's peccadillos that emerged during her stay with Hughes was the attraction to candles, especially in lieu of electrical lighting. "Nico was a true specimen: among other things, she thrived only in the gloom—the gloomier she could make the atmosphere around her, the more radiant she became," noted Warhol in *POPism*. "Fred was back and forth to Europe a lot. When he arrived back at the apartment one night with all his suitcases, he stumbled into the living room and found that he couldn't switch the lights on. He saw a candle flickering in another room around a corner, and then Nico walked in holding a candelabra. 'Oh, Nico! I'm so sorry!' he said, suddenly realizing that Con Edison must have turned off the electricity. 'I just remembered I forgot to pay the light bill, and here you've been in the dark all this time!' 'Nooooo, it's fiiiiine,' she said, positively beaming with joy. She'd had the happiest time of her whole life, drifting around there in the dark for a whole month."

These idiosyncrasies became cemented in Nico's mythology. Appearing in *Eye* magazine, an article later in the year titled "On the Eve of Destruction, What Was Andy Warhol's Gang Up To?" also helped to bolster Nico's vampire-like lifestyle. The exposé featured a behind-closed-doors look at the Hughes/Nico household, stating, "Nico sleeps or stays sequestered all day (sometimes playing the organ), then goes out to Max's Kansas City, a restaurant hangout for representatives from art, fashion, and movie worlds, until the wee hours. When she returns, according to Freddy, she climbs—fully clothed—into the empty bathtub where she sits all night composing songs…Meanwhile, Freddy stumbles, bleary-eyed, into the bathroom and is always surprised to find Nico sitting in the tub." Though barely a year had passed since her debut on stage as the Velvets' blonde bombshell, the press had already embraced Nico's radical change.

———

Nico had been practicing the harmonium constantly, spending her days focused on writing lyrics and mastering the instrument. Though few people seemed to understand her new direction, the ones that did were impressed. "The next phase of Nico was the real Nico. She was doing her own songs and she performed them for me on her little harmonium and I thought they were magnificent. They were so startling. The songs just spoke for themselves," said Danny Fields. This was the first time that Nico felt the music was hers and that she was able to pull from her own experiences, ideas, and feelings for inspiration. When asked where the lyrical content came from, Nico said, "It has to do with my going to Berlin in 1946 when I was a little girl and seeing the entire city destroyed. I like the fallen empire, the image of the fallen empire."

Nico felt it was her art, not her appearance, that was, for the first time, being engaged with. "In the '60s, in the Velvet Underground period, she's like a mirror, and she plays so much with mirror images that anything she might say in the press is not really her, it's that mirror image," Bockris says. "Later on, she's more her own person;

she's not so much refracting the light of the Factory, or the light of Warhol."

The hours spent working by herself paid off, at least in Nico's mind. She confides these feelings in the *Twen* interview, remarking, "I write the music independently of the lyrics. I play the organ and I write everything that comes to my mind…I never think about it, things just happen. Really. I have little reason. When I tell you that I became a songwriter, I do not mean that I meant it. One day I had a song, and that was the beginning. Everything happens somehow. They are not coincidences, everything is predetermined. I am very fatalistic."

Having crafted the songs for the new album, Nico now needed a record label that would put them out. She was concerned that her reputation as a model, actress, and Superstar would be detrimental in her transition to serious solo artist. She turned to Fields for help. "She was so afraid," he said. "She knew that she had this great beauty and this great mystery, but she was so worried ('but I want them to know my songs') and people would say, 'Yeah, yeah. Now she writes songs. What a day. What else does she do?' But look at those songs; they're amazing. The great art songs of the '60s."

Fields was perfectly positioned to bolster Nico's career. In 1968, he was working at Elektra Records and had immediate access to the label's president, Jac Holzman. "Danny was close to the whole Warhol crowd," said Holzman. "One day, he brought Nico in. I knew who Nico was, and she brought in her little harmonium; she sat, and she played. Was it off the wall? Unbelievably so. But so what? It's not gonna be an expensive record to make and she's an interesting artist and let's just see what happens."

Fields has a similar memory of the day he brought the singer in to see the label president, which he shared in a 2002 magazine interview. "At that time, I think I had established some credibility with Jac because he thought I had an ear for the future, as it were. He has wonderful taste, and I kinda knew that he would see through the legend, the myth, the beauty, the goddess. I don't think he wanted to fuck her. Jac simply recognized good songs—that was the essence of Elektra. And he saw that in Nico, even though that was the last thing you imagined about her. Nico wasn't known as a songwriter but Jac saw something beyond the fact that she was an actress and had been in the Velvets and was associated with Andy Warhol." With the support of Holzman, Fields signed Nico to the label. "Even though it wasn't technically her first album, it was the first album of her music, of her as a musician. I don't know anything about music, but I know it's extraplanetary," he said.

24

The marble index of a mind forever
Voyaging through strange seas of thought, alone.
William Wordsworth

During a visit to Fields in his apartment, Nico found some much-needed inspiration. "She sat and read books of poetry looking for a title. And she found it in Wordsworth. 'The Marble Index of the Mind Gone...' She liked that phrase. She was a poet," said Fields. Nico read the title to Fields, who agreed it would work for the project. "I don't know how much Wordsworth she had read but she ran it by me and I found it sufficiently Gothic, pure, and lovely and meaningless. She is an extraordinary poet in a language that was not her own...She had a wonderful gift for discovering the English language on the spot. That's what she did. If it's a word or if it's not, I don't care. That was the way she expressed herself. She knew what she was saying, *you* knew what she was saying, but it certainly wasn't conventional emotive English expression at all. And yet it worked."

According to Ultra Violet, Nico wanted Warhol to design the cover for *The Marble Index*. However, it was rock photographer Guy Webster who ended up taking the pictures for the cover of the LP. Webster was already well known for his LP art and included among his credits the Rolling Stones, the Byrds, and Nico's labelmates the Doors.

"She was sent to me by Elektra Records," Webster tells me over the phone from his southern California studio. "They said, 'We want you to photograph somebody: Nico.' I said, 'Oh, I know who Nico is, I saw her in the Fellini films.' They told me that she was singing with a different group, and that she was a poet. I said, 'I'd love to meet her, send her to me.' They did. We got along great, right from the very beginning. I had this big estate in Beverly Hills, and I took her up to my guest house, which was as gigantic as a studio. We also went out the next day and did stuff outside with her on the hill. It was a lot of fun. She had that deep German voice, which I liked. I thought of her as a Nazi killer—I'm not joking! I actually did, because I didn't know any tall German women at the time.

"She was absolutely beautiful, stunning. I photographed all of the top actresses in Hollywood, but Nico was different. She was tall like a fashion model, had long blonde hair... She was a model and she knew how to pose; she knew how to look, she knew how to do makeup. When we went out and shot pictures, she was very easy. She moved beautifully, she lifted her arms in the air like a goddess... it was beautiful! And easy to photograph, so that's it—she was a real model.

"For the actual shoot, she came in and the light was very dark. I lit it with one light. She had the white hair, and I'm going to make it turn dark because I wanted it against a white background. People always asked how I did it. I did it in a dark room, very high contrast. I made a large 16 x 20 print and I sent it to Holzman. He loved it, and that's what was used for the cover."

The image is a dramatic black-and-white close-up of Nico's face. Her hair is deep black, matching the top of her shirt and the heavy eyeliner and eyelashes. The background is a softer shade, but still contrasts harshly with the white plane of her face. Her cheekbones provide the only other shadow in the picture.

Though he remembered his time shooting Nico fondly, Webster only saw her once again, this time several years later in Spain. "In the early 1970s, my wife and I were living in Minorca, Spain. I would go to the American bar every morning. People like the Stones and the Who and the families of those groups would come there; it was a very hip place to hang out at the time. So I'm sitting having coffee at the American bar, and its foggy... really foggy. I can barely see down the main avenue, and I see this dark figure with a long cape, and I thought, 'God, that looks like Nico, I can't believe it!' As she's getting closer, she yells out, 'Guy! You got any drugs?' I say, "Shut up, you can't do drugs here. If you do, you go to jail for six years automatically. Everybody was paranoid; if you had a joint you were scared, because the Guardia Civil would turn you in and you'd go to jail. I said, 'Nico, I'm so sorry I can't give you anything. I love you!' She said, 'See you soon, goodbye...' And she walked off into the fog. I never saw her again."

25

It took three sessions in May of 1968 to produce *The Marble Index*. Elektra Studios at 962 North La Cienega Boulevard in Los Angeles (now West Hollywood) was the primary location where the tracks were recorded and mixed, with Frazier Mohawk noted as producer.[92] Mohawk had already worked on several albums, including LPs by the Paul Butterfield Blues Band and Kaleidoscope (the band who had opened for Nico at the Scene). But Danny Fields gives Nico's former bandmate John Cale, who was brought in to help proceedings, credit for being the one who made the songs work. "Frazier Mohawk is the producer of the record simply because Jac wanted somebody connected with the record company there. He didn't want it to be completely up to the artistic eccentricity of this duo. But in fact, that's what happened," said Fields in a 2002 interview. "I don't think there was literally one creative input from Frazier Mohawk. Not to denigrate him as a producer, I'm sure he did good work elsewhere, but he couldn't move into that partnership speaking any language that they understood. Frazier Mohawk had nothing to do...he just sat there. John [Cale] just created those arrangements on the spot."

Though an unknown quantity in the producer role, Cale shaped *Index* into its otherworldly form. "The songs were already in Nico's head," he said later. Yet his contribution as collaborator, arranger, and uncredited co-producer was indelible. "Before I did *Index* I didn't know I could arrange," he said, "but then I got lucky and found a very strong personality like Nico who threw me against the wall and I had to come and bounce back."

The process wasn't easy because, according to Cale, when they worked together the two could be counted on to fight at "every opportunity." Each song presented a separate challenge, as the harmonium was not an instrument that was ever truly in tune. Cale, being a multi-instrumentalist, added a variety of different elements to the mix, including glockenspiel, bells, mouth organ, and bosun's pipe, as well as the expected electric viola, piano, bass, and guitar.

After recording finished, Cale kicked the singer out of the studio, locking the door behind her. Two days later, he let Nico back in to hear the final results. "You've got to remember that on those solo albums she was really in pain," he reflected. "Afterward she'd burst into tears of gratitude. It's that whole thing of self-loathing and the discovery of her personality." These qualities infected the music itself, as fan Steven Morrissey, lead singer of the iconic Mancunian band the Smiths, mused: "I was enormously comforted by her isolation and depression."[93]

The final album clocked in at just thirty minutes. Producer Mohawk later said that both he and Nico were heavily stoned on heroin during the fast-paced sessions, making Cale even more indispensable, and claimed that the LP's length was intentional, as "that's all I could listen to. Fifteen minutes a side seemed about right. Myself and [engineer] John Haeny spent maybe a day or two mixing it. We couldn't listen to it all the way through. It kind of made us want to slit our wrists... After it was finished, we genuinely thought people might kill themselves. *The Marble Index* isn't a record you listen to. It's a hole you fall into."

26

If I'd gone ahead and died, I would be a cult figure now.

Andy Warhol

On June 3, 1968, Valerie Solanas entered the Factory. Solanas was known to Warhol, having appeared in his movie from the previous year, *I, a Man*. She was also renowned for her extremist views on feminism, which she collated in her manifesto "Society for Cutting Up Men" or "SCUM." The document railed against the patriarchy, arguing that men had ruined the world and only women could fix it for the future.

Warhol was not alarmed by Solanas's arrival, thinking she was looking for money or wanting to pester him about a script she had previously left with him. Hence, the artist was completely surprised when the woman removed a .32 automatic from a paper bag and fired at him. Two shots went astray before Solanas succeeded in hitting Warhol in the chest. The bullet went into his right side and straight through him, coming out on the left side of his back. Warhol later told friends, "It hurt so much, I wished I was dead." Solanas then turned to visiting art critic and curator Mario Amaya and pulled the trigger. Though her shot went astray, she wasn't deterred and fired again, this time hitting him near the hip. Fred Hughes was also in the room as the entire horror show unfolded. He may have thought he had escaped the mad woman's wrath, as Solanas sauntered over to the elevator and pressed the button to bring it up to the Factory. However, instead of leaving immediately, she walked back to Hughes and aimed the gun at his forehead. She again pulled the trigger, but the firearm jammed. She reached for her backup piece, a .22, to finish the job. But the lift arrived, and instead of cutting down the terrified Hughes, she went to the waiting carriage and left the scene of the crime. Solanas gave herself up not long after in Times Square, explaining the reason why she had attacked Warhol could be found within the pages of her manifesto.

While Warhol lay bleeding, waiting for an ambulance to arrive, Billy Name had tears streaming down his face as he cradled the artist's head in his lap. Warhol's only response to the situation was, "Please don't make me laugh, it hurts too much." One report claimed that Warhol was clinically dead when the paramedics arrived. The artist was quickly rushed off to Columbus Hospital and placed in intensive care. He went on to spend two months in the hospital, recuperating from the various surgeries needed to bring him back to health. The attack left him having to wear a surgical corset for the rest of his life to hold his organs in place.

David Croland clearly remembers getting the news of the attack. "I was with Nico and Susan at my apartment on 71st Street. The phone rang, and it was Viva Superstar. She said that Andy had been shot. We were all a little freaked out. I said to Susan and Nico, 'We're going to the hospital to see Andy. We don't know if he's going to live or die.' Nico did not want to. She said, 'No, we're not. We're going to stay here because they're shooting Superstars possibly.' So I said, 'So what do you want to do?' And she said, 'We'll stay here, we'll light a candle and some incense, we'll smoke a joint, if you have any marijuana'—which we probably did. We just stayed in my apartment with the lights off and the candles burning, until we heard from Viva that Andy was alive and would possibly pull through."

Nico was terribly shaken by Warhol's brush with death and wrote a new song specially for him called "The Falconer." She did not think the people around him had taken the shooting seriously.

Physically, if not mentally, recovered, Warhol and Elektra Records held the premiere of *The Marble Index* at the Factory on September 19. The evening promised a "playing of the album," which was to start "promptly at 8:40 p.m.," with "wine, supper and dancing to follow." A newspaper write-up highlighted the happening, as it marked the first party that Warhol had hosted since being shot. "Before I thought it would be fun to be dead. Now I know it's fun to be alive," Warhol said in the piece. The album is described as "an ear-piercing 16 minutes that everyone said was beautiful," including Warhol. Adding further to Nico's growing mystique as the queen of weird, the artist confided that "Nico spent the whole summer writing it [*The Marble Index*] in the bathtub. She works well there." Nico had by this time changed her hair color and is noted as being "a tall redhead who refuses to give her age ('I'm too old to talk about it')." Taking the opportunity to promote her album, she tells the reporter that it is "like a movie. It has all the senses and it is in my line." When asked if she thinks the LP will succeed, she confidently replies, "Of course. There's very little good music around."

Nico seems equally eager to develop the album in a postcard she wrote to Danny Fields around the same time, in which she refers to British DJ John Peel and a song title from *The Marble Index*:

Danny Fields
c/o Elektra Records
1855 Broadway
New York City
10025
USA

They won't let me back past the frozen borderline. Please send Record to John Peel in London & François's movie to Hamburg c/o Mr. EHRFELD Metro Nomex Records. Release due in three weeks' time.
I love you! Nico.

Nico continued her promotional activities, giving a "guided tour" for *Eye* magazine "of the legendary Rock Castle in the hills of Los Angeles—the dreamlike mansion where the stars stay when they can't bear being away from home." The piece strived to showcase an unbeatable list of musical movers and shakers who had graced the "the electronic Olympus, the hip Versailles, the Taj Mahal of sound," with Nico providing the inside story: "The list of tenants reads like a social register of rock 'n roll. Nico has lived here, as have Bob Dylan, The Doors, the Jefferson Airplane, the Grateful Dead, the Lovin' Spoonful, Andy Warhol, the Who, Barry McGuire, Tiny Tim, and yes, the Beatles'. However, instead of lending a knowledgeable voice to the article, Nico seemed melancholic and already nostalgic, longing for an era that had ended only a year earlier: "She speaks in her tentative manner about the Castle's special meaning to her, of the idyllic isolation it provides from smog and groupies." As she leads the reporter from one room to another, the article becomes more like a historic account of strangers, not the intimate recounting of someone's personal history: "'This was Bob Dylan's room,' says Nico, guiding me to the first now-empty chamber off the stairway. Large windows overlook a garden, resplendent with afternoon sun. 'He had a beautiful desk here where he spent a lot of time writing songs, and he had a huge bed here, but now it's all gone. He wrote so many beautiful songs. You can see why he liked it here.'"

Toward the end of the tour, Nico brings the reporter back to "a goldfish pond in the garden...'There are five small deer who live down here near the fountain. It's just like living in a forest. And all the overgrown garden, it's like Gothic ruins,' she says wistfully." The theme of sadness and longing continues to the end of the piece, with Nico confiding, "The Castle used to seem so happy to me. But now it seems sad. I had some wonderful times here, but I could never live in it again. It is a very unusual place in the world." It is hard to work out whether Nico was openly showing herself in the piece or if she was simply adding fodder to the spooky moon goddess persona she had newly inhabited. The closing line complements her Garboesque traits only further, as Nico says, "A twenty-two room castle can be awfully lonely place for just one person."

While Nico was beginning the press cycle for *The Marble Index*, speculation about her former lover, Alain Delon, was unfolding. On October 1, 1968, the body of Stevan Marković was found in a public dump in the village of Élancourt, in Yvelines, west of Paris. His mouth was gagged, his body bound and wrapped in plastic. Marković was the ex-bodyguard and close friend of Delon. The death saw Delon come under investigation because of his purported association with several notorious French gangsters. During his questioning by police, Delon confessed that there had been an attempt to murder his wife Nathalie as well. While driving in Paris, she had discovered that one of the wheels on her car had been loosened. Luckily, she noticed it before it came off completely. Several other threats to Delon and his family were recorded by the police after the death of Marković; there were also rumors that a colleague of Marković was intending to kill the actor. Delon asked for permission to carry his own firearm, which was denied. Instead, he was given a police guard.

The Delon element was catnip to the press, who started dogging the household in Boulogne. Nico was very concerned for Ari's safety, though Ari recalled that his grandparents were the ones who took action after the murder. The incident provided them with the impetus to send the young boy away to a boarding school near Versailles, which he attended until he was a teenager.

———

The Marble Index proved to be so different to any other popular release of the time that even critics seemed confused about how to classify or describe it. "I can't make out a single real word," said the reviewer in the *NME*. Its uniqueness hindered sales, as neither journalists, customers nor even Elektra Records knew the right way to market this strange creation. Danny Fields tried hard to help Nico in any way he could, though she did not have formal management or a booking agent to organize concerts. Her own admitted dislike for performing live or engaging enthusiastically with any of the promotional opportunities that were presented to her doomed the album early on to be a sales flop. In *Follow the Music*, Elektra president Jac Holzman recalled, "She'd call up and, in her low moan, tell you, 'I'll be in on Tuesday, set up some interviews.' Tuesday would come, and no Nico. Eight months later, she'd call again. 'I'm back in town.' You would say, 'What about those other times?' 'Oh, I couldn't do those, I had to go to Rome.'"

An interesting artifact from Nico's promotional activities is a script dated December 17, 1968. It starts off with an introduction, followed by a bunch of interview questions. The most likely answers that Nico will give are also included ("'Why did you give up modeling?' A: She became bored with the work…she'll explain"). The replies also illustrate how the image of the lone, rambling, vagabond figure is being perpetuated and encouraged ("'What inspires you to compose music and words?' A: She's a poet…She gets her ideas mostly just walking around the city…she lives alone…is imaginative…A dreamer…").

Despite all of Fields's efforts, *The Marble Index* did not sell well. "Restricted sales but a beautiful album," *Record Retailer* said in the spring of 1969. Years later, in *Please Kill Me*, a reflective Fields said, "When I think of what I did at Elektra—I fought with The Doors (Jim Morrison and I hated each other); I signed the MC5, who they fired; I signed the Stooges, who they dropped; I signed Nico, who never sold any records." Yet even if Nico had been enthused and dependable during the album's promotional cycle, in all likelihood it would still have experienced low sales figures, as its icy, gloomy lyrics and musicality were just too weird for most consumers. "It's an artifact, not a commercial commodity. You can't sell suicide," explained John Cale in a 1977 interview with *Sounds*.

I haven't time to be a cliché.

Nico

Working on *The Marble Index* proved to John Cale and the higher-ups at Elektra that he could deliver the goods in the studio. Discussing the label's reaction to the LP, Cale reflected that "that album allowed a lot of European angst to come out and it was really something. We got carte blanche, which didn't normally happen...[Elektra boss] Jac Holzman told me how much he liked it, which was how I came to produce the Stooges." The Stooges were a Danny Fields discovery, hailing from Michigan. Soon after Fields signed the group, they were brought to New York to start recording with Cale. Lead singer Iggy Pop (born James Osterberg) had already publicly confirmed his admiration for the Velvet Underground and Nico. When asked in an interview with *Jazz & Pop* magazine to name his favorite contemporary artist, Pop responded, "I like the Velvet Underground and I'm one of those very few people who really, really like Nico's music. I love her last album [*The Marble Index*]." The trip marked the first time the singer had been to any major metropolis, and it was transformative. "I was meeting a lot of people who were unlike anyone I had ever met," Pop reflected when I spoke to him. He has a great sense of humor and is disarmingly honest and kind, and his memories provide one of the most thoughtful and honest portraits of Nico. "A lot of people who were interesting were artistic people, cultivated, literary in a sense—kind of like my father was. But they weren't strict like that. They were also more rockin', like me. This interested me. It was confusing. There weren't people like that in the Midwest. A lot of these people gravitated around Andy Warhol and his art scene. Among them, I got to know Nico."

Nico had taken up residence at the Chelsea Hotel and was already starting to think about her next album. She thought the artists' boarding house would be the perfect place to let inspiration flow and took to going with Cale to the Stooges' recording sessions, which were taking place at the Hit Factory studio.

"I don't remember the specific first time I met Nico. It's probable that I met her through Danny Fields, but it's also possible that I met her in our studio through John," Pop confides. "I do remember she was present at a number of the sessions for the first Stooges album. My earliest memory of her is sitting there with John Cale in the booth. She would sit there going, 'Yaah, yaah, this is good...better than the Velvets.'" Nico watched and listened, knitting throughout the sessions. "The two of them [Cale and Nico] looked like refugees from *Valley of the Dolls* or something," says Pop. "It was very gothic-looking." Cale's outfit made a particular impression on the young lead singer. "John wore a great big, black, velvet, hooded cape like Dracula. It had pink velour inside. The two of them would sit there. It was kind of like the Addams Family...it was like Mr. and Mrs. Munster," says Pop. "I got along with her right off." So well that soon after their initial meeting, the two became an item. "The next night or so, we went to Steve Paul's club, the Scene, to see Terry Reid play. Jimi Hendrix showed up and we jammed with him," recalled Pop's Stooges bandmate Ron Asheton. "After the show, Iggy and I had a beer with Hendrix. Iggy was walking around with Nico, and I was just sitting there snickering, because she was leading him around like he was her kid. She was so tall and he's so short—they were holding hands, real lovey-dovey. She wouldn't let him out of her sight." The two would often eat lunch at Max's. Nico made it obvious to everyone that she had dibs on the new arrival from the Midwest. Pop biographer Paul Trynka recounted one particular evening, when photographer Leee Black Childers and actor Jaime Di Carlo spotted the pair standing together, with Nico's hand thrust firmly down the front of Pop's trousers.

Danny Fields was not at all surprised by this new romance. "You kind of expected that Iggy would be someone Nico would fall in love with," Fields asserted. "He was everything she would like in a guy: wounded, brilliant, fragile but made of steel, insane, demented. So, it was no surprise. Nico fell in love with everyone who was extremely brilliant, insane, or a junkie. I don't want to seem cynical, and if I knew it was going to make such history, I would have had a tape recorder, but at the time it was, 'Ho hum, Nico's in love with another poet.'"

During the recording sessions, the Stooges used the Chelsea Hotel as a base for writing songs. It was there that Pop remembers "keeping company with her from time to time." He eventually wrote some of the lyrics for the Stooges track "We Will Fall" in reference to having to wait for Nico at the hotel. For him, their age difference was part of Nico's allure. "She was nine or ten years older than me and I knew she had been around more than I had. I never really thought about it, until one day I saw her passport. It was sort of like having a premonition of what was going to happen to me: years later, I was gonna end up in Berlin. I remember that the picture was black and white and very stark and very German-looking. The name on it was Christa Päffgen. I saw the age and the whole thing...I thought, 'Woah!' I didn't know what to make of that, but I thought, 'Wow! This is something else!'

"I was really thrilled and excited to be around her," Pop continues. "She was older and from somewhere else, and the first foreign person I can remember having a lot of contact with, and I really liked that. I liked that her accent was from somewhere else...everything was from somewhere else. And she was extremely strong. She was like hanging out with a rock singer, like hanging out with a guy, except she had girl's parts. It was the only difference. Otherwise, it was like a guy. A tough-minded, egotistical, artistic kind of guy."

In another interview, he went into more detail, saying, "She didn't want to be cuddled or anything. She didn't want me to whip her either." However, Pop did witness her uncertainty about what she would do next and how she fit in to the changing culture. "At key times, she would show tremendous vulnerability, and all of a sudden it would all fall off," says Pop. "And I would see, here's someone over thirty, not a model any more, not a commercial entity in the big business called America... What the fuck is she going to do? Once in a while, that side of it would show itself in the way she would get flustered over something or just sort of be off to the wind. She had a great sadness about her."

Nico's vulnerability and isolation touched Pop, who recognized a damaged woman who was not sure where to turn or what to do. "You know, [I was] a young, smart-ass rock singer trying to make an impression in New York City, hanging out with a very lost girl, a very lost and fragile personality. I think she was on the rebound. She didn't really have any relations with the Velvet Underground any more. She wasn't a top model any more... she was just kind of floating around. I think there had been an affair—with this one, with that one... whichever musician."

The duality in Nico appealed to Pop, who could appreciate, even at his young age, a soul who was adrift despite all of the outer trappings of success. "She had all the accoutrements of a really groovy international gal—the right boots, the right sheepskin coat, the right hair and she knew people on the right level—and yet she was fucked up, she had a twist to her." Pop was one of the few people that Nico opened up to, the singer recalling, "She was never the sort of person who would lie in real life, but she did work in an Andy Warhol enterprise for a while, and Andy Warhol's directive on how you do an interview is lie! Lie! You must lie!"

Once recording with Cale was done, it was time for the Stooges to return to Michigan. They had taken up residence in a farmhouse

—or "Fun House," as it was referred to—located in the middle of a cornfield. Nico decided she would follow her new amour back to the Midwest. "When Iggy said, 'Nico's coming,' it was like, 'Hey, well cool, we don't care,'" said Stooge Ron Asheton. "When Nico moved into the Fun House, we hardly saw her, because Iggy kept her up in the attic. The only time we saw her was when we practiced, and we resented her being there because we had a big rule—nobody allowed in the practice room, *especially* a woman." The tall German in residence did cause tension among the bandmates; as Iggy says, "The Stooges didn't want any girl in the house, especially one who had a very deep voice. They would imitate how she talked."

Nico would watch the band practice, clearly interested in what the young group was creating. "She would come to our rehearsals. We're just these guys rehearsing in this tiny, little, miserable, destroyed former living room of a farmhouse. She would stand right there and watch and listen to everything we did. The songs were just these primitive riffs, with me kind of caterwauling. She was very attentive to it and checked it out. She said once [*does impression of Nico*], 'You are better than Lou.' I think that was because she was just pissed off at Lou. That's what I think! That was the only time I ever heard her...she didn't express [anything bad about the Velvet Underground] or flappability, but she did say that. Maybe she liked the Stooges that much—I don't really know."

In many ways, she was the teacher to Pop's willing student. "She'd be very opinionated about my work and this, that and the other thing," says Pop. But it wasn't just his art that Nico was tutoring the twenty-one-year-old in; she also introduced him to some of the more refined aspects of adulthood. "She taught me how to eat pussy. She said one day, 'You know there is something very nice you can do for me that would make me feel very good.' So she showed me about that, which was a good thing to learn."

Nico did occasionally take up the role of rock'n'roll den mother, whipping up her vegetarian meals for the unsuspecting young men.

"She'd try to cook for us. She'd cook pots of brown rice every day and sometimes serve fresh fruit, but mainly brown rice and vegetables, and it would always have so much Tabasco and hot sauce that nobody could eat it—but she tried. She had an ear infection and she felt the Tabasco would clear her out," remembers Pop. Regardless of how edible Nico's culinary attempts may have been, they were often accompanied by expensive tipples that were new to the Midwestern boys. "She'd make these great curry dishes and just leave them on the table with really expensive wines," said Ron Asheton. "That's what got us all back into drinking, the great wines Nico turned us on to." Nico's choice of booze also made a huge impression on Pop. "The first time I ever had a Beaujolais, that was from Nico. Before that I just had Ripple—a very cheap, very sweet wine. It was the time of year when the Beaujolais wines were coming into season. They mature in September, so she was excited. 'We must find some Beaujolais wine!' There was a place called the Big 10 Party Store up the road from the Stooge house, and they had it. I had never had a European wine or anything and I took to that like a duck to water. I was drinking a bottle a day of that and doing other drugs." He adds, "Nico liked to drink." The wines were not just a lesson in being a sommelier; Nico was also teaching Pop how to navigate the music industry. "She'd feed me red wines with French names I'd never heard of. That's how I learned all that bullshit, that's how I learned to modulate my voice . . . and speak to record company executives."

Nico's choice of food and drink reflected her conflicted persona. "She had a mix of so many things. There was a little bit of a top model in there, someone who knew her way around France and made love to Alain Delon and had been in very, very nasty New York and survived. Then there was a little bit of just a very typical somebody who would wear an alternative dress and eat brown rice. Little of this, little of that. Really, really, truly interesting person."

Yet for all her seemingly sophisticated ways, Nico had genuinely fallen for the young singer. According to Danny Fields, "Nico would call me all the time from Ann Arbor, saying, 'I don't know eeeff he loves meee enymore, he's ignoring meee, oooh, he's so meeeean to meee!' I'd say, 'Well, I guess you picked kind of a hard guy to have an affair with.' You know, sorry, but what else is new?"

Nico was also an influence on Pop's early stage presence. "The more we were together, the crazier she seemed and the crazier I became," recalls Pop, adding, "You know, she was not like the girl next door. She had a way of shaking things up. She had insights, and she would let you know her insights in a briefly worded passage, with 110 percent assurance that she was right. She'd tell me [*does impression of Nico*], 'You must wear your hair to hide your face. Your face is not to be seen.' That was one. Another one was [*does impression of Nico*], 'You are not yet fully poisoned. Lou is poisoned. Bob Dylan is poisoned. You have not yet got to poisoned. You need to poison,'" says Pop. "She meant I had too much humanity." Looking back, he is clearly moved by how true Nico's assertions turned out to be. "In retrospect, it was like having my own little Greek chorus or something. Or an oracle. I had an oracle on my hands, that is what I had!"

When Nico was in the crowd, Pop began trying out more chaotic versions of his stage persona during gigs. "There was something about her presence that kept me constantly edgy. And I had some of my most dangerous and some pretty nasty shows [with Nico in the audience]. A couple of them were stopped by the police. When we were working in Michigan, she was coming with me to the shows. I didn't know what that was, whether I was trying to impress her or some influence—I am not sure." Nico inspired Pop to make the live shows ever more provocative. A couple of occasions particularly stick out in his memory. "It was getting colder, and she gave me a sheepskin embroidered jacket which she said Jim Morrison had given her. I don't know if it was so or not, but probably true—she's not a liar type. One of the gigs I drank all the wine and then broke the wine bottle over the microphone in the middle of the finale because I thought the broken glass would look cool in the light. Which it did, but it cut a teenage audience member. It was sort of controversial. Then there was another gig—it might have been the last time she came to my gig with me—she was there at the show in Romeo, Michigan. I stripped off and sort of counterattacked the proletariat of rural Michigan. I got arrested by the state police. The band tried to smuggle me out in the trunk of a car, but they [the police] grabbed me."

Nico's time with Pop illustrates that she wanted to have an intimate, close bond with someone; however, she may have not been equipped or known how to make such a situation last. The romance with the young singer was no different: short, but impactful for Pop. "It's not a long period of time that I spent together with her—maybe a month, I don't know. But it was important to me," he later said. Bandmate Asheton had a slightly different spin on the situation, saying, "Nico stayed a long time, about three months. Iggy never said if he was in love with her or not."

One artifact to come from the romance was a short film shot for "Evening of Light," a track on *The Marble Index*. It was a special song for Nico. "I had a toy piano on 'Evening of Light,' a piano for little children, and I started playing and we used that," she commented later. François de Menil was determined to make a film with the singer, and it was decided that they would make a video for the song. Nico had met de Menil while she lived with Fred Hughes. De Menil became obsessed with the singer and proposed doing a project with her; however, she had recently relocated to Michigan to be with Pop. De Menil was heir to the oil equipment firm Schlumberger fortune, so when Nico insisted on having him drive to Michigan to film there, there were no financial obstacles. She also told the aspiring filmmaker that he must feature Pop in the project. De Menil did just that. "I think it really pissed off de Menil," recalls Pop. "At that time, the equipment was really bulky. He didn't look thrilled about the whole thing, but he put it all in a station wagon and drove to Michigan." Filming for the video, which was shot on 16 mm, took place in a barren, icy potato field neighboring the Fun House. "There are a lot of farms around there," says Pop, "and it was she and I and the third person was the Stooges' road manager [John Adams] at the time."

The video captures a red-haired Nico, looking hauntingly angelic in a white robe, strolling across the desolate land, before lying down on the ground. Iggy wears tight-fitting leather trousers and a gray T-shirt with the word "RATIONAL" emblazoned across the chest. His face is painted mime white, his features completely obscured. Doll parts are scattered across the landscape as Iggy carries a cross. The final scenes are of the sun setting as the cross is erected and burned against a dark sky. It was a challenging shoot. "It was very physical. I did it because she asked me to. I wasn't going to turn her down. We ran around and around this potato field and mimed with plastic limbs. I never made much sense of it…but I needed dinner that day," says Pop.

The film is eerie, gorgeous, and incredibly atmospheric. Pop credits Nico for coming up with the concept and the symbolism. "She probably wanted that imagery and told the guy, 'Find me a place where we can burn a cross.' A field was just probably convenient as a place where you could start a fire and nothing was going to happen. But, also, the potato has a deep history with the German people. I think it was Charlottenburg castle in Berlin where the first potato cultivation in Europe went on. It was early, and they love their *Kartoffels* in Germany. The look of that field certainly matched the song, so maybe François has some credit there. The guy was not a hick. He barely deigned to speak to any of us. He was a New York guy supported by an important trust fund, so he didn't really talk to me. I don't remember who said what. I just remember I was out there going, 'Shit, this is hard! I'm getting tired here!' When you're on the spot, you definitely try to perform and do the best you can do. As it turns out, it was a wonderful thing. It's probably the only video I've been in that I've ever liked!

This one was all right. It was her video, not mine, and the music was great."

When presented to Elektra as a possible promotional vehicle, *Evening of Light* was swiftly rejected. Attempts by de Menil to get the video broadcast by other media outlets were equally fruitless. However, decades later, Pop is proud of the final result of that afternoon spent in the cold fields of the Midwest. "What a great song. It's a real mind-fucker."

Ron Asheton had similar memories, saying, "We all went out to this farm, and Nico got John Adams to be in it, too, because he looked like a sphinx: big, long, light, curly red hair. It was the dead of winter and we were sitting looking out this picture window, laughing, while they put these mannequin arms all over the field—John with no shirt on, and Iggy with no shirt on, doing nothing. Boy, it was real artsy."

Nico departed Michigan and Iggy not long after they completed filming *Evening of Light*. According to Asheton, she left behind an unpleasant reminder: "I remember after she left, Iggy came downstairs looking for some advice. He came up to me and said, 'Well, I think something's wrong, maybe you can tell me what this is?' So he whips out his cock, squeezes it, and green goo comes out. I said, 'Buddy, you got the clap.'"

However, it is Nico's artistry that has stuck with Pop. "In my way, I loved her. I had a great admiration for her," he says. "She was a great, great artist. It was just a real kick to be around her. I'm absolutely convinced that someday, when people have ears to hear her, in the same way that people have eyes to see a van Gogh now, that people are gonna just go, 'WHOOOAAA!'"

200

III: EXISTENCE

29

Nico first met Philippe Garrel in 1969, through her friend, actress Tina Aumont. Aumont was shooting a movie, *Le Lit de la vierge* ("The Virgin's Bed"), with the model Zouzou and an underground star named Pierre Clémenti.[94] Garrel was looking for music to score his new project, and Nico hesitantly offered her "Warhol" song, "The Falconer." This was the start of an almost decade-long relationship, one that was based on creativity and addiction.

True to Nico's usual taste, Garrel was three years her junior but just as offbeat as she was, with Paul Morrissey describing her new suitor as looking like "Laurence Olivier doing Richard the Third." "He was all hair with a pointed nose sticking through," Morrissey continued. "You thought he should have been surrounded by snarling hounds and a raven on his shoulder. But he was terribly quiet and slightly pretentious—just the sort of person Nico would fall for then, of course." Pauledith Soubrier, Ari's aunt, had a similar recollection of Garrel, stating, "There was nothing to see above his neck but an immense mass of dark hair. My mother looked at this figure standing there, went right up and swept the hair from the center across either side of his head. She tugged the hair aside like it was a pair of curtains, to look at the face. He was very bony."

Garrel came from Parisian entertainment royalty, his father being revered screen actor Maurice Garrel. Young Philippe seemed poised to be the new *enfant terrible* of French underground cinema, having made his first movie at the age of sixteen. By twenty-five, he had completed six features, though none was ever widely released. This combination of pedigree and weirdness was appealing to Nico, who soon began collaborating with the upstart.

While embarking on this new relationship, Nico received some terrible news. On July 3, her former lover Brian Jones was found motionless at the bottom of his swimming pool. Though an autopsy revealed a heavily enlarged liver and heart—most likely the result of his heavy drug use—the official cause of death was "misadventure" by accidental drowning. The rock royalty were shaken. Nico despaired at the loss of her former beau, while both the Who's Pete Townshend and the Doors' Jim Morrison wrote poems in homage to the Stones' founder.[95] During an appearance on a U.S. television show around the same time, Jimi Hendrix dedicated a song to the fallen musician. Within two years, both Morrison and Hendrix would be dead, like Jones, at the age of twenty-seven.

By the start of 1970, Nico had begun shooting what would be the first of seven films with Garrel: *La Cicatrice intérieure* (*The Inner Scar*), which became the best known of these collaborations. Nico was not sure when the project would be finished but did not care, saying in an interview, "This new one is very important to me. It's so powerful. We did part of it in the American desert and part of it in the Egyptian desert...I don't know when we'll finish it. It doesn't matter, there's no hurry because it's a very timeless thing."

It took two years to complete, as Garrel would often take breaks from the production in order to find the additional funds required to finish it. Filmed across three different, barren terrains, *Scar* is composed mostly of long, simple, linear tracking shots, with minimal editing during scenes. What little dialogue there is was written by Nico, usually moments before the camera began rolling.[96] She also provided five songs for the soundtrack, all of which went on to be featured on her third studio album, *Desertshore* (which came out at the end of the year). In a postcard to Danny Fields, dated January 12, 1970, and sent from Luxor, Egypt, Nico confides:

Dear Danny, I am getting nostalgic over the old life of living so solitary. Can you do anything for me in NY? I would follow your advice. The movie is O.K. but does not take me into my world. Love you, Nico.

Ari accompanied his mother during filming and appeared throughout the movie.[97] He recalls the clashing dualism of living with Delon's mother and spending time with Nico, saying, "The beginning of the school year coincided with the shooting of *La Cicatrice intérieure*. I was part of the adventurous life of Nico and the most avant-garde of French films. We were reclusive in a palace, fed broth and Coca-Cola. I can still see myself on all fours on the carpet of our room, building castles while listening with my mother to the tape of Procol Harum." Ari's vivid description dovetails with the bleak but beautiful vistas in *The Inner Scar*, which are as prominent as the characters themselves. The film mainly features Nico, dressed in loose, flowing robes, Pierre Clémenti, wearing nothing, and Garrel drifting across the various endless landscapes.

Upon release, the film was applauded and panned equally, seen as either a stark, visionary expression of cinematic genius or the result of two junkies with a camera and financial backing. The *New York Times* summarized it best, saying, "Clémenti speaks French; Nico sometimes complains in English and sometimes declaims in German verse, and sometimes sings for musical background on the soundtrack. There are no subtitles. The people, never more than two at a time, move through a variety of landscapes from glacial to nearly tropical—but that are always, in some manner, desert. The people may walk or run or ride a horse, or drive a flock of sheep or even sail a little boat—but almost always they are in movement... In such stark, unyielding simplicity there is surely a good deal of pretension." Garrel admitted to taking LSD to "prepare" for the film, which must have added to the strange, non-linear sequences that make up the movie in its entirety. One *Time Out* reviewer wrote,

"You need a bloody big spliff to enjoy this. A miserable couple who you would not wish to meet at a party [Garrel and Nico] are joined by a naked weirdo [Clémenti] . . . with a bow and arrow and a desire to set everything on fire. That's about it, frankly, unless I fell asleep, which is likely."

The film's title, and much of the very subjective "plot," refers back to deep-seated pain, hurt and regret. In an interview, Nico recalled the genesis of the film, saying that "it started out with Philippe having had electric shock treatment. And that's how he called the film, 'The Inner Scar,' which is you know, madness. It's a scar in the brain. I was with him while he was in this clinic, near Rome. I was in the same room. And they sent me out a few times before giving him electroshocks. I didn't know it until I discovered it. It was horrible."

At the start of the production, Garrel was sewing his own clothes. He eventually began also to make Nico's wardrobe, resulting in the two of them often being dressed similarly in flowing, almost medieval garments, usually in black or white. The bond was made even stronger by their simultaneous further descent into heroin addiction. Drugs became a tool for wielding power, and one of Nico's former lovers claims that the relationship was abusive. "Garrel was Nico's . . . nightmare, for years," says Robert King. "He wanted her to make films with him. She was initially good about it, and then became bad about it. That's what I know."

While with Garrel, heroin became the most important thing in Nico's life. Previously, she had smoked the drug; by 1970, she had been taught how to liquefy and inject it. It is still unclear when the transition between the two methods of administering the opiate occurred or who guided her in the different techniques. People who use heroin typically report feeling a surge of pleasurable sensation—a "rush." The intensity of the rush is a function of how much drug is taken and how rapidly it enters the brain and binds to the opioid receptors. After the initial effects wear off, users will usually be drowsy for several hours, their mental function is clouded, their heart function reduces and breathing is also severely slowed, sometimes enough to be life-threatening. These numbing elements allowed Nico to function, to temporarily forget the past and the uncertain present. As she stumbled across former acquaintances and friends, they were almost unanimously shocked by her new look and devasting addiction. "It was extraordinary. I had not seen her for some years, and I was dismayed. She wore orange–red dyed hair, long but severely cut, and terrible clothes. When I first knew her, she was uncontaminated," said her pal Carlos de Maldonado-Bostock, "but now she was contaminated beyond belief. I hardly knew what to say. In fact, I didn't know what to say. I simply couldn't speak. It was as though some terrible tragedy had befallen her. I was appalled." Paul Morrissey was equally upset, saying, "She came back to New York soon after with Garrel and she looked hideous. She had been one of the most famous blonde models there was, an icon to thousands of people whom she'd never meet, and here she was with this awful crimson hair and unshapely clothes and screaming to the world, 'I don't want to be beautiful anymore.' It was tragic to see this change. This is the time when the drugs got heavy. This was the start of the slide down to hell. It was this Garrel guy who turned her round. She had become artistic, and she did what she thought artists do—go mad, get wired, go to hell."

The drugs momentarily assuaged the acute loneliness inherent in Nico, while driving a wedge between her and those who cared for her, making her more isolated than ever before. Danny Fields emphasized this point, saying, "She didn't seem to help herself in many instances, but she felt she could indulge those impulses because there were always men around. There was always a cushion of guardians. There was a Paul Morrissey or there was someone in place there...Andy Warhol. We all took care of her. And she knew that was there. She knew that she could do frail and helpless. Getting a phone call in the middle of the night. 'Oh, Danny, I must have some heroin. Can you give me $10?' And I'd have to tell her, 'Nico, not for that. Leave me alone. It's the middle of the night.' People would say to me, 'You talk to her like that? You know, she's *Nico*.' But you *could* talk to her like that. 'Fuck off, Nico. Not for that. I love you. Goodbye.' Click. But she knew who loved her," he concluded. "At the end of the day, we would be there for her as much as you could, but you can't be there for a junkie. I'm sorry. You can't." The drugs also stripped Nico of her sense of humor, with scoring the next hit becoming the most important, if not only, priority. "If she hadn't been jonesing she would have laughed at that herself," said Fields. "That's the way she was. She loved the absurdities of life."

30

At the start of February 1970, Nico received some horrible news: after several years dealing with debilitating Parkinson's disease, Grete had passed away in Germany. Nico was no longer subsidizing her mother and had rarely been in touch during the last several years of Grete's life. Without money or other relatives, Grete had eventually been shipped to the town of Bürgerhaus, where, according to Helma, she was placed in an "old people's home for the nervous and seriously ill" and told that she would stay there until her death. "From then on, the social welfare office took over everything. Isn't that terrible?" said Helma.

Though Nico had ignored her mother the entire time her health was deteriorating, she rushed to attend the funeral. "She never visited her mother at the clinic," said Helma. "She only came to bury her. She was all in black, in deepest mourning for her mother, kneeling at her bed with the biggest crocodile tears and complaining, 'Mother, Mother! I didn't want it like this!' Then she was really done. But, as I said, she had never had time for her mother [once she became ill], she never cared for her."

Margarete Päffgen was buried in Grunewald Forest Cemetery, located in Berlin. Nico eventually wrote a song, "Mütterlein," about her, which ended up on *Desertshore*. One reason that Nico may not have attended to Grete at the end was the probably all-consuming nature of her own addiction. Recovered former users often recall that during the throes of their sickness, life would revolve entirely between scoring and using, with little to no regard paid to any other part of their existence. Nico was likely no exception. Another possibility could be that seeing Grete would have thrown her further into her downward spiral of angst, originally fueled by her separation from Ari. Whatever the reason for her disregard, Nico must have been shaken by the loss of her mother. Grete's passing officially made her an orphan, and with the exception of her cousin, Aunt Helma and Ari, she was now entirely alone in the world.

Between shooting *The Inner Scar* and playing random shows, Nico lived with Garrel in the Montparnasse Hotel, located in Paris. Eventually, Garrel's father offered his son a luxury top-floor apartment, located on the narrow rue de Richelieu, near the stock exchange. Upon moving in, the younger Garrel stripped the space of all modern "necessities." Out went the electricity, gas, hot water, carpets, furniture, stove, heater, lighting and any sort of formal decoration. The only nod to aesthetics were the walls: Nico and Garrel had decided to give every surface two thick layers of black enamel paint. A large overcoat of Garrel's doubled as both mattress and bedding. This morbidly depressing atmosphere was aided by the few things that did make their way into the home. "There were dead pigeons by the window, grime on the floor and the ledges, bird shit, stale grease, rubble, debris, dust," said a friend in Richard Witts's biography. "The most sensational feature was the fireplace. It had not been used in years, just a big black hole in the wall. But cascading from the grate was the most magnificent heap of cigarette packets I had ever seen. It was like a ski slope made of tiny cardboard boxes. Scattered amongst the packs were thousands of dog ends, crumbling cigarette tips flung from the four corners of the room. It took your breath away." Sometimes Ari joined the pair in the squalor, the limited entertainment on offer based around what was free. He recounted, "All three of us went to visit the museums, or we went for long walks on the docks. We walked a lot because we were really very poor. Then, invariably, we returned to Philippe's apartment, which was neglected in the extreme, butts spilled on the ground and a chimney torn off, most often without electricity. We did not even have cutlery and we ate with our fingers the cheese and the rice."

Despite living in a horrifyingly grim abode, Nico had no plans to leave Paris. She had been dropped by Elektra and, while she had written a few songs, did not have a label or any infrastructure to help her.

———

Back in New York, a young producer named Joe Boyd was making a name for himself. He had already discovered singer Nick Drake and was producing the Incredible String Band, who were signed to Elektra. It was there that he came across Nico. "I would go in their [Elektra's] office all the time and grab promo copies of new releases," he tells me. "On one of those visits, I got a hold of *The Marble Index*. When I played it, I was stunned. I just thought, 'Wow, this is really out there and wonderful.' It's unlike anything else, and I just thought it was astonishing." The haunting album stayed with Boyd long after his first listen. "Some months later, I happened to run into Jac Holzman and told him how much I loved the record. He basically said, 'Yeah, it's a great record, but it didn't sell, so we've dropped her.' And I said, 'You've dropped her?!' And he said, 'Well, yeah, what can you do...'"

At the time, Boyd was starting a new venture with Warner Brothers. Working with Mo Ostin and Joe Smith, the label was called Reprise, and Boyd was keen to get Nico on the roster. "I still hadn't met either John [Cale] or Nico, I just had this enthusiasm," he says. Boyd struck a deal with Ostin: a new Nico record could be done if Cale did the arrangements and the cost was low.

Though he did not know Cale personally, the two men ran in the same circles, and Boyd was able to track down a phone number for the ex-Velvet. "When Moe gave me a cautious green light,

I just picked up the phone to John and introduced myself. I said, 'Would you be up for doing another record with Nico? You and I can co-produce it, you can do all the arrangements.' I think I mentioned a figure of what I could carve out of the budget for him. He said he'd be delighted to."

Though Nico would have been deep into her drug use and co-dependent relationship with Garrel, it was the creative process of making the album that Boyd focused on throughout our conversation. When asked if Cale brought any of the baggage from the Velvet Underground days into the project, Boyd says, "Whatever had gone on between them with the Velvet Underground, he had gone ahead and done *The Marble Index*. I think he liked the idea of having projects that were independent of Lou [Reed]."

Once Boyd and Cale had come to an agreement, things moved very fast. "We met in New York, and he called Nico. We recorded *Desertshore* in three days or something." Nico "was very self-contained," says Boyd. "It's not like she sat down and said to John, 'Oh, I have this idea—what do you think?' I think she said, 'This is the song,' and then John figured out what to do with it in terms of the arranging and overdubs and things like that. The core of everything on that record was Nico seated at the harmonium with the vocal mic."

The Cale/Nico relationship "wasn't super-friendly," says Boyd, though he recalls that "they teased each other a bit. John would roll his eyes periodically at things that she would do or say, but I think that he was intrigued by her as a performer and as a singer, as a foil for his artistic sensibility." The one track that stuck with Boyd in particular, even decades on, was "Afraid," with its desolate lyrics "You are beautiful / and you are alone." The song was purely autobiographical for Nico; as Boyd says, "I don't think she had the ability to write things that weren't about her."

While the last bits of overdubbing and engineering took place, Boyd found himself with a gap before the project could be completed. During this time, he was introduced not only to Ari, who was with Nico at the time, but to some of the New York underground, whom he had never come into contact with before. "I'd gotten to know Nico in the course of making the record, and we had some strange friends in common, like Amanda Lear.[98] I'd never seen the Velvets live and I'd never met John until that point." He found Nico "curiously funny. She had a bit of a sense of humor, although it was hard to find sometimes."

In retrospect, Boyd says Nico "was a kind of naive painter...a character with no training who had something unique in her personality that was striking and original. I don't know what would have happened if she hadn't met John, and whether or not anybody would have noticed her, but there is something absolutely compelling about her singing and her songs. It's not complex music, but she was a tortured person and she put it all out there—that's what you ask from art. I think she's a very interesting character. In America, there is Janis Joplin, Jim Morrison and Jimi, all this stuff. In the middle of this, you have these two weird Europeans: John Cale and Nico. They bring a completely alien sensibility right into downtown New York and create something startling, stir people up. They make people look at things a little differently."

The cover of *Desertshore* was a still from Garrel's movie *The Inner Scar*. Showing Nico sitting atop a white horse that is being led by a little boy through a barren landscape, it cemented her dedication to her personal and professional collaboration with the filmmaker. Like *The Marble Index*, *Desertshore* met with mixed reviews from the press and Nico's inner circle alike. Cale did all the arrangements on the album, as well as playing all the instruments, with the exception of trumpet and Nico's harmonium. He also provided harmony vocals on "My Only Child." He was impressed by Nico's progress as a musician, commenting how on *Desertshore* "Her singing was more confident, and I was surprised to hear how her songs had become more musically coherent. The melodies became more adventurous, beautifully constructed, too. She focused much better on having subtle, simple lines and shorter phrases. And she started writing changes—contrasting sections, even." This may be because many of the songs were incredibly personal, including "The Falconer" (inspired by Warhol after his 1968 shooting), "Janitor of Lunacy" (inspired by the death of Brian Jones), "Mütterlein" (inspired by her mother) and "My Only Child" (inspired by her son). Ari also made a guest appearance on the LP, speaking in French on the seventy-two-second interlude "Le Petit Chevalier." *Rolling Stone* later branded the track "a chilling little chanson reminiscent of *The Village of the Damned*."

Paul Morrissey for one liked the new Cale/Nico collaboration even less than its predecessor. "She'd play me her new records with her songs on, and I had to say, 'Oh, Nico, these songs are so hard to listen to! I don't think anyone else can sing these songs, and I don't know that you can either,'" he said. Iggy Pop, on the other hand, was blown away upon first listen. "A favorite New York memory, which was a big one for me, happened while she was working on *Desertshore*. She had a room at the Chelsea, and we bumped into each other. She invited me to come up and play some of her new songs for me. It was just a very bare hotel room, and she had her harmonium in there. I sat down and she played 'Janitor of Lunacy' for me. For an audience of one. That was really 'Wow!' For me, that was one of the very few times in my life I've been witness to what I would call 'complete' music. Here was someone making the music and the melody and the ambience and the literature all at once for me without benefit of a stage, proscenium or lighting or a ticket or any of that shit. It was complete and the quality was so high. I thought, 'Wow. Wow.'" Cosey Fanni Tutti is equally complimentary about *Desertshore*, saying, "What's so strong about Nico is that she comes across as this kind of androgynous person with her voice, but she has this wonderful warmth about her and vulnerability—but also honesty—when she sings. She brings something to it that I don't think a male voice could have done."

When the record was commercially released in December 1970, *Desertshore* received little commercial recognition. Like *The Marble Index*, the album obtained a small cult following upon first hitting the shelves but was overlooked by most large magazines and the public in general.

———

"I met Nico in 1970. She lived at Paul Morrisey's house on East 81st Street for a while. That's where I was staying, so we kinda 'lived' together for a couple of months," recalls Vincent Fremont, the former executive manager of Andy Warhol's studio. He had begun working with Warhol at the Factory and was already staying with Morrissey when Nico appeared in New York, around the time of *Desertshore*'s appearance in the stores. It is likely that she was back on the East Coast for its release. "She would cry almost every night; she was very depressed," Fremont tells me. He already knew who Nico was before meeting her. However, he was surprised at how different she looked by the time they began sharing an apartment. "I had a big crush on her while I was in high school, when she did the *Velvet Underground & Nico* album. But when I met her, she had already changed her hair to red."

Underneath the beauty, Fremont quickly discovered that "there were a lot of facets to her. She would tell me about her life. I never had sex with her or anything, but I would sit on her bed and listen to her stories. It wasn't walking down a rosy path. She was a troubled soul. She was raped as a young woman by a GI. She was just complicated. She was on drugs by that time. She would show me photographs. We became fairly close. I was a good listener. I just remember her crying a lot. I'd stay up with her."

Like she had while living with Viva, Nico constantly practiced her harmonium, much to the dismay of her new roommates. "She

215

used to play that harmonium and she would sing. Paul Morrissey would start pulling his hair out, saying, 'Nico, can't you write something more commercial?' I mean, it would literally make you want to slit your wrists, it was so depressing. She'd be singing along and driving us crazy."

31

On January 17, 1971, Nico appeared on stage with John Cale at his first post-Velvet Underground solo gig, at the Roundhouse in London. Cale accompanied Nico on piano and viola during some of her songs, the singer later telling an interviewer for *Record Mirror* that the two were "still best friends...we have the same taste in music." She goes on to say that she would like to continue working with Cale, "if he wants to work with me, but I might change my music. But if I want to change my music I have to start playing different instruments"—something she never did. Nico revealed that she was working on a new film with Philippe Garrel, taking on the role of "a movie director who gets killed by a big camera in the end. I think it is every movie director's wish to be killed by his camera. They get obsessed with their function and to them nothing is more important than their camera." This particular project never came to fruition. On one of the few occasions when Nico acknowledges her appearance and any hindrance it may cause her, she concludes by saying, "I would really like to write film score music, but I don't know how to get into it. People don't believe that a beautiful girl can do that!"

In February, she recorded a four-song BBC session for John Peel. The radio DJ had a reputation for championing music from outside of the mainstream, and Nico was no exception. Her appearance on the show, performing alone, accompanied only by the haunting harmonium, bolstered her importance in outsider culture. Two tracks were from *The Marble Index* ("No One

Is There" and "Frozen Warnings"); one was from her recent album *Desertshore* ("Janitor of Lunacy"); the fourth, "Secret Side," was a new track, illustrating that Nico was working on fresh material. Peel was reportedly dazzled by Nico's voice, but less so by meeting her, as the singer walked out of the studio during an on-air conversation with the DJ. Peel noted this interaction, writing in his diary on February 4, 1971, that Nico was "stunningly rude" and "Andy Warhol NY super cool rat shit."

By April, Nico had secured some New York shows at the Gaslight club. Though these gigs never actually took place, a series of recordings exist from practice sessions held at the apartment of music industry friends Richard and Lisa Robinson from April 9, 1971, where she was joined by Lou Reed. It is unclear whether Reed planned on accompanying her during the shows, but the tapes offer great insight into the complicated Nico/Reed dynamic. Reed has been hailed a genius, but he clearly needed Nico, at least in the early Velvet days, to position him for this future exaltation. As her addiction became worse, Nico saw Reed as a possible ray of hope. This material mostly features the two going through old Velvet Underground and *Chelsea Girl* material, rather than any of the newer tracks from *The Marble Index* or *Desertshore*. The recordings show a tenderness between Reed and Nico, who joke throughout the sessions and return each other's banter:

(*Reed begins to play guitar over playback.*)

Reed (*tuning guitar*): [I hope?] we're in the right key. Can you play that again?

(*Playback begins again, and Reed plays guitar chords over the top; possibly chuckles.*)

Nico (*upbeat*): It's just so low. It's lower than my lowest song!

At many points throughout the more than an hour's worth of recording, Reed is kind, reassuring, and patient with the singer. Her link to Paul Morrissey as her guardian and mentor is still obvious, as she says, "Morrissey gave me a lecture... the other day, on how I shouldn't despise these songs that I liked very much one time." Reed says, "I know you can do it," as Nico worries that she won't be able to perform the *Chelsea Girl* material correctly:

Nico (*animated*): Because I know the lyrics of that one and (*quietly*) [our one?]. The other one, the Dylan one. "I'll Keep It with Mine." (*laughing*) "These Days," I forgot! (*upbeat*) So I will have to learn from (*quietly*) what I've taped just now. (*animated*) So, we can go over the other three now and then "I'll Keep It with Mine."

Reed: Then we're gonna have to rehearse on Monday.

Danny Fields makes a cameo on the tapes, acting as Nico's cheerleader, friend, and confidant, as per usual. As the two discuss what songs should be included in her set list, it is clear that Nico, though demurring somewhat while in the presence of Reed, is still set on performing her new material:

Fields: You wanna do five songs?

Nico: I mean, from the old... the old.

Fields (*over Nico*): Is that a fifteen-minute set? Oh.

Nico: And then my own.

Fields: How many songs all together?

Nico: All together?

Fields: Yeah...

Later on that same day, another taped conversation between Nico and Fields reveals frustration on both sides of the relationship. Nico is annoyed by her label Reprise's lack of promotion for the release of *Desertshore* and tries to rope Fields into aiding her again. Throughout the chat, Fields is thinking about different opportunities and ways to help Nico, from reconnecting her with former bandmates and producers to getting her gigs and creating a track record that a label or promoter could get behind. It seems that Nico, under the influence of tequila, had broached the idea of Fields managing her, but did not get the enthusiastic reply she had craved. This sets the tone for the first minute of the conversation, in which Nico is less talkative.

Nico: What do you want them to do?

Fields: Well, it would be nice if they took out an ad or something.

Nico: I know, really. They should do that—an ad.

Fields: Really. They're usually very good about it. Best company about that.

Nico: Really? (*upbeat*) I thought Elektra was better (*laughs*). Remember they had a whole-page ad?

Fields: Yeah, I was there nudging them. Because I was there, yelling at them. If you don't have anyone there, speaking for you, it's hard to get something done, you know...I'll speak for you. I have to see; I just have to get rid of this job at Atlantic.[99]

Nico: Because, yeah, the night...I don't know if I was drunk or you were disinterested...(*trails off*).

Fields: No, I wasn't disinterested. I just felt that I didn't know what was happening.

Nico (*laughs*): Oh yes...You don't think that, umm...It's really...(*annoyed sigh*) I don't know how to say it (*laughs. Pauses*) I thought that nightclubs for my sort of music wasn't the right thing, the right place, but...(*trails off*).

Fields: Well, I think it's a good place to be.

Nico (*possibly disappointed*): Just for a few days—it's okay.

Fields: I think it's okay. Then we can get a lot of people in there to see you and everything. Maybe we can get a booking agent in and see what can be done, you know?

Nico (*quietly*): Yes.

Fields is obviously trying to get Nico to start thinking about ways to promote herself and get her career back on track. His personal frustration with his current position is clear, as he gently tries to nudge Nico into some sort of action. He then starts to think of other people whom Nico could work with, including "Lewis" (Lou Reed):

Fields: Are you in touch with Joe Boyd at all?

Nico: No, no, he...

Fields: What about John [Cale]?

Nico: John...

Fields: Would you like to do an act with Lewis?

Nico: Sure.

Fields: Lewis said he would like to do something with you.

Nico: Yes, I would like to, but what do you mean—an act?

Fields: Perform together, sing each other's songs, I dunno, like Sonny and Cher.

Nico (*quietly, possibly smiling*): Oh no, I can't do that. (*Danny laughs.*) I only want to sing my own things now. Maybe sing one song...but not more. Because that's...(*laughs and trails off*).

Fields: Because we were listening to the tapes of the Velvet Underground and they were playing "I'll Be Your Mirror," and Lewis pointed to the speakers and said, "Do you think I could work with her?" (*laughs*) I said, "Sure, that's a good idea."

Nico: I could always sing that song, "I'll Be Your Mirror." But I don't want to sing the others.

Fields: Yeah, I know. We should think about it; we could put you and John and Lewis...and somehow make John director, musical director. That would be fabulous. As a first start—this is nice.

Nico: But he hasn't got a moral left now.

Fields: Who?

Nico: John. Because he is being paid for just sitting back...[100]

Fields: That's what I am too. I know how it feels. (*Nico laughs.*)

Nico (*upbeat*): It feels terrible, doesn't it?

Fields: Yeah, it does, really. It's not dignified at all. It's not nice, you don't have any pride or anything. You just feel awful. Like, you just hate the people that you work for, they just look like pigs. It's awful.

Fields's attempt to bring Nico and Reed back together again is interesting, as is her positive response. The conversation then moves on to Cale's new undertaking as producer for the Stooges:

Nico: Tell me, what is your...your (*quietly*) business model?

Fields: That is my business. I'm waiting. The Stooges didn't work, because Iggy was on junk all winter. (*Nico gasps.*) I know, you're telling me.

Nico (*shocked*): Iggy? He's on junk now?

Fields: He was, he's off it now. But he almost died once. And then he stopped, and he hasn't taken it since, but it was terrible, though. He would throw up all night, before the job, and it was just…(*Nico laughs.*) He was missing work, running into debt, and was hustling for money. Man, it was just awful. I sent them money. I thought it was going to go for rent on the house, and it went for junk. (*Nico exclaims off mic.*)…They weren't working, and it was just really low. But then he almost died one night…

Nico: Did he take that much? (*laughing*) How much?

Fields: I don't know how much; it was a lot. He almost died, and he just stopped right then and there.

Nico: Is Jim…Jimmy[101] back with them?

Fields: No, he hasn't been with them for a year…so I've been the only one, that's why I haven't been able to go out and work for them, because there's no one to…

Nico (*cutting across him*): Are they still very popular?

Fields: Well now, they're starting to work again this week for the first time in months. And everybody wants to see them. So I guess they'll be pretty popular. If we can keep them working and keep them straight…They should get very big pretty soon. The price went up. When they start working, they're making almost four thousand a night now, which is not bad; between three and four thousand a night. If they do that regularly, then I'll be able to take enough money from that to be able to leave them and just start a little office and get a secretary.

Nico seems to be desperately looking for guidance or hope. Fields had provided a stable, unerring support system throughout these years of her solo career. The trust she has in him is clear in her bald honesty. Nico rarely, if ever, shared her opinions of her counterparts or her aspirations and true feelings with anyone—especially journalists, in the few interviews that still can be found. Her comments here to Fields reveal that there is a tension—perhaps jealousy on Nico's part—toward Reed's and Cale's continuing success. Equally intriguing are Nico's enquiries after Pop; her tone and temperament when discussing the singer provide an important illustration of the tenderness she still felt toward her former flame.

Nico then confides to Fields that she is feeling more confident about her performance style, having improved from even fairly recent shows. She also shares an aspiration to play at a much-revered venue, showing either great hope for the future or total delusion:

Nico: I'd like to play at the Carnegie Hall.

Fields: Wouldn't that be wonderful?

Nico (*laughs*): Because I'm really not afraid any more. When you saw me two years ago, a year and a half ago, it was nothing like that. (*Fields agrees in background. Nico is animated*) Nothing like that now! It only took me three appearances to get rid of that.

Fields: How are you fixed for money?

Nico: Well, I am okay now, because Fred [Hughes] owed me some (*quietly*) and he gave it to me.

Fields: If you need a little more, I can always let you have some until you start.

Nico (*smiling*): I still owe you for the dentist (*laughs*).[102]

Fields: So, don't you think it's a good idea for you to play there? 'Cause everyone could come and see you who's important. And maybe we could get things done. And then if you get good reviews, we could stick 'em back to Warner Brothers, then they'll really get excited and do something. 'Cause they always like to have a working artist. I always figure if they're gonna invest money, it's best to invest in somebody who's working. Because that's the only way you really sell records, is to have someone working—you know that.

Nico (*possibly having not listened to what Fields said*): What? What?

Fields: That you have to go around and appear places to sell records.

Nico (*animated*): Yes, I know. Absolutely.

Fields: So, if Warner Brothers knows you're working, then maybe they'll put something behind your record.

Nico (*quietly*): Yes.

Fields: It's just a good idea to start soon... I think it'll be good. I'm sorry if I didn't sound encouraging the other night. I didn't mean to...

Nico (*quietly*): No, I thought it was me. (*Fields disagrees in background.*) I thought it was me, because I've been drinking tequila.

Fields: I drink tequila too. I'm drinking Southern Comfort lately.

Nico: Which?

Fields: Southern Comfort.

Nico: What's that?

Fields: It's bourbon and peach brandy.

Nico (*upbeat*): Ooh, bourbon!

Fields: It's very sweet and strong. Janis [Joplin] used to drink it all the time.

Fields drawing any comparison between the two singers, however benign, is still chilling. Though Nico's ambitions are obvious—wanting to play Carnegie Hall—so is her growing desperation. This is only exacerbated by the fact that her gigs at the Gaslight never happened and a lack of any sort of management or booking agent to represent her. Shortly before the shows were to take place, Nico had to leave the country.

———

Even the ever-supportive Fields has "despaired" at one particular Nico anecdote. Eyewitnesses still cannot agree on what actually occurred, with multiple versions and details added, edited, or subtracted, depending on who is (re)telling the story. The known facts: sometime in 1971, Nico was sitting in El Quixote, the Spanish restaurant attached to the Chelsea Hotel. A young Black woman, Emmaretta Marks, was sitting adjacent to the German singer with another group of people. Marks was a favorite of Jimi Hendrix and had a starring role in the musical *Hair*. She was talking within earshot of Nico about racial inequality and the challenges that she faced. In Nico's mind, almost any kind of suffering would have paled by comparison to what she saw and experienced during her early years in Nazi Germany, and Marks's comments were apparently too much for her. From here, however, the account of what happened in the restaurant is inconsistent.

In one version of the tale, John Cale recounts, "The woman [Marks] was apparently saying, 'How I've suffered! How I've suffered!' Nico didn't have time for Yanks who claimed to have a raw deal. Nico shouted back, 'Suffering? You don't know what suffering is!' Then—wham!—she threw a glass of beer at the dyke. I can't remember whether Nico told me she intended only to throw the drink and not the glass... but anyway, she threw the glass with the drink in it and the glass smashed against the woman's head and cut her face open. The woman needed something like twenty stitches in her face. I can believe it happened. Nico had paid more dues than this woman, but she never spoke about it. That's what annoyed her. It kind of broke the dam." In another interview, Paul Morrissey dismisses race as being the catalyst for the attack, saying, "She was black, she was white—who cares, frankly? The only fact you can glean from it is that Nico smashed this glass in the girl's face. Because of it, Nico said she had a contract out on her from the Black Panthers. Sure...!"

Joe Boyd heard a different version while working on a project about Jimi Hendrix. In his account, it is Nico's insecurity, not Marks's race, that caused the altercation. "We interviewed a lot of girls who had been involved with Jimi. There was this decadent scene in New York, and a lot of it centered around the Chelsea Hotel—not the Warhol side of the Chelsea, but in the restaurant [El Quixote] next door. We were talking to two girls, and they talked about another girl [Emmaretta Marks] who had been involved with Jimi or had been around in that scene. This girl [Marks] was really cute, funny, and lively. She was the male center of attention—the men couldn't get their eyes off her. She was sitting opposite Nico at this booth/table. According to these girls, at a certain point Nico couldn't take it any more and picked up a beer bottle. She smashed it on this girl's head and cut her badly. According to them, this girl went to the hospital and filed a complaint with the police, but I don't think Nico got arrested. They said that Emmaretta's brother had some friends that basically sent a message to Nico saying, 'You're not welcome in New York any more.' That's why she left New York and never came back." Vincent Fremont also remembered the event, saying, "One night she came home with Joe Dallesandro.[103] She'd cut somebody's face in a bar with a glass. We had to whisk her away. Joe took her to the airport and got her out of the country as quickly as possible."

An interview with Fields in the *Guardian* featured a similar version of events. "Nico was, I dunno, feeling neglected, or drunk, but suddenly she said, 'I hate black people,' and smashed a wineglass on the table and stuck it in the girl's eye. There was lots of blood and screaming. Fortunately she just twisted it around her eye socket, so the glass never reached [the eye] but it's not like she was being cautious... She had to get out of town. She was away for a while. This crossed the line. I'm being driven beyond reaching toward someone you love. There's some point where you have to say, 'I love you, but I cannot get close anymore.'" In another conversation with Fields, he clarified things further, saying that such racial remarks were usually just Nico being ironic or poking fun, and the comment itself had been taken out of context. It may have been meant as tongue-in-cheek because she was frustrated and annoyed, rather than it being a confession that she actually "hated Black people... The time with the broken wineglass, she flew off the handle, as it were, and [it was] obviously an *extremely* unusual thing for her, i.e. to be violent in any way. Something snapped that evening," says Fields. The ramifications of the violence witnessed by Nico in the early part of her life cannot be forgotten, he argues, stating, "When you come from Germany in the war, there is a lot that you're not sure about. You grow up being bombed—this was her childhood." Fields is the first to highlight the importance of context, saying that to refer to Nico simply as racist is "insufficient, and kind of comical. She loved Leonard Cohen and she loved Lou Reed, she loved Bob Dylan—she loved all these Jewish guys... She didn't belong to anything. It was news to me that she even registered what color people were; she seemed above that. It was a pose, an act." In another piece, he goes further, saying, "She was so far from being a Nazi."

There have never been definitive answers as to why Nico attacked Marks, what kind of injury was inflicted with the glass, if the Black Panthers were involved or if Marks had any affiliation with them. Based upon her temperament and the circumstances, the most likely explanation is that the outburst was the result of a combination of Nico being frustrated and various intoxicants. What is certain is that Nico *believed* it was unsafe for her to return to New York for many years after the incident. The repercussions stayed with her long after it happened. "I remember one afternoon we decided to have a hamburger at Max's," said Iggy Pop. "Just ourselves in the front, no scene or anything. That afternoon, the subject kept coming up that there had been a controversial physical altercation with another woman. All I remember is that her reply to me was just very matter-of-fact. She had a very deadpan way of expressing herself. It wasn't comic at all or odd, but she basically said, 'Bitch had it coming.' The concept, although she put it in a different way, was [*does impression of Nico*] 'She was not nice,' or something like that."

In a 1975 interview, Nico admitted that it was in "a fit of madness" that she "cut the face of a young girl, a black panther,"[104] going on to claim that "The police were looking for me and the black panthers, so I couldn't go back." She also revealed that the attack was "not provoked" and that she had "just lost [her] mind" during the episode. When asked if she had ever done anything to make up for it, Nico responded, "I mentioned it in one song. I mean, they are listening to my music all the time anyhow, so they will have understood it." In a 1985 *Melody Maker* piece, she again admits to being inebriated when the incident occurred.[105] When asked about her thoughts on the Black Panthers, she answers, "I'm a little afraid of them, because I once hurt a girl's face and she was a member of

The Black Panthers. I was high on angel dust and had been drinking, not much, and I hit this girl's eye with a glass, and she had 17 stitches, and they were looking for me. I was hiding in New Jersey, and then I had to leave the country." Nico concludes the piece by saying, "It was an accident, it wasn't intentional." She retreated back to Philippe Garrel's dismal flat in Paris, once again seeking refuge from herself in Europe.

————

On the morning of July 3, 1971, Nico saw Jim Morrison for the first time in several years. Morrison had relocated to Paris with his girlfriend Pamela Courson, in an attempt to escape fame and celebrity, while concentrating on his poetry. His once slim physique had become bloated by alcohol, a full beard obscuring the globally famous chiseled cheekbones. Nico, meanwhile, now exiled to the French capital, was living in squalor with Garrel. She had no idea she was in the same city as her former paramour until she caught a glimpse of him in a black car driving past her as she walked down the Avenue de l'Opéra. Though she attempted to wave him down, Morrison didn't see her. Later that evening, he was declared dead after suffering heart failure. It was exactly two years to the day since Brian Jones had died.

In a letter to Danny Fields, postmarked July 16, Nico reports having been to Morrison's grave. Her disgust at the lack of visitors and decoration at his resting place is palpable as she remarks, "Jim's grave did not resemble that of a hero, I had been the only person to visit & it struck me very hard." Indeed, for his first several years in the legendary Père Lachaise Cemetery, the final resting place of other legendary figures such as Oscar Wilde and Edith Piaf, Morrison's body lay in an unmarked grave.[106] Nico also voices concern for the repercussions of the incident with Marks and clearly wants to return from her exile in Paris to New York:

Can you give me some information about the Girl Emeretta, please. Will I be able to return soon. Though I do not desire anything now and I hope that there won't be much to take...Can you give me an answer.

Love & kisses
Nico

During the 1970s, Nico was on a continuous quest for a record label and any sort of artistic advice. Her letters to Fields illustrate a woman who was still attempting to cobble a career together, alone. "It annoyed me so much to be told that Nico disappeared from music in the Seventies," complained Tina Aumont in Richard Witts's biography. "Music was a part of her daily life, and she made a lot of concerts. It just shows how cut off America is from Europe. Nico's problem always was that she didn't have a manager. There was no one to plan her musical life. There was no coordination or publicity." This drove Nico only deeper into drug use, as getting a fix became an escape from her troubled past and uncertain future. Heroin, however, further isolated her from the few relationships she still had, with people like Fields, who had been her unerring lifeline, becoming tired of her repeated requests for money to fund her addiction.

———

John Cale had invited Lou Reed to join him and Nico at a gig in Paris on January 29, 1972, at the Bataclan. The three began practicing for the show—a surprising turn for Reed, who was notorious for hating to rehearse.[107] According to biographer Victor Bockris, the Bataclan show illustrated "just how ambivalent Reed felt about his solo career." Besides the prep time with Cale, Reed also spent an entire day reviewing songs with Nico in Paris. The show was a triumph, with all three artists presenting old and new material in an acoustic format. While most of the pieces were performed by Cale and Reed, Nico still stood out as a haunting and singular artist. The gig was recorded, eventually being released as a sixteen-song live LP. Reed was "so moved by the experience with Cale and Nico that he suggested the three of them get back together, but they turned him down," said Bockris. Cale was finding success as a producer and solo artist, while Nico had released three solo albums and was starring in avant-garde films with Philippe Garrel. As Bockris explained, "At the time, they both appeared to be in a stronger position than Lewis [Reed]."

In a March 13 letter to Danny Fields, it is clear that Nico is once again looking for options, fishing for support, and is not sure what to do or who to turn to:

London March 13th
Dear Danny,

What is happening to you & the old world? . . . I have been here over two weeks giving interviews to all the musical papers, I also sang at the Round House [*sic*].[108] I cannot say that it is a very classical peace [*sic*] but in spite of that it was refreshing. Joe Boyd had made the arrangements for it against his feelings. He also wants to produce my new album. I don't know if it is to please me, or if it is to send down the peoples [*sic*] throats. Have you any suggestions at all? In any case John Cale, where is he? A reporter from *Friends* magazine seemed to know that you have returned with Elektra. How is Jac Holzman? I would return to NY but I am scared that nobody wants to know me anymore. If you see Leonhard [*sic*], tell him that if it hadn't been for him, Philippe would still be crazy, from too many Electroshocks. The movie "LA CICATRICE INTERIEURE" is nearly finished.[109] Ari gave a beautiful picture as the little white knight on it.

Please let me know how things are.
Yours faithfully,
Nico.
P.S.
I still love you

It is not clear who "Leonhard" is, but one guess is that it is a reference to her old friend and admirer Leonard Cohen. Nico repeats her ongoing fear of coming back to New York, as well as her concerns about Garrel's unstable mental state. Her worry that "nobody wants to know me" indicates some understanding of how the attack, her poor record sales, and her notoriety may have damaged her reputation as any sort of commercial artist. The heroin problem only exacerbated the worries and made any actual challenges even harder to surmount. In retrospect, Fields wondered how Nico—and Garrel—were financing their basic existence, let alone a raging drug problem, saying, "Who was paying for any of this?" and throwing his arms up in the air with puzzled despair.

Nico and Garrel continued to collaborate together, releasing the second part of a trilogy that had started with *La Cicatrice intérieure*. *Athanor*—meaning an alchemist's melting pot—is a twenty-minute silent epic that is as dreamy and nonsensical as its predecessor. Starring Nico and another actress who went by the singular name of "Musky," *Athanor* is in color and features shots of an unclothed Nico throughout. Her figure is not the diet pill sinew of *Sweet Skin*, but the more filled-out curves of a woman. One synopsis of the film describes the plot:

Athanor (Nico) is searching for fire. A flame is always at the foreground. Nico naked in tombs, looking at herself in circular mirrors, Nico in castles, keeper of the fire. Nico and Musky as medieval princesses. *Athanor* is a film about fire.

Psychedelic singer-songwriter and former Soft Machine member Kevin Ayers seemed to have an ongoing infatuation with Nico throughout the 1970s, but he always refused to talk about what relationship he had with her, if any. "I never kiss and tell," he said tartly, when asked in a 2007 *Guardian* interview whether he and Nico were ever involved. It is not clear how they first met or if their connection was anything but professional, but Nico was indisputably an inspiration for Ayers throughout the latter part of his career. One example appears on his fourth studio album, *Bananamour*, which features a track called "Decadence" that is an incredibly unflattering depiction of Nico. The damning lyrics read as if written by an embittered lover or a jealous friend, going on to claim that the subject is "suffering from wear and tear"—an obvious dig at what was considered to be Nico's fading beauty.

It is unclear what caused Ayers to hold his decades-long bitterness toward Nico. It could be that the singer rebuffed his advances during one of their interactions. Regardless of Ayers, Lou Reed found a different sort of inspiration in Nico. In Dave Thompson's book *Beyond the "Velvet Underground,"* Reed publicly and rabidly praised her solo records, saying, "Those albums are so incredible, the most incredible albums ever made. *The Marble Index, Desertshore*...you try to get a copy. You can't get 'em, you can't order them. They're in bins someplace. I have orders in five stores. They've disappeared off the face of the earth."

In July 1973, Reed released his third solo studio album, *Berlin*. Nico loved it, even writing her former bandmate an enthusiastic five-page letter praising the work. Billed as a concept album/rock opera, *Berlin*'s tracks are centered around topics familiar to Nico: a doomed couple and their struggle with drug addiction, abuse, and depression, among other uplifting themes.

Though she had been marketed on her albums and in the press as a paragon for being alone, Nico was rarely without a paramour of some sort during the 1970s. It was at the Opéra Comique in 1973 that Lutz Graf-Ulbrich first met the singer. It is understandable that Nico was attracted to the young guitar player. He was head-turningly handsome, with high cheekbones, a tall, lanky build, and blond hair. Graf-Ulbrich was equally enamored with Nico when she took to the stage. "Nobody knew who she really was. There was a strange aura, and lots of rumors, and nobody knew what to make of all that. Before we met she was already a mysterious thing," he recalled. It is hard to tell if Graf-Ulbrich himself is remembering his own interactions and thoughts from the time or if he, too, has fallen into the abyss of endless Nico myths. "When she performed, it was really strange, with her harmonium and the way she sang. The audience was very enthusiastic. I was stunned. And of course we talked," he said. "There was a party...and she took me aside. She saw my record cover and she said it was strange and frightening. Her aura and personality were just so strong that I felt like a little boy. I was 22 and she was 36."

In 1974, Graf-Ulbrich's band Agitation Freedom broke up. Now performing as a solo artist, he stayed in France, and was once again doing the festival circuit when he came back into contact with Nico, this time backstage. After having accidentally drunk tea laced with acid, Graf-Ulbrich found Nico, like a ghostly aberration, seated in front of him, donned in "a red cloak like a curtain." The German singer asked Graf-Ulbrich where he was staying. Upon learning that he did not have a hotel for the night, Nico offered to help him out. "I went to her room and said bye and she said, 'Oh no, you're not getting away.' She was naked on the bed and she was very good looking. I was too shy; I went back to my own room. She was amazingly beautiful, the most beautiful woman I had ever seen," he continued. "Her symmetrical face with her full lips, her big eyes, her perfect body...I felt paralyzed by her beauty and did not know what to say." The two were reunited in the morning and found they were both going to the French capital. "We sat together on the train to Paris and I played her all of my songs and the whole thing started," he recalled.

Upon arriving at their destination, "She invited me to her home. She was living together with filmmaker Philippe Garrel, who was not really pleased that I appeared with her." Graf-Ulbrich's memories of the Paris space are just as disturbing as others' descriptions. "The dreary four-room-apartment on the fifth floor had black walls and almost no furniture. The flat had been given to him by his father, the renowned actor Maurice Garrel. There was a fridge, a piano, two beds and a mattress. The whole flat was covered by a layer of dust, the kitchen seemed rarely used. Dusty, old dishes were piling up in the sink."

Neither an in-house lover nor a vile abode were enough to put Graf-Ulbrich off from embarking on an affair with the singer. "I worshipped her. I was a fan and madly in love. But she was still together with Philippe Garrel," he recalls. Graf-Ulbrich's own admission of both "worshipping" Nico and being a "fan" of hers, on top of the differences in age and experience, must have put them on an unequal footing from the start. Looking back, he says, "My years with Nico were the most intense times of my entire life." Graf-Ulbrich was young, eager and earnest, in contrast to many of the hardened characters whom Nico usually surrounded herself with. "Nico generally liked philosophers and drug dealers and gangsters and anything like this. I was an exception to this," says Graf-Ulbrich. And though clearly wanting attention from the men around her, Nico was not interested in public displays of affection—at least with Graf-Ulbrich.[110] "She didn't hold hands in public. She called me her 'German friend.'"

By the time Graf-Ulbrich came into Nico's life, she was in the clutches of full-blown addiction. He remembered her being "so hard to follow as a person, even though we were really close. I could never tell what she was thinking." Nico's substance abuse problems had made it even more difficult to read her, with Graf-Ulbrich recalling, "When she was taking heroin, she went even further away." In an attempt to be more intimate with his new lover, Graf-Ulbrich decided to try the drug. "After a while, I gave in to her. I only took it for about a year and a half, maybe in '74, and by '76 I was done," he says now. "I was addicted, but more to Nico than to the drug. I took it because Nico took it. She told me, 'It's good, take some.' I wanted to be on her level. I wanted to understand her. It's hard," he continues, "if you love your partner and you can only watch her drifting into other spheres and you can't follow. At some point I started to take heroin as well and became a junkie. Our relationship was . . . well, I adored her. I was incredibly proud to live this life by her side. And, of course, I didn't feel like I was on the same level that she was. Heroin became an important aspect of our relationship."

For Nico, the drugs provided relief from her own mind and present surroundings. She spent a lot of her time "sitting around hallucinating," recalls Graf-Ulbrich. It also meant she was incredibly uninspired to work on her music. Gone was the woman writing lyrics by candlelight and practicing the harmonium for hours on end. This may also have been the fallout from the sales failure of her two previous LPs, a lack of management and no clear path forward—all of which created a perpetual roundabout of despair, drug use and isolation. "I remember she once said, 'I wrote already albums with a lot of songs. That's enough, what more do people want?'" recounts Graf-Ulbrich. The few shows she did were to keep the threesome—Nico, Garrel, and now Graf-Ulbrich—in drugs, not to try out new ideas or revisit old material. "She wasn't working on songs all the time. There were two concerts in a month or something," he says. "She would rehearse right before a concert or a few notes occasionally."

Soon the cycle of searching for drugs, scoring, and using became the central focus of Graf-Ulbrich's life. "We were always looking for it. I consider addiction to heroin an interesting way to live. It may sound perverse, but you always have a goal." Perhaps because of his infatuation with Nico, perhaps because of the short period in which he found himself entrenched in the dependency pattern, his description of the time sounds almost romantic. "We bought some heroin on the street. You see the weirdest places and meet the strangest people. It's like being in a gangster movie." However, nerves were wearing thin and tensions rising in the filthy apartment. Garrel was not pleased with the addition of Nico's new lover to the household. "He was angry and jealous," notes Graf-Ulbrich. "I said to him, 'Come on. Let's not fight, this is ridiculous.' He and Nico were more like brother and sister. It was an uncomfortable situation."

Nico's downward spiral was trying at best, alarming at worst—especially for old friends and acquaintances. Contact with her was often initiated by her need to "borrow" money to score drugs, putting strain on already fraying relationships with former colleagues. Vincent Fremont told me about the singer's infrequent visits to the Factory post-Velvets. "Andy [Warhol] was uncomfortable because he knew the reason she was there was to try and get some money, and he didn't like to give money to people who might abuse drugs. It was complicated and layered with her sad life," he says. "She would show up, but she wasn't part of Andy's world anymore. The drugs really did a number on her. She was still beautiful, but heroin did take its toll physically, besides everything else. Her beauty was fading…"

Though now ruling her life, the opiates only underscored how deeply disturbed Nico was. "I remember realizing just how miserable she was," Fremont recalls. "She may have thought that whatever she was on would help [numb her pain], but it didn't really mask the unhappiness."

———

Off the back of *Berlin*, and proclaiming to the music press that he loved the John Cale/Nico albums, Lou Reed made a bold decision: he would put himself forward to produce an album for his old flame. By this point, Nico had no record deal, was playing shows only sporadically—just enough to barely eke out a living—and was in dire straits. Between her raging heroin habit and lack of income, Reed's offer was a lifeline. He asked her to stay with him at his small apartment on East 52nd Street in New York for the duration of the recording process, taking the pressure off Nico, who had to pay only for transportation. This was good, as there was not a dime to spare. She somehow scraped together enough money to pay for an airline ticket, packed her few belongings—the harmonium and some candles—into a bag and left Paris, the hope of a new start seeming to sparkle on the Manhattan skyline. This could be a chance not only to get her career back on track, but to progress what she and Cale had started with *The Marble Index* and *Desertshore*. This could be the big break. Things were finally starting to look up.

However, upon arrival, Nico found that her former bandmate's generosity had disappeared. Instead, he went about teasing her with drugs, showing Nico how much he had, then declining to share the stash with the befuddled German. Nico's desperate situation becomes even clearer from an anecdote that Victor Bockris shares. The writer happened to be at Reed's house during one night of Nico's stay, and he clearly remembers Reed's cruel treatment of the chanteuse. "One night I go to his [Reed's] place, and there is Nico. You've got this little apartment, with a couch and a round breakfast table with chairs around it. Nico is sitting in one of these chairs. I'm sitting on the couch, looking at her. Lou is sitting in a chair; we are in a triangle. I'm astonished to notice that Nico is giving me the eyes, inviting me over with her eyes to her table in a seductive way. I just begin to move. My ass is maybe one inch above the cushions of the couch. Lou whispers to me across the room, 'You don't have a chance!'

"I sit down at this tiny little round table. Me and Nico started to talk, and we had chemistry; it's not so much sexually, just mentally. Lou at that point comes over and tries to get into the conversation. Nico closes him off by looking at me and refusing to acknowledge him. Lou then takes a bag of white powder out of his pocket and waves it in front of her. Her face lights up. It turns out he had been taunting her the whole time she has been there, pretending to offer her drugs but then refusing to give them to her. We are talking about speed...where you shoot it up. Reed interrupts the conversation and breaks the contact between me and Nico. Now Nico's mind is more on getting the drugs from Lou than it is on talking to me. It was very cruel. The next day, he actually threw her out of the house and then refused to ever see or talk to her. He really, really fucked with her horribly. She was very needy of his collaboration for a record, and to entice her all the way across the Atlantic—telling her, 'You can stay with me'—and then suddenly just throwing her out...it was one of Lou's truly horrible things to do."

Luckily, one of Reed's people came by and saw her sitting outside his apartment and took care of her. Says Bockris, "You see him do this to Nico, who was, at that period, trembling on the brink of not looking so good any more. She had a lot of majesty. Then Lou waving a bag of speed in her face—it was distasteful."

Bockris stresses how crucial to Nico's career a Reed/Nico collaboration could have been. "The reason that what Lou did was so mean is because it was a turning point for her. It was 1974; she could have gone on to go higher [in sales or prestige], or she could have gone on to the track she went on to, which is essentially a ramshackle track. You keep going, but you make records in a couple days, nothing is like it used to be. You are on a different level in the rock business. You are on a lower level. You do not get the same kind of treatment, the same kind of studios, the same sort of musicians."

Upon hearing of Reed's behavior with Nico, John Cale rang his former bandmate up to read him the riot act. According to

Bockris, "The Nico episode [was] a bone of contention between them throughout the decade," with Cale admitting, "Right through the seventies, I hoped Lou would write her another song like 'All Tomorrow's Parties,'[111] or I would tell him I was working with Nico on her new LP, whichever it was, and he'd just say, 'Really?'—nothing more, not a flicker of interest. He could have written wonderful songs for her. It's a shame and I regret it very much."

Bockris praises Cale for being one of the few steadfast friends and colleagues that stood by Nico through all the trials and tribulations. He also argues that not only Nico's gender but her appearance played a massive role in how she was presented in the media. "The way she has been treated by the press is largely dominated by the fact that she's not just a woman, but she was a world-class beauty. Any independent creative expression by a woman will come with an enormous amount of heavy beating by a male-dominated press. That's why Cale was so important; he tried to protect her to some extent from that stuff. Cale is really heroic in this story; he really does stand by her." Jonathan Donahue of Mercury Rev agrees, telling me, "I think that John [Cale] was probably one of the few men in her life that encouraged her and allowed her the space to grow. He watered the plant; the other ones just overshadowed it."

In her diary, Nico rarely wrote anything about Reed. However, one comment does stand out, especially in light of Bockris's story. She confides, "Lou Reed is a very loyal Person when it comes to Andy's ideas. When it came to me, there was only jealousy, Refusing of letting him program me." She goes on to give a seething critique of one of Reed's performances, possibly referring to the March 31, 1977, show at the Eissporthalle in Berlin, Germany. "One time in Berlin, about fourteen years ago, Lou was giving his second Concert in Berlin, on which occasion I made a Guest appearance, but it all went wrong because of lack of Lou's musical Arrangements on the songs that were twice too slow for me to sing. The Place was deserted according to the Crew's Expectations."

During this period, Cale was signed to Island Records by Richard Williams, who had left journalism behind to do A&R at the label. Williams and Cale brought Nico on board, with the idea that the record they would make together would be the third and last installment of a series that started with *The Marble Index*. The resulting album, *The End*, followed a similar structure as previous Nico/Cale efforts, with Nico first laying down vocals and her harmonium, then Cale coming in to build layers of sound and texture to complete the tracks, with instruments ranging from the electric viola to the glockenspiel, bells, and a bosun's pipe. "She only had a limited command of the instrument," recalled Williams of Nico's efforts on the harmonium, adding, "Because she played fewer notes, it restricted her singing and it became literally monotonous, but not in a pejorative way." Cale also recruited former Roxy Music members Brian Eno and Phil Manzanera to guest on the album. The new LP included a haunting cover of the Doors song "The End," as well as the German national anthem, "Das Lied der Deutschen." Nico's decision to perform and record "The End" for her album of the same name was not an accident; the song was part of her ongoing homage to the man whom she perceived to have changed her life.

Nico continued to show her support for Philippe Garrel by using stills from their newest collaboration, *Les Hautes Solitudes*, on both the front and back cover of her LP. Once *The End* was released in autumn 1974, the reviews began rolling in. Reactions were not unlike those received for her two previous albums; journalists were confused, horrified, or downright disturbed by Nico's newest offering. One writer called her rendition of "The End" "far scarier than The Doors' original"; another penned, "It's her interpretation of Jim Morrison's 'The End' that really chills to the marrow, that song's 'Oedipus' sequence being sufficiently visual to be scary as hell"; while *Creem* contributor Richard Cromelin noted, "If Morrison sang it as a lizard, Nico is a sightless bird, lost but ever so calm, somehow knowing the right direction. She is the pure, dead marble of a ruined Acropolis, a crumbling column on the subterranean bank of Morrison's River Styx." Many writers were put off by Nico having the audacity to take on the Jim Morrison classic, showing a special kind of misogyny in their comments. One journalist argued that "*The End* is full of these confused, purposeless characters—each, with the possible exception of Manzanera, expert at that throw-so-much-crap-at-the-wall-and-some-of-it-is-bound-to-stick technique. This time, for me, it doesn't. This time we've got a fair smattering of the proven Nico 'weirdness' formula as tried and tested on 'The Marble Index' and 'Desertshore' and a new 'Sing-alonanico' approach where the Ice Maiden, the first of the meta-groupies, takes on…Jim Morrison's 'The End.'" Even the marketing material played on the dark nature of the record's content, with advertisements featuring the tagline "Why Waste Time Committing Suicide When You Could Buy This Album?"

Equally controversial was her inclusion of the German national anthem. It is likely Nico chose it as both a tongue-in-cheek gesture and an indictment of her home country. Yet these two ideas were often lost on reviewers and audiences alike. Music journalist Peter Hogan called the track "truly chilling," noting that "though probably intended as camp cabaret…today [it is] just plain sinister…as it turned out, this wasn't the end, but maybe it should have been." At a Berlin gig, Nico's rendition of the song—complete with passages that had been banned after 1945 on account of their Nazi associations[112]—induced a riot. "[Brian] Eno making air-raid noises on his synth, Cale pounding his piano, Nico intoning 'Deutschland über alles,' cushions flying—it was quite something," Williams later said of the gig.

Besides the press's view of *The End* as both contentious and completely different to anything else, Nico's changing appearance shocked journalists, who seemed to take joy in critiquing her look.

Their commentary frames her as a 1970s version of Miss Havisham, a Dickensian character who is rotting away within her own house-turned-mausoleum. "The very high priestess of Weird sips whisky backed by six tall candles and a gold crucifix," notes Steve Lake in *Melody Maker*. "They don't come much more Gothic than Nico," adds Peter Hogan in a different review. "The wailing harmonium, the vampire-priestess voice (like cold marble and cobweb-covered crystal), the chiseled beauty turning to decay, the solemnly intoned tales of madness, desperation and death: her whole act is like Brecht and Weill crossed with Edgar Allan Poe."

———

One day while out at lunch with John Cale and Kevin Ayers, Richard Williams had an idea. What about putting a bunch of Island artists—in this case, Brian Eno, Cale, Ayers, and Nico—together in a showcase concert and recording the whole thing? The idea came to fruition at the Rainbow Hall in London on June 1, 1974. The LP of the concert—referred to as the "ACNE" album (an acronym of the participants' names)—was released in a then miraculously fast three weeks, with only one Nico track, "The End," making the final record. Cale, Eno, and Ayers all join her on the song, as well as Ayers's former Soft Machine bandmate Robert Wyatt and Mike Oldfield, fresh from his global success with *Tubular Bells*.

Journalists did not hesitate to describe Nico in derogatory terms, many of which framed her as a spaced-out freak. For example, though a *Melody Maker* piece concedes that Nico's performance style is "fascinating to watch," this is a point-and-stare situation, as "her facial contortions and sudden switches of expression [are] often alarming." The journalist goes on to claim that "attempting to actually communicate with her is at times like trying to make contact with an autistic child...Much of the time she seems distant, as though troubled by some half-remembered dream. Often she doesn't appear to hear the question asked or will counter one question with another."

For Nico, the ACNE show was "very convenient for a certain promotion of a certain album"—most likely meaning the actual ACNE LP itself. But Nico was no fool; she realized that the tour de force of musicians at the June 1 gig would provide a needed boost of awareness to her own endeavors. She did not like the way that the ACNE LP turned out. Though she never said so, this may have been because only one of her songs featured on it. Publicly, she renounced the production and admitted going along with other people's plans instead of guiding her own career. In an interview with *Melody Maker*, she said, "I thought it [the LP] was very badly mixed. Going backward and forwards and together. It sounds like fake Arab music. I was disappointed by the record and the concert. I said to John and Eno that we should not do the show at all. We did not even get a proper appearance, just drifted in and out…I don't want to put anybody down…but just because we are all on the same record label doesn't mean that we will accept anything…At the moment I am just being drawn into other people's happenings. I am not doing what I want to do."

Though Ayers had released an unflattering portrait of Nico via his song "Decadence" the previous year, she agreed to supply guest vocals on a track for his fifth studio album, *The Confessions of Dr. Dream and Other Stories*. However, neither of them was happy with the final version of the song, the hauntingly named "Irreversible Neural Damage." "When I sang on that song, 'Irreversible Neural Damage,' it was a misconception," Nico later confided. "I don't like what they did to it. I don't think Kevin's happy with it. It should have been just straightforward, like two children singing together." Her appeal to Ayers, Nico contended, was a result of him being "very taken with what I'm doing, and the idea of being German. You see, he is kind of attracted to Marlene Dietrich."

For his part, Ayers once again sounded like a disappointed

Nr. 3326

Köln-Lindenthal, den 14. April 1939.

Die Mutter des un-

benbezeichneten Kindes hat mit dem Kantorist Hermann Wilhelm Paßgen, katholischer Religion, wohnhaft in Köln Luxemburger Straße 47 am 30. Dezember 1938 die Ehe geschlossen (Familienbuch Nr. 397 des Standesamts Köln-Lindenthal) Das Kind ist gemäß Beschluß des Amtsgerichts Köln vom 13. März 1939 ehelich geworden.

Der Standesbeamte

Köln-Lindenthal, den 19. Oktober 1938

Die Margarete Berta Schütz, geborene Schütz, ohne Beruf evangelisch wohnhaft rechtskräftig geschieden seit dem Ehefrau des 8. Oktober 1937 von dem Maler Rudolf Paul Emil Schütz wohnhaft in Berlin S. 42, Prinzessinnenstraße 13

hat am 16. Oktober 1938 um 17 Uhr 30 Minuten zu Kerpenerstraße 32

ein Mädchen geboren. Das Kind hat den Vornamen erhalten:

Christa

Eingetragen auf mündliche — schriftliche — Anzeige des ermächtigten Beamten der Frauenklinik

Anzeigende

Die Wohnung der Frau ist in Köln, Meister-Gerhardstraße 10/12

Vorgelesen, genehmigt und unterschrieben

Der Standesbeamte

Eheschließung der Eltern am 7.8.37 in Hardenberg Berlin

1. bezw. Geburt der Mutter, (bei unehelichen Kindern) (Standesamt) Berlin XIII B Hardenberg Nr. 477).

2. Eheschließung des Kindes am in (Standesamt) Nr.).

3. Tod des Kindes am 13.07.1988 in Ibiza, Provinz Balearen Spanien (Standesamt Berlin (West) I Nr. 654/1988).

Nico's birth details as registered on her mother's registration card, or *Meldekarte*. The third entry on Margarete Berta Schulz's card states: "born on October 16 1938 at 17.30h in Köln-Lindenthal, Kerpenerstraße 32 a girl. The child was given the name Christa." Kerpenerstrasse, in Köln-Lindenthal, is in Cologne.

Young Christa was placed at the Kinderheim Sülz orphanage for seven months in 1940. It was then the largest orphanage in Europe.

A child walking through the rubble in Berlin, Germany, following Allied bombing during World War II. Nico would have been seven years old. Photographed circa 1945.

Nico posing in 1956. When asked how she dealt with the idiosyncrasies of modeling, she responded, "I was an alien . . . I did not take it seriously. I could laugh . . . because I was playing the part of Nico."

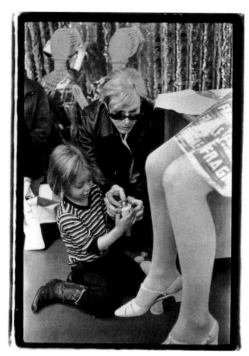

Andy Warhol kneels on the ground to help Ari operate an aerosol spray can aimed at the legs of his mother, Nico, in the Abraham & Straus department store, New York, in November 1966. The event was held to highlight a one-wear, disposable dress, available in "whitest white twill of Kaycel R," that came with a do-it-yourself paint set.

Nico with American art dealer Irving Blum and Andy Warhol in Los Angeles, California, 1966.

INTRO: NICO

ONE OF ANDY WARHOL'S SCREEN ACTING DISCOVERIES HAS BEGUN A NEW CAREER AS A

RECORDING ARTIST. HER NAME IS NICO AND YOU MAY REMEMBER SEEING HER IN SOME

OF THE UNDERGROUND FILMS IF YOU'VE BEEN UNDERGROUND LATELY...OR YOU MIGHT WELL

RECOGNIZE HER FACE FROM HAVING SEEN IT ON A MAGAZINE COVER. NICO WAS A TOP

FASHION MODEL FOR SOME TIME, BEFORE SHE BEGAN AN ACTING CAREER. SHE'S

HERE WITH US FOR THE FIRST TIME TODAY AND I'M LOOKING FORWARD TO MEETING

HER...HERE'S NICO.

.... YOU AND OTHERS OF ANDY'S SUPERSTARS USE ONLY ONE NAME. HAVE YOU A LAST

NAME?

       (SHE'LL TELL: 1. SHE WAS BORN IN GERMANY
               2. CAME HER AS A MODEL FOR TOP U.S. AGENCY.
               3. EARNED A GREAT DEAL OF MONEY, as A MODEL HERE IN U.S.

.... WHY DID YOU DECIDE TO GIVE UP MODELLING?

       (SHE BECAME BORED WITH THE WORK...SHE'LL EXPLAIN)

.... BUT YOU'VE LIVED ALL OVER EUROPE AND SCANDINAVIA...WHY DO YOU

PREFER LIVING HERE?

       (SHE'LL EXPLAIN...SHE WORKS BEST HERE)

.... DO YOU WRITE ALL YOUR OWN SONGS?..I UNDERSTAND YOU'RE GOING TO SING FOR

US. WHAT INSPIRES YOU TO COMPOSE MUSIC AND WORDS?

       (SHE'S A POET...SHE GETS HER IDEAS MOSTLY JUST WALKING AROUND THE CITY...
       SHE LIVES ALONE...IS IMAGINATIVE..A DREAMER. HER ORGAN, WHICH SHE
       USED TO ACCOMPANY HERSELF, IS A "HOLY" ORGAN WHICH SHE PURCHASED AT
       MANNY'S MUSIC STORE IN MIDTOWN MANHATTAN)

.... WHAT ARE YOU GOING TO SING?

       (TITLE IS "NO ONE IS THERE")

Una Baines, keyboardist for the Blue Orchids, says, "[Nico] did say her only regret was not being born a man. I think she wanted the same privileges and power that men have. She felt people were only interested in her looks. She wanted something more substantial. She wrote songs in her second language. She was fluent in seven. The song 'No One Is There' was about [Richard] Nixon. It's superbly written. She is still not appreciated for her talent."

Contact sheet taken
in the London
Docklands in
summer 1965
for Nico's first
promotional film,
for the song "I'm
Not Sayin'." Taken
by either Peter
Whitehead or his
assistant Anthony
Stern (they used
the same camera).
It was Whitehead's
first commission
for Andrew Loog
Oldham.

Nico with members of the Velvet Underground at Phillip Law's house in Los Angeles, 1966. Pictured are Maureen Tucker (with hand on window frame), Sterling Morrison, Lou Reed, and John Cale.

Nico performs with the Velvet Underground at Steve Paul's nightclub, the Scene (West 46th Street), New York, January 1967.

Nico appears on British television show *Ready, Steady, Go!* in 1965 to promote her single "I'm Not Sayin'" / "The Last Mile." Record producer Andrew Loog Oldham says, "Looking back at it, the B-side is better than the A-side."

Nico with Brian Jones in the audience at the Monterey International Pop Festival, Monterey, California, 1967.

DJ and producer of *Chelsea Girl* Tom Wilson with Nico at ABC studios, New York, in June 1967.

Nico poses for a portrait session in circa 1967.

Nico speaks into a microphone at the Dom in New York, April 1967. David Croland describes her performance as "incredible . . . It was like Marilyn Monroe, she was lit from within."

Nico in the garden behind the Portobello Hotel in London, 1974. In June that year she took part in a live concert at the Rainbow Hall, performing with Kevin Ayers, John Cale, and Brian Eno. The LP of the concert—referred to as the "ACNE" album (an acronym of the participants' names)—was released in a then miraculously fast three weeks.

Nico performing live in front of graffiti which reads "She runs through the world like an open razor, and you might get cut" at the Mabuhay Gardens, San Francisco, in December 1977.

The house on Effra Road in Brixton where Nico lived in the 1980s. "All she had was a little bag and a little red radio," says Barbara Wilkin. I once said to her, "'You have nothing, Nico!' She replied, 'It's the only way to be really free.'"

Nico in 1985. She was starting to reassess her health, says drummer Graham Dowdall. "She was in a much better place by then. She'd say things like, 'This is the best I've felt since the 1960s.'"

The Foresters pub in Manchester, which Nico describes in her diary around 1986. "Manchester reminds me of Berlin, in a way," she said in an interview.

Nico's grave is marked on the cemetery map where she is buried in Berlin, although a proposal to name a square after her in Cologne was denied because of her "drug career."

A stone cherub wears headphones at Nico's grave in the Grunewald Forest cemetery in Berlin, where she is buried with her mother.

Nico by Trafford Parsons, Spirit Studios, Downing Street, Manchester. Mural on the gable end of Spirit Studios, near Piccadilly Station in Manchester.

schoolboy with an unrequited crush, commenting, "Nico is a woman you can only use for specific things, her voice and presence. I could certainly use her again, work with her on something. I don't know if she'd ever want to use me on anything. I doubt it. But making something together, an album, I don't think that's possible. We fight too much." Nico does get some revenge on Ayers in the *Melody Maker* piece. When asked if she liked performing with Eno, Nico aligns herself with the synth player, answering, "Oh yes...a lot. He's great, incredibly talented. But don't even speak of that terrible concert. I should never have agreed to do it. Because I don't enjoy Kevin's kind of music—it escapes me completely...Kevin's music is just fooling around."

———

Nico and Philippe Garrel's latest collaboration was first screened in December 1974. Called *Les Hautes Solitudes* ("The Outer Reaches of Solitude"), the film was shot in black and white and featured no script, no subtitles—just silence. Summarized as a "biographical film about Jean Seberg, loosely based on Nietzsche's *Anti-Christ*," upon release the movie received the same sort of sniggering condescension as the previous pieces. In a *Melody Maker* interview, the tone of withering delusion cast upon Nico is palpable. Her deadpan sense of humor and dry delivery are not considered, her comments being taken, and reported, as straight facts: "Much of Nico's time of late has been spent in planning what she describes as 'The Perfect Picture' in conjunction with filmmaker Philip Garel. 'Philip is doing everything possible to make himself a pile of ashes,' she says somewhat enigmatically. And Nico's contribution to this piece of celluloid? 'Lyrics, sound, and my acting ability. I play the role of a person that's opposed to female emancipation.'"

In her diary, Nico reflects on the way she is perceived by others, providing a contrast to—and perhaps an explanation for—her interview commentary: "I don't want to be anybody's Talisman. Would you ever wish to be, would you ever hope to be, when all the Politics are mistaken." She is clearly aware of how the press is positioning her—as a faded, out of touch loony—begging the question of why would she want to give revealing interviews to those who had already made up their mind about her, having placed her as the "talisman" for junkie disaster? When Nico does refer to her drug use in her diary, it is always matter-of-fact; she does not glamourize her addiction, though the press often allude to it as being part of her appeal to a certain type of fan. Her answers in the media often show her dry humor and perhaps the same wind-up-merchant exasperation that is illustrated by her inclusion on *The End* of "Das Lied der Deutschen," as a means of holding a mirror up to the very press and public who were so quick to ridicule and judge her.

The Inner Scar had taken several years to complete; now Philippe Garrel and Nico were moving at a fast clip, adding to their cinematic collaborations with great speed. April 1975 saw the premiere of the rarely screened *Un ange passe* ("An Angel Is Passing") in Paris. In Garrel's eyes, the project fulfilled its purpose, which was "to show love to my father." While the movie may have been meant as "a portrait of Philippe Garrel's father, Maurice," the Internet Movie Database summarizes the film very differently, saying it is about "A woman sitting on a bench, silent, filmed long and closely."

Nico's musical output, however, was not as robust. "Nico had no management for a while, because managers don't want a junkie as a client. So she didn't play a lot of concerts, and that was really difficult for her," says Lutz Graf-Ulbrich. "Money which we earned from Nico gigs was directly spent on drugs and was always short... We ourselves were poor as church mice!" Though financially desperate, Nico was still recognized everywhere she went, her fame a stark contrast to her poor health and squalid living conditions. The reality of her poverty often forced her to steal in order to survive and feed her addiction. "I was invited to parties still and people would look at me and point at me and say, 'Look, that's Nico!' But I would be slipping the cutlery into my pockets and making sure I got a lot of drink and a free lift home," she notes in her diary. Her appearance, once striking for her often being clothed in head-to-toe pristine white, was now ragged. "She always wore this big, black robe and carried the harmonium over her shoulder. She was like someone from another world, I guess also because of the drugs," Graf-Ulbrich said. Not all of her family and friends were as accepting of her as her lover Graf-Ulbrich. In a letter to Danny Fields, Nico recounts the treatment she received from her former mentors Paul Morrissey and Andy Warhol, while admitting to adopting a pitiful look:

> Dear Danny, when will we see each other again? It has been
> so very long & all my old friends, like Paul & Andy, are all
> kind of hostile toward me, because I do not see myself running
> around like a doll. I look more like a prehistoric figure with rags
> hanging around her & worn out boots.

Eventually, Graf-Ulbrich began playing and traveling with Nico. One tour of the south of France in August 1975 found the two reunited with a bunch of other musicians, including Kevin Ayers, for the Arles Festival. On a day off, Graf-Ulbrich recalled everyone "hang[ing] out in and around the pool, philosophizing or just looking at the gracious young groupies in their tiny bikinis"—everyone except Nico, who instead was "sitting under a parasol fully dressed in her black clothes despite the high temperature reading *The Book of the Dead*." It was during this concert that Garrel decided to use Graf-Ulbrich's and Ash Ra Tempel's music as the soundtrack to his forthcoming film, film *Le Berceau de cristal* ("The Crystal Cradle"), featuring Nico, Anita Pallenberg, and Dominique Sanda. Though the deal was "sealed with a handshake," the musicians "never saw a penny" in payment for his use of their songs.

When not on tour, Graf-Ulbrich lived with the singer, at one point even decamping to his parents' house in the Charlottenburg area of Berlin. "When I invited Nico, they said, 'Of course she can live here with you,' even [with her] having the curtains closed during the day and getting up very late, with her long black dresses and the white makeup…She was, of course, a bit strange to look at for my parents. They were very open-minded, even if they were typical Germans. I said from the start that I wanted to be a musician, which for the parents wasn't the best choice for a profession. But they were always very supportive. They always have been." But even the most accommodating families have their limits. Once Graf-Ulbrich's mother and father figured out that there was heroin in the house, the duo were asked to leave, once again adjourning to Garrel's wretched apartment, where conditions were still unbearably bleak. Though having used Graf-Ulbrich's music in his film, Garrel was still uncommunicative. "The winter was cold. Philippe used to hang around in his fur coat and smoked one cigarette after the other, always until the very end…He just stared into space. Nico had a small room with her bed and her harmonium. When she had concerts, she was rehearsing her songs, but only then," Graf-Ulbrich recounts. His own accommodation was equally minimal, consisting of "a mattress in the room in front. Apart from that there was only an old piano, a TV set and a harpsichord, no other furniture."

———

Even though she had been scared for years about possible retribution by the Black Panthers following the Emmaretta Marks incident, Nico still could not resist returning to New York, and the Chelsea Hotel itself, the scene of the horrific event. In 1978, she moved herself and Graf-Ulbrich back into her old haunt, right in the wake of Nancy Spungen's death. Spungen had been the notorious girlfriend of John Ritchie, better known by his stage name of Sid Vicious.[113] The couple had been abusing drugs and became addicted to heroin before taking up residence in the Chelsea. Their stay was punctuated by each of them publicly abusing the other, both mentally and physically, and ended abruptly on October 12, when Nancy was found in the couple's bathroom, having bled out on the tiled floor following a single fatal stab wound to the stomach. Vicious was immediately arrested and charged with second-degree murder, to which he pleaded not guilty before being released on bail. Nico was aware of the tragedy, writing in her diary, "Staying at the Chelsea Hotel once again in 1978 shortly after Nancy had been stabbed in a room without a window, very nearly became my own fate...drifting into a bottomless pit..." The reference to "drifting into a bottomless pit" does make it seem as though Nico was aware of how dire her situation, with her own addiction, had become; the terrible reality of moving into the Chelsea directly after Spungen's grisly passing, following a life riddled with drug problems, was not lost on her.

The Chelsea was at the center of many alternative cultures. Joe Bidewell was Nico's neighbor during her stay, and later performed with her and John Cale. For him, the hotel offered both affordable shelter and the opportunity to rub shoulders with like-minded creatives. "I went down to the Chelsea, which, to tell you the truth, had a really bad reputation at that time. It was inexpensive and run down. You literally would see needles on the floor; people would come in and shoot up in the bathroom. This was all pre-Aids. As for the junk scene in New York City, it was still rampant, of mythological proportions, at that point in time. I'm from the Midwest, and I had no interest really in doing hard drugs, except from a literary point of view. I always thought that it was sort of romantic. Fortunately, my Baptist upbringing kept me from indulging. I did have to deal with the theft and the different things that went on because of so much rampant drug abuse in the city. I had personal experiences with stuff getting stolen [*laughing*], that sort of thing. A kid from the Midwest finds out pretty fast...But the Chelsea was really a mecca. I would walk into the lobby, and there's Uma Thurman in the middle of a photo shoot—this is the building that I live in! One day I walked out of my door and there was Allen Ginsberg."

Like Bidewell, Jim Tisdall was a New York transplant who later toured with Nico during her time in the U.S. Before installing themselves in the Chelsea, Nico and Graf-Ulbrich stayed with Tisdall. "I didn't know Lutz until I met Nico," he tells me. "But my brother John and our mutual friend Blaine Johnston knew her and Lutz in Berlin, so when Nico came to NYC, they asked if she could stay at my loft on 17th Street and 5th Avenue, and I agreed." Tisdall enjoyed Nico's company, recalling, "I remember her style of dress made me think right away of hippies. She seemed very serious, but I soon realized that she had a wry sense of humor. She was a good house guest and was considerate to me and to my girlfriend, who shared the loft with me. I did notice that she seemed a bit ill and soon learned about the drug problem. I found her conversation quite interesting; she would respond to things creatively and honestly. Indeed, I quickly concluded that she had a poetic sensibility, and this was reflected in her conversation in unexpected and fascinating ways." Nico and Graf-Ulbrich's stay was short-lived, as the duo soon got the room at the Chelsea Hotel. Graf-Ulbrich recorded the same events in his autobiography, recalling, "After we had filled out the immigration papers, we were welcomed by Blaine together with his old pal John Tisdall at JFK Airport. John had a car, so we drove through the winter snow of night-time New York City. Nico had told me a lot about the Chelsea Hotel. She had met Leonard Cohen here, with whom she had had a heavy romance. She showed me a scar on her wrist from that. Also Bob Dylan had written songs here. We lived in the first floor, room 121, just across that [sic] room 100, where not so long ago Sid Viscous [sic] had killed his friend Nancy. At the Chelsea Hotel everything seemed possible."

Though it had been several years since her tenure in the Velvet Underground, Nico was still being judged against her blonde, svelte image, by both the press and herself. "Nico's physical appearance—slimmer and released from the telltale puffiness of our last meeting—was matched by the brightness of her answers and easy wit…Time's tugged at the corner of her eyes a little but she's still a strikingly beautiful woman," starts one article for *Sounds* in April 1978.

In an interview with Graf-Ulbrich and his wife Daniela, Daniela says, "You [Lutz] told me she was always putting on makeup and that she was very concerned with her appearance. And that she used that as an excuse, like she didn't want to be beautiful anymore so she gave it away." Graf-Ulbrich replied, "It's true. She could be insecure. When we were living at the Chelsea at one point she had put on a lot of weight. And she didn't like that." Nico's own Aunt Helma was mortified by what she saw as the demise of her niece's great beauty. "In the end, she wanted to be as ugly as a witch," Wolff asserted, continuing, "She wanted to destroy herself. It was a campaign of annihilation against herself." Tisdall also recalled, "She was a bit out of shape when I met her, due, I assumed, to the addictions and to the drinking. She didn't dress the way a model and film star might, but more like a hippie. I wondered if she had adopted a Baudelairean[114] attitude. I also felt that she had succumbed to the pernicious theory that you have to engage in excess in order to develop artistically. But these were my own thoughts, not explicitly said by her. She did keep a copy of *Fleurs du mal*,[115] and I think the poet's work was an influence." Of the consistently brutal press remarks, Tisdall notes, "Snark sells. Mean people like to take down those who have had success and who they envy." To the public, Nico did not seem bothered. When asked by a journalist for *Sounds* magazine, "Does time passing make you sad? Aging?" Nico replied, "No. It's, uh, very boring."

One piece, written in a June edition of *ZigZag* magazine, offers a rare glimpse into Nico's personality, noting, "She's dressed in black cape, rust-colored Cossack-style trousers and her trusty boots. She smiles and laughs a lot, while still retaining this detached charisma, her voice rich and Teutonic. All in all, we get along like a house on fire, much to my relief. I soon realize that it's best to let Nico steer her own course..." The article goes on to showcase Nico's intellect, a characteristic rarely commented on, as she shared that "I read a lot, I like to read. I prefer Nietzsche of all. Then I like some English poets: William Wordsworth, Lord Tennyson, Lord Byron, Shelley... Shakespeare sometimes, but Tennyson is the best of all. He's an incredible Romantic, it's just so beautiful. You find everything there. In Shakespeare you just find death." Such acknowledgments of cognitive engagement were exceedingly uncommon, with most publications—and people in general—still infatuated with Nico's physicality.

———

For all her outward bravado, Nico was very much doubting herself and her future. A letter sent from Barcelona to Graf-Ulbrich, dated September 15, reveals this inner turmoil. Her reason for being in Spain is unknown, though she writes:

> Dear Lutz,
> I was here in the city all the time & am back to Paris today. As always, there is a losing streak...Your Nico

Another piece of correspondence—undated but likely from the same period—echoes this despair, Nico once again seeming to be looking for something to help or inspire her, and once again coming up empty:

> Le Côte d'Azur, Cannes
>
> Dear Lutz,
> I'll go back tomorrow night after I've missed everything. Except for some interesting dreams. Everything seems pretty unimportant to me here. Nico.

Things were about to get worse. After returning to Paris, Nico left her harmonium in the entrance hallway of the apartment she shared with Garrel, coming back soon after to find that it had been stolen. Penniless, without even her beloved instrument to provide comfort, she found some solace in providing vocals to a track on Spanish electronic band Neuronium's second album *Vuelo Químico*. This happened by accident, as the singer found herself in the same studio while it was being recorded, and reportedly was so moved by the music that she wanted to contribute. She speaks more than sings excerpts from poet Edgar Allan Poe's "Ulalume" on the track. The specific passages of the poem she uses are a poignant counterpoint to Nico's own circumstances—especially their references to October, the month of Nico's birth—the bleak and unrelenting text a reflection of the singer's own circumstances:

> The skies they were ashen and sober;
> The leaves they were crispéd and sere—
> The leaves they were withering and sere;
> It was night in the lonesome October
> Of my most immemorial year;
> It was hard by the dim lake of Auber,
> In the misty mid region of Weir—
> It was down by the dank tarn of Auber,
> In the ghoul-haunted woodland of Weir.

I am a pagan. But I am religious too. I guess religion also exists in a pagan, like pagan exists in religion, because it was there first.

Nico

I was in fashion too long. Every year or so, something else is fashionable, I like to be an innovator.

Nico

In 1975, two young British teens, Steven Bailey and Susan Ballion, met at a Roxy Music show in London. Glam rock was fading out, and there was a void for music that reflected the frustration and lives of young people. In the UK, punk rock soon filled the chasm, with the Sex Pistols leading the charge most visibly. The band were notorious for causing controversy and grabbing headlines with their foul mouths and rebellious attitude toward conventional British norms. Ballion and Bailey started following the group. Inspired by the Pistols' lack of any traditional prowess on musical instruments, and possessing the chutzpah but not necessarily the virtuoso skills to get up on a stage and perform in front of an audience, the duo, having rechristened themselves Siouxsie Sioux and Steve Severin, decided to form their own group. At the same time, another band dropped out of the upcoming 100 Club Punk Festival, giving Sioux the opportunity to approach Pistols manager Malcolm McLaren and suggest she and Severin should fill the spot. McLaren agreed. Though having no other musicians and no band name, the two quickly recruited some friends to create a line-up (including Sid

Vicious on drums), and on September 20, 1976, they performed a twenty-minute set—consisting mostly of an improvised interpretation of "The Lord's Prayer"—as Siousxie and the Banshees.

Though Severin and Sioux had viewed the gig as a one-off, they soon found themselves being asked to perform at other shows. They quickly found a permanent drummer and guitarist, and by November 1977 were appearing on Tony Wilson's *So It Goes*, on Manchester's Granada TV. The following month, they recorded a session for John Peel's BBC radio show and were featured as the cover stars of the UK weekly music magazine *Sounds*.

By early 1978, the band was selling out venues in London. Sioux's lyrics, makeup, and clothing, crossed with the desolate musicality of the Banshees, created an aesthetic that up until now had rarely been heard or seen in pop music. For Sioux, Nico was the foundation of her inspiration. She often cited the German singer as an influence, from her vocal stylings to her pronunciations. "Nico had an otherworldly character which was enhanced by the choral quality of the organ she used," Sioux said. "I was struck by the pictures on the records, how beautiful she was. It was the first time I'd heard such a deep voice and that made an impression on me. She was a mature dark angel." Jane's Addiction guitarist Dave Navarro echoes this sentiment, having been "a huge Banshees fan," and can similarly trace his own musical education back to both women. "I know Siouxsie was a huge Nico fan; you can hear it in her voice. That low, overly mixed sound, where the vocals are a little bit too loud in the mix, but it's good," he asserts. "When you have a singer like that, someone who has so much personality, you want to capture as much of it as you can, so you crank that shit up. I had a small love affair with her [Nico] that she's unaware of." Nico's trailblazing music, Navarro argues, created an opportunity for artists like Sioux to experience more mainstream success, by providing a blueprint for the exploration of unconventional subjects and singing styles. Looking at the album charts from 1978, this is true. In the UK, there were a few other off-center artists making a dent in the male-dominated market, with Kate Bush, Blondie's Debbie Harry, and Patti Smith all appearing in the bottom half of the top 100 of that year. In the U.S., though, it was a bleak landscape for anything other than the omnipresent disco and classic and adult-oriented rock (AOR). "She [Nico] opened the door for a lot of singers who had an unusual take, a darkness to them. People were discovering that they were identifying to those feelings and emotions. Even if you're not lyrically following along, there's a sentiment—a melancholy—that goes along with just the sonic part alone that can take you into a different space," Navarro tells me. "Some days you can get lost in the story; some days you can get lost in your own head; some days you can reflect on morbid past experiences; and other days you can have hope for the future. That's the beauty of music. Whatever frame of mind you're in dictates how you hear the song at that time."

It was not just her albums that made Nico distinctive; it was the entire package, "the way she presented herself, all black clothing," says Mark Lanegan. "I read something by someone who a lot of people give credit to as the first goth musician. I think it was Peter Murphy [it was]. He said, 'Nico was Mary Shelley Gothic; everyone else was Hammer Horror movie Gothic.'"

By April 1978, with punk rock now entrenched in the rhetoric and culture of the disenfranchised youth, two of the movement's original architects, John Cale and Lou Reed, toured the UK separately, heralded as heroes. Soon Nico managed to land some gigs, as venues and promoters assumed the songstress would be met with a similar reception to that of her former Velvets bandmates. They arranged for her to open for several buzz bands of the moment, including the Adverts, Siouxsie and the Banshees, and Cabaret Voltaire, in what was sure to be a hugely successful combination of punk forefathers and post-punk provocateurs.

First up was Nico playing with the Adverts and the Killjoys at the Music Machine in Camden, London, on April 28. Among those present was Peter Clarke—otherwise known as Budgie, the drummer for the Banshees. We exchanged several emails in which he told me about the shows with Nico. "Amidst those awed by her returning presence lurched the kind of pug-ugly bottle-throwing punks," he recalled, as Nico sat "alone on stage with her harmonium and voice," before being "forced to beat an undignified retreat as her performance was punctured by flying cans and glasses." Journalist Kris Needs was also in attendance, writing later in *ZigZag*, "They threw glasses at Nico when she played her first British gig in nearly four years at the Music Machine. For her, it must have been a striking contrast to the blissed-out hippies in deck-chairs who rippled apathetically at her last London performance; supporting Kevin Ayers at a Hyde Park free concert." Needs was a Nico fan and saw the gig as both a musical triumph for her and a bewildering indictment of the burgeoning post-punk scene, noting, "The annoying thing was [that] the Music Machine gig was a success. She went down a storm, with Nico-lytes coming from as far as Scotland. It's just the punky morons who left any sour taste, probably plucking up the guts to throw glasses at the single female sitting onstage." Needs notes Nico's incredible bravery throughout the whole experience, saying, "No one else could have held a crowd like that with so little…Of course it's easy to criticize Nico and some did. But what she's doing isn't easy. It's unique and strange. And deceptively melodic. She is unpredictable, erratic, a law to herself."

Undeterred by the horrendous reception she had received in London, Nico soldiered on to play with the Banshees that September. The band had just crossed over from the punk underground to the charts, with their debut single, "Hong Kong Garden," scoring a UK top 10 slot. With their success came a less anarchist, more conservative fan. Severin summed up the punters, saying that they were all confronted with a crowd "who had never been to a Punk concert before. Nico was the last thing they expected to hear." Once again, the hapless chanteuse was pelted with rude epithets and bottles. She finally left the tour in Cardiff. Giving a death stare to the audience as she prepared to walk off the stage, she pulled herself to her full near six foot height and said, over the ranting crowd, "If I had a machine gun, I would shoot you all."

As this unfolded, a horrified Budgie sat backstage, disgusted by what he saw. "I stood on the stage at Hemel Hempstead Pavilion and watched her sitting alone and bewildered as these Neanderthal cowards pelted this lone woman with abuse, missiles, and phlegm. She fled the stage in tears and the Banshees, enormous fans who were trying to help her, were incensed." While this sort of experience may have been so traumatizing as to make other artists never want to perform in public again, Nico was fearless. Just a few weeks after the Cardiff show, she was booked again at the Music Machine, this time with experimental electronic band Cabaret Voltaire, the Pop Group and Linton Kwesi Johnson. "It was probably one of the best line-ups I've ever been on," Stephen Mallinder of Cabaret Voltaire tells me over a cup of coffee in Brighton. "Nico created a small explosion in the hinterlands of culture."

Regardless of how bad her drug addiction had become, Nico never missed a show. Cosey Fanni Tutti recalled attending a gig and watching a clearly smack-sick Nico attempt to perform: "We went to meet her at the Marquee. She was in a really bad place. The drugs had taken their toll on her. We went backstage to meet her, but she was totally out of it. Because she had to go on stage any minute, we thought we'd catch up with her afterward. We just said, 'Hello,' but she was nowhere. Then she went on stage and she had one of those moments where she starts and then drifts and then stops and then has to start again. I think it was about three times that she sort of started and drifted off and stopped again and started again before she got going. The audience weren't very kind to her at all. I was so upset by that. Nobody's taking any notice of her struggle! The bands backstage were just drinking and ignoring her. I thought, 'Do they not know what she is? What status she has here?'"

At the end of 1978, Nico played a gig in Paris. It was notable because it was here that she met Corsicans Philippe Quilichini and Antoine Giacomoni. The pair made a striking duo. Quilichini was a white-reggae bassist, while his friend Giacomoni was a young, attractive, gay photographer. Both were taken with the singer and pledged to find an opportunity to collaborate together. Giacomoni even charmed a hesitant Nico into posing for a series of photographs,[116] most famously featuring her posed in a graveyard. But new friends were not enough to make her stay in Europe. Lutz Graf-Ulbrich had decided to go back to New York to pursue his music career. With no other options presenting themselves, Nico followed him. "I winced because that meant I'd have to pay for her ticket as usual," he recalls. "She said, 'Don't worry. After two weeks there I'll have a gig and everything will be all right.'" On the plane ride from London back to the East Coast, Nico was told that Sid Vicious had died of a heroin overdose. She had got to know him through Siouxsie and the Banshees and had been contemplating getting him to play bass on her next album. The news upset her. She had lost another friend, one she felt close to, as the deceased punk had also spent time at the Chelsea and had an all-encompassing drug problem. "She was really shocked," Graf-Ulbrich recalled.

Soon after landing and getting settled back in the hotel, Nico connected with Jane Friedman. Friedman was managing John Cale, and she took the newly arrived Nico under her wing, booking her to play with her former bandmate at the hot club in Manhattan, CBGB.[117] The venue, which had originally opened in 1973 as a dive bar, had recently become the place for the emerging punk and new wave scene, with bands like Talking Heads, the Ramones, and Blondie all using it as a launch pad for wider mainstream success. The gig was announced in the *Village Voice* and tickets sold out within two hours of going on sale. With a few weeks to go until the February 19 show, practice commenced, with Cale bringing his viola to the Chelsea. Even their old friend Andy Warhol was excited about the mini-Velvets reunion. After seeing the singer backstage at a Clash gig two nights before she made her New York return in Cale's show, Warhol wrote in his diary, "...we got backstage there was Nico! With John Cale! And she looks beautiful again, absolutely beautiful, she's finally thin in the face."

The night of the gig, the whole entourage was forced to take a public bus to get to CBGB, as heavy snow had made it impossible for cabs to navigate the streets. Graf-Ulbrich was not impressed by the neighborhood that the club was located in, saying, "The area around the CBGB was not the finest. There were bums all over the place and the houses were looking rather desolate." The soundcheck was rocky, with Nico having problems remembering the start of a song. Unable to read music, she depended solely on touch and sound to find her way around the harmonium keyboard, but this technique was failing her, as "She tried with both hands on her keyboard, but bass-line and melody just would not come together," Graf-Ulbrich remembered.

Nico harbored resentment at being what she perceived as the warm-up for Cale's main event. She would often have several drinks before gigs, and the CBGB show was no different. The pre-performance pints were followed by alcohol ordered from the stage during her turn. By the time she came off stage, after several encores, Nico was fairly drunk, bordering on incoherent. Unfortunately, this was when Friedman asked her if she would be okay to play the second of the two performances scheduled for the night. Nico was not aware of the additional engagement and was not pleased with this news. She told Friedman, "No one has told me about two shows. The fee is much too low for that. No way!" Somehow, amidst much crying and shouting, Graf-Ulbrich and Friedman got Nico back onto the stage for round two. Graf-Ulbrich recalled the night, saying, "The audience welcomed her with a huge applause and she began singing. She was still so upset that her long notes turned into long sobs, although she kept trying to get herself under control. The concert was about to become a disaster. The audience laughed, cheered, booed, and encouraged her. In the middle of a song she stopped and shouted all her rage into the mike: 'Nobody told me that there would be two shows. I am sick of being the Opening Act of Mister John Cale! The money they pay me is not enough for two shows anyway!' And she left the stage right away, leaving behind a stunned audience."

Cale and his band took to the stage, but Nico was far from calmed down. Once Cale had finished and the crowd was dispersing, she exploded. She could become violent and unpredictable when she was mixing alcohol and methadone. Graf-Ulbrich remembered, "She screamed, ran from table to table and pushed down the chairs which had been put on the tables to clean up the hall. She asked for the owner, to beat him up. Nobody could stop her. Several security guys tried to calm her down, but they all were scared, because Nico really got going and seemed uncontrollable."

Despite her atrocious outburst, Friedman still managed to book Nico three nights back at CBGB, from March 8 to 10. These were heralded as her official comeback shows. Not having to share the spotlight with anyone else, Nico was on fine form, even shouting down a disorderly audience member, as captured on a bootleg:

Nico: This is a song from my album that has not been released.

Heckler: Yeah!

Nico: Some of you people seem to be pretty drunk. Well, so am I.

Heckler: We wanna hear some rock'n'roll!

Nico: You shouldn't have come to see me then.

Heckler: Funky. Get funky, baby. Yer funky but chic!

Nico: I don't think I want to continue unless some people shut up.

Heckler: Why don't you get off?

Nico: Oh shut up, will you? If you have anything to say, go out of here, get out of here, will you?

Heckler: Can't we talk?

Nico: No, you can't, damn it!

Off the back of the successful CBGB shows, Cale forgave Nico's outburst, bringing her along to play further gigs with him. By this time, Joe Bidewell was performing in Cale's band, which was known as Sabotage. "Nico joined that outfit for a brief period and just did dates with us," says Bidewell. "We hit it off from the very beginning. I thought she exuded a lot of class. She wasn't at a great spot in her life for a lot of reasons that are documented, but she always was a lady." Bidewell did several gigs with Nico and Cale, but one was a favorite. "A memorable gig was at the Mudd Club.[118] Nico was playing by herself on the harmonium, and it was very dark. Just what you know Nico to be. At one point, people were making so much noise that she looked out into the audience and in her thick Germanic accent said, 'Shut up, you little punk-heads!' The whole history of what she represented was lost on a lot of these club kids who had come to the Mudd Club simply because it was 'the' place to go. They didn't realize the gravity of the moment, because it was Nico! By herself on the harmonium, playing before the John Cale band...It was lost on them."

Jim Tisdall also attended Nico's first solo CBGB show. "She asked me why I had not brought my harp; apparently she expected me to be part of that concert. Later, when Lutz went back to Germany, she invited me to fill in at some gigs that she needed an accompanist for around NYC. Her vocal performance, full of irony and deep pain and anger, seemed to evoke the ghosts of all the victims of the murderous Nazi regime. It always gave me chills to be on stage with her then. It was musically interesting, emotionally honest, politically brave and, in short, a real performance event."

265

Sparked by the excellent press reaction to the initial CBGB show, a new set of Nico dates was put together, with Tisdall again in the mix. "In addition to accompanying her on almost all of her songs and playing solo between sets, I helped interact with the club management, 'counted the house' and got the show to start and end on time, got us to and from our lodgings, and [other] such typical details," recalls Tisdall.

It was not a glamourous affair. "The whole thing was on a budget—just a van between cities, and usually staying at someone's house who was a fan or friend of the venue," he says. "These kind people were uniformly interesting and artistic, so they made the rigors of the tour much less exhausting and much more fun. The show was easy to set up—just two musicians requiring a few microphones. Nico would do a set, I'd do one to three numbers, and Nico would do a second set. The audience seemed to know her work pretty well and would often applaud a song they recognized just from the first few bars of musical introduction.

"Backstage was sometimes just a little tense, as Nico would suffer a bit of the jitters before going on. But nothing extreme. Often we would have met some new friends, and they would be invited to spend time with us backstage, which helped keep the atmosphere friendly, relaxed, and interesting. Usually, fans also would want to meet after the shows, so it was a nice social atmosphere."

Despite the resurgence of interest in her career, drugs were still at the center of Nico's daily routine. Her dependency continued to impact on new as well as old relationships. She had added alcohol to her nightly annihilations, further compounding her mood instability. "Drinking was one of her addictions," says Tisdall, "and addiction is torture. On the last night of the tour, in Cleveland, when we were surrounded by fans after the concert, Nico suddenly and very publicly accused me of having withheld money from her, of cheating her out of her earnings. This so outraged me that I announced then and there that I would take nothing for myself. I handed over my own earnings to her and I left, returning to NYC on my own. In retrospect, that was a young man's dramatic reaction to having his honor impugned. I know she was having withdrawal symptoms at that point. At this distance in time, I don't really hold it against her or take it personally."

Tisdall also remembers the daily hunt for opiates, saying, "The hard part [of the tour] was Nico's inability to reliably get the drugs—methadone especially—that she needed at that point to function at all well. To the outsider, opioid and alcohol addiction is a lot of unpleasant emotions and activities in pursuit of a dubious and potentially permanent rest. One hates to see the addict in such dire distress, and one cannot help but dislike the turmoil that comes with the addiction."

In *Please Kill Me*, poet and musician Jim Carroll revealed his own run-in with Nico during a gig in San Francisco, most likely on the tour Tisdall played on. "I was at the Mabuhay Gardens, which was like the CBGB's of San Francisco, and I was trying to hit on one of the girls in the Go-Go's," said Carroll. "I had this really good coke, so I'm doling out some lines in the manager's office, and we're doing some and then all of a sudden Nico comes in. She sees the coke and says, 'Is that cocaine?' Then she says, 'Oh, you are Szhim Carroll. I read about you. You are so skinny. I am so fat.' She was really large and she looked pretty bad. I said, 'You sounded great. Here, have some coke.' She was really thankful. She said, 'Oh, this is very good cook.' I said, 'Thanks. Coming from you that's a real compliment.' It was that period when she was really on junk."

Amidst the tour dates and the drugs, Nico still managed to shoot another movie with Philippe Garrel. The project began filming in 1978, with Nico enthusing about their newest collaboration across several press interviews. "This film is very special because it's a revival of the first movie ever made: *La Lumière*," she told Kris Needs in June 1978's *ZigZag*. "It's a silent one. It's amazing. I'm the lead role this time. It's a very unusual film...When I stand on the roof of the opera it's amazing I don't fly off because it was such a wind, such a storm that it might just have taken me away with my cape. It was spreading out almost like Batman. If I had let it go...but I didn't. I wrapped myself in it!"

The end product, titled *Le Bleu des origines* ("The Blue of the Origins"), is a silent black-and-white piece, lasting forty-nine crackling minutes. Filmed on a hand-cranked camera, the movie has a decidedly and purposefully primitive look to it, harking back to the days of the first silent films. One synopsis summarizes the action: "At the top of a neo-classical building, a man looks at the sky, a woman reads, hair in the wind."

Nico seemed to fluctuate in interviews between ambivalence and resentment toward Garrel. Her former stark enthusiasm and praise for the filmmaker had evaporated, replaced by unmistakeable resentment and anger. "He's being very good to himself but I couldn't say that he's being very good to *myself*. Because I could do better without him. I mean, he can *not* do better without me," she told *Sounds* in April 1978. *Le Bleu des origines* was the seventh and last film Nico and Garrel worked on together. It also marked the end of their off-screen, decade-long relationship.

———

While Nico was making movies, nursing her heroin addiction, and trying to land a new recording contract, Ari, having now been legally adopted by the Boulogne family, was struggling to come to terms with his parentage. The taking on of his grandmother's surname started a lifelong battle within the young man, as he tried to figure out who he was and where his allegiance lay.

Ari's memories include one of Nico's "legendary" visits to Bourg-la-Reine, where the Boulognes lived. It illustrates the dilemma of a young man who wants to see and know the mother he has been taught to fear by his grandparents, who were most likely trying to shield the vulnerable boy from what they thought was a damaged woman. "I was busy doing my homework when she rang the famous door of Avenue du General Leclerc," he writes. "My grandfather walked along the long corridor leading to it from the house, he glanced behind the small shutter, closed it, did not open the door and, coming back to us, let it go: 'It was Nico.' He went back to sit in tense silence. I had been unable to react. Subsequently, my grandparents surrounded their fortress with a pit of silence and invisibility and did not hesitate to make the same blow to her at a time when they had deprived her of any news of me."

The young teen was caught in the middle of an unwinnable war between the mother he wanted to know and had been taught to fear and the proposed stability that Edith offered—uncertain, as it came with the baggage and rejection of his father, Alain Delon. He claims that his mother sent him letters, though his grandparents maintained they rarely, if ever, heard from the singer. In one piece of correspondence that Ari says he received, Nico tells him that she had known where he was for months and claims not to have known of his adoption. His grandparents put the adoption between them, reminding Ari of the stability they had provided. However, this had the opposite effect, instilling not comfort but further feelings of confusion and isolation within the boy. "I was beginning to be frightened...of the abyss of my abandonment," Ari writes. "According to them [the Boulognes], there was no other way out [than to be adopted]. I was overwhelmed: it was in my own 'interest' to reject my mother."

Meanwhile, Ari's infrequent communications with Nico only fueled his internal turmoil. Desperate for any form of solace, Ari began shooting up smack. "This bewitchment helped to blunt my resentment toward my mother," he reveals. "My obstinacy in disavowing it [heroin] vanished. The ritual of heroin addicts was then still new to me and exercised irresistible charm. The spell began with the attraction of the syringe itself, before the flash. The pleasure continued with...the proud contemplation of my dilated pupils in a mirror."

Now seventeen years old, Ari finally reconnected with Nico. Most of the details involved are blurry, if they are even recalled. "I do not remember the sequences that led to our reunion," he says, though it happened in "the winter of 1979...I found her in an apartment where Ernest Hemingway had lived." An entire childhood's worth of questions, animosity, and rejection lay within the young man. "What were our first words?" he asks himself. "Have we talked about adoption? Did she tell me about all her vain attempts to talk to me on the phone or to see me? Have we together sought to understand what has happened to us? Or, on the contrary, did we instantly erase all this disorder in this complicit silence that enveloped us afterward? Describing this moment is impossible. I just know that the dream reality became *the* reality." None of these issues were discussed. Nico's state, however, may have played a part in the lack of any airing of emotions. "My mother was 'smashed,' and I was not shocked," Ari recalls. However, he, too, may have been high, as he notes: "No doubt I was myself." After all the years of hurt, loss, resentment, and grief on both sides, heroin provided a shared field of experience and a source of bonding for the pair. "Without feeling the need to tell [each other] anything, we found ourselves on the same ground, somehow equal," Ari confides. "A child and a mother merged. Neither solemnity nor affectation nor drama. It was as if we had never left, as if we knew each other perfectly well. No verbal overload was necessary."

In *Nico: Icon*, Lutz Graf-Ulbrich also remembers this poisonous sacrament between mother and son, saying, "She gave him heroin. You can only shake your head. I mean...what can you say to that? A mother giving her son heroin, I don't understand that." While it does seem horrifying, it may also be understandable. Nico did not have much experience as a parent and was presented for the first time in over a decade with her child, who was almost a fully grown adult. The drug provided, as Ari astutely recognized, a mutual bond, without them having to dissect the tangled, complicated, and messy emotional baggage, the very thing that had driven both of them independently to take up the substance in the first place. Graf-Ulbrich said that "Nico had told me that she got Ari hooked on smack. That's why I recounted this in the film *Nico: Icon* and then this information was out in the world." Later, Ari told Graf-Ulbrich that someone other than his mother introduced him to the drug. However, the teen and his mother had a relationship that was bonded further by the use of opiates. Nico's only child admitted to Graf-Ulbrich that he and his mother did use heroin together, often even sharing needles.

35

The two of them now reunited, Ari would often accompany his mother on the road, their mutual addiction creating a bond while temporarily preventing any actual feelings, regrets or emotions from being expressed. Shows were Nico's main source of income, which meant her relentless touring schedule did not let up as 1980 arrived. Money was desperately needed just to keep the horrific withdrawals from smack at bay. "The heroin was the reveler who dispensed with all justification, or the obligation to go back...it was indeed the mediator of our merger...A cloud of love and opium..." said Ari. Echoing Lutz Graf-Ulbrich's memories of living and being on tour with Nico, he continued, "We were a magical and thrilling couple. [The intensity of our life] suddenly covered all the gaps in our history. I was with her now and no one could separate us any more. Living with her became an absolute adventure, terrible and enchanting at the same time."

———

"I'm only going by what Nico said to me. I do not doubt her for a minute, because she wasn't really a person who made up stories and stuff like that," Nico's former beau Robert King tells me. "All this crap that people write about her is stupid. It's their personal angst that they're taking out on her. Because she probably sacked them and got a different guitarist, drummer or whatever...I'm only going to say what is the truth, because she deserves the truth." The Nico he describes is a harsh contradiction to the reserved, withdrawn persona that is depicted so often. "She was a very...playful person...inquisitive. I was lucky enough to know her son, and also I was really close to her family, in a bigger sense, so for me I can see it from a different perspective than all these other assholes. I don't know why they do that. Does it make them [feel] great to insult somebody in such a way? I don't think so."

When asked how he first met Nico, King laughs, saying, "Well, that's an interesting story." Newly arrived in London, he found himself moving into a flat in Ladbroke Grove. At the time, when not on tour, Nico was living in the same neighborhood with the two Corsicans she had met at her Paris gig in 1978, Philippe Quilichini and Antoine Giacomoni, and Quilichini's girlfriend, Nadette Duget. It was here at the flat, located on the corner of Cambridge Gardens and Ladbroke Grove, that King first encountered the icon.

"I was sitting in the kitchen, and my flatmate said, 'You've got to meet somebody I think that you would like.' And that was Nico. It was funny as fuck." For King, the attraction was immediate. "I just hooked my claws into her," he laughs. "She was older, but as good-looking as she was when she was young. A commanding presence; she had charisma and a very soft...innocence. I used to think that before I knew who she was, because I knew her albums. The press never gave that image." When asked who made the first romantic advance, King immediately confides, "Oh, it was her."

He does not agree that Nico stopped caring about her appearance. "When I knew her, she was getting older and starting to, shall we say it politely, 'spread.' It used to panic her greatly. She was aware of what people said about her, what people wrote about her. If you think of what you know about Nico and her image, and then marry that to reading depraved libel and newspapers about her, that's essentially what it is—depraved libel."

When asked to explain who the woman behind the mantle was, King responds, "The real Nico?" He contemplates this, before saying, "Okay. The day that Charles and Diana got married, me and Nico decided to make spaghetti Siciliana, which is essentially a can of anchovies pounded down into paste, fried with garlic and tomato, then served with pasta. Unfortunately, we were taking heroin. We also decided to take these purple haze acid tablets, two each. So we ended up watching Princess Diana get married to Charles while we were wallpapering the apartment with spaghetti Siciliana. For about a month, the flat stank of rotten fish! It took weeks of washing the walls for the stink to go. So that tells you how much of an 'Ice Queen' she was."

While some biographies have alluded to Nico asking others to refer to her as Christa, King, like everyone I asked this question of, has no memory of her ever going by any name other than Nico, in private or public. "She didn't ever use her own name, ever," he tells me. "She always referred to herself as Nico because she was being 'Nico.' She got sadly caught up in the trap of being the persona, the pop star. And that's really what kept her in the hell of heroin addiction. People expected her to be on the drugs, and they allowed her to continue that persona. Part of it was that she recognized being the supreme heroin queen was kind of a unique status, if you understand. When she was in the Factory, she was competing with Edie Sedgwick and the other Superstars for an identity. The Velvet Underground and heroin had a huge impact on people."

King regales me with a story of Nico having eyes for an Afro-Caribbean man who lived near her. "Every day in Ladbroke Grove, we used to go to this pub on the corner. There used to be a van parked up there. This band called Rip Rig + Panic[119] used to live

274

in it. At lunchtime every day, me and Nico would go to the pub—obviously out of our heads on heroin—for a Guinness. We'd buy Rip Rig + Panic a drink, and Nico would always want to play pool with Sean [Oliver, the band's bass player], because she had crush on him. Sean was a wee black guy with an Afro."

Nico's mastery of so many languages surpassed King's expectations, her abilities illustrated by one of her daily rituals. "Her English was good; she used to do the *Times* crossword. I was taught by Jesuits when I was a kid, so I was educated properly. I used to read *The Times*, and every cunt used to think, 'Why are you reading that, when you should be reading other, less highbrow shit?' But Nico loved it. The first time she saw me doing it, she just said, 'Oh, I'm so glad you read *The Times*.' I said, 'Why?' And she responded, 'Because I love the crossword.' I thought, 'WHAT THE FUCK!' So I gave it to her, and she did the whole thing in two hours! After that, I used to get *The Times* for her every morning so that she could do the crossword."

King also met Nico's former bandmate and paramour Lou Reed, with whom the Scottish singer was not impressed. "One time, Lou Reed came to stay. The guy's a cunt. He walked into the house and said to me, 'Boy, make me tea!' It's the wrong thing to say to me...because I'm crazy, I'm seriously crazy like...[*laughs*]. I just put him in his place. He apologized afterward." King may have been one of the few men ever to stand up for Nico; his face-off with Reed is even more incredible as it marks someone siding with the songstress over the already glorified lead man. Reed's rise and deification only increased as the years passed, while Nico seemed determined to see how low she could go.

The relationship with King eventually ended. Without King, Nico would again lack any semblance of security, instead having to depend on her teenage son for this. Ari was unclear if the breakup saddened his mother, as she "rarely showed her emotions."

Though her addiction held her captive throughout the late 1970s, Nico was still writing music sporadically and already had a title picked out for her new record. "Of course I have new songs," Nico declared to *Sounds* in April. "I've been waiting to put new songs on an album for the past two years, and I didn't want to sign with just anybody. I don't think it's wrong to disappear for a while. It's better, I think. Because somehow you accumulate—throughout the events that are happening to you, the events that you're facing constantly, and you just see things much clearer. While you're working at a particular subject it's important to disappear for a while. My music is not accidental. If you want it to be an accident, it is an accident, but it can also be something else. It can be very well thought out." "I have just enough for an album, which is going to be called *Drama of Exile*," she told *ZigZag* magazine in June.

However, finding a home for the record was proving to be a challenge, with Nico commenting in the book *Beyond the Velvet Underground*, "I've been sort of disappearing and reappearing... I went to Los Angeles thinking I could sign a record contract. It may have been easier if I'd have been more patient about it. I left after two months." She hung on, though, telling journalists that "I've signed it in my head. I think I definitely would like to sign with Arista, because it's like being in the same boat with a few friends (Is Lou Reed still there?)... that are important on the music scene right now. So why should I be with a different company? So maybe we can make the whole... *exposure* or whatever you like to call it... make it a *parliament!*"

By the start of 1981, Nico and her flatmates had decided to work together to produce the singer's fifth studio album. Duget would be the executive producer, with Quilichini taking on Cale's role as arranger and producer. The album would mark a departure not only in terms of the studio team, but in its sound, Nico trading in her trademark bleak, stripped-back vibe for a variety of faster-paced songs. "It was really boring, all that quiet stuff," she noted. "And having been a member of the Velvet Underground, rock'n'roll is something I have to do at one point, even if only for one album. I want to combine it with Arabic music. I am part Turkish. Well, my father was part Turkish. I've been disappearing. I've been disappearing from myself. I've become a total stranger to myself, and that's why I title the record *Drama of Exile*... Because it's a drama being a stranger to yourself." *Drama* was also to include two covers: David Bowie's "'Heroes'" and a Velvets track. "I always wanted to sing 'Waiting for the Man' but Lou wouldn't let me," Nico said. "Lou was the boss and was very bossy. Anyway, I know a little bit more about the subject now than I did then. I find it something to occupy yourself with, running up and down the city." Nico claimed that the choice of these two particular songs was carefully thought through. She chose "Waiting for the Man" "as a tribute to Lou and because I wanted to sing rock'n'roll. I'd never done it before and it's such a great rock'n'roll song. I'm looking at it as a new song. Apart from having so much choice I thought I could do one or two songs from Lou Reed's *Berlin* album, but they're all so suicidal." The Bowie track was picked because it was "not quite so destructive." In addition to new producers and a different sound, Nico was also considering changing the packaging that the record came in, noting that she wanted to include a lyric sheet. She had not inserted one before as "Cale and a few other people always thought that this would take away from the myth that was built around me if I put the lyrics on the sleeve."

Ari eventually made his way to the flat to join his mother.

Besides being an aspiring record producer, Duget was a well-known heroin dealer and kept control of both her boyfriend and Nico through the drug. Nico could not function without daily doses of her "medicine" and became completely reliant on her female flatmate to supply her with the necessary fixes. "My mother showed some distrust of the 'Corsican bandits,'" Ari writes. "She reproached them for leaving her in need for hours in the house, in the company of only the cat. In fact, they still had more drugs while she carried her diva junkie cross. The daily gear of my mother, I was soon to discover and even manage it in part: without her ration she could do nothing. In the pale lights of this city, I had plunged into the unfathomable abyss of heroin."

Amidst this bog of addiction, recording for *Drama of Exile* began in April/May 1981 at Gooseberry Studios in the Tulse Hill neighborhood of London. Independent label Aura Records, owned by Aaron Sixx, advanced the cost of production. While her previous albums—with the exception of *The End*—had been almost entirely Nico and Cale, *Drama* featured an entire band, including some notable names: oriental string instrument expert Muhammad Hadi; drummer Steve Cordonna; Ian Dury's sax player Davey Payne; percussionist J. J. Johnson of Wayne County's Electric Chairs; and Andy Clarke, who had previously played keyboards on David Bowie's album *Scary Monsters (and Super Creeps)*. Later, Thierry Matioszek was brought in to do electric violin and backing vocals, with Gary Barnacle providing additional sax and drums later. Quilichini played guitar as well as produced.

There are two conflicting accounts of the recording and release of *Drama*. One is from the perspective of Duget and Quilichini and is told by journalist and mutual friend Bruno Blum, while the other is from Aaron Sixx, who signed Nico to make *Drama*. I spoke to both of them to get the two opposing views directly from people who were actually there. The definitive truth may yet to be revealed, but both parties vehemently believe their version is what actually occurred.

I spoke first to Blum. His points come across with a surprising urgency. "For the past thirty years, a lot of lies have been spread about this, and no one is here to tell the true story of what happened," he argues passionately over the phone. As a journalist, he often found himself in London, as it "was the capital of music at the time." Blum confirmed that both Duget and her boyfriend Quilichini were heroin addicts. The two had produced an album in Jamaica for a reggae group called the Congos, before returning to London.

At the time, Nico was living with Duget and Quilichini in an apartment with a large living room, where the three would often gather to watch television together. However, it was the drugs that were the main draw for all of the occupants. "There was quite a lot of heroin around at the time...very good heroin from Thailand, the best heroin you could get. It's the holy grail for junkies. I think a lot of the reason that Nico was staying there was because there was such good heroin around," Blum hypothesizes.

His recollections of the singer come via the lens of his background as a writer, as at the time he was thinking of writing a book about the Velvets. An outing to the pub, under the premise of interviewing Nico for the possible tome, did not go as well as Blum had hoped. "Nico, who was in her forties at the time, looked like the ghost of herself. She had put on some weight; she was not looking as striking as she used to. I bought her a drink and asked her questions. Quickly I understood that I knew more about her life than she cared to remember. She just stood there listening to my questions, had absolutely nothing to say and stared at me. Maybe she just wasn't interested or didn't remember. She just didn't seem to remember anything, even the Velvet Underground times. Her mind was blank, and she would just say 'Yes' or 'No.' I could feel that it would be very difficult to work with her."

At this point, according to Blum, Nico's whole existence had come to revolve around the opiate. "I remember Nico being very friendly, although a little cold and shy at times. She was just desperately strung out to get more smack. Whenever she talked to me, it was often related to trying to get me to get heroin for her. It was really pathetic. One day she heard I was there. She came out as I was on the staircase and said, 'Bruno, can you please ask Nadette to give me some heroin, please? I am sick, you must help me.' Nadette was very harsh; she said, 'Tell that bitch she's had enough today!' It was that kind of vibe. There was this guy from a band called Scars [Robert King] who was around a lot; he was good friends with them."

Living with Nico, Blum argues, was not a pleasant experience, as she "was such a mess. Nobody would deal with her. I'm not trying to say anything bad about her. I'm just trying to say that she would act erratically. Here was Nico, a 'finished' legend. Her connections had run out, and Nadette Duget came and got it together," he concludes.

Trying to build on her and Quilichini's success with the Congos, Duget connected with Aaron Sixx. Blum tells me that Sixx agreed to pay for studio time to make a new Nico album, while Duget consented to "deal" with Nico, which basically meant providing the singer with a place to stay and drugs, and keeping track of her overall—a huge undertaking at times, as "You never knew what Nico was going to do. She could be a lunatic sometimes or disappear."

Blum was among the few invited to the studio for the recording of *Drama of Exile*, describing the scene as "secretive. No journalist was around in the studio that I know of, because Nico didn't like people to be around when she was recording...but I was there."

It was about halfway through the recording process that Blum recalls problems starting to pop up. "JJ, the drummer (whom I lived with at the time), came up one day and said, 'Guess what, we've fallen out with Aaron Sixx.' Sixx had decided that he did not want to spend more money on studio time. According to Nadette, he took the tapes and disappeared...They had gotten all of these great musicians to record, and it was all gone! They were really pissed off with him. I don't know what happened...probably some junkie business. The album was nearly completed and only two songs were left to do. They had done at the time what is called 'a rough mix.' It was not finished; it had no sound effects, the vocals were not done. He took the tapes thinking that the album was done! He had even taken some of Antoine Giacomoni's pictures! Nadette and Philippe started some kind of lawsuit."

The flatmates went back to take another crack at the record, this time using Duget's money to finance the undertaking. As all of the musicians had already rehearsed the songs, it took only a week to re-record the album in its (new) entirety. "Nico did her vocals. Antoine did the pictures with Nico's son Ari; they were all taken in London and on the Tube. I'm not sure how Nadette got the money together," Blum confides.

However, just as they finished the second version of the record, they were distraught to discover that Sixx had pressed up an album featuring the rough mixes from the studio. Blum's horror at this is still palpable all these years later. "Sixx had released an album that was unfinished that he'd paid for! He did not even credit the musicians correctly. They were so mad because he had not only taken the tapes and not allowed them to finish the record, but he had now released it."

Blum asserts that Nico had been paid by Sixx for the undertaking. He claims that though she may not have liked the fact that the project with Sixx was incomplete, Nico would "sign anything" for money. However, at the end of the day, Blum asserts, "It was all junkie business."

The appearance of Sixx's version snuffed out all plans for Giacomoni, Duget and Quilichini to release their re-recorded *Drama*. According to Blum, the original rough mix pressing had a devasting impact on the flatmates. "Nico didn't like it, Antoine and Nadette were mad, and Philippe wasn't coming out of his room much and taking smack a lot…he was pretty fucked up. It killed their spirits completely," Blum confides. All their conversations began to revolve around the record and Aaron Sixx. About a year later, a deal was struck with a French label to release the second effort with extra tracks. There was little coverage of it, though, as "it had already been out," Blum says. "It was all a mess... That record, in my opinion, is Nico's best work. Maybe Aaron Sixx had some problems with them, and maybe he had some excuse for doing this, but certainly it wasn't cool. No matter what he says—and he probably did try to get Nico's approval—the record he issued on Aura was not on."

Quilichini and Duget ended up going back to Corsica. They ran out of money and their "career was broken," according to Blum, because of "this whole problem with Aaron." Blum tells me that "Nadette died of anorexia a few years later," but he thinks her death was actually caused by having a "broken heart." He is not sure how Philippe passed away, or if it was related to heroin. Either way, "It was all pretty heavy."

Blum saw Nico one last time, when the singer played at Heaven in London. "I went backstage with Antoine, Philippe, and Nadette. Nico was there, hazy as ever. She was very friendly with Nadette and Philippe... there was no way anyone could say that she had fallen out with them. She played this really spacey set with the harmonium. It was very cold and very strange."

From his home in Los Angeles, Aaron Sixx tells me what he recalls of the experience. "'If you harken back to that time, there weren't many women musicians around,' he says. 'The few who were in the scene all knew each other to some degree.' This may be why Nico attended an Annette Peacock show at the Bataclan in Paris. Sixx was working with Peacock at the time and recounts being approached by Nico after the gig. "There was a tall woman with a long black overcoat and a scarf or two around her neck. She came up to me and she said, 'Can I meet Annette?' And I said, 'Why do you want to meet Annette?' And she said, 'Oh, I know her from New York.' Annette was in the dressing room with the band, so I said, 'What's your name? I'll mention it to her.' And she said [*imitates languid German accent*], 'My name is Nico.' Obviously, I knew who Nico was. I said that the French record company were throwing a dinner for all of us, why didn't she come with us? So Nico came along. We were talking a bit; she was talking to other people. I remember she was very aloof and standoffish...not very friendly. Nico was never engaging with anybody in the time I knew her...and she never smiled or laughed or anything. It was always dead serious."

When she did speak, anecdotes about Reed were often a feature. "She was forever telling stories about Lou—Lou this and Lou that. We signed Lou at Arista [where Sixx also worked], and he was a total fucking handful as well! He was very creative, but...Nico and John Cale and Lou...there were stories and truths and mistruths." Despite the rumors he had heard, Sixx told Nico to contact him if she ever found herself in London, where the music executive was living at the time. "That was it," he tells me. "I didn't even think about it again."

However, Nico did not forget Sixx's offer. Several months later, she got in contact with him, saying she was looking to make an album. "She came with a French/Vietnamese woman whose name was Nadette Duget...who turned out to be her drug dealer. She knew absolutely nothing about management or music or anything. She was a drug dealer—end of story. The producer was her boyfriend, Philippe Quilichini, who was a French Corsican guy. The only experience they had was in Jamaica, which was not a good sign for anybody in the music business." Yet these red flags did not put off Sixx, who thought he "could do something with Nico." After she played some demo tracks for him, Sixx agreed to draw up a contract and work with the singer. However, the process quickly began to go downhill. "I said that I would pay for the studio and the musicians and so on. There was an advance, but I'm pretty sure the advance was going to be paid when the record was finished, because I did not trust Duget and Quilichini. They did not look like drug addicts, and I actually never thought that they were. Nico, I could tell by her attitude and by her teeth—they were in pretty bad shape by then, which obviously is a sign of somebody who's done a lot of heroin."

A visit to the rented Notting Hill flat confirmed Sixx's suspicions. "Nico was very overweight and wearing three layers of clothes. I never saw her without a long dress/skirt and an overcoat. She covered herself up almost totally. She had dark hair at that time. I figured out that Duget was supplying the drugs. But at the point when we started working together, I didn't know how bad Duget was."

Not far into the project, more red flags started popping up for Sixx. The first was Duget's refusal to sign a contract with him. "She kept giving excuses," he recalls. Despite any misgivings, Sixx still booked a studio in south London so recording could start. "Quilichini started putting together the musicians he wanted," Sixx tells me. "I said that I would pay for everything. When they were recording, they'd go back to Paris every once in a while and then come back again. Recording was going well, and I was keeping on top of it. It was sounding really, really good. The songs Nico wrote were great and they were originals." However, though the basic components of the LP had been recorded, Sixx still had not received a signed contract from Duget.

"I made it totally clear that as long as I'm paying, this is my album," Sixx recalls. "She [Duget] kept going off to Paris…obviously my ears were up. I knew to be on the lookout; it's not the first time I'd been confronted with something like this. It's something you encounter in the music business over the years." One day, his worst fears were confirmed. "On a Saturday morning, the studio calls me and says, 'Hi, Aaron, we just want to give you a heads-up that Nadette called us yesterday to say she's coming over to London to pick up the tapes.' I said, 'What? All right, fine, you don't give anybody any tapes. I'm coming right down to pick them up.' So I went down to the studio and I picked up all the reel-to-reel tapes. Obviously you can figure out what they were trying to do...[inferring taking the tapes without signing the contract].

"At some point Nadette and I talked. 'What are you doing?' I said. She said, 'They're our tapes and we can do with them what we want, and we didn't sign the contract.' I said, 'Look, excuse me, but I paid for the studio and the musicians! They're my tapes, not yours.' So she says, 'Oh well, we're going to sue you!' I took the tapes and mixed that album."

Some accounts have said that Sixx paid off a studio engineer for the reels, then paid Nico to keep quiet—or a variation of these themes. He denies these claims. "The £2,000 sounds right to Nico, but not to the studio," he said of any advance paid. "The studio doesn't just let you go in for days and days [without paying]. I was paying them directly. If there was money exchanged, it may have been the last part of what was owed for the studio. For all the recordings, it was not £2,000."

The sleeve of Sixx's version of *Drama of Exile* is very dramatic. Pictured emerging from a London Tube station, dirty, graffitied walls behind her, Nico looks drained and haunted, draped in thick layers of black, indiscernible clothing. "I picked the album cover shot," says Sixx. "Giacomoni showed me a bunch of pictures of Nico. They were mostly the standard head shots, and I immediately said, 'That's the one we want.' So that's where it ended." Lawyers eventually got involved on both sides, with no clear resolution. "The end result is that it went back and forth."

Nico would still periodically contact Sixx, always looking for money. "'Aaron, I need some money' [*laughing*]. That was her opening line, not 'Hi, Aaron, how are you?' And I would say, 'Nico, stop this bullshit. You need to get away from Nadette.'" Sixx claims that the advance Nico was asking after had already been included in the fee paid to Duget for production costs and studio time. Yet it seemed Nico either didn't understand this or hadn't been informed by her "manager" of the arrangement. "From Nico's standpoint, that was an advance to her that she kept wanting to get," Sixx tells me. "At the end of the day, when I knew Nico her main interest in life was drugs. It wasn't music anymore or anything else. And that's why she was with Duget," he concludes.

Sixx deduced that the Duget/Quilichini version of *Drama* came from a few cassette copies of the sessions. Once back in Paris, Quilichini took the demos he had, re-recorded parts and combined them with a scattering of new material. This is why there are "two" *Drama* albums. "They stitched together the *Drama of Exile* album as their *Drama of Exile* album with a different cover. The cover of it has a black and white image of Nico in a cemetery with a big long over-coat," Sixx informs me. He was not happy about the advent of this alternative version. "I put a stop to that immediately. Technically, that was never, ever allowed to be released, but it's impossible to stop everything."

———

Sixx's account of the passing of Duget and Quilichini conflicts with Blum's story, but is equally tragic. "Duget and Quilichini were driving back to Paris on the motorway and had a head-on crash. Duget was killed outright immediately, and Quilichini died a day or so later. That put an end to Duget and Quilichini. They left the music business and the earth!"

IV: END

During all of the *Drama of Exile* tribulations, Nico was at her lowest point. Broke, addicted, and reliant on people awed by her celebrity status to provide her with drugs, a roof over her head and the basic necessities, the future appeared ever bleaker. "I think one of the reasons Nico ended up working in Britain so much was because she was very friendly with Neneh Cherry and her band Rip Rig + Panic," Phil Jones tells me over dim sum in Manchester. Jones was a Mancunian booking agent who worked with Alan Wise, managing and booking various bands. "Rip were based in Ladbroke Grove. Neneh helped get her into the Rough Trade booking agency, who in turn got her onto one of our nights at Rafters."

Located in the St. James Building on Oxford Street in Manchester, Rafters was a club that showcased new and cult artists. In 1981, it was run and promoted by Alan Wise, one of the music provoca-teurs responsible for championing some of the most iconic artists to come out of Manchester during the 1970s and '80s. "I think Alan is written out of the story," says Phil Rainford during our interview. At the time, Rainford was a face in the northern scene, having been the original singer for post-punk band and Factory Records sign-ing the Durutti Column. Rainford worked with Wise, eventually being hired by the promoter to do the sound and help out with any duties while Nico and her band were on tour. "Alan was one of the founders of the Manchester music scene. He was putting on gigs for people nobody had ever heard of way before Tony Wilson.[120] Wilson brought Alan in to help him. Without Alan, hardly any of this [the iconic 1980s/'90s Manchester music scene] would have happened," Rainford says. Aaron Sixx's memories of Wise are similar. "Alan was one of the guys who started Factory in Manchester. He was a rich, Jewish, Manchester boy, overweight and very nice. He always had a smile. He was very, very witty and got along with most people."

Wise cut a memorable figure, being larger than life in stature as well as personality, which helped make him both a catalyst for new music as well as a controversial figure within the community. "He was like your cartoon character of the big, myopic Jew," Rainford recalls. "He could be a real bully because he was big. He was six foot something and fat as well. He had a big physical presence and always looked forty-five from about the age of twenty. He was misogynistic—he was most of the horrible things you could think of," Rainford continues. "But he was also one of the most brilliant guys you've ever met. He was bitingly funny. A lot of people didn't like him and didn't like his humor. He and Tony got on quite well, but as far as the media was concerned, Al didn't fit into that suave and sophisticated thing that Tony was."

Though having already had a solo career for over a decade, Nico's name did not immediately ring a bell with Wise. "The Rough Trade agency had got in touch with Alan, saying, 'We've got an interesting cult artist called Nico.' Alan said, 'Who's he?'" says James Young. Young would later be drafted in by Wise to arrange and play keyboards for the singer. Promoter Nigel Bagley also remembers getting asked about the German singer. "We were booking artists for the Rafters nightclub in Manchester in 1981 when I got a call from an agency telling me that Nico was in a pub in London, was a mess and was borrowing money off everyone. The person said, 'You can book her, but I've no idea if she will turn up.' I'd had the Kevin Ayers, John Cale, Brian Eno and Nico *June 1, 1974* live album since I was twelve, which led me to *The Velvet Underground & Nico*, so it was a chance to put on my childhood heroine. I booked her for £200. Then the agency called back, asking, 'Can you get her some heroin?'" Jones remembers how "her arms were horrible," though he notes, "but otherwise she didn't look as if she'd been taking heroin for years."

Rainford was the one who was sent to retrieve the singer from the train station and bring her to the gig. "She had this chap in tow [Robert King]. She's got this harmonium thing with her; he's got an amp and a guitar. I picked them up from the station and took them to the hotel we had them in and then took her down to club." It was there that Wise first met Nico in the flesh. In *Nico: Icon*, he recounted, "I thought she was quite charming, the day I met her. She was walking down the steps of Rafters. I was walking out. She was traveling around just on her own with a guy called Robert. They had no money, no food, and she seemed a free spirit, looked a bit desperate. So that immediately attracted me. I liked her immediately. From the first second. And I did not even know who she was."

Everyone who was anyone in the Manchester scene turned up that night for the show. "At that first Rafters gig, New Order, Tony Wilson and the Factory Records lot were on the guest list," says Jones.

"I knew the Velvet Underground, but I didn't really know who she was," remembers Michael Wadada during our chat. He would eventually tour as a sound engineer for Nico. "I met her for the first time when she played in Manchester at Rafters. She just seemed kind of relaxed and easygoing at the time, but not wanting to engage with anybody. She was pretty washed out commercially. Nobody would book her."

Una Baines was familiar with the Velvet Underground through her bandmate, Mark E. Smith of the Fall. "I was about sixteen when I met Mark. He was into the Velvet Underground. I just loved them. It was love at first listen. I just thought the songs were so incredible. They had that dark and light thing. All the really strong, powerful stuff, like 'Heroin,' and then all these really delicate songs, like 'I'll

291

Be Your Mirror.' That is how I heard of Nico. We used to get all her solo albums. Just think, for English being her second language, she was such an amazing writer. Titles like 'Janitor of Lunacy'—what a title! Nobody sings like Nico. I was a totally smitten fan. I learned how to play all the tunes on the piano for lots of her songs."

Baines had a new band, Blue Orchids, which was being managed by Wise at the time Nico was booked to play Rafters. "We went into Rafters," says Baines, "and I will never forget the very first time I met her, because I was so nervous. She had very long auburn hair, and all we could see was the back of her head. She turned round and just kind of smiled at us. I'd only ever seen pictures of Nico the blonde model; obviously, this was a much older version. She just had this incredible face and these green eyes. I was in awe of her. You could see that face had lived a life."

Baines may have been one of the only people in the audience already familiar with Nico's solo work. "Nico was really down and out at the time," says Young. "She had no money; all she had was her harmonium. She had a really serious habit. Okay, she had a name, but it was not a name that would attract a huge following or audience. Because this was just after punk. It was the new wave time. People would reference Nico, but they wouldn't necessarily pay money to go and see her."

According to Jones, "Everybody had heard of her, but nobody knew what she did." He and Wise were immediately blown away once Nico began to perform. "Everybody went, 'Bloody hell!' Her singing 'The End' by the Doors was unbelievable, high drama. Then she did the flipping German national anthem, 'Deutschland, Deutschland über alles,' alone at the harmonium. We thought, 'Fucking hell, what's she going to do next?'" Nico then went on to perform some of the Velvets classics, Jones remembers. "She sang 'Femme Fatale,' 'All Tomorrow's Parties' and 'I'm Waiting for the Man.' Alan Wise was enthralled. She had nowhere to stay, and he said, 'We can't just let her go.'"

Phil Rainford has a more detailed account of what happened at the end of the first Rafters show. "I took them [Nico and King] back to the hotel. The next day, myself and Al went to take them back to the station. [King] was in the bathroom, and we were talking to Nico. She started crying. We were a pair of softies, going, 'What's the matter, Nico?' She said [*does impression of Nico*], 'I have nowhere to go. No money and nowhere to go. Nowhere to live in London.' It was like, 'Oh.' You don't expect this. The guy that was with her was a musician. Both heroin addicts. We couldn't afford to keep her in a hotel forever. We took her back to either Al's or another friend of ours who had a spare room. It became obvious within a couple of days that they were running out of heroin. I talked to Al about what we were going to do. By this time, Al was absolutely fascinated by Nico. He had become a bit obsessed. Al always fell in love with somebody within a day."

Rainford and Wise shuffled King onto a train back to London, then turned their attention to Nico. Her main priority was getting some heroin. She was in luck: at the time, Manchester had some of the highest-grade opiates in the world. "By this time, Nico'd moved into the spare room at Alan's," Rainford tells me. "He got a bit fed up with her and tried to dump her on me and my girlfriend. We had a really nice house at the time. My girlfriend was a middle class girl from Northern Ireland, quite Protestant and straight up really! After a few days of Nico being in the kitchen, jacking up heroin in her feet, my girlfriend said, 'I want her out of here!' Nico only lasted a few days. That was the end of her staying at mine. She went back to Al's. It was clear that we had to get her working so she could live."

Wise had a slightly different version of events. "I found her some-where to live, she'd been touring but she liked Manchester because of the Victorian architecture. Initially she was staying in a Polish hotel in Whalley Range (what do you get for your trouble and pain?), the Polex, owned by a war hero. It was very cheap, she didn't have much money. After that, she came to live in Didsbury with me, only briefly, then she moved to the other side of Manchester, a beautiful area called Prestwich Park (house was called Moresby), it was Victorian."

Rainford remembers, "She had no money, absolutely no money. She was about forty at the time, but she was a forty-year-old woman who was at the end of her career and at the end of her tether and didn't know what to do with herself and had no money whatsoever. Al decided it was his mission to resurrect Nico's career."

Nico's life, Wise thought, was "the past: Berlin, the war, what she'd done, modeling, why she didn't like it." Yet he also saw the complicated and often misunderstood woman underneath the years of mythology. "I spoke to Andrew Loog Oldham about her; he said that when they'd met, she'd been very 'Harvey Nichol's' [sic] meaning nice clothes, bright attire, fairly upbeat, what you might consider a 'Lightweight'; but her personality changed because of her opiate use. She got into that culture. Had she not got into opiates she may simply have been a lighthearted German Folk Singer, as 'I'm Not Sayin'' suggests. The heavy Marlene Dietrich stance came later. Oldham said her character wasn't like that at all. She could be moody, but I'd have said it was because of all the drugs she took over the years. Her mood altered every few seconds but she could talk and be charming and witty. She said what she did and got on with it. She was one of the last Left Bank Bohemians. She hadn't had a formal education in the sense that she hadn't gone to university, which she regretted and said was because of the war, she always read good books: Dostoyevsky, Solzhenitsyn, quality English writers. She liked being solitary but she'd also socialize. She wasn't a snob; she'd hang out at the local pool hall, strike up a conversation with a bum."

After years of Nico having no proper management, Wise appointed himself to the task. "She needed to perform to get money for drugs, and the next thing we knew, Wise had bamboozled her into letting us co-manage her," recalls Jones. "She didn't trust any-body, and she had no reason to because she had nobody looking after her affairs, which is why Wise was perfect for her. He put her life into some sort of order, gave her a base and gave her work. The only work she could do was sing gothic songs to a slightly bemused audience. We put her on our books and got her a lot of work, but she didn't fit in. Everyone wanted to hero-worship her. They were all in awe of her and a bit scared of her. I think a lot of people tried to 'woo' her."

The relationship between Nico and Wise was complicated. "He was absolutely besotted with her," says Young. "It was like a husband and wife, but with no sex! Which is possibly like a lot of husband–wife relationships! A lot of serious rows, a very highly emotional relationship. Not what a typical manager–artist relationship is. There'd be fights and screaming, all that! And at the same time the opposite. It was Alan who gave her the complete [works of] Oscar Wilde; it was Alan who would take her out on the moors to see beautiful bits of landscape and go driving up to the Lake District to see where Wordsworth lived and take her to Haworth, up to Brontë country. They had that. Both sides.

"It was very intense. Alan wanted a real relationship with her, but nothing ever happened. He said once that she said to him [*does impression of Nico*], 'Oh, why don't you just rape me?' Because he was staring at her in a lustful way, and she could read him. It was just a very, very intense relationship. But I think most of Alan's rela-tionships were; it didn't matter to him that they were highly emo-tional." Young continues, "She got the management she deserved in that kind of way…Alan, he wasn't a great visionary manager and he really didn't understand music, but he really saved Nico. He saved her life.

"They lived by constantly tearing at each other like a crazed married couple," he concludes. "At the same time, they were close friends. I would say that apart from Ari, Alan was closest to Nico. I was never that close to her; my relationship was more professional. I realized early on that getting close to Nico meant sharing a propensity for addiction. Alan was a Valium addict, and his father had a chain of pharmacies. He understood the chemistry of need, he could facilitate. He responded to people who were ill, whether physically or psychologically. He went under the sobriquet of 'Doctor' and took damaged people into his care."

David John Haskins, better known as David J, became aware of Nico through listening to the "banana" album. "The first time I heard the Velvet Underground would have been in 1973. David Bowie was talking about them being an influence. Then I went out and got the first Velvets album and just loved it to bits. It's a desert island disk for me. Top 5. It's timeless. I love the flavor that Nico brought to it, both musically and visually."

J's personal memories of Nico dovetail with her often-discussed combination of beauty and sadness. However, he also brings a humanity, a levity to the singer that has been ignored and over-looked. "I thought she was stunningly beautiful," he tells me during our chat. "I saw her in *La Dolce Vita*, the Fellini film. She looks very mysterious and very enigmatic to me. I was fascinated with her right from the start. Then, when she started to make her own solo albums, I was really into that. I loved the fact that she adopted the harmonium as her instrument of choice, because I think that was a perfect accompaniment. I saw her live in the late '70s. She was just solo with the harmonium. She ended the set with her version of the Doors" "The End," which was just so deep and beautiful. It was packed! Everyone was very respectful; it was a real listening audience. It needed to be because what she was doing was quietly intense.

"She was melancholic and wallowed in sadness. She once said [*does impression of Nico*], 'I am only happy when I am sad.' That's true, because she saw the beauty in melancholia. It's the Portuguese word *saudade*, which is this...there's no translation in English, but it means longing for that which is lost. It can be a person or a place or just a feeling. She's very much like that. I think that is very evident in her music and her persona. She has that feeling, that bittersweet...it's a nostalgia that's beyond nostalgia. It's a longing and a yearning, and it's sort of like a sweet ache. That sweet ache is in her music. It's something that I very much related to, and still do. There is a darkness to it, but there is light in there as well. I think she was a hypersensitive person. She was truly gothic in her presentation—beyond the obvious outer trappings of wearing black. It's a deeper sense, an old sense. Beyond fashion. The gravitas of the gothic is there. It's far too simplistic and reductive to simply say she was the 'Garbo of goth.'"

J went on to found one of the most influential post-punk bands, Bauhaus. The group is hailed as being one of the pioneers of gothic rock music, a genre rife with dark imagery and melancholic lyrics. The band's lead singer, Peter Murphy, had already met Nico, when she showed up during a recording session for their 1981 LP *Mask*. J recalls, "She'd previously met Peter; they exchanged numbers and he invited her to the session. He told her to come by any time as we were in London for two weeks of studio work. We [the rest of the band] weren't in on this. I think Peter was out of the room when the intercom buzzer buzzed. I'd just finished playing my bass part. The intercom comes on and went through into the studios on a speaker. We hear [*makes buzzing sound*], 'Hello, who is it?' [*does impression of Nico*] 'It is me, Nico.' We thought somebody was having a laugh. 'What? Who?' 'Nico. It is me.' Then Daniel [Ash, Bauhaus guitarist] goes, 'Yeah, and I'm fucking Lou Reed!' 'No, it is really me!' Pete came in then and said, 'Oh, it's Nico! Let her in.' We were like, 'What? It really is Nico?'

"She comes in with her black robes, clutching a bottle of mezcal, some limes and salt. She taught me how to drink mezcal; it was the first time I'd tasted it. I sat in the corner with her because I'd done my bit and the others were doing their overdubs. We were kind of snuggled up. I just got whisper-chatting with her. I loved this little smile that would play around her features; it was this sad, soft smile. We were just talking, and I thought I'd just float this boat out there, thinking she'll probably set it ablaze, this little paper boat, which was to ask her about the Velvet Underground. But she didn't; she engaged. I said, 'What was your favorite Velvet Underground song that you sang?' And she said, ' "I'll Be Your Mirror." ' She said she always loved that song, and she told me she didn't like 'Femme Fatale,' and I expressed my surprise. I said, 'Really? I love that song! You didn't like that?' [*does impression of Nico*] 'Well, I like the song but I don't like the way that Lou sings "*femme*." He sings "*fem*," "*fem*." I tell him, "Lou, no. It is [*pronouncing it correctly*] '*femme*.'" ' Then she says, 'But of course, he is stubborn and belligerent so he speaks still "*fem*." Ruined it for me.' "

J is on the whole very respectful of Nico, yet even he makes a point about her appearance. "She looked somewhat haggard, but she still had a beauty. It was poignant because she was so stunning, but obviously needle-damaged. I remember when I was sitting next to her in the studio, I smelled this aroma. She wore this very heavy, heady, pungent perfume that was intoxicating, but underneath that was this weird chemical smell that comes from the drugs. That was disturbing."

Nico joined Bauhaus to perform a version of "Waiting for the Man" several times during the following months. One of these performances, at Fagin's in Manchester on October 23, 1981, was recorded. J remembers the first time this collaboration happened was at none other than Rafters in Manchester. "When we did that first gig in Manchester, she was there because Alan Wise was her manager. He was also the promoter for our show, and she was with him, just watching us soundcheck. She approached us when we finished and requested that we do a song with her. She said we could do a Velvet Underground song. 'What do you think, boys?'

We said, 'Yeah, great!' She went into our dressing room on her own. The security guy said, 'That woman's in there. I think she's doing some drugs or something, sticking a needle in her bum.' Apparently, she was shooting up in there. She came out, and he was laughing. He didn't know who she was. He was this big black guy with a thick Mancunian accent. I felt sad for her that she still was an addict to that degree. I felt sad that this guy was laughing at her and there was no appreciation of the artist that she was.

"Daniel and I went back to the hotel. I remember we worked out 'Waiting for the Man' by sticking our guitars into the sink to amplify them in the hotel room. We just worked it out there and then. We didn't rehearse it with her at all; we just did it. They did it as a duet, Peter and Nico. She loved it, and then she wanted us to be her permanent live band afterward and go on tour. She said [*does impression of Nico*], 'Can you boys be my band? Play live all over Europe? Be great.' We actually considered it for about twenty minutes and then decided no, this is crazy. We'd got our own thing going on, so, 'We can't do that, Nico. Sorry. Sorry, love.' But then she turned up again and we did another show. That was in Salford, just outside of Manchester. That was a better version of 'Waiting for the Man,' but it wasn't the one that was recorded and released on a record. That was the first time [in Manchester]. Somebody just recorded it on a cassette player in the audience."

Nico also regaled the young bassist with stories of paramours past. "She once gave me a list of her ex-lovers; it was very funny. We were in a hotel bar after we played with her the first time in Manchester. I was sitting with her having a drink. She had a crush on Peter Murphy. He was over on the other side of the room, and she was looking at him adoringly. She said [*does impression of Nico*], 'Peter is a very beautiful boy.' I said, 'Yeah, yeah.' She then said [*does impression of Nico*], 'I have known many beautiful men. I've had many lovers.' She started to go through this list [*does impression of Nico*]: 'Bob Dylan, Lou Reed, Jim Morrison.' It went on and on. [*does impression of Nico*] 'I have loved and lost. Peter, he is very beautiful boy.'"[121]

J argues that Nico's artistry has often been overshadowed by the men in her life and her problems with drugs. "The lasting legacy is her music. It's stripped down to the essence of the emotion that she is conveying. It's bare bones, and it's so minimalist and immediate. She's totally unique. What is really key as well is when she was born and the shadow of World War II that loomed over her, and she was very aware of that. The Nazis and all of that. Berlin. She's a product of her time, but a very singular personality who is being influenced by that time in history and commentating on it in her own creative way. She's seeing it through a very singular lens. It's a very acute observation. We are precariously seeing that world, and I feel privileged to have seen that, and we can still do it by listening to her music."

38

Once he had her settled in Manchester, Alan Wise quickly began straightening out Nico's business affairs, which were a tangled mess after more than a decade of disregard. One of his first tasks was to go through her various contracts and record deals, chasing money and royalties on behalf of the singer. Aaron Sixx remembers when the new manager started taking control of Nico's affairs. "Alan gave me a call to say that he was looking after Nico. I obviously told him what the story was with Duget holding things up, and I said that I need Nico to sign off on the contract. Without that, I'm wasn't going to do anything! So he said, 'Leave it with me and I'll do it.' She signed off the original contract, and she signed over the publishing to the songs on the album to me." Now under Wise's care, Nico's sporadic calls to Sixx asking for money dwindled. When business needed to be discussed, it was Wise, not Nico, picking up the phone. "I would speak to Alan, not Nico," says Sixx. Wise also began to book shows and look for a band for Nico, using his relationships within the local artistic community to move things along quickly. "We hooked her up with musicians, and Manchester was her home for years," remembers Phil Jones. Indeed, Nico did live in the city for over seven years, on and off, one of the longest (almost) continuous stays she ever had in a single place.

———

Nico's usual routine was not what one would expect of an internationally known former model and icon. Her days were often spent in bed, shooting up, or trying to score drugs. Her haunts included local pool halls and pubs, and she could be seen riding her bike around the neighborhood. James Young has argued in interviews that this "period of perceived disintegration was not necessarily all sordid demise and the destruction of a talent but instead an extension of Nico's redefined personality. She took pride in her graying hair, sagging skin, and needle-marked arms because they were the antithesis to everything she had once been told she was wonderful for." "She was a very modest person as well," recalls Barbara Wilkin. Wilkin got to know Nico well during the singer's time in Manchester. She eventually had a major role in the singer's life, acting as a friend, de facto tour manager, and confidante. Now a yoga teacher, Wilkin emanated a calm, soothing beauty as she welcomed me into her home to talk about Nico. Her first meeting with the singer occurred by happenstance. "I lived in Holland at the time. A friend who was a journalist came round one day. He said, 'I'm going to a concert. I'm going to see Christa Päffgen. Do you want to come with?' I thought, 'Who is this woman?' I went with him. He and a friend wanted to interview Nico after the concert. Blue Orchid was the support act. I was interested in drumming, so I was watching the drummer all the way through the first act, and then when they came out again with Nico.

"After the concert, my friends disappeared to do the interview. Suddenly, the drummer [from Blue Orchids] was next to me. He said, 'Why [must you only] look at me like this? I dropped my sticks! You made me all nervous!' That was how I met Toby Toman.[122] I was with him for four and a half years, eventually moving to England to be with him. Anyway, back to Nico: my friends couldn't find her. They were going around the hotel, but Nico was in the dressing room. I was the only one left there. Everybody had gone, so Toby said, 'Come into the dressing room.' That's when I first met Nico.

"I found her very scary. She was just sitting at the end of a table. Toby said that I was German, and she just looked me. She didn't look at anybody else. I went, 'Mmm,' and looked away. Then she says in German, in a deep voice, '*Du brauchst doch keine Angst vor mir zu haben. Ich bin eine alte Frau.*' That means, 'You don't have to be scared of me. I am an old woman.' I didn't know what to say. She took an interest in me because of the German aspect. She wanted to speak German so we could secretly talk about everybody around us. She didn't like very bubbly, pretty girls going around [*makes bubbly, pretty-girl sounds*]. I think she liked me because I was quiet. I didn't talk a lot and I can listen. I always was just around as Toby's girlfriend to start off with.

"She didn't expect much luxury. She wasn't a diva...she was one of us. She did her concerts. Sometimes she wasn't very well, and she had to do them anyway. But the show must go on, and she was very professional."

Manchester-raised artist Stella Grundy was just sixteen when she saw Nico perform at the Manchester Library, a set that was "beautiful, powerful, and dark," in a room "thick with cigarette and marijuana smoke." She tells me over a drink at the Dry Bar in Manchester about how it was a transformative experience for her as a teenager. "I was enraptured. From that night on I decided I wanted to be an artist, writer, singer—anything to be part of this world." Grundy also recalls Nico's regular appearances at nearby watering holes. "She didn't like fans of the Velvet Underground mithering her about those times, although she was happy to write messages and autographs for people when asked. I've been shown a few of these items. Some people were unkind to her and took advantage, though." Grundy saw this up close as her boyfriend at the time even went backstage and stole Nico's heroin needles, as some sort of cultural memento from the "queen of the junkies." She even recalls being told that "someone had stolen her diary."

A young Steven Morrissey was also greatly impacted by the

presence nearby of the legendary singer. "I was enormously comforted by her isolation and depression," recounted the Smiths' lead singer. "She lived nearby and [could] often be seen whirling about glamourous Manchester in a long black cape humming [*Desertshore*'s] 'Le Petit Chevalier.'" His close friend, artist Linder Sterling, lived in the flat above Nico at one point during the singer's time in Manchester and has clear memories of Nico starting her "morning" in early afternoon with "a tumbler half-filled with brandy." Before moving out, Nico gave Sterling a key piece of performance advice: "When you sing a high note, you should imagine it falling to the floor and all low notes rising up."

New bands especially were reverential toward the singer. "We realized what an icon she was later when we put her on in London and Siouxsie [Sioux], Duran Duran, and all these film stars turned up," recalls Phil Jones. Una Baines remembers Nico's appearance in Manchester as being exciting for the young artistic scene that was emerging. "I think a lot of the people who actually worked with her were fans. They were Velvet Underground fans, at least. Nico was an important figure in music history. I think there was a lot of respect for her." These new converts were especially significant, as Nico felt abandoned by her old friends and paramours. "She used to say all the time, 'They've all left me, they won't ring me back.' But why would you?" Jones wonders. "She was a bit of a leech and didn't have any regard for herself. The only one who did was John Cale. Lou Reed (to my knowledge) never got back to her. Maybe once…[Paul] Morrissey did occasionally. She knew how good it was to name-drop, but she wanted to name-drop more Buzzcocks and New Order in those days. She'd cottoned on that those were the new kids. She liked the fact that all this was going on in Manchester and she could be a bit of a godmother. She liked the fact that she was a bit of celeb and people were a bit in awe of her—Tony Wilson called her 'ma'am'—but she also really liked normality," Jones continues. "On Sunday nights, we would go to the Kwok Man in Chinatown for a Chinese meal. Alan took her to meet his family at Christmas. She liked the pubs in Prestwich, where she could play pool and be anonymous."

Barbara Wilkin agrees. "She met a few people because of Alan, who would introduce them, but it wasn't like the New York scene for her when she was younger. She was in her forties when she was here. She did a few gigs, small gigs. People came to see her and talk to her. Obviously, she would take note of 'This is so-and-so.' She didn't really socialize in the scene, the music scene." It seemed incredible to music fans that the former chanteuse of a legendary New York band was living in their city. "I saw her being searched by police in the Spinners Arms—a then-notorious pub in Hulme," said fan Richard Hector-Jones. "My friend whispered: 'That's Nico,' and I was thinking: 'What the fuck is a star from the Velvet Underground doing in this shithole?'"

The combination of respect and an ability to blend in with the crowd was also alluring to Nico. "People just accept you for who you are rather than what you are," says Young about the city's scene. "I think she felt more relaxed there because of that. She could go to the pub and shoot a bit of pool. She liked to do that, and it'd just be her, not like, 'I've been playing pool with Nico!' It wasn't that. There's much more of a Nico thing now than there was then. Thirty years ago, it was quieter, she was a minor artist. She was no big deal." However, the almost inevitable talk about 1960s New York had become annoying. Young recalls most people wanting to hear her stories from the Velvet days, with no interest in what the singer had done as a solo artist. "If they [people approaching her or at interviews] just wanted to talk about Andy Warhol, the Velvet Underground...I think she sort of accepted it. That was okay at first. But if people didn't want to talk about *The Marble Index* or *Desertshore* or what she's doing now or a concert that evening, then that would really piss her off, understandably. That [the 1960s scene in NYC] was twenty years back for her! It's like

306

they expected her to be frozen in time. People would bring up the past constantly."

"Spider" Mike King had just moved back to Manchester after a stint in London when he got the call from Alan Wise. "I'd always been a fan of the Velvet Underground," the guitar player tells me one autumn afternoon over some pints in a Manchester pub. "When I was nineteen, I had my first acid trip. We just listened to the *Velvet Underground & Nico* album all the way through for hours—put it on again, put it on again, put it on again... So I was really nervous when Al asked me to do a few gigs in England with her.

"I was very nervous when I met her. She was not too aloof but was interested to know if I could hack it; this was kind of like an audition as much as anything. I played a few tunes—'All Tomorrow's Parties' and a couple of others—and got this sign, a nod of approval: 'Yeah, yeah, he'll do.' I was in for the English gigs. She was very charismatic, though not chatty. She was a doyenne of rock nobility to me. I had a great deal of respect for her. I was a bit in awe."

Openly and repeatedly doling out admiration for his friend, King's experience of working with Nico contradicts other accusations of her being an unskilled artist. "When I was doing the solo gig with her, it struck me how fantastically unique her timing was on her vocals. She had her own unique voice and her own way of how to deliver and project. She would draw in the audience with the way she delivered her song. Her timing was very interesting because if I was playing the guitar with her, I would have to follow her voice—it's not like you could just play the song in a regular way, bar to bar, strict timing. Every time I played it, I had to vary it, to follow her voice, because her voice changed the timing according to the mood that she was in, however she felt she wanted to project her voice on that particular night.

"She had this mystique about her which people found very alluring and very attractive. You read that she was a bit of a 'naive' artist. Absolute bollocks. She knew exactly what she was doing. I never heard her hit a wrong note, though she could be a bit dodgy when she'd had a drink; it wasn't good when she'd had a drink. Her poison of choice was wine.

"She was great. I loved her loads. And she had a great pair of pins."

Graham Dowdall was new to the Manchester scene when he started playing drums with Nico, a transplant from the capital. He was happy to have escaped London for the more collaborative northern scene. An abundance of disused industrial buildings meant cheap rehearsal spaces, making it an ideal place for aspiring musicians to incubate.

Dowdall relates to me over the phone his initial encounter with Nico. "I went up to a rehearsal at one of the most grottiest places you can ever imagine, on a very new road in north Manchester. Nico was there, looking pretty scary. The microphone didn't work, so Nico, being the trooper that she was, sang in the first rehearsal with no mic. As soon as she opened her mouth, every hair on my body stood on end and I thought, 'Yes, I'm having this!' Her singing voice was just so powerful. That was me joining."

Led by Wise, the Manchester community provided Nico with a security and stability that she had not experienced in a long time, if ever. The artistic scene and the history of the city were a perfect fit for the last bohemian. "I think she was aware that there was a scene—Joy Division, dark music—or maybe she just liked the cheap heroin," said Martin Bramah, the guitarist for Blue Orchids. "But she didn't see the grubby, industrial city I grew up in. She'd gaze at the Victorian architecture and say: 'This is so romantic.'"

39

James Young was a handsome, fair-haired scholar, about to start his Master of Philosophy degree at Jesus College, Oxford University,[123] in November 1981, when he received two unexpected visitors who would change the course of his life. "There was a knock at my door and I opened it and there was my old friend Alan Wise and a German lady with him." Young did not recognize the singer. "Big woman...strange eyes. And he [Wise] introduced me and said, 'This is Nico. A friend of mine.' The name rang a bell...but didn't, you know..." She looked very different to the blonde visage Young was familiar with from the 1960s. "Nico, yeah. I'd heard the Velvet Underground, of course: 'All Tomorrow's Parties.' This Nico was different. She was not the beautiful blonde in front of the Velvet Underground; she had dark brown hair, she looked kind of tired and a little bit unhappy. Straight away she wanted to use the bathroom. I had no idea what was going on and she was a very long time in there."

Young became concerned when his guest did not emerge from the loo for over half an hour. "I said, 'What's going on?' and my friend said, 'This is NICO...you know, from the Velvet Underground.' 'Ah, right!' It all made sense then. Then I knew why she was in the toilet for so long. After some time she reappeared, looking a lot better, looking fresher," Young said. "She'd colonized the bathroom and then the next thing she wanted to do was take over my kitchen. She carried this saddle bag with her and she'd produced a bag of dried lentils. She then proceeded to give me instructions on how to make good lentil soup. I remember her being quite cross that I didn't have the right spices. She made her lentil soup and that was a good lesson. And then in her typical Nico way, she took over my life." As Young later said, "It was the end of my academic life and into something else. Into a time tunnel, from which I never emerged."

Young found himself drafted by Wise into being Nico's pianist, and eventually her arranger. The well-mannered academic became part of the motley crew making up Nico's backing band, a group he described as consisting of "a swing jazz bebop drummer, a kind of a guitar hero playing Pete Townshend, leaping around...a smacked-out bass player, and a college boy playing piano [describing himself]." Yet in Young, Nico found both a creative collaborator and an accidental biographer. "You did have to force her to be creative, but she could do it," says Phil Rainford. "She would pull it out of the bag, but Jim [Young] did most of the music. That's when Jim would come in. Jim would write nearly all the music for the stuff and never got credited, which was a rip-off." In 1992, Young wrote a memoir of his years working with the singer, the by turns hilarious, snarky and sad *Songs They Never Play on the Radio*. In *Nico: Icon*, he confides, "[I decided to write the book about Nico] for money. And I wanted to celebrate an aspect of my life and other people's lives that [doesn't] normally get much attention in rock literature: Failure."

———

In Manchester, Nico began to open up and develop real relationships. "The thing about myths and about mythologizing people is that actually you don't get the real person behind it," says Rainford. "You don't get that very sad, broken, lonely woman that we first met. We did grow to really love her and feel protective of her. She was just a human like anybody else. She had all the failings of everybody, like you and I have. People forget that. She found within Manchester people that did care about her and were friends with her. I don't

310

know if she actually ever had friends before, to be truthful."

Having authentic relationships did not come easily to Nico. "There was a sense of a really solid identity of 'I'm Nico,'" says Young. "Whoever this personality was, whether it was Christa or Nico or whoever the fuck it was, it was that sense of self-assuredness. She's not pretending to be somebody else; she's not trying to blend with other people. You accept her, that's why most people felt uncomfortable with her, or guys were afraid of her, because she would not adapt. Her identity was very secure. Which also made it hard for her to make friends."

Phil Jones describes Nico as being "very funny... You could have a real laugh with Nico because she got jokes and used to love people telling her proper jokes," he notes. "She often didn't get them straight away, though. She used to like English sarcasm."

Nico did not have many possessions; she never even had copies of her own records. Everything she owned fitted into a large holdall. "She had few clothes," recounts Rainford. "You know how women have huge handbags so you could go live abroad for a year? Well, she had one of them. This handbag had its own eco-culture in it. It was so big and had so much stuff in it. She had not much more than the clothes on her back and whatever was in this handbag and the harmonium. She didn't have a wardrobe or a suitcase. In the few places that I've seen where she's lived, she didn't have dresses or a rack of clothes." "Everything was in a big leather holdall—her whole world," Spider Mike King concurs.

While Rainford was shocked by such minimalism, he quickly learned that such an existence was not new for the singer. "As I got to know her over the years, I began to realize she'd lived like that for a very long time. After the war, she described to me how they lived in one room in the basement of a bombed-out house, as everybody in Germany was doing at the time. She was a really successful model in her younger years, and they just moved from one place to the next doing the catwalk shows, staying in hotels.

I think that's what she was used to. She wasn't materialistic in the sense that she liked a lot of possessions or anything. She was very happy in one room. She very rarely came out of the room.

"She used to have a couple of silk scarves, and whatever room she went into—whether it be in a hotel or at mine or at Al's—she'd put one of these scarves over the lamp and light a few candles. She was very happy watching telly. She liked cartoons: *Bugs Bunny* and things like that. Mine and her favorite were the coyote one, *Road Runner*! We used to sit giggling at that. She also liked a show called *Your Life in Their Hands*, where they would actually film a surgeon doing a live operation. They'd do things like lung transplants or heart transplants or operations to remove a cancerous ball from somebody's stomach. We were both quite fascinated by it. We would watch that, usually in her room or in my room, depending on where we were."

For the most part, Nico liked to stay at home when not performing. "You had to force her to go and socialize," says Rainford. "Once she got out there, she would sit in the corner of the room and hold court. I used to think, 'Is she really dumb, or does she just not say very much?' She wasn't dumb, obviously, because she could speak lots of languages. You wouldn't have her on a chat show as the entertainment. I think she just wasn't that socially adept. It's quite often a thing: you hear of somebody being enigmatic; actually, when you meet them, they're just quite boring, nothing to say. With Nico, I quite liked the silence. We could just sit there having fags and a beer and not say anything. I quite liked it; as much as I'm a talker, I also quite like sitting with somebody and being silent."

Phil Jones, who attended the opening of legendary Manchester nightclub the Hacienda with Nico in May 1982, recalls a similar homebody. "We went to her house, and it stank of the patchouli oil she used to wear and all the incense she would burn. She was always in bed. It would always take ages to get her out of places. If we were going somewhere for a night out, she'd be up and ready; but if we were going to get her for a gig, she'd still be in bed whether it was 7:30 a.m. or 5:30 p.m. She didn't walk around town. Wise used to drive her everywhere."

Though she had been both a sex symbol and a fashion icon two decades earlier, Jones saw no evidence of either during Nico's time in Manchester. "She never wore heels, always those flat biker boots. I never saw her in anything else. She was almost six feet tall, but she was broad from the top. She always wore big clothes, never let any of her femininity out. She was very unfeminine." Young concurs, saying, "She was almost proud that her teeth were rotten, her hair was gray. Her skin was bad; she had needle tracks all over. I mean, she liked that...it was her aesthetic." Her fellow former Factory Superstar Mary Woronov even wrote in her autobiography that she was "shocked to see Nico's teeth were rotting away" when the actress went to the singer's gig at the Whisky a Go Go in Los Angeles.[124]

Manchester friends and colleagues sensed that Nico was tired of her looks being her most talked-about attribute, yet she did not see herself as any sort of trailblazer. "I don't think she'd have labeled herself a feminist because she hated any form of ideology," says Una Baines. "She did say her only regret was not being born a man. I think she wanted the same privileges and power that men have. She felt people were only interested in her looks. She wanted something more substantial. She wrote songs in her second language. She was fluent in seven. The song 'No One Was There' was about [U.S. President Richard] Nixon. It's superbly written. She is still not appreciated for her talent." Young agrees, saying, "She concluded that taking heroin and wearing black clothes was a renunciation of the world, almost like a nun would do, so she could concentrate on being an artist. Black on black, motorcycle boots, pre-goth, badass."

Though having had relationships with some of the biggest icons of the twentieth century, during the 1980s Nico did not partake in romantic affairs for the most part. "She was not a sexual being," Young says. "Certainly, I hear stories about when she knew Iggy and those times, but she was very prudish with us. She was quite disapproving of sexy talk. She would tut us when she thought we were being inappropriate. Fucking hell, there she is shooting up and she's telling me! Boys' talk—she didn't like that kind of thing. Then she would suddenly come out with these things. It would suddenly pop out, and there'd be silence in the van. [*does impression of Nico*] 'You know I prefer it the Turkish way [anal sex].'"

Spider Mike shares similar memories. "All the time I knew her, I only ever saw her with one man," he recalls. "It was on the American tour, with a roadie that we had from New York. He was recovering from a heroin addiction. He had a sponsor or a mentor. All the time we were on the road, he was making phone calls back to New York to this person, because he was trying to keep off heroin. But Nico got her claws into him, straightaway.

"By the time we hit San Francisco, which was about a week after the tour started, he was sharing her bed. And she got him back onto the junk as well. She was mercenary in a lot of respects, and that mercenary aspect of her was part of her survival instinct. She'd pick and choose who she wanted to be with and where she wanted to go. And she lived that kind of free bohemian life. I've never seen her in a relationship with anybody, except that one-off," Spider says. "She isolated herself, cocooned herself within herself. She wasn't extroverted, she wasn't making friends easily, but she chose who her friends would be very carefully. It was partially her natural personality, partially the heroin—and it was a nightmare if she couldn't get heroin."

Scoring heroin, by any means possible, was a top priority. The mood on the road depended entirely on whether Nico had been able to use that day. Always having the drug on hand became of paramount importance. "We got a certain amount of heroin into the States in the harmonium," Spider Mike tells me. "It ran out about halfway through [the tour]. It was a nightmare, trying to get her stuff, total drama. If she had her scag, she was fine. She actually believed it kept her younger. I don't know if she ever ate. She'd perform great—fantastic, charismatic performer. She was fine with heroin, absolutely fine. But if she didn't get her heroin, she'd start drinking; if she was drinking, she was absolutely useless when she got on stage."

Alcohol caused many problems at the shows, from lyrics being sang incorrectly to Nico's ever-escalating erratic behavior. "She'd forget the words, she'd be staggering around, her eyes would be bloodshot—it was the worst thing," Spider Mike recalls. The entourage would do anything to prevent this happening, as Nico drunk was horrible to behold. "Everybody would be mad-panicking to try and score some scag, because we knew what the alternative was going to be. It was best if she junked up [*chuckles*]. But she was never really high, just maintaining, and she never looked like she was high."

Nico's ability to use great quantities of opiates without them seeming to have any outward effect on her shocked the guitarist. "In the afternoon before we played the Naples gig, we went for a soundcheck," says Spider Mike. "There were two junkies in the band besides Nico. There were compartments at the back of the stage—cubicles that were curtained off, makeshift little dressing rooms—and they were sat in one of these cubicles. I looked in. On this little table in front of the mirror I saw an English newspaper. I thought, 'Oh, great!' They screamed, 'Aaaagh—what yer doin?' Inadvertently, I'd picked up the newspaper upon which they'd put the heroin that they'd just bought on the streets of Naples! I was, 'Oh, sorry, mate...sorry about that.' They're scraping around on the floor, trying to get whatever bits they could recover. About an hour later, one of them was in the emergency ward of the Naples hospital, fighting for his life because this junk that they'd bought was fucking shit. If they'd had more of that junk, they'd both be dead. But they got some for Nico, and she was fine! Her tolerance was astounding."

Blue Orchids guitarist Martin Bramah highlighted some of the challenges of traveling with Nico, as tours often revolved around scoring drugs for the singer. "When we were on the road, there was a lot of waiting around unsavory parts of town—she would post letters full of heroin to herself at the next hotel—whereas in Manchester, she had a dealer."

Rainford also has stories of sketchy characters and heroin being delivered via the mail. "I'd been thrown in the deep end. I'd never done any sound before in my life. Driver-cum-soundman. We used to have this guy [whom Wise had found] called Baggers. We were doing a tour of Europe, and I'm going to Al, 'What are we going to do about the heroin?' 'Don't worry,' say Al and Baggers. 'We're just posting it to the hotel, there'll be some stuff there.' Sure enough, that worked for a few of the gigs. Then we got to Scandinavia. We got to this hotel and there was no heroin. No letters. The guy on the reception said, 'No, it has arrived,' and he was blackmailing us. Baggers paid him some money to get the heroin, but then the guy said, 'No, I've sold it.' One of the things I've always admired about Nico is that even when she was really sick because she'd run out of heroin, she still went on and did the gig. They weren't great shows, but she went on and did it."

Even though Una Baines respected and admired Nico, the drugs were ultimately one of the reasons the Orchids decided to stop working with her. "We had an experience going through customs after a tour of Holland. Nico OD'd, and they radioed ahead and searched everybody, with sniffer dogs and everything. All me and Martin [Bramah] had was a bit of grass in a pipe, which we threw in the sea before we got back! We knew where she kept her syringes—in her Marlboro packet. We didn't know where she'd hid her drugs, but . . . She was as cool as a cucumber. They didn't find anything, and when we got through, we went to the nearest pub, and Nico said [*adopts a deep German voice*], 'Did you see how I hypnotized the dog?' They searched her clothes and everything and they couldn't find anything. She's seasoned—she's gone through this many times before. I thought, 'I can't go through this, I've got a baby at home.'"

Despite these issues, Nico would always ultimately deliver what was needed. "She'd write bits of poems on a fag packet and stuff like that," recalls Phil Rainford. "She would come up with them in the end, with what were really quite deep and profound lyrics. She was really soaked in mid-European mythology. A lot of her lyrics were things she read as a child or as a teenager in Germany. Quite often these deep and meaningful lyrics, or deep and translatable lyrics, were based on the myths of Germany. The myths of mid-Europe."

———

After making many movies with Philippe Garrel, sometime in 1982 Nico decided to work with another director. It is unclear if there was a specific incident that caused a rupture between Garrel or Nico, or if the opportunity to do a film with someone else just came along. Either way, Nico being in a movie made by anyone else but Garrel created a definitive break between her and the filmmaker, after more than a decade of on and off co-habitation, collaboration, and shared addiction. The new project was as esoteric as any Garrel film, the new director—the Spaniard Joaquín Lledó—as art-house-friendly as her previous collaborators. The resulting sixty-five-minute-long drama, *La Vraie Histoire de Gérard Lechômeur* ("The True Story of Gérard Lechômeur"), reunited Nico with her *Inner Scar* co-star Pierre Clémenti. The vague plot outline revolves around workers being hanged during a strike at a steel mill. Nico is cast as the heroine, an "ideal anarchist." Another lighthearted rom-com it was not.

40

Manchester proved to be an ideal home base for Nico. She had management, friends, and a place to stay. "Alan Wise did a pretty good job—the band played to packed audiences," says her friend and former lover Lutz Graf-Ulbrich, "though she wrote in her diary that she'd much prefer to play at the opera house for an opera audience, instead of all these punk clubs." Phil Jones asserts that the lack of recognition was an ongoing vexation for the singer. "She understood she was doing something very different, and that was her frustration. When she sounded her best was with the Blue Orchids. She could get that 'Velvet-y' thing which pleased the punters, and then she could do all her dramatic bits at the end," he notes.

Una Baines recalls, "We'd become her backing band and also opened for her, so we did two sets. I loved it. I think she realized I was a bit of a fan. She used to let me soundcheck her keyboard, which I just took as a fucking amazing honor! She was very disciplined, she always did a really professional performance. The clichés about her aren't fair. I think because she was a woman and she was so beautiful, the fact she took heroin is the focus, not her music." Baines says that Nico's shows were always done "to a very high standard. When she got a new band, she had to teach all of the material to everybody. That's hard work, doing that." One time, Blue Orchids' drummer Toby experienced Nico's tutorials firsthand. "She didn't really suffer fools very gladly," says Baines. "We were working on the song 'Vegas.' The drums are so complicated, and she really put Toby through his paces to get it right."

Baines sees a great disparity between a woman whom she describes as a consummate performer and the drug-addled mess portrayed by the press. "When it come to the music, she was really kind of strict," Baines asserts. "You really had to do it exactly how she wanted it to be done. She had pride in her work, and that never wavered. She was very, very professional."

Though Baines and others found a connection with Nico through music, this could only go so far, as drugs seemed to form the core of Nico's life. "To become emotionally close with Nico you would have to share something with her," James Young said. "That was usually a form of addiction. She lived in a dream world, you know—and it's not just because of the opiate. She did live in a different dimension. It all went back to her violent childhood. She couldn't move on from the shock of being brought up in Nazi Germany. That experience closed her up emotionally."

Having met Nico on the day the Orchids performed with her at a club called Scamp's Disco in Oxford, Young quickly found himself enjoying the same turbulent touring life. He had never been on tour with a rock band, let alone a group composed of several drug addicts. It was a shocking experience for the young pianist. "I had no real understanding of what went on in that kind of world," Young said. "I was a library creature, I was a bookworm. So suddenly seeing people shooting up in the van with the needles stuck in their ass... The guys were drinking and driving and doing all these taboo things, things that are forbidden, illegal, and dangerous. Nico would sit there, kind of chain-smoking Marlboros, occasionally she'd have a shot. So the van was just kind of a bog of everyone smoking, of everyone smoking hashish, the smell of heroin cooking. It was just this incredible toxic stew. I tried to open a window once, and Nico said [*does impression of Nico*], 'Are you some kind of fresh air freak?' She could take over any situation. You know, she was an alpha female. She didn't like other women around, she only liked really the company of men. She liked to dominate and get her way, and I guess we all accepted that. The only way we could survive Nico's absolute self-absorption and selfishness was through humor and absurdity."

Sound engineer Michael Wadada describes the shows themselves as "really amazing" yet often riddled with problems, as the group played in cities and countries that did not put on many, if any, rock shows. "Her gigs were very unusual," he recalls. "For instance, the one in Czechoslovakia, we had to get into the town center in Prague and look for a red car [with the organizers in it] because it was illegal to do gigs. We couldn't find it. Alan Wise just said, 'Come on, we'll just check into the big hotel here and wait while they find us.' They eventually contacted us and then took us at the time of the gig to the place. It was some kind of college. We got there and everybody was sitting, waiting. There was nothing there. We had just arrived and had to set up in front of them. I was asking, 'Where is the PA?' and somebody pointed to something that looked like a home stereo. They were just patiently sitting there. They loved it. We were doing something that was very dangerous. In fact, after the show we were told that the police had found out and were hitting the guy who had put it on."

Responsible for sound on the tour, Wadada often found himself battling Nico's dual use of the harmonium. "She used to use it as an ashtray. It was always squeaking. She'd sometimes put an ashtray on top of it, and other times when it wasn't there she'd just do it directly into the harmonium. It was always, 'These notes aren't working!' and then I'd brush all this cigarette ash out of it, because harmoniums are very mechanical." The instrument was equally troublesome for Phil Rainford. "This squeaky old harmonium leaked all the time, so mic'ing it up was a real problem. She'd be pumping this thing, going [*hums a tune*], and you'd just be hearing [*makes whooshing air sound*]. The air! It was old, so all the air would be leaking out, making it really hard to amplify."

It was sometimes a challenge separating the substance abuse from the talented individual. "Could I trust Nico? Ultimately, no. And if that sounds hard, well that's how it is, because heroin addiction or alcoholism reduce your needs to a very simple thing," said James Young. "It's kind of like a religious conversion. Could I have trusted Nico artistically? Yes, absolutely. Nico, the pure artist, was deeply inspiring. When I first went on tour with her, I would stand at the side of the stage, because she used to do a twenty-minute solo spot—just her and the harmonium. I'd watch from the wings of the stage and I just remember thinking: 'Yeah, I get it. I absolutely get this.' Because it was something unique."

Between episodes of debauchery and madness, a softer side of Nico sometimes emerged. One such memorable event happened during Young's very first tour with the singer. "The van was parked near a tree with some blossoms on it. She picked these blossoms off the tree, I think it was forsythia or something: long, slender, thin branches with these little yellow blossoms all the way along. She broke these off and stuck them all around the interior of the van. I thought, 'This is rather nice! Who knew?' I'd rehearsed with her for a month and she had only shown me the darker side. Then suddenly she's putting all these blossoms around the van. What a lovely thing! It was just a contradiction of who I'd seen her to be. I liked that, the fact that she could surprise me."

Despite the constant touring, Nico still found herself with very little money. "We were very poor, all the money was spent on drugs," recalls Ari. "I remember that miserable Christmas in London in 1981. My mother was on tour." Una Baines met Ari during this time. "We went to London and we stayed at this very ostentatious flat that had a big gold Buddha in the hallway," remembers Baines. "Nico'd run out of money, and we were just so in love with her we wanted to put all our money together and buy her some heroin. And Ari was going, 'No, this is what she does. You cannot do that!' He was telling us off and saying, 'Do not do that, this is what my mother does. Don't fall for it.' He was such a handsome young man. I don't think he was into drugs at that time. I think he was more trying to look after Nico, be the parent, but he knew what she was like."

From 1982 through to 1988, Nico was to play more than 1,200 shows, traveling back and forth between gigs and Manchester continuously. "When I joined, it was like being recruited by Alan to what he called 'the good ship Nico,'" says Young. "At first it was chaotic. There were some ad hoc dates in England, to sustain Nico's habit. Then we went to Italy in March of 1982, just as the Falklands War was on. The promoters were asking why she wasn't blonde.

"We did a six-week tour of America in 1982. That was a bit of a baptism by fire. Didn't get paid; East Coast to West Coast and back again with no air conditioning, squabbling all the way, vile motels with cockroaches, Nico withdrawing…it was just nuts. I was naive enough to think I wasn't naive. What the fuck was I doing, this college boy, wandering around the Tenderloin district in San Francisco trying to score heroin?

"When I look back on it, when I knew her Nico was somehow renouncing everything in her past. Paul Morrissey said it was a renunciation of everything, of all the glamourous model stuff, so that she could become an artist. That took guts."

Spider Mike King recalls that it was less Nico the artist, more her as a relic from the Velvet Underground that attracted fans to the shows. "People would go to the gigs out of a weird curiosity. They wanted to see, to have a taste, a flavor of something they'd only heard about that was a such a dynamic circumstance of the '60s. By this time, Lou Reed was a great solo artist. I think people saw Nico as being part of that. They would not buy a record necessarily, but would go to a gig to check out that vibe because they'd heard her on the 'banana' album. It's just about as simple as that. It was curiosity."

On the road, Nico was rather quiet. However, the long stints in cars led to contemplation, which sometimes caught up with the singer. "There was a time when Nico was in the back of the car with me," Spider Mike recounts. "We'd been traveling for hours, and she started gently sobbing to herself. I put my arm round her and said, 'Are you okay?' 'Yah,' she said, 'I just think of things from the long ago.' That was the only time I had ever seen her express herself with any sadness or emotion—she was very stoic. We never talked in the car. Well, the guys would, but her, absolutely not, no. She would just sit by the window."

Nico's choice of songs for her set list could be a source of controversy, according to sound engineer Phil Rainford. He would often try to get an idea of the crowd before Nico took to the stage. "Sometimes I used to try and gauge the temperature of the gig and who would be there. Sometimes I'd say to her, 'Don't do "Deutschland über alles" tonight.' She'd say [*does impression of Nico*], 'Why? Why? It's just a song.' But she knew what connotations it had for some people. Sometimes she was quite a bit of a devil's advocate in that way. I tried to talk to her a few times about it, and she would just say, 'I like the song.' It actually really suited her doom-laden voice. In a way, I sort of saw it as how Jimi Hendrix did the national anthem of the United States on guitar. Some people thought he was making fun of it and some people thought, 'Oh, look, a new modern version. That's great.' I think she just saw it like that. As an artist, she was allowed to do what she wanted, and it was up to other people what they thought of it. They had to interpret what she meant. Whether she was making fun of it or whether she thought it was just a good song or whether she knew it would cause controversy at some concerts, I don't know, because she would never say. She saw it in the way that Jimi Hendrix did: 'I've got the right to do this and I've got the right to do it how I want it. It's up to other people how they interpret it.' I thought, 'Well, that's fair enough. I can't argue with that.'"

It was that song that Nico decided to play at a show in Naples, Italy, leading to a near riot. The country was deeply divided at the time between anarchists and fascists, some of whom thought a Nico gig would be the perfect place to protest. "The fascists were throwing coins at Nico," says Spider Mike. Showing her steely resolve, Nico stayed on the stage, continuing to perform while she was pelted by a constant stream of items. "She went up to the mic and said [*does impression of Nico*], 'You are all fucking arseholes—fuck off!'" laughs Spider Mike. "In the midst of this the cops arrived, and the show was stopped after about half an hour. She was still performing through it all."

The fascists and the anarchists then started fighting each other, with Nico and her band eventually given a police escort back to their hotel. The pandemonium of the previous day led to Nico having to hold a press conference in Rome, the location of the next show. "She was at one end of this room, and the paparazzi—the press—were interviewing her," recalls Rainford. "I was stood at the back, watching her hold court. She had 'em in the palm of her hand; she was great, so charismatic. They were saying, 'What does it feel like to be a living legend?' That was one of the questions. Her reply [*does impression of Nico*]: 'I feel like I have stepped out of an oil painting!' Great, fantastic, brilliant!" At the show that evening, police with guns lined the balcony, as local law enforcement did not want a repeat of the insanity in Naples.

Rainford has many memories of simply having fun with Nico on the road, revealing a silly, human side to the singer that is not often discussed. "We used to sing together quite a lot," he says—you can hear a smile in his voice even over the phone. "Both of us were big fans of the American songbook: Frank Sinatra and Ella Fitzgerald. When we were traveling, quite often she'd sit in the front with me, driving everybody else mad in the bus, and we didn't care! 'Fly Me to the Moon' and 'My Funny Valentine' and stuff. We had that sort of connection. Even in her room we would do it: 'Do you remember this song, Nix?' and we'd start a song and we'd both sing it. But it was only the American songbook which we both really loved.

"Once we were in some hotel in Italy. I don't think we had any money to pay for the hotel bill, so, if I can remember it rightly, we said, 'We'll put on a wee concert.' It had a little hall as a dining room and there was a piano in there. It was me, Nico and Jim [James Young]. She and I got up and sang 'My Funny Valentine.' It actually went down really well. Italians love Frank Sinatra songs, though I don't know if they particularly liked Nico's doom-laden middle European angst." Such glimpses under the "Nico" facade offer a softer, arguably more authentic persona and an insight into what might have been, if not for the addiction issues.

The high jinks continued as the band made its way across various countries. "In Naples I was drinking late at the hotel bar. I had a tab, on James [Young's] room," Spider Mike laughs. "I was really getting hammered after the gig. I eventually struggled from the bar to my room and threw myself on the bed. This voice goes [*does impression of Nico*], 'Spider, what are you doing in my bed?' I said, 'Nnnna—what? No, this is my room.' 'No, Spider, you are in the same room but a floor above.' She was in bed with her boots on and her big handbag on the floor. Apparently, the hotel had accidentally given me the master key, which opened all the rooms!"

Fun aside, Nico's drug problem always seemed to hinder any real progress for the singer. She was her own worst enemy in this sense. "The regret is that she didn't make more music in Manchester," said promoter Nigel Bagley. "She had signed some messy deals which prevented her recording. We put her in the studio with Martin Hannett,[125] who shared certain behavioral habits [a heroin addiction]. A single, 'Procession,' worked well, and 'All Tomorrow's Parties' on the B-side was sensational. So we gave her £1,000 to do an album and she ran away to London. It turned out that she didn't have any songs but didn't want to admit it. Heroin stopped her writing."

People were still drawn to her, perhaps because she seemed so insular. "She was perceived as a strong female artist doing her own thing, but on the other side of that was her vulnerability," says Stephen Mallinder of Cabaret Voltaire. "She could never work with other people. Probably the only way she could work was if she was performing to herself, singing to herself. You get the feeling that there was a necessity for her to do this, to perform, probably as a way of verifying/reassuring her existence, but it wasn't ever something you got the feeling she particularly enjoyed. In some ways, I don't think she needed an audience or other members of a band to articulate what she did. The strangeness of her music—she was like a lost, mournful figure. Her gigs felt like a cry in the dark. You get the feeling she would've done it if there was no one else in the room, because it felt like she was exorcizing demons."

Nico was aware of how powerless her addiction rendered her in nearly every way; she was at the mercy of Alan Wise to book her shows to pay for the needed heroin. "Had I more money, I would have more power, but somewhere along the line there would be compromise," she says in her journal. "Everything that I do has to be true. The slightest upset would bring bad luck; of that I have had enough lately. The Karma that seems to turn on me faster than my worst enemy. My own karma, a different environment would do her good, Ibiza for one month after the German Tours, for Christmas that would be. As long as I can sing and not get tired of it I will be happy."

"Nico was in a man's world," says Barbara Wilkin, "especially when it was about the music, but she needed her money. [The men in the band] could be mean to her. Some comments made about her when the boys were all together I thought were really horrible. Sexual comments like, 'She's had so many men you can throw a plate in there.'" Graham Dowdall was one of the bandmates with whom Nico had a good relationship, and he knew a person who was much different from the cold, disconnected persona repeated so often in the media. "People see Nico, the ice queen—the sort of utter darkness that she lived in this world of coldness. I'm always eager to disabuse that as it was Nico's stage persona. She would paint on the white face to go on stage because she knew which way her bread was buttered. That's the way people viewed her, the way they *wanted* to view her. She wasn't entirely like that. She was my mate and she was actually a very warm person at times—a lot of the time. She was, to some extent, in control of the creative stuff around her, though she was also very happy to delegate some of that creative process in a knowing way. She worked with people that she trusted and believed in as creative musicians. It wasn't just, 'Al Wise knows this person, and they'll work with me because they'll work for peanuts.' I was kicked out of the band on numerous times, from working with Nico in the early days, because of some of the people around her, because of the idea of playing gigs for nothing, and all that sort of thing. And each time, after a certain amount of time, I would get this call [*does impression of Nico*]: 'Oh, Dows! It's Nico! Things are much better now. I really would want you to join the band again and play with me.' It's like that! She wanted certain people to be around her, and luckily I was one of them. I quit three times, and she asked me back twice, and Al [Wise] asked me the other time." Unlike the myth that she was a negative, malignant presence, Dowdall describes a supportive musical mind. "She was actually really positive and encouraging to work with."

However, being on the road constantly was a grind. "She had a pool of musicians," Wilkin notes. "It wasn't always the same. Tours were different, depending on who was with us. Normally, it was a hired van with equipment, and everybody chipped in. Nico liked to sit behind the driver. At one point, we had a van which Alan bought. A nice Talbot. She was dead jealous that I was driving. She said, 'I used to drive the Velvet Underground!' I don't do her voice well [*deepens voice*]: 'I used to drive! I can drive!' Alan wouldn't let her, but I think for some reason she thought I would. She started putting her knees in my back. Finally, I let her take the wheel at one point. We came out of a tunnel, and she says, 'I want to drive now! Okay?!' We stopped the car. Nico was trying to drive and it was going [*makes surging noises and gestures*]. Then she killed the engine and she just cried. She couldn't do it any more, but I'm sure she could in the past. Maybe she hadn't driven in donkey's years."

Journalists often preyed upon the obvious changes in Nico, openly crowing with palpable delight at what they framed as the demise of a former world-class beauty. An especially disturbing example of this is an *NME* review from 1983, written by a female contributor. She seems incredibly happy at seeing Nico's very public, unapologetic transformation from the blonde bombshell of the 1960s to the mature performer. "I mean that there was something unbearably pathetic about a once-beautiful woman, now around 40, conducting a public search for some vestige of her former self," Cynthia Rose writes. In tearing her down, nothing is off limits, from Nico's voice to her appearance, as Rose continues her annihilation: "In this situation, every phrase Nico sang or mumbled took on an irony that might have been awful if it hadn't by now become so truly banal. There she stood, intoning 'All Tomorrow's Parties' in a voice an octave deeper but with no increase in its three-or-so note range—wearing her own 'hand-me-down gown' of sheepskin coat, sloppy black polyester pantsuit and cowboy boots." Rose even seems to deride Nico for daring to look like herself, crucifying her for not still being the cool muse of the Velvets. "One by one, the motley company blundered through those simple, churchy folksy tunes once rendered perverse by Nico's sliding delivery, deadpan dramatics, and former hard white-blonde giant-German self," she asserts. "The only result was a messy, uninteresting demonstration of how sorry a sight vices from cough syrup to self-pity can produce in the flesh."

Rose is exactly the kind of audience member that Barbara Wilkin despised. "There were many gigs we were at and the crowd only wanted to hear the Velvet Underground stuff. As soon as she sat there with the harmonium, people started talking loudly over it. I often felt like going, 'Shut up and listen!' But I didn't. Now, I probably would. Then, I didn't. Sometimes she would just [*makes sighing noise*], stop, have a drink. She would start again because she didn't have a choice. She could just hear the audience talking so loud."

Nico knew her heroin problem had destroyed many of her previous relationships but still could not stop. In her diary, she even seems to almost accept that she has no other choice but to continue the spin cycle of touring, scoring, using and poverty, writing, "In every human journey there's a point of no return." Dowdall saw this for himself. "I think she felt that her conspicuous addiction caused a lot of her old, American-based people to distance themselves from her. I think a lot of it was men who'd used her, but they'd moved on. There was a lot of that. They'd claim they don't want to look back at the junkies and stuff like that. Or they didn't want people to know that they were still users. They just wanted to distance themselves. There was something scurrilous about Nico that they just didn't want. A lot of them were trying to paint a cleaner picture. In the '70s, it was okay to be a bit scuzzy, but in the early '80s I suppose even Lou Reed was trying to maintain that he was clean." However, Dowdall disagrees with the claim that the drugs extinguished her artistry. "It is incorrect to say, "Oh, it's such a tragedy that heroin destroyed her creativity," he says. "Heroin didn't destroy her creativity. A lack of heroin at times made her not the nice person that she could be when she had it! And I think the period before we met her, it probably slowed up her creativity and allowed her to be influenced by some horrible characters. I don't think heroin actually diminished her creativity."

He also has a problem with the assertion that Nico was a compulsive liar. "She would embellish the truth to the press, because the truth is never always a good story for the press," he recalls. "She used to have this character that she would put on. It's not dishonesty, but there's a hiding behind something in that. She never said anything to me that I was able to say later, 'Nico, that wasn't true, what you told me. You lied to me about this. You lied to me about that.' None, actually. I can't think of a single example." Phil Jones also had issues with the allegation of Nico systematically making up stories. "If she told you something personally, it tended to be true," he said. "In Oliver Stone's Doors film, there's a scene where she gives Jim Morrison a blowjob in a lift. She would have been really affronted by that. She'd read this sort of thing in books and tell me: 'That never fucking happened.' She never was a femme fatale. She just got hit on a lot by very famous people. I think she was abused along the way. She told me five times: 'Jim Morrison was the only man I ever loved.'"

Most of her unsavory acts were related to drugs. "I can think of lots of examples of her behaving badly—but not lying," says Dowdall. "Most of her bad behavior was to do with heroin. When she was short of heroin, she was a monster! I had to physically throw her out of my house—not that she was being particularly horrible, but because she was going to be. We always used to stop off at my place on the way back from European tours because I was south London, and always by the time she came back she was sick [from withdrawal] and she'd be trying to ring her dealer in Stoke Newington. He was often not there, so she would say, 'Can I just sit in your house and wait for him to ring?' I am thinking to myself, 'I really don't want a sick junkie in my sitting room.' 'Oh, it's so warm and nice in here! You have tea and a fire!' And it's like [*makes groaning noise*]. So I have actually had to throw her out: 'Nico, sorry. Go home.' This is the Nico that I knew, as a person. She'd come down here, we'd smoke a joint in front of the gas fire and we'd drink tea. She was a warm and friendly mate."

41

Jane Goldstraw first came into contact with Nico in the early 1980s, when her partner was rehearsing for a tour with the singer. The two women became close. "I was living in St. Paul's Road with my two children and their father. I'd fallen asleep on the futon couch, and I got shaken awake by Nico. I remember the first image I saw of her was how tall she was, this kind of looming figure! She picked me up by my shoulders and kissed me on each cheek and said, 'You look like something out of a Mucha poster!'[126] They were a set of art posters that were around. I was flattered."

Goldstraw is a soft-spoken, gentle woman. Up until now, she has never been interviewed nor talked about her relationship with Nico, but over several emails and phone calls she opened up to me, providing precious insight into the singer. My interviews with her were some of the most important and eye-opening that I carried out, as she is one of the few females who knew the singer outside of the mythology that always preceded her in later years. Not being an artist allowed Goldstraw to get to know Nico without any previous expectations or context, simply as an individual with no parameters.

"At the time, my children's father wasn't a heroin addict, so I'm not sure what she actually came around for. They might have been talking about music, but I also think she needed some medicine [heroin]. Alan Wise was her manager, unfortunately. He brought her around to the house probably thinking that my partner would know where to get some."

Goldstraw made Nico some coffee, thinking nothing of it. However, the singer quickly became a frequent visitor, finding solace and a rare kindred spirit in the young mother. "Over the next few weeks, she started to come by more. She was living on Singleton Road, a couple of roads away from where I lived. I got to know her…on a different level [than other people around at the time]. I wasn't in the band, I didn't take drugs. It was just me and the children. She became my friend. I think she was depressed. Her skin had this very sallow, waxy color and she didn't wash her hair very much. I think she was a very lonely person. But so was I.

"[Alan Wise] would make sure that this woman only had enough [money] for a couple of days' worth of medicine [heroin]. He would write the most ridiculous lists [for her tours]: two quilts needed, two pillows needed, meal for sixteen…petrol. In other words, he was keeping all the money. [Wise] kept her so that she needed him for that small amount [of money] that she got. When she would come around, she would tell me how disgusting he was. He kept walking into her room and things.

"I got hold of him one day and said, 'What are you doing! Leave her alone!' He said, 'Oh, she's talking rubbish, she's exaggerating.' I said, 'No, she's not. Leave her alone. She does not want you to touch her.' You know, people were there for who she was, but they never actually *saw* her for who she was. She played with my children; they loved her!

"Apparently, I made her favorite soup—potato and leek. I would be cooking, and she'd just tell me funny stories. One day, she came into the kitchen and said, 'I think your husband's wife is a bitch.' I turned around and said, 'Oh, okay.' Even though I wasn't married [to him], I wondered what I had done. I said, 'Why?' And she replied, 'She left three children with him to bring up, and you have to bring the younger ones up.' And I said, 'No, no, you've got it wrong. Those are our children.' She was completely freaked. She said, 'Dirty pervert!' I actually laughed. I thought it was funny. She said, 'No, no, you're so young, this is not right!' I told her it was okay, but she just kept saying, 'No, it's not, he's a pervert.' She was so funny at times, you'd have loved her [Jane was thirteen when she met her partner, who was twenty-one].

"She really was my friend, a very interesting woman. She'd tell me all sorts of things about her childhood—having to step over Jewish people that had been shot and things like that," Goldstraw recalls. "When we were on our own, she'd play the piano. We'd sing together and we'd tape it…we used to have fun."

Nico told Goldstraw that "She didn't like women; she liked *me*. Apparently she fell in love with me…I had to fight her off! It was like, 'No, listen, you're my friend, that's it. I'm sorry, I am not that way inclined.' She'd say, 'Oh, you're too shy. Why are you so shy?' I'd say, 'I'm not shy, you're my friend.' We'd go down to my local shops that I'd been going to for a few years. She'd put her arm around me and say, 'This is my new girlfriend. I'm in love with her.' I'd just stand there. I'm quite small—I'm only five foot three—and she'd tower above me with her arm around me. It never bothered me."

Goldstraw was not awed by Nico's legend or status, simply viewing her as a close mate, without any expectations. This allowed Nico to open up and feel accepted in a way she seldom experienced. "I think she liked me because she knew that I didn't want anything off her. I wasn't hanging around her for who she was and what she had," Goldstraw hypothesizes. "I hate using the word—it was normal." It was the everyday rituals that Nico seemed to most cherish, as she had never had the chance to have such mundane experiences herself. "I cared for her, I really did care for her," Goldstraw says. To be the object of such unabated affection was rare for Nico, for whom gestures of kindness with no expectations attached were few. Goldstraw recalls one instance when Nico's deeply buried need for this kind of interaction became visible: "I went into Manchester city center one day, and this shoe shop had a sale on. I'd noticed

333

that Nico's boots were getting worn. I remembered that she liked espadrilles. I found these espadrilles in black that went right up to your knees. You could tie them, and they were size ten! I got them for her. She was so thrilled! She said, 'I haven't had a present for so long!' She actually looked like she was going to cry. She hugged me so tight, and I thought she was going to break my ribs! She never had them off her feet."

This vulnerable, "real" side of the singer was glimpsed by few throughout her life. Moments like those the singer had with Goldstraw were few and far between, yet they illustrated who the woman under the myth may have been, and how Nico's unconventional childhood may have stunted her ability to connect with people. Arguably, in her younger days, building the myth of Nico, not necessarily ardent passion, may have fueled the same-sex relationships—or at least the singer's perceived need to include such anecdotes as part of the mystique surrounding her. However, later in life, it would have been a deep-seated need to be loved and accepted for the "Christa" core that fueled the forging of romantic entanglements, regardless of gender. Nico's protective mantle and the later haze of addiction seemingly shielded her from further hurt and pain, while shutting off the possibility of the authentic young girl inside to heal and flourish. "I remember how badly treated she was too," says Goldstraw. This made any genuine connection that much more important to Nico.

With Goldstraw, Nico could just *be*, which must have been a rare occurrence. "I think sometimes she just craved to be herself, and she could be that with me because I didn't want anything from her. We'd watch a film or sing. She rode her bicycle around Manchester, and we'd take my dog and kids and walk across the moors. One of her sayings: 'I'm sick of this shit! All of these people just want to take from me.' Earaches, Nico suffered a lot of those. I remember her having cotton wool in her ears a lot. Tiger Balm was one of her favorite things; she would rub it on her temples and wrists for headaches. If she had a cold, she would rub it under her nose. She gave me my first tub of it. I would often make her fresh lemon tea with honey."

Around the same time, another woman came into Nico's life who would end up playing an important role. Barbara Wilkin met the singer through mutual friends at a concert. A year and a half after her first interaction with the singer, Wilkin was summoned to Nico's hotel room while the singer was on tour in Amsterdam. A fan had left a "special" cake heavily laced with hashish in her dressing room. The baked confection did not get to its intended recipient, as Wise ate it and proceeded to become gravely ill. "Alan had a very, very serious turn on that, because he never would touch any drugs like that," says Wilkin. "Emotionally, he was a bit unstable anyway, so that really sent him into panic mode. He suffered for about two years, I think. He never really recovered from that." Wilkin found Wise in bed and very ill. "Nico was sitting there [*does impression of Nico*], 'Oh. He's not well.' She had lit all these candles for him. Alan then said, 'Could you come along and help with this tour?' I was already helping out on the road, a little bit here and there. The next thing I knew, I was on this European tour."

Wilkin accompanied Nico on one of her attempts as an adult to reconnect with the Päffgens. "We tried, Nico and me, to see them [the Päffgen family]," says Wilkin. "She wanted me to come with her because I was a German. Her German was good but a bit rusty. Nico said she still always hoped she had some kind of inheritance from that side of the family. They owned the big brewery in Cologne and were very rich. We figured out where they lived; she had an address. Typical German house. It was a flat; we had to go up a couple of flights of stairs. We went to the door and knocked on it. We said who we were and it was just [*makes dismissive noise*]. We got the door pushed in our face. Door closed. There was nothing she could do."

If I was writing my book, I wouldn't really spend much time on
Nico. In my world, she didn't loom that large. She was just a
neighbor. Famous, so interesting because she was famous.
She was a bit of a casualty.

John Torjusson

In 1984, Alan Wise decided it would be a good idea to rent a house
in London. It would be a base for any shows in the capital and
save Nico and the ever-changing entourage of musicians around
her from having to drive the four hours it took to get to and from
Manchester. Brixton was picked as the location, with the contingent
moving into an imposing residence at 23 Effra Road. The landlady,
Mrs. Chin, was not made aware of the nefarious character of some
of the artists and drug addicts that she had taken on as tenants. "I
think Alan got the flat here because of the Fridge nightclub," asserts
John Torjusson, referring to a venue nearby. Torjusson lived two
houses down from Nico.

Brixton was still recovering from the well-publicized riots that
occurred in the area in 1981. The largely Afro-Caribbean community had been deeply impacted by the recession and was suffering
from high unemployment, poor housing, and a higher-than-average
crime rate, leading to serious economic and social issues. An ongoing combination of perceived lackadaisical policing in dealing with
crimes against the Black community and police brutality toward
them culminated in what became known as the "Brixton uprising,"
leading to protesters and police clashing between April 10 and 12.

The main riot—dubbed "Bloody Sunday" by *Time* magazine—took place on April 11 and resulted in almost three hundred police and forty-five members of the public being injured. Over a hundred vehicles were burned, with more than half of those belonging to the authorities. Thirty buildings went up in flames, with almost a hundred and fifty being damaged. A *Guardian* report claimed that up to five thousand people were involved in the event.

The disturbances meant prices for would-be renters were low, the area now an urban wasteland of charred architecture and boarded-up residences. "A room was rented to us by a housing association. It was supposed to be £2 each a week, but hardly anyone ever paid it," admits Torjusson, giving a flavor of the time. "It was a bit bad of us not to pay it, but that's the way it was in those days. A lot of Brixton was empty; nobody really wanted to live there. There were a lot of building sites, a lot of ground zero-type areas with demolished houses. All along the railway, it was just wasteland. You'd get a lot of Rastas sitting around the fire. It was great. Brilliant. They weren't intimidating or anything."

Torjusson met Nico via her sometime housemate, Mancunian poet John Cooper Clarke. Clarke had amassed a cult following during the late 1970s and early '80s via regular live performances, building a reputation as a "punk poet." Torjusson first ran into him at the local art house cinema, the Ritzy. "In those days, it was showing late night double bills," recalls Torjusson. "They served nothing except carrot cake, homemade by one of the staff. We thought this was a real extra, because normally you'd never see that sort of thing. No popcorn, just carrot cake. My sister worked there, so they would often let us in for free. We'd watch a John Waters movie or some German films. Hardly anybody was in the cinema, but then we noticed Cooper Clarke: his silhouette and his big hair. I just shouted at him, 'How are you, Clarkey?' He turned around. I'd never met him before that. He'd been seen walking around Brixton, so people knew that he was a resident. He came and sat with us and

337

had a chat, and he was very good company. Witty. He came back to our house that night and stayed up all night. Then he showed us where he and Nico lived. We met Alan [Wise], the manager. In the house was anybody who Alan was working with." Torjusson has a vivid memory of his first glimpse of where Nico lived. "I remember the bloody bedsheets in her room," he says. He would quickly become friends with the singer. "She would come round in the middle of day and say, 'Let's go to the pub,'" he remembers. "She was sort of slow-moving, slow-speaking. Quite an Amazonian figure, tall and quite big." Torjusson was impressed by her total mastery of English. "She spoke it like a native. It wasn't like a foreign-language speaker." However, he remembers his neighbor as being "a little bit zombified." "Cooper Clarke would sometimes tease her just to get a reaction from her. Something like, 'If we don't sell enough records, we'll have to put you on the street,' and stuff like this. She'd get angry. Most of the time they just sort of jogged along okay, those two. They were friendly enough, but not matey. They were both using, which is 90 percent of why things were like that, I think.

"There were a few other people who used to come round to our house, who were into the same kind of thing. Once they heard that Nico was living nearby, they'd quickly run over there. I remember feeling a bit bad about telling them that she lived there because then they hooked up. She didn't really look beyond having twenty quid to go get some smack. I thought she was a drug casualty. I thought, 'Here is somebody who has been in the Velvet Underground and has been famous and made records. You should have something to show for it.' That's one thing. Another thing was her way of talking: half a sentence, and then she'd sort of drift off into her own world. Both her and Cooper Clarke would fall asleep all the time with a fag and then burn themselves, watching some TV programs. But Cooper Clarke could still be witty and funny and tell jokes. He was supposed to be writing a book at the time based on *Moby Dick*. He never got past the outline. I never remember Nico doing anything artistic like writing or anything, or even talking about music, really. I think she was trying to do methadone, but if there was any heroin around, she'd do that as well. I never saw her quit, really, but I saw her on methadone, so I presumed at that point that she had run out of heroin or that maybe she was trying to quit. To me it was always on–off."

Nico's appearance shocked her neighbor. "She'd never show any skin apart from her face. She was quite portly, but not fat. Long brown hair, not dyed. Brownish face. Not much movement in the face. Long sleeves, leather trousers, motorbike boots open. She never changed her clothes," recalls Torjusson.

"She didn't like to bathe too often," Barbara Wilkin affirms. Outward embellishment was not a priority to Nico, who mostly saw it as an impediment to being taken as a serious artist. "She didn't want to be pretty. She always said, 'The only thing I regret is that I wasn't born a man.' She felt as a woman, she didn't count," Wilkin concludes.

"I think that her appearance was a way to facilitate her art, and she didn't want any distractions from that," says James Young. "I think she figured that glamour was a surface thing. Ornamental and useless. I think she worked that one out—she was smart enough! Why else would she suddenly start wearing very plain things, very dark things? Because she wanted something else to resonate and for people to focus on. I think that was what it was about. It was quite shocking as a young guy, when you're with this woman who was obviously stunningly beautiful when she was younger, and she wasn't old, but who was seriously neglecting herself."

Danny Fields agrees with Young. "Her relationship to her own beauty is so conflicted and damaged," he says. "She loved having rotten teeth—oh, I mean, that says it all. She did one show in 23rd Street at the Squat Theatre [in New York]. I went backstage and she was really big and fat and her teeth were all gone. And I saw her just enough to say, 'Hello, I love you,' and then that was it."

Wilkin's memories parallel what Fields saw. "Nico looked bad at times because of the drugs. Especially when she was still on the heroin. I think that if you're on heroin, you don't care so much about bodily hygiene. Her teeth were pretty bad. She actually lost one at one point. She wouldn't go to the dentist properly." Yet regardless of her appearance or addiction, Wilkin underscores that Nico "would always turn up for her concerts and gigs, so that's not lazy. She would also be on time, unlike John Cooper Clarke, who when I worked with him I had to tell him an hour and a half before to get him on time!"

Wilkin also called 23 Effra Road home for seven months. "Alan [Wise] lived downstairs, and Nico had one room. I remember one time we came back from tour and the phone was cut off. People came, junkies came and used all the spoons. The carpet looked horrible in the living room, with all the tipped drinks. I did clean the place quite a few times, and Nico appreciated it. She didn't like all that mess and stuff, but she would not clean." Wilkin also noted how few possessions Nico owned. "She didn't have many clothes either. All she had was a little bag and a little red radio. She used to tune in to stations on the short wave, trying to find some Arabian music and stuff. We liked that. Or Indian music. You didn't get that in those days, you didn't have the internet. I once said to her, 'You have nothing, Nico!' She replied, 'It's the only way to be really free. If you have more, you're not free any more.' She did stuff which was not going to be popular, but she did it because of art. She was a true artist."

Just as in Manchester, when not on tour Nico preferred to stay in. "Whenever you went to her room, it was always really hot and muggy and stuffy, with loads of Marlboros and the smell of hash," says Young, who also stayed at the Brixton abode. "Never a window open—no way! She liked that cocoon feeling: TV glowing in the corner, no fresh air, no 'I'm going out to the park.' No. No interest. We'd sit and watch TV; you'd make comments with the TV on. Instead of the fire glowing in the corner, it would be the TV. It would be on till closedown. It wasn't twenty-four hours like it is now; at midnight, it would switch to white and [*makes static noise*]. They'd leave it on for that! In Brixton, I got back late once. There's John Cooper Clarke [*makes nodding out gesture*], so I switched it off by mistake. And he's like, 'I was watching that!' [*makes static noise*]. Nico was the same. It just used to be on, and you sat around." Mornings were not a popular time either at 23 Effra Road. "She wouldn't get up in the mornings, no way!" laughs Young. "She was nocturnal. She wouldn't appear until late afternoon."

Nico would occasionally socialize in Brixton, which was a very racially mixed area. "We sometimes used to go to the pub together. She liked to do that: drink a beer and play pool. She wasn't only wine, wine, wine," says Wilkin. "She even tried to fix me up with a boy. She said, 'You've been single for long enough! He's very nice!' She confessed that it was the owner's son from this pub. They were Rastafarians. Nico always gets accused of being racist, but she was not." Torjusson agrees. "I don't think she had a big racist philosophy or anything, she'd just be irritated by people. She wouldn't bite her tongue and say, 'Oh, these people!' She wouldn't mind saying, 'Oh, these black people!' or something. Most people wouldn't say something like that." Graham Dowdall also has issues with the constant accusations of racism leveled against Nico. "I think it's become part of the legend," he says. "She chose to have a Jewish manager. Alan is very Jewish. He didn't find that that was a compromise for himself. We had a security guy that was black, Yankee Bill. Nico was very friendly with him. I've seen her hanging out with black people. She lived in Brixton, when Brixton was very black! I don't think she was a racist. I think that politically she was very complex."

Nico also had her routines in the neighborhood. "She would go to the separate Greek shop to get her yogurt. She liked Greek yogurt," says Wilkin.[127] "Then she would go to the West Indian baker to get the West Indian bun. She loved eating that, so she lived on that for a while! I think when she was a model she had to always look perfect and she had to starve herself. She once said to me, 'All we had to eat was an apple and an egg in the morning, and then we had to wait all day to get little bits in the evening.' She also said, 'I only have to look at food and I put on weight.' When I knew her, she was a strange eater. She never would eat in public. She would eat by herself in her room and she might eat very unhealthily—just have chocolate and white wine when she was on the heroin. She would cook sometimes. When we were in Brixton, she said, 'Okay, I'm cooking,' and she'd make what we called the Nico Soup, which was a stew with red lentils, carrots, potatoes—just a stew. She was vegetarian. She wouldn't eat meat. I don't know when she became a vegetarian, but she was a vegetarian all the time I knew her.

"She liked to have somebody around at times when she needed something," Wilkin recalls. "When I would be back up in Manchester, she would say, 'When are you coming back?' She used to come into my room frequently. One time I told her, 'I can't sleep,' so she gave me some methadone. It poisoned me! 'Try some of this. It tastes like cough medicine,' she said. The next thing I know, I thought I was dying! I managed to keep it down but was not in a good place. She stayed around and lit a candle. She was meowing at the window at a cat for ages [*meows*] to distract me. Then I was okay."

Wilkin thinks that the combination of drugs and heartbreak were detrimental to Nico from an early age. "Slimming pills, which are basically speed, will do your mind in. I think the thing which happened with Alain Delon was very upsetting as well. She honestly was in love with him, or thought she was in love with him. I think she had a deep, deep loneliness inside."

Wilkin also speaks of a practical side to Nico. "She would always say, 'You always have to have an onion in your house,' just in case you have to cook something. Another time when we were on tour in Barcelona, she said, 'Come on, let's go out.' We liked to just sit on the boulevard. She liked Campari and ice. Campari was like fresh orange. We were people-watching, speaking only in German."

"I think the people around her amused her," says Young, "our little tour party: Alan and the musicians, we were a little tableau of freaks and weirdos! She saw our little games and our strategies, falling in and out of love with unsuitable girls. She'd seen it all before a thousand times. She was mean about anybody's girl. Or if anybody invited a girl into the van! Or invited their girlfriend along! The looks would be like [*growls*]! She was the queen, and there was no competition—no other women allowed. Didn't want them around, didn't trust one of them. What the basis of that was, I wouldn't know. Whether or not that went back to the modeling years and that competitive thing…I wouldn't know what the reason for that was. But she did say many times that she didn't like women."

"I think she was a bit contemptuous of the world and thought people were soft," says Torjusson. "You live in a place with no electricity, no heating—that's all right as long as you've got a bit of smack. When I went to her place, it was barely furnished. My place was barely furnished as well, but I thought, 'She's an older woman, she might have a bit of comfort or something.' Also, I thought, 'She's a famous person, so where's the reward for fame?' Nothing except a pair of leather trousers and a harmonium. No place of her own.

"Nico would get on well with masculine types. I think that's why she liked Una [Baines]. In those days, Una would compete with the men in anything and would think nothing of hitching across Europe with macho lorry drivers. Alan was a bit like that, he was a bit old-school sexist and stuff, and I think Nico thought that was fine. She relied on Alan for organizing everything, and I think Alan quite liked that, he liked looking after her."

Wise would go between Manchester and Brixton. There was only one bathroom for all of the rotating roommates, and Nico "used to complain about Al's smells," says Young. "[*does impression of Nico*] 'I'm not going in there, he's been in there! You go in! You go in!'"

343

Torjusson has a less odoriferous memory of Wise, saying he was "a good guy" and "a doer." "He'd organize things. In those days, none of us drove, but he'd go, 'Let's drive out to the New Forest or some place in the countryside to some Buddhist retreat.' We would just have a meal and a chat. He liked to drive and talk. That was the really good thing about him. He had quite a number of different people turning up in the flat. He would be quite keen to have girls around."

Wise and Nico's relationship continued to be "really, really complex on so many levels," says Graham Dowdall. "Al worshipped Nico. Al wanted to be with Nico in a sexy way." He then recounts an incident which "sums up their relationship better than anything else." "Nico was in London and went to the Brixton flat. Al Wise was in Manchester. Nico spoke to Al on the phone and—she told me this story, so no doubt that it's true—she said to Al, 'Al, I'm staying over in London, is it okay if I use your bed?' He said, 'Yeah, Nico. That's fine.' So she goes to bed. Al Wise jumps on the last train from Manchester to London, arrives in Brixton. 'Oh, there's only one bed, I'll have to get in bed with Nico.' In her words, 'I woke up, and he was just masturbating between the cheeks of my arse, the disgusting pig!'"

Another resident of the Brixton pad was John Cale. "I remember him coming up the stairs with two crates of beer, and I was thinking, 'He's really sorted out for beer!' I'd never known anybody who buys beer by the crate before," laughs Torjusson. Young describes his former flatmates'—Nico and Cale's—relationship as "very affectionate... He was someone she trusted," he says. "Old friends. They knew each other before they were really famous. It's different. If you're a famous person, you can only be with famous people and relax with them, because other people might want something from you."

John Cooper Clarke claims to have been "star-struck" by living under the same roof as "two-fifths of the Velvet Underground... As a housemate, she was very tidy. No trouble at all," he claimed. He was not overly close with the singer, however. "I can't remember ever having any kind of searching conversation with her. There's nothing I can relate that would puncture her mythological status. She was the kind of artist that people project a lot of themselves onto, very self-contained. Self-possessed. She moved around in her own micro-climate of glamour."

Ari would also make visits to Brixton. "She was so proud of having Ari," Wilkin recalls. "She said, 'I was the most organized that I ever was. When I was pregnant and knew Ari was coming, I got everything sorted out for him and bought all his clothes and everything.' Then Ari was taken away from her. Alain Delon's mum took him, and then she missed a lot of his childhood. When he came as a young man to Manchester, he was nineteen. He was very green behind his ears. He soon also became a drug addict. I'm sure they slept in a bed together, they just cuddled. Maybe it's strange for other men to think, 'How can you cuddle a young man?' but I think they just cuddled to make up for lost time."

Torjusson once spent New Year's Eve with mother and son. "I think Ari was a very lost kind of person," he says. "Their relationship was very close and quite intimate in terms of body language, but strange as well. The usual chatting or talking about things didn't seem to be there. It was quite silent, but quite close as well. He would lean against her on the sofa. Ari was obviously more animated and alive because he was still young then, but Nico was quite silent and quite happy to watch telly. Both in their own worlds, but I think they were both under the influence as well at the time. It's not exactly a great way to grow up, with a mum like Nico. She was a bit incapable of looking after herself."

Young offers a different view. "She had a strong sense of self and identity. There's a kind of regal thing. A lot of people were afraid of her or felt uncomfortable with her or felt they kind of had to creep around her, and she didn't like that. She used to say, 'Most people are afraid of me.' Because she did give off this air of real self-containment and a kind of inner strength. I wouldn't say she was lost at all, but there was no master plan. She instinctively knew where to go! It wasn't an ambition; it was more an immediate sense of 'the next thing is this.' But I don't think she saw further than one step ahead. I don't think she thought, 'In twenty years, I'm gonna wear black and write my own songs with a harmonium,' or 'I'm gonna be a singer-songwriter.' It's 'I'm gonna try singing.'"

It is understandable why people—like Torjusson, who repeatedly said he was just a neighbor, not necessarily an insider—would get the idea of Nico as a distant personality. It was a common opinion. "I think she really had the measure of people. That's why she kept her distance, I think. She could really see a fool from a distance," Una Baines asserts.

James Young agrees. "She was an intelligent woman," he says. "Her mind worked on a different wave. I wouldn't even say she was slower, she just existed in a slightly different dimension to the people around her. People would think that she was stupid and say rather cruel things. She wasn't fast and smart, but she could read people very intuitively. She had a kind of street savvy." Though she never received any formal education as an adult—and incredibly aware of this seeming flaw in her character—Nico "was an autodidact. She liked to read," says Young. "She was 'unschooled,' as it were, but did like to read serious literature and didn't read trash. People like to caricature her as being morose—not really, no. She did like dark stuff, but it wasn't the corny goth thing either. I think just temperamentally she was melancholic and heavy. But I wouldn't say that necessarily meant a death wish or an obsession with death. She'd always be lugging around some enormous volume of something or other. For about three years it was the complete Oscar Wilde! Or she'd have [Samuel Taylor] Coleridge or [William] Wordsworth or William Blake. She was really into Blake. It's not light reading, all that stuff." Indeed, Nico's love of books and reading is evident throughout her interviews, as well as in her own notes. In her diary, she says, "The book I am reading is so well written. *Sanctuary* by William Faulkner, after *Light in August* it is rather stimulating." Ed Sanders of New York band the Fugs also recalled often seeing the singer at the Peace Eye bookstore in the 1960s: "Nico used to hang around the Peace Eye in the afternoons. She would sit and read books."

––––

Wilkin says that Nico rarely spoke about her years with Philippe Garrel as it had been "not a very nice time. All about drugs and not very safe." In Torjusson's memory, Nico had consigned any physical intimacy with men to the past. "I played music all the time but never professionally. I played Nico a song of mine, and she got the wrong idea. She thought I was coming on to her. She was like [*does impression of Nico*], 'I'm too old for this kind of thing.' She did say to me, 'I'm past relationships,' or 'I'm past that kind of thing,' because she thought I might have been interested in her myself. I wasn't there 24/7, but my strong impression was her sex life was behind her—she was not a sexual being. Not the energy for it. Not the appetite for it."

Dowdall shares a memory from touring that perhaps reveals Nico's view on sexual intimacy at the time. "So Nico wasn't having sex. In the early days, she was pretty fucked-up with heroin and she wasn't really eating a lot. She'd eat cheese rolls and custard. But a couple of times when we were on long boat journeys somewhere in Scandinavia, she had a cabin. She was bored. She'd come up to myself and Eric [Random] and she'd say [*does impression of Nico*], 'Why don't we go to my room and we can have a *partouze*?'[128] I didn't know what a *partouze* was, to be honest. She quickly explained what a *partouze* was, and I declined. There were several moments, several of those kinds of experiences, where she was bored and thought she'd fill the boredom with having sex, with either me or Eric or both of us."

———

As 1984 wrapped up, Nico signed a new record deal with indie label Beggars Banquet. "There was no big ceremony; it just happened in an office," recalls Phil Rainford. "We talked to Martin [Mills, founder of Beggars Group] for ages. Then we went and had a bit of lunch at a pub down the street. That was it. A lot of the excitement about getting signed was that the money would facilitate buying more drugs—heroin was the focus. At that time, she'd hit rock bottom. It was a way of building up her self-esteem again. It was good for her and good for everybody else because we all got bits of work out of it." A celebratory Marlboro cigarette was raised to the career resurrection. "Marlboro fags! She always had Marlboro fags!" laughs Rainford. "She also liked a beer. She wasn't a big drinker usually. I don't remember her thinking, 'I'll have a Martini on the rocks, shaken, not stirred.' She just liked a beer. If you see a lot of the pictures of her, you'll see there's a beer on the table."

———

After a lifetime of experiences shared with icons and notables, Nico seemed happiest surrounding herself with locals in her Manchester neighborhood and people she met through Alan Wise. "She didn't really socialize with the Manchester glitterati or hang out in clubs," said Nigel Bagley. "Hooky [Peter Hook from New Order] would occasionally turn up . . . her heroes were from a previous generation; the Bob Dylans and so on. She once asked me round for dinner, and there was this bizarre scene of Nico cooking couscous with one hand and cooking up heroin with the other. I was thinking: 'I hope she doesn't mix them up.' She has such a dark image, but there was so much funny stuff, and she was wonderfully deadpan. We met the film director John Waters who asked if she would sing at his funeral. She said: 'Call me when you're dead.'"

Hook had been a Nico fan for a long time before she lived in the northern city. I caught up with him between sessions mentoring young artists at a British university. "I used to do the sound for the Stockholm Monsters,[129] and we ended up doing a tour supporting Nico," he says. "Nico was pretty bad. She was barely eating. She was a mess, and she looked a mess, to be honest. [Her addiction] made her very miserable, very grumpy. Alan Wise was such a dirty old fucker that just used to plague her. She had hit rock bottom. In the concerts and stuff, she wasn't good. Alan Wise always used to say, 'Nico is the only act in the world that can only play anywhere once.' I'd go, 'Why?' And he'd say, 'Because she's so fucking bad and so miserable nobody'll ever have her back.' It was actually really, really sad. She used to do that cover version of ' "Heroes" ' [*does impression of Nico singing it*]. It was the most miserable fucking thing you'd ever heard in your life. I did feel exceptionally sorry for her at that point. But, in her defense, she kept going. She had stamina. Nothing could keep her down, which was absolutely incredible."

The state of Nico's health and career was a sobering example for the young artist. "As a musician, to watch Nico come down as much as she did, it wasn't something nice to witness. I'd say, 'Hello, Nico. How are you?' And she'd say [*does impression of Nico*], 'I'm so fucking miserable, Hooky. I am so fucking miserable. I live in fucking Prestwich. I live with addicts. Alan Wise is always trying to fuck me up the arse.' I was like, 'Oh God, I'm sorry I asked!' She really did wallow in it. A great character despite it."

Though Wise has been heralded as Nico's savior by some, Hook saw an unsavory side to the relationship. "I remember she did a tour of eastern Europe because Alan Wise…he didn't help her career, let me put it that way. He ended up taking her round all these really odd places in eastern Europe because they were the only gigs he could get her. He ended up taking her further and further afield. She nearly ended up at the North Pole under his guidance, God bless them both.

"He was telling me this wonderful story. They came back from Berlin on a coach, and there were fifteen men and Nico, all the band and the roadies and Nico. When they got to the East German border, the East German soldiers pulled the truck over and pulled them all off. They put the men against the bus like they were going to line them up and shoot them, and they kept Nico with them. All these East German soldiers were there, all armed, and they put Alsatians on the bus to search for drugs. Nico, first she just started patting all her pockets like she was looking for something, and they were all staring at her. And then she found something in her pocket and she pulled it out, and it was a heroin joint. She lit it, stood in-between two East German border guards, and smoked it. The fifteen of them were cacking themselves and she was just laughing. I just thought, 'What a woman.'"

Hook's bands shared the same studio as Nico, and he recalls how "She couldn't pay for a session once, so she gave the owner her harmonium, the one she used to play with her feet." The instrument "wheezed like an old bloke that smoked sixty fags a day for fifty years. We always used to laugh as Joy Division, and then as New Order, at this harmonium. But no one ever disturbed it as it was Nico's harmonium." Hook eventually bought the studio, but by then the instrument had disappeared. "It's so sad," he concludes, "as now you'd obviously treasure it."

43

As 1985 started, work began on an album for British independent record label Beggars Banquet. Alan Wise called Aaron Sixx to tell him about the new project. After all of the issues with *Drama of Exile*, Sixx "didn't really want to be involved" in any new Nico undertaking. According to him, Wise said it was John Cale whom the label had originally wanted to sign. Nico had been added because she was inexpensive. "Alan told me that Beggars wanted to do something with John Cale," says Sixx. "They weren't really interested in Nico, they wanted Cale. Nico was somebody that was very easy to work with. Cale could control her easily, given all the history. The story I got via Alan was that Cale said he would work with Beggars, but it has to be a Nico album." Whatever the genesis of the reunion, the duo were back in the studio after a decade apart. A name had already been chosen for the LP: *Camera Obscura*—a darkened box with an aperture for projecting the image of an external object onto a screen.

Recording started in March at Strongroom Studios in London. This time it was Cale, not Nico, who was suffering. "John Cale was actually worse than Nico," recalls Graham Dowdall. "He was coming to the end of his period of excess, so he was taking reasonable amounts of cocaine but drinking phenomenal amounts; he was getting bottles of champagne and crates of Grolsch delivered." Nico, however, was starting to reassess her health. "She was in a much better place by then," says the drummer. "She'd say things like, 'This is the best I've felt since the '60s.' I think she felt like it was an opportunity to get back into the game properly." Cale, too, noticed a change in his old friend. "She had a lot of depth in her personality that she didn't have before, better lyrics and sensibility. She wasn't as abrasive as she used to be," he said. "She's very together, a great lady, for somebody who most people don't associate with being a professional musician. She's very determined, has a very professional attitude toward her work." Even though he may have been battling his own demons, Cale still came through for his former bandmate. "He had this production genius, and it was incredibly exciting to work with him," says Dowdall. "He and Nico were like old mates, and it was pretty focused. John believed in her as an artist and he wanted to make sure she got a good album, under budget and on time."

Camera Obscura also formalized the relationship between Nico and some of the musicians with whom she had been regularly working. The record was officially attributed to Nico and "the Faction," the name given to her backing band. Dowdall recalls, "The core Faction was me and Jim [James Young], with Eric Random being the third member. The relationship between me, Nico and Jim was a really, really positive, creative relationship. We'd come round here to my studios; this is where we would rehearse often and demoed all of *Camera Obscura*. She trusted both of us hugely, musically. She was a little bit socially removed from Jim and was closer socially with Eric and myself, because Jim—love him!—he's a bit Oxford. We used to call him 'Gentleman Jim' and make jokes about how he had a butler who would clean his house and all of this silly stuff. And Nico was really in on that joke. She'd take the piss out of him for being this Oxfordian kind of character; obviously, Nico was from a different world. And I suppose Eric, myself and Nico were a little bit more street and a little bit more rock'n'roll than Jim. But she really trusted him musically and in terms of finding ways to support her melodies. I suppose the writing of *Camera Obscura* was a pretty pleasurable experience. It's a flawed album; it's not perfect, but some of that's down to Cale more than it is down to Nico. I'm proud of it."

The final touch was the silver and black cover art designed by Factory Records maverick Peter Saville. Saville had already created iconic LP artwork for Joy Division, New Order, John Cooper Clarke, Roxy Music and Wham! when the opportunity to work on an image for *Camera Obscura* came up. Speaking to me from his studio, Saville confesses, "It was quite a thrill to unexpectedly do something for Nico. I didn't meet her; a photograph was chosen and we made an acknowledgment to Warhol in a very '80s way. I had an American assistant [Chris Mathan], who designed the Nico sleeve. It's a hybrid of a sensibility of the '80s whilst acknowledging the prominence of Nico... The idea of doing something for Nico was like a moment of connection between the Velvet Underground and Warhol. It was irresistible."

Positive reviews began coming in for the album upon release. "She might be pushing 50, but she still looks a debauched 30," said Dave Thompson in *Melody Maker*. "Not for her the ravages of time. Perfectly preserved, she'll run forever, baffling 21st century anthropologists with her note-perfect impersonations of an industrial computer with a Greta Garbo fixation... Listening to Nico is... essentially a cathartic ritual, best experienced with the shutters pulled tight and the gaslight casting eerie shadows on the wall." Noting the new direction of the songs—"It is not classic Nico... there's no 'Janitor of Lunacy,' 'Julius Caesar' or 'Genghis Khan'"—Thompson writes, "But hell, a Nico album's a Nico album, and, accepting that John Cale's overwhelming presence should at least win him a co-billing in the credits, there really is no one else who could have made a record like this one." Mark Lanegan agrees. "I think Cale just appreciated her art and loved her as a person, even though by all accounts neither one of them was the easiest to get along with," he says. "They had something special between the two of them where they created great art, and that's really all that matters—making great art."

Other reviewers were not as gracious, once again dragging out the tired analysis of Nico's destroyed countenance. "She raises a hand to her face, feeling the lumps and the lines, her past marked out in secret codes," writes Don Watson in the *NME*. "Suddenly conscious of how badly she had applied her makeup this morning…her pale, powdery face, its lumps like a relief map of the modern age. Underneath all that fat was a face she once knew. How terrible she looked now," he concludes.

———

By 1986, Nico was going back and forth between Brixton and Manchester, if she wasn't on tour. A revealing Australian interview illustrates the nomadic, unstable lifestyle of the singer. After the DJ welcomes her to Melbourne, Nico responds, "I've not quite arrived yet." She goes on to tell him that she doesn't have a home, and even her passport notes her transient existence: "It says '*ohne festen Wohnsitz*,' which means 'without a fixed address.'" She claims that she prefers it this way, "as it's like being married when you have a home. God, it's terrible." Attempting to establish common ground, the interviewer says that living in Brixton must be very "intense," a nod to the neighborhood's racial tensions, reports of which had been shared around the world. Nico shoots him down, answering witheringly, "Not as much as people make out; Hell's Kitchen on the Lower East Side [*sic*] in New York is much more dangerous." In another interview, Nico is asked why she lives in Manchester. "Where I live right now reminds me of Berlin," she replies. "Manchester reminds me of Berlin, in a way."

Though claiming to enjoy the lack of permanence, Nico returned to Manchester not long after getting back to the UK from Australia. This time, Ari came with her, taking up residence with his mother.

In Manchester, Nico's appreciation of the city shines through via her diary, as she writes of local pubs ("Tonight we shall go for a drink at the Forrester's") and of being inspired by the city's history, referencing former residents Karl Marx and Friedrich Engels ("The real reason for my Residence here In M.[anchester] are Karl Marx And his friend F.[riedrich] Engels"). She even takes note of her neighbors and their culture, documenting, "The Jewish New Year is the most religious time of the Year and all the People are fasting during the day, I wonder if they can touch their Baking ovens themselves, or if they'll burn their fingers doing it. On Singleton Road they did burn their fingers."[130] An entry from October 25 shows how comfortable she feels in the city, saying, "Now that I am back in M[anchester]...I slept so very well here, I am mentioning it because that doesn't happen often that I get any decent sleep."

The last place Nico lived in Manchester was in the Century Park neighborhood. In 1988, the house was divided into flats and sold to a young married couple, making Nico an unwanted tenant. Homeowner Janet Wraeng recalled the gruesome state of the place when she found it:

> She ended up in squalor...that's the only way I can describe it. I know it's my house now, but at the time, it was appalling. There was water dripping everywhere. There was no heating. It was quite shocking, really...for someone to be living like that. Especially someone who knew so many rich and famous people, someone who moved in those circles...and she ended up in a squalor [sic] bed sit. It was quite shocking. She left the house in a taxi and we just stood there and watched her go. Literally [all of her possessions] fit in the back of a black cab. That was her whole life in three, four bags.[131]

With the encouragement of friends, and feeling comfortable in Manchester, Nico finally quit heroin. It was a long time coming, according to Phil Jones. "It was a different time, and I think we should've put her in a care home, got her cleaned up and she could've flourished. It was almost a Shakespearean tragedy. She was vulnerable, and all those people ignored her," he says. Sixx also recalled conversations about Nico's substance abuse. "I remember talking to Alan about the heroin problem. He said he'd get her into a methadone program." That is exactly what happened. "She decided to stop, and to get on the methadone," said Ari in *Nico: Icon*. "That was in 1986. She never took heroin again."

Jane Goldstraw remembers when Nico finally decided to embark on quitting smack. "She just said she'd had enough. She'd had septicaemia[132] and she'd had to go into hospital for about a week. She wanted me to brush her hair because she couldn't move, she couldn't get out of bed...She had a drip in and things," Goldstraw recalls. "The doctors told her that if she got septicaemia again, she would die. Once she came off heroin, she started looking really well. It was a huge difference, as she had got to a point on the drugs that she looked dreadfully ill."

Besides being almost fatally sick, the combination of encouragement from Wise and the imprisonment of her reliable drug dealer also helped tip Nico toward starting a recovery program. But though now off heroin, she was far from living the "clean" and "healthy" lifestyle that has often been attributed to this period of her life. Methadone is an opioid, originally created to help people in extreme pain, and it is often used as part of a treatment program to help people beat heroin addiction. However, it is not a "cure" and it has its own side effects. "Methadone is a horrible drug; it zombifies people," says Young. "She was on that evil 'chemical cosh' methadone; in my view it was methadone that contributed to her demise. I didn't like what it was doing to her. I guess it made her easier to manage—no more running around to find a connection."

Though off heroin, Nico was never completely "clean." "Nico clean? You kidding?" laughs Young. Whether it was white wine, the occasional beer imbibed while playing pool or hashish, Nico still partook of various other substances. "She preferred to smoke hashish, not weed," echoes Barbara Wilkin. "She didn't roll ordinary joints but what she called 'New Yorkers'—pure hashish in rolling paper—which she smoked with pliers all the way to the end—quite a skill without burning your lips. She also would share 'ordinary' joints or pipes if others were offering. I think she was happier on that, and without the hassle of getting the other stuff in seedy and dangerous places." Wilkin also notes that by this point, Nico "didn't have any veins left suitable to inject herself."

While using any drug at all is often frowned upon in recovery programs, this may have been the form of harm reduction that worked for Nico, dialing down the chaos of the previous decades. Though Young and others now argue that the methadone possibly had more far-reaching effects on her health, the singer's immediate improvement once she came off heroin seemed evident after years of a life that revolved around scoring and using.

Throughout the final pages of Nico's diary, there is a vivid determination to stay off heroin and stick with the methadone plan— her "medication." Her observations show how she is noticing, and appreciating, the world around her:

> They're cutting the trees down in the Garden and I like those trees. The new landlord seems to be rich but unromantic...Never mind, they were doing it on Singleton Rd. too, and I was furious, those clean-cut assholes have a lot to answer for...The little boy downstairs is too small to understand, but he would agree with me about pruning the trees, and the grass they're going to cut as well. Time for Ibiza, because of my Medication, it isn't easy to just live anywhere. At least it doesn't include Australia and Paris, because I know now where to go.

Here Nico is identifying where she feels comfortable traveling, her routine and plans no longer revolving around scoring heroin, instead focusing on places where she knows she will be able to stick to her methadone program. A later passage flips this around, as here Nico is "scoring" a check from a record label, while again noting the world around her:

As sure as it had to be today, my first check from Beggars Banquet and the sun is shining a perfect October day in these Northern Regions of the Globe. Some trees have real gold leaves…

Nico documents her healing in the pages of her diary. "Starting Monday, I will get my medication from Prestwich hospital and I am extremely relieved on this matter." She began to ride her bike more and take on responsibilities that she had never contemplated engaging with previously, like getting a bank account of her own. She marvels at each small victory, writing, "Opening a new Bank account has been easier than I thought it would have been, at least they can negotiate my checks instead of myself having to do so. The convenience is staggering."

The idea of past and present clashing against each other is a repeated motif. In a passage marked as being from "Tuesday morning, afternoon," Nico references two ghosts—one the previous resident of the house she is living in, the other herself—once again flipping between first and third person (the "long gone ghost"):

When a man from the council rapped at my door, asking for Fiona, a long gone ghost, this girl is too much, a life full of struggling for some false recognition. Bringing or rather getting facts all mixed up. Last night they showed some excerpts of "La dolce Vita" on T.V.

While addiction had held her hostage for decades, it had also created a persona which defined her—both to herself and to others. In her recorded thoughts she appears to be coming to grips with the time she has spent as a "ghost" herself because of the drugs. "My superstition being justified each time I did not keep my promise. Perhaps [someone] will change me the check from America, Something to show that I have lived there," she writes on October 3—again, a reference to existing, as if previously, when on heroin, she lacked subsistence. There is a constant push/pull in her words, between wanting/yearning to have permanency of any kind and the fear of taking this step. "The walls are shelter from the cold and rain," she notes, as she looks for furniture in the form of a settee for her home. "What the hell am I going to sit on. Some of us have the walls and others have the furniture," she argues, as if picking necessity (walls), while longing for, yet scared of, comfort (furniture). This internal tension is underscored when she realizes, "If I should go to Australia then I would abandon the damn furniture anyway," as if tossing away any actual acceptance of having a stable and homely place of her own. In a later entry, she writes, "Oh yes, I feel very privileged being here at this very moment, the walls are alive and well, what the hell is going on there, Someone is coming through the walls." It may be that she feels secure, but also that "walls" in this context refers to her ability to connect with others, something she has not done in a significant manner for a very long time.

Nico also seems to be taking her various critics to task, at last striking out, if only in her own personal notes, at the decades of cruel and unfair depictions of her perpetuated in the media. "A Newspaperman doesn't even have enough creativity to write a piece on somebody without needing a Tape recorder, even so they don't get the right picture. One's Identity is at the mercy of some spook story, totally untrue or out of focus, a big Lie. A good Newspaperman gives a credible Portrait of the Individual," Nico argues.

Nico is clearly starting to plan, or at least contemplate, an existence beyond a next hit. "Human nature is clumsy dealing with the future in such a futuristic way of invention," she writes. She looks to other stars for guidance, noting how old they are, as if to prove to herself that she can still be relevant at her age. "Bette Davis is still doing it, with as much as Parchment paper over her skinny face and body. Being thirty-five years my adversary. Lillian Gish being forty-three years older than myself. Marlene, she's still singing sometimes, when she runs out of money, if she runs out of money. Unless she was dealing with creeps like myself."

Nico returns to her lament about poor management, noting, "Somehow I never managed to find the Person to take care of my business." Yet this time, she admits that being without heroin is making it difficult to see not only the decisions she made before, but also what she must take on; being stoned would be an easier escape: "I expect some changes in the near future, my lucidity is half killing me, or should I say my Intuitions." Her dance with her own mortality still lingers at the forefront of her mind, as she writes, "Crossing Bury New Road past midnight last night on my bicycle, a car honked his horn at me as he passed, did he think I was suicidal, crossing the street just avoiding a crash excites me."

James Young also noted how the new, heroin-free version of Nico was less fatalistic and more hopeful than he had seen her in the past:

We were talking about death, as you do after a good spaghetti dinner. "I've got so close to it, so many times...it's like you begin to see it. First, when you're young, it doesn't exist. Then later it's a shadow, indistinct. Then you begin to recognize it as it gets closer..." Though she'd been intimate with the deaths of others—her father, murdered by the Nazis; her mother's death of cancer in a mental asylum; the execution of the American sergeant who'd raped her; the grave dust-laden air of Berlin; she'd also monitored her own mortality in her songs and in her life. Other people's deaths are not the same as your own.

Yet through all the internal damnation and inventory, Nico seems determined and excited to begin a new chapter in her life. "The moment is mine, and he who takes it is an Intruder to Here and Eternity. Unless you allow the occasion to happen you cannot think of yourself as a convincing actress," she writes in one passage, while in another she declares, once again using walls as an analogy to explain the changes in her life, "Winter penetrating these old walls, October, November, December 1988 this will be the most important turning point of my life, I better believe it too."

44

Tragically, as Nico entered this turning point in her life, Ari suffered a mental collapse, landing him in a Parisian mental institution. In his autobiography, he touches on the incident, but not in a great amount of detail. Nico's anguish is recorded throughout her journal, as she vacillates between worrying about her son, having hope and trying to spend as much time with him as possible. Within the entries about Ari, she reflects on her own flaws and troubles, even referencing Alain Delon. In one paragraph, she writes, "It frightens me how much we are alike sometimes, when I am bored I would also take anything to get rid of my depression, but you can't just take any old thing that'll make you crazy and insane."

Indeed, though now more than two decades had gone by since Ari's birth, Nico still remained angry, hurt and frustrated by her ex-lover. A letter in her diary, seemingly written for Ari, illustrates this:

Monday morning, today I managed to wake up a little earlier than normal and I shall go to see your father this evening. Perhaps we can talk some sense, or must this go on for another twenty years? Today has been the most destructive day since I came here, as soon as one involves other people even if they belong to the family it turns out to be a disaster, at the moment I have nothing to lose and everything to win.

Such notes directed to her son were not uncommon in Nico's diary, with the subject often being Delon, according to Ari. "She never ceased writing letters that she often did not send," he asserts. "And this correspondence never had a destiny other than myself. You who had left him. This obsession she had to reconnect with the flamboyant feelings that tied her to her carnal memory! This father who was more inaccessible than a star."

Now off heroin, Nico began to gain clarity. Even critics commented on her staying power, with one saying, "Possibly the only rumor about Nico that hasn't circulated so far is that she was once a man...Nico hardly needs such a drastic career boost. She is weird enough already." But Nico did need a different way of managing her life. She started to express frustration at the constant, demanding tour schedule, which brought what she perceived as little return. "My Management doesn't do me justice at all...I will not yield for less than three hundred, even that is an insult. If I sing long enough on some busy street corner I'll make enough to pay my rent. My Gas and Electricity is about to be cut off. This undervalued fee for the original Underground is uncomfortable. It creates all sorts of inconveniences. Like catching a cold because some other guys are driving the car that I should drive."

Pressure was mounting to once again return to the studio and make a new album. Nico was not excited about this prospect, writing, "When they say, that it's time for a new Album they mean I should repeat myself once again, the damned music nonstop and loud." Her patience with her schedule, her band and the music business in its entirety had run out. Yet the grueling days continued, as she still needed the money shows provided to survive. A letter to Lutz Graf-Ulbrich from February 1986 illustrates the global scope of Nico's tours:

Bondi 17 February 1986

Hello Babies, I'm here on tour with my group in Sydney, where we had three days of great success. It is summer here and very hot when we arrived. Since I've been here, it has cooled down. All the best, Nico.

Another entry from her diary further revealed her feelings, as she writes:

> The End of the month the damn Tour in Germany is starting,
> I am not in the least excited about it either. If anybody dares
> to be cheeky on this Tour, I will break his face. I shall tell them
> upfront, so it doesn't come as a surprise. They are unable to
> get a Concert together on their Name alone and are only using
> my Name to try and make it. This whole Music business [is]
> starting to bore me very much.

Amidst all of the exasperation, Nico seemed to be rediscovering a trace of her self-worth. She recognized that she had hit rock bottom, writing, "But nothing can give me a bad reputation anymore." She even calls out various bootleg recordings of her shows that had been made into poor-quality LPs as a quick source of cash, saying, "Even my Musicians and my Manager have tried to destroy my Music; either by playing badly or else by bringing out some cheap Production on Live tapes." Yet Nico saw herself as the proverbial phoenix from the flame, concluding the passage with, "All that cannot harm me, because my singing will always prevail. There isn't such a thing as my singing being bad, not even if I tried to be."

James Young shared Nico's irritation, but for different reasons. "At the end of 1986, I left [the Faction]. Nico wasn't doing anything new. If I'm really honest, I left in the hope that she'd say, 'Don't go, let's work on new material.' It had got to the point where it was just going round and round revisiting the same venues, playing the same music, and that carried on." Young wanted to provide Nico with a new direction in which she could take her music. "I'd get accused of being a prima donna because I'd always try and push her into doing new projects, which she'd always resist. I remember I was always trying to hit on her with new ideas. I said, 'I wanna do a German album and do German songs. We could do Kurt Weill! If anybody could do a Kurt Weill thing, it should be you! You were in Berlin! You're German. If anybody could do it...!' [*does impression of Nico*] 'I wanna sing my own songs. I don't wanna do it!' Just stubborn, stubborn, stubborn! I just saw so much potential. It was so fucking frustrating.

"She did like classical music, and I wanted to do a contemporary treatment of Schubert's *Winterreise*. That would have been amazing! Bringing in electronica, bringing in strange sounds that would not have been present in Schubert's world, but with her—wow! And some of her amazing lyrics. She may have been scared to bust out on her own completely, to leave behind the security of doing three or four Velvet Underground songs and then the rest of it all hers. To suddenly start doing stuff that these serious classical musicians do, it was probably terrifying. But that was the exciting thing, and I just couldn't get that through to her. Endlessly frustrating. I used to really nag her about it, and I think she got pissed off with me as much as I got pissed off with her."

Possibly to alleviate some of the pressure from her musical career, Nico returned to film, making an eleven-minute short with writer/director Sylvain Roumette. Called *L'Interview* ("The Interview"), the movie features Nico and her former lover Philippe Garrel's father, Maurice. The black-and-white movie begins with Nico looking into a mirror, touching up her makeup—a contrast to the idea that she did not care about her appearance. She and the elder Garrel are seated side by side, with Nico holding a notebook and pen. Behind them is a piano, and they appear to be in a living room setting.

The conversation bounces between the two, with Garrel first appearing to talk about the use of silence and actors in his films, then Nico seeming to read back from her notebook what he just said, interpreting it while adding her own flourishes and ideas. Every so often, an off camera voice directs and comments. It is unclear what the movie is trying to expound. It does, however, capture Nico's innate ability to both speak French fluently and be effortlessly captivating in front of the camera, bringing drama and a regalness to even the most pedestrian of movements, such as when she dons dark glasses and sips some sort of beverage from a snifter at the end of the movie.

———

The new year started off with a startling event. On February 20, 1987, Andy Warhol was admitted to New York Hospital, where his gall bladder was successfully removed. He seemed to be recovering; however, complications flared up and he suffered a sudden cardiac arrest. He died on February 22. Less than two weeks before, on February 10, Warhol had mentioned Nico in his diary, saying how "everything just looks right when she does it," referring to some "raggy clothes" that he had seen her wearing. Nico does not mention the passing of her former friend and mentor in her journal, but his death would most likely have saddened her. It may also have helped begin to set her free from the past, which Warhol had played such a large part in creating. Now off heroin, Nico was starting to think clearly for the first time in decades.

In his excellent book *Songs They Never Play on the Radio*, James Young recalls seeing Nico in 1987: "I'd hardly seen her for the best part of a year, and there was a distinct change in her. She looked older but seemed happier." Her diary captures this, as she seems to be making an inventory of her life, as if awakening from a dream. Manchester provided the stability she needed not only to let go of her addiction, but to begin to take responsibility for herself. Passages written throughout the year evoke the changing of seasons, but also the evolution of Nico.

The prospect of writing as a new outlet for expressing herself clearly excited Nico. It is clear that she is starting to set goals for herself—possibly for the first time:

In exactly three months and four days The book and the Record must be finished. This typewriter is beautiful...yes, it's true: if I write three thousand words every day, in one month [*sic*] time my book can be finished...When I write in this style it only coordinates my Plans, and I have a clear focus on everything.

Even when feeling uninspired, Nico still puts pen to paper, showing the same determination that propelled her out of Germany in the first place, while indulging in some self-reflection at the same time:

It's late and I find it hard to write anything of interest, except for the Girls on the Street that are very fashionable with their braids, some look healthy and others don't, I am working on mine by just letting it grow for the rest of my middle-aged life, it sounds like Paradox looking at myself in the mirror.

Writing provided Nico with something she felt she could control. Her thoughts on her own music at the time when she was using the journal on a regular basis make it seem as if she feels she no longer has ownership of her art. The book she is hoping to pull together will be her doing, and she is navigating the way it comes together without the intervention of anyone else:

Writing this book is going to take some time and nobody is going to steal any more of mine. Wherever I go in future the typewriter will be my companion, if that makes any sense at all. What am I talking about anyway, Smalltalk.

She expresses resentment toward her own band and believes she has been taken advantage of, stating, "All those young Musicians make me laugh having the nerve of demanding anything at all.

They act like Superstars[133] and want to make it running around on my expense, any more of that and it'll be the End[134] of their playing with me. If anybody thinks that nothing has changed or going to and that I refuse to sing for one hundred pounds a show they must be mad. Until now I have not budged to all these whims." On methadone, a strong, determined Nico emerges, as she swears "on the Name of my only child that nobody will steal from me anymore."

By this time, after more than 1,200 shows in just a handful of years, Nico was sick of the perpetual cycle of being on the road. The actual performance was always the same as well, surely making it exhausting and mind-numbing for everyone involved. Nico underscores this repetition, documenting in her own diary, "Tour is starting in ten days is crazy, when my tonsils hurt already. People think that tomorrow is a good day to rob me of my precious time." James Young also recalled her desire to stop playing so many gigs, noting, "She was tired of the endless tours and now just wanted to do the occasional well-paid prestigious show." Even gig attendees who were fans started to see the toll that nonstop performing had taken on Nico. In March 1987, a Brixton local named Andy saw her show at neighborhood venue the Fridge. "There weren't many people there. We stood right at the front and watched her with her little harmonium," he reflected. "Best thing she did were the old Velvet Underground songs. She was still very striking looking with a charisma that was noticeable but looked old and worn out. She looked like she might have been a bit of a junkie or something like that. Her skin wasn't too good. You never can tell, can you? I wouldn't like to judge somebody just on their appearance. But the voice was good. The backup band too did a good imitation of the Velvet Underground. They did 'Waiting for the Man.'"

———

Just as Nico was in the midst of all these emotional, professional and personal breakthroughs, tragedy struck once again. Ari fell into a coma for two weeks. It is unclear if this was due to a mental breakdown, a suicide attempt, an opiate overdose or an adverse reaction to a cocktail of drugs. It seems likely from Ari's diary and Nico's own notes that contact with Alain Delon had been attempted, with the ultimate result being rejection.

Guilt clearly dominates Nico's consciousness, as she writes of herself in the third person, documenting the struggles with her own recovery and touring:

> Code of Honor: Promises that I can't keep and feeling like a traitor, an unloyal mother, only to preserve nervous energy for the days of the end of this month when just before each performance she's just about to drop. One time, shortly after the show, in Halifax she nearly did not get back up. The heaviness of stone. Weighing that against a slow reducing dose, over two years on Methadone.

Much of the later part of Nico's diary is composed of her detailing her trips to and from the Parisian hospital to see Ari and her attempts to stick to the methadone:

> The sound of the life-support machines is something else and I shall put it on my next Album. When I come back on Tuesday perhaps they will let me tape it, without seeming bizarre. The Doctor must have thought that you have a funny mother, asking for Methadone. How could I leave M.[anchester] without enough of my Medication, they gave me a whole day's supply, amazing…

Nico portrays herself as the protective parent, discussing Ari's progress with nurses and doctors, specifically one Hedi Dahoud, who attended to Ari. Reviewing her diary, it appears that she tried to be with Ari as much as possible, the guilt of not being with him until this point clearly cutting her to the bone: "I can feel my nerves go bad, now is not the time to go insane, so it is slow motion for me, until this extensive nightmare is over...My dreams have not exactly given me the most of comfort. Three o'clock in the morning and I should go to sleep in order to wake up easier." Her notes are filled with details of her visits to Ari and his slow steps back to health:

> Today is my third day here and in a few minutes I am going to see my Ari baby at the Hospital...
> It's quarter to one p.m. and my Ari baby has just had his lunch at the Hospital in Paris...
> I am sitting next to you by your bedside my Aribaby...
> My Ari baby is much better than I expected.

At one point, Ari's doctors asked for a meeting with Nico, which she was not pleased with: "In the morning Ari's Psychiatrist wants to see me, if he chooses to be cheeky, I will tell him something." Nico ends up confiding to the doctor the family history of drug problems, but she feels that she is not believed or heard, writing in her diary:

> Sitting in your Psychiatrist's chair yesterday was an Experience, him asking me all these Questions about my maternity. I forgot to tell him that my father was an Opium addict and that I was conceived an Opium addict, nobody would believe me. The microscopical Vision of the world in my early childhood was something hard to deal with.

The longer Ari is in care, the more Nico's trust in the medical system crumbles. Her frustration at her inability to really help him is obvious, as she feels he is not receiving the correct care nor being housed in an appropriate facility:

At this place in Paris, Le Centre de Readaptation, it is a narrow building, most Patients are getting strong Medication, better get the hell out of there for they make you crazy, I would not be surprised if they do tape telephone conversations.

Delon is a specter who constantly haunts both mother and son. Nico's notes are filled with frustration, loathing, and desperation. "Wherever I may wind up tonight, I haven't a clue, to go and see Ari's father without a warning I might as well throw a Petrol bomb into his Office," she writes. "One hour ago I tried telephoning your father and... he wasn't back yet. It would have been useless to even try to see him tonight." Even as Ari lay in the hospital unconscious, Nico still continued to reach out to Delon, hoping he would finally accept her son.

He never has.

Besides her book, which she wanted to call "Moving Target," Nico was working on a new record and new projects. She had a small role in the Christel Buschmann film *Let's Kiss and Say Goodbye*. Not straying from her track record of art house esoteric, the movie is "A study of the alienated people who frequent the Ballhaus Barmbek dance hall, including an obese groupie, an old man reciting poetry, two young women and a regular dance employee."

Nico also went into the studio to record guest vocals with synth-pop new wave guru Marc Almond. The track, "Your Kisses Burn," appeared on Almond's fourth studio album, the appropriately named *The Stars We Are*. Almond had been a long-time fan and was delighted at the prospect of finally getting to work with one of his inspirations. "Nico was a mysterious figure, enigmatic with that great musical and artistic connection to the Velvet Underground and Warhol, which were things I was obsessed about at school," he said. "And of course that wonderful intriguing voice, icy and remote yet warm at the same time. She made a sound I'd never heard before—maybe some sort of a gothic punk Marlene Dietrich. The first time I heard her music was with the Velvet Underground, but I bought *Desertshore*, *The Marble Index* and *The End* and liked them more. There was also her musical association with Brian Eno, which made her more intriguing. When I became a musician, she was always at the top of my wish list for a duet of some sort."

Almond used his prior success to convince his record label to let him bring Nico in on his album. "I was so nervous to contact her and EMI were not really for it at all, as you can imagine. I wanted to make sure that she was treated like the legend and the star I felt she was. EMI balked at her demands, but I was insistent. It turned out she was lovely if fragile, and we played pool[135] and drank tea and talked for ages. The song was a problem, it turned out to be a bit too complicated, too orchestral for her and she began to deteriorate as the day went on and the methadone took effect. She still managed to deliver that wonderful Nico voice. We left on warm terms with plans for a better track more suited to her."

Nico still had tour dates lined up, much to her chagrin. "The last time I put her on," recalled promoter John Keenan, "she was in her leather trousers, and asked: 'Why don't more people see me? I will be dead soon.' I think she thought that, at 49, she was through; that generation thought everyone was past it when they got to 50."

Besides some solo shows, Nico played several gigs with John Cale. James Young was involved in these appearances, including those in Japan. Most of the Faction were reunited, acting as a backup band for both Cale and Nico. Nico would go on before Cale, much to her displeasure. "Nico didn't like the idea of us playing with Cale," Young writes in *Songs They Never Played on the Radio*. "It made her feel more marginal, more of a warm-up act. So on the way to every show there were rows about who was doing what, and the order of appearance, and the fact that Cale absolutely refused to perform a number with Nico." I asked Young why there was a stark contrast between Cale's formerly supportive role in Nico's life and the hard-line attitude during this tour. "Looking back, I think it was to do with John's iron determination to stay clean. He had just got off addiction to both alcohol and cocaine, and he was super-focused on staying fit and healthy. Letting Nico in on any level may have seemed some kind of threat to that, a doorway back to old habits. He relented later on, if I remember correctly, when we played the same bill in Brussels at the Grand Palais [1987/88?]...I think they sang 'A Child's Christmas in Wales' together."

At the time, Nico's constant touring had taken away much of the cachet of her shows, as their frequency made each proceeding one less special. Young noted this, saying, "Compared with her last tour of Japan, which had been successful both in audience rapport and in financial terms, this was a half-hearted affair. They'd seen Nico the year before, but this was Cale's first trip to Japan and so there was more of a novelty value attached to his appearances. Novelty is intrinsic to success in Japan...Famous but not popular was the verdict on Nico."

In June 1988, Lutz Graf-Ulbrich organized a festival called "Fata Morgana," named for the mirage that can be seen in deserts, among other places. It was to be held at the Berlin Planetarium, with five international artists composing and performing music inspired by the desert. Graf-Ulbrich immediately had Nico in mind as a possible participant. Her love for that landscape was well known: from *The Inner Scar*, which features several different barren terrains, to her time spent with Jim Morrison in Death Valley, it was her favorite place. When Graf-Ulbrich asked her what desert she wanted to write about, Nico answered, "the Moon."

Graf-Ulbrich had seen Nico sporadically since her recovery. "When I met her in her last years...she was very calm and gentle, and soft and not aggressive at all," he said. By the time of "Fata Morgana," Nico had been off heroin for two years. "She had lost weight and was slim again," said Graf-Ulbrich. "I had the impression that she felt quite comfortable in this period and that she had calmed down a bit from all her struggles with drugs."

Faction members Graham Dowdall and James Young joined Nico for the "magical performance." "There was a little stage, maybe 250 seats, the Planetarium machines were working," recalled Graf-Ulbrich. The absence of heroin made a marked difference to how Nico approached shows. "Nico's new positivism also implied a more self-conscious awareness of the music and it affected me to the degree that, for the first time in a long while, we were both paralyzed with stage fright," said Young. Dowdall has great memories of the performance. "The gig in Berlin was fantastic!" he says. "It was a glorious experience. She was on methadone by then and she was pretty healthy. She wanted to refocus, to do another bunch of original, strong material from a fresh, clean perspective. We thought it was the beginning of a really exciting new period. She was funny. I've got a photo of her climbing through the window to get into the dressing room. It was the only way you could. She was just sparky. Her aunt [Helma] was there. She was on form.

"Lutz had done this brilliant thing of getting us there. We spent three days of writing music in the planetarium. Everything was nice. She was in her home city. It was just great. She was just buzzing." He goes on to recall a specific funny memory: "She had these boots that jingled. They were really useful because if we were misbehaving or talking about her, we could always hear her coming because of the jingling of these boots." The last song Nico performed that evening was "You Forgot to Answer," the track she had written for Jim Morrison. "I think she felt like it was an opportunity to get back into the fame properly," says Dowdall. Young concurs, telling me that Nico seemed to be back on track, ready and wanting to do a new record and get in the studio. He describes her as being "really fired up" to start a new chapter of her life and career.

Young remembers Nico being in pain but refusing to take any medicine at the "Fata Morgana" show. "At the last concert, Nico kept saying, 'I've got this headache, I've got this headache!' She had taken to wrapping a kind of turban around her head, real tight. She claimed it really helped with the pain. I told her that she should see a doctor. She just looked at me like, 'Oh, come on.' She didn't want to get medicalized."

After the show Nico spent the night at Graf-Ulbrich's, as she was sick of staying in hotels. "She counted the money and was happy about the deal, but complained, as always, about the 'expensive' musicians," Graf-Ulbrich recounted. She confided to her old friend and former lover that she was sick of constantly being on tour and wanted to concentrate on writing, only booking gigs at big venues, like opera houses. She announced that she was going to once again seek refuge in her beloved Ibiza, where she would spend three months working on her book and catching up with Ari. Nico then invited Graf-Ulbrich to join them. Graf-Ulbrich turned the offer down, before driving the duo to the airport.

At the terminal, the staff wanted to charge Nico extra to bring along her harmonium. "She really flipped out and got very upset," recalled Graf-Ulbrich. "She kept insulting the entire ground staff of the company. That's how she entered the plane. One flight attendant gave me advice to look after her. 'The way she gets furious, she won't live much longer!' I just shrugged my shoulders." Though originally deciding against accompanying Nico and her son on the trip, Graf-Ulbrich later changed his mind and bought a ticket, the plan being to meet up with them in Ibiza. "I had this answering machine message from Ari that said, 'It's so nice, come to Ibiza with us!' And so I bought this ticket the next day."

Reading Nico's diary, she seems mindful of how vulnerable she was to backsliding into using. She also reveals, again, an awareness of the damage she had done with her substance abuse. She writes on March 18, 1988, "I still think that I am rather apt to taking heroin again, my mind does not function like it should, but as soon as a change of Scenery will refresh my Imagination."

The trip to Spain represented a blank slate of opportunity for Nico, both health-wise and financially. Jane Goldstraw saw her a couple of days before she left for Ibiza. "She was actually looking really well when she went on holiday," Goldstraw said. Phil Jones and Alan Wise had also finally sorted out Nico's tangled past album sales, culminating in an unprecedented cash flow. "We finally got her royalties for her—a lot of money. So she was able to come off drugs, decamp to Ibiza and live a normal life with her son," Jones recalled.

Young also noted how important the trip was for the singer. "I think Ibiza meant for Nico a refuge, a place of re-evaluation where she could live a less chaotic existence for a while," he said in Helen Donlon's book *Shadows Across the Moon*. "But it might also be that she was reimagining and wishing to re-enter the ethos of an era that was now gone. For European intelligentsia as well as bohemia, the Mediterranean, during the immediate post War period, represented something life-affirming after all that horror and destruction: the sun, the sea, fertility, Picasso, Matisse, Robert Graves, Lawrence Durrell, Bardot, Loren..." Highlighting the complicated and conflicting parts of Nico, Young continued, "[She] was definitely not a party animal...Nico was a bohemian, yes; a junkie, sure...but also a puritan."

46

In Ibiza, Nico had found her spiritual and emotional home. Her return in 1988 was an opportunity for her to fully embrace a heroin-free lifestyle and her budding writing ambitions and to forge a new start with twenty-five-year-old Ari. She even told a journalist as she left the UK, "I'm flying to Ibiza. It's my favorite place. I think I'll die there." The myth of Nico being obsessed with darkness is a prevalent leitmotif. It may have been more that death fascinated her and she knew how to play the macabre persona up to the media, as it was what they—and the fans—expected. In an interview in Berlin in 1975, she is asked, "Are there still any human beings around that you love?" Nico answers, "Yes. Death for example. (chuckles) Definitely."

It may have been the death of the "Nico" persona that she wanted, however. In her diary, she may have been hinting at this. She references her birthday, marking a renewal, when she first began taking opiates heavily (most likely the diet pills when she was twenty-one) and became internationally known as "Nico." She writes, "One is only once in a lifetime seven times seven years old. In sixteen days exactly will that happen to me, in sixteen more days I might be dead twice. But when she comes alive again, you better watch out for that shadow somewhere not far behind you." This shadow may have been the repressed, authentic Christa. "Warm, naive again," Ari notes of her temperament in Ibiza. "She thought that running a flower shop was the most beautiful job in the world." Alan Wise also recalled this fascination, saying,

"Toward the end, she wanted to work in a flower shop until she found out the wages. She went to a florist's to ask how much they paid. They told her £150, she said 'I can't live on a £150 a day.' They said no, it's £150 a week. She liked flowers." "She wanted to focus on writing—only writing—poems, autobiography, and other books," Ari concludes of Nico's plans.

She and Ari had been staying with a friend who went by the name of "Russian George" in a cottage close to the nearby Sant Josep Road. In mid-July, Ari was ill. Nico nursed him, taking the opportunity to make up for lost time, even biking in extreme temperatures to get her son water. Ari writes, "I had salmonella and she took care of me like a real mother, cooked me rice so I'd only drink the water it was cooking in. On 13th July, she went into town to do some groceries and buy some water; there was no drinking water where we lived. She pushed her bike over seven kilometers, under the fiery sun of July, with two jugs of ten liters of drinking water, as well as some food and bread. I recall her arrival, I was sat in the shadow, sickly, she was sat on the chair beside me, exhausted."

On July 17, Peter Hook happened to be in Ibiza and saw Nico at the end of the four days that Ari notes Nico spent caring for him. Hook and his New Order bandmates were in Spain to record their latest album, *Technique*. "We'd heard Nico was on the island and she'd actually got clean. That coincided with us getting really dirty. We had been out all night and decided to get breakfast Bloody Marys. We were sat in Ibiza town in a café. Lo and behold, who walked past but bloody Nico with Ari. We knew them both. We knew how difficult Ari could be, so we hid.[136] She didn't see us. They went in another café and had something to eat and drink. It was breakfast time. It was like 11 o'clock in the morning. She decided to cycle back to Santa Eulària, which is a long way."

Once back at the cottage, despite it being over 32ºC outside and the hottest day of the year, Nico decided to head back down into town in order to buy some hash, pedaling the eight kilometers to get there. She had been complaining of a bad headache and thought the medicinal properties of the drug would ease the pain. As James Young had seen her do before, she wrapped a large piece of black fabric around her head, as she believed it would help alleviate her discomfort and protect her from the sun. According to Ari, she spent almost an hour in front of the mirror, getting her makeshift headdress just right. She then asked Ari to pump the front tire of her bike, but seeing how weak he still was from his illness, Nico went ahead and filled it with air herself. At precisely 1 p.m., she left the cottage on her bike, heading down the hill, donning sunglasses and with a copy of Mark Twain's semi-autobiographical travel novel *Roughing It* tucked into her black coat. "See you later, darling," she said to Ari. "I saw her go down the dirt and rock road and disappear behind the pine trees," he recalled.

Afternoon turned to evening, and Nico still had not returned home. At first Ari, still sick with diarrhea, was not concerned about his mother's absence. "The night of the 18th, as she wasn't back yet, I wasn't too worried, thinking she was sleeping over at some friends of hers, in Figueretas," he writes in his memoir. However, when Nico did not return the next day, Ari started to get anxious about his mother's whereabouts. Though still ill himself, he began to look for her:

> The next morning, no Nico; at noon, I was worried. I struggled down the large path going from *la finca* to the road; we lived two and a half kilometers into the mountain. I took the bus, went to the hospital—the very one, I would learn later, where she was refused treatment—to obtain medication for diarrhea. Then, I walked to my friend Manolo, who was the only one who had a phone. We called the police: nothing. Clive [Crocker], a long-time friend, arrived later. We called hospitals: Insular Hospital, the Cruz-Roja, where she was also refused admission; then the last one, the biggest, slightly out of town. A

380

doctor answered us: "Yes, you can come, she's well." We jumped in Clive's Jeep and went to the hospital right away.

Clive Crocker recalled the hunt for Nico. "'Has someone been brought in?' 'Yes, yes.' We finally found her. We went to the hospital," he remembered. "Once there," said Ari, "the doctor, with vivid emotions on his face, told us: 'I'm sorry, it was the wrong person.'" Crocker continued: "They said, 'She was in here.' 'What do you mean, was?' 'She died.' We didn't know why they were speaking of her in the past tense." Ari, Crocker and their friend Manolo, who had also accompanied them to the hospital, were then asked to go to the morgue to identify the body. "Manolo entered the room with me; Clive, her old friend, couldn't. I kissed my mother on the forehead, then left to puke behind a car parked in the entrance of the hospital." Crocker lamented, "It was a terrible sight; she was so dour, lying there."

Lutz Graf-Ulbrich got the call from Ari that Nico had passed away. Having bought his ticket earlier the same day, he was greeted at the airport by "headlines of the newspapers everywhere: 'Icon Dead.'" Even in death, Nico was defined by the men in her life, as Graf-Ulbrich recalled arriving at the terminal, only to see the "*Berliner Zeitung* headline: 'Nico: Death of a Star from Berlin Reveals the Secret Love Drama of Alain Delon.'"

Ari brought Graf-Ulbrich back to the *finca*. He showed his mother's friend around the house, then offered Graf-Ulbrich the use of Nico's bedroom. "When I entered, I felt strange," Graf-Ulbrich recalls. "Her organ was standing there, and next to it her high boots. It was as if she had just left the house for a walk and would come back any moment. Ari had asked me to bring a cassette from her last concert...He put it into the recorder. We were listening to it and each of us was crying silently." Ari also loaned Graf-Ulbrich Nico's diary, which she was hoping to turn into a book.[137]

Graf-Ulbrich eventually went to the hospital to get a last glimpse of his old friend. "The terrible look on her face of..."—Lutz pauses to find the right word—"...aloneness."

No one knows exactly what happened to Nico. Various theories and versions of events have been batted around since her passing. One story has her falling off her bike and rolling down an embankment, with passersby calling for an ambulance. An alternative is that a taxi driver found her slumped on the side of the steep road that goes down Figueretas hill, her bicycle on the dusty ground nearby. Some newspapers declared that she was "thrown" from her bike, then suffered an injury which led to her passing. One website even went so far as to use Nico's fatal accident as an example of why it is important to wear a bike helmet. Sunstroke has been blamed, as well as undetected underlying medical issues, which may have arisen from years of drug abuse or been hereditary or set off by the methadone or caused by the fall. There is no definitive answer.

It was noted on the medical records that a young couple had brought Nico to the hospital but left without providing their names or contact information. In the attempt to find out what exactly had happened, Graf-Ulbrich and Ari took to the airwaves in Ibiza, asking for those involved to come forward and identify themselves. A German girl and a Spanish guy responded and related what had happened. The couple had seen Nico ride by them on her bike as she traveled into town. In her book *Shadows Across the Moon*, Helen Donlon retraces (with James Young) what is thought to be the exact path of Nico's last journey:

> We walked on past the giant elevated clock that also serves as a barometer at the top of Vara de Rey, we turned uphill into Via Punica and stopped at the exact spot where Nico had fallen off her bicycle. We took photos in the shadows; in the urine-scented alleyway just off the main drag of Avenida Espanya, where the blazing summer sun had by now turned the afternoon into an eternal siesta. The alleyway contained a dowdy and old-looking flower shop and no other signs of life.

James pointed out the sad irony of the florists being probably the last thing she saw before she fell off her bike: apparently she had been considering retiring from the world of touring and opening a flower shop herself.

According to the couple, they later found her on the side of the road, next to the upturned bike, near to where the Hotel Montesol used to be. The two tried to talk to her, but she had become paralyzed on one side and could not communicate—a horrible irony as she spoke seven different languages. The duo also claimed that Nico was waving a book by Oscar Wilde[138] around with her one good hand. They took the singer to a Red Cross hospital, which would not admit her; the staff there thought she was a vagrant and "refused to deal with her because of the state of her arms...shattered with needle marks." A second hospital would not see her as she was a foreigner and did not have health insurance. A third also barred entry, asserting that Nico was just an old hippie who had been out in the heat too long, her heavy, dark, woolen clothing adding to their disgust. Finally, a fourth hospital, the Can Misses, agreed to take her in. Though she was unable to speak, at the entryway Nico vehemently shook her head and attempted to say "No," her lifelong lack of faith in traditional medical practices most likely having been further underpinned by her recent experience with Ari's care. Ignoring her pleas, a nurse put the singer onto a gurney, misdiagnosing her as having succumbed to sunstroke. She was left on a hospital bed, drifting in and out of consciousness.

In the morning, a doctor finally examined her and realized that she had suffered a cerebral hemorrhage, leading to a large quantity of blood leaking into Nico's brain. The medical staff attempted to give her lifesaving injections. Tragically, after over a decade of intravenous drug abuse, there wasn't one viable vein via which they could administer the medication, leaving Nico to suffer a slow death alone in a hospital room, horribly aware of where she was but

383

unable to speak, unable to ask why nobody was helping her. No one recognized her; they thought she was just another drug casualty. She officially passed away at 8 p.m. on July 18, 1988.

———

In a 2017 interview, Lutz Graf-Ulbrich was asked whether Nico had any phobias. He answered, "The sun. And that was what killed her in the end." In another article, he goes on to say, "She was 49, but it was more a miracle that she survived so long. She outlived her colleagues who died much earlier, because of drugs or whatever. She was so strong, and she'd had such a full and rich life." Paul Morrissey blamed her passing on the Spanish care system, saying, "Nico died from not having health insurance in Ibiza." "She didn't even reach this thing we call 'Saturn return,'"[139] mused Andrew Loog Oldham during our interview. "Mind you, the years she put under her belt, she still qualified." Victor Brox shared Graf-Ulbrich's shock that the singer had lasted as long as she had. "It's ironic, given her inclination for romance, that her death was already mythic," he noted. Her fellow Superstar Viva, sounding vindictive to the end, added, "To survive all those years and then fall off a bike to your death seems a little cruel. When I heard the story I said, 'I bet she was stoned.' She outlived most of the others—Edie, Jim Morrison, Tim Hardin, a lot of the Factory people, even Andy himself. It's kind of hopeful news for junkies. She's their Saint Nico now."

More than thirty years later, Peter Hook is still upset that he did not get to say goodbye properly. "I always regret that. There's quite a cautionary tale in it, to see her on that day that she died. That was a real shock. I felt really stupid with that one, honestly. Shame."

"I feel sure it could have been prevented in some way," James Young says, reflecting on her death. "If she had been in Manchester, then Alan Wise would have insisted she saw a doctor...a real one."

Ari has precious memories of the last days he shared with his mother in Ibiza. "A fortnight before her death, we went to the hotel El Corsario together to drink a beer. Through a small window, she showed me where she lived thirty years ago, on a boat stuck to the quay, with Alejandro, the cousin of Juan Carlos the current king of Spain, who at this period, in 1958, was a friend of hers," he recalls. The Nico he describes sounds serene and content: "She was going through her memories, and was beautiful, very beautiful again, at peace; I would almost say happy. Looking, in the shadow of the *finca*, at some old books about Ibiza, illustrated with photo engraving…What I miss is kissing her or hugging her or holding her hand. She would turn up and say: Hello Arilein! Let's go to the café and have a beer. She had a very low voice, like that.

"It's the sun," Ari concluded. "I know that killed her. Definitely."

There is a theory that Nico may have known that she was unwell and had limited time left. "Last year I was talking to Ari," Young said in *Shadows Across the Moon*, "and he thinks she knew she was dying. So now, ultimately, I guess there was another agenda. She went to Ibiza to die. She didn't want to die in Manchester, or Berlin or Paris or New York. She wanted to die in a cradle of life. As a girl she saw Berlin on fire, watched the death trains to the camps roll by, lived her dream life literally in a graveyard. The Mediterranean would bathe her body clean, bleach her bones, return her to the source …for Nico, Ibiza represented freedom: freedom from the world and, ultimately, freedom from herself. It was a place she chose to live, to reinvent herself…and to die, a free woman."

47

Twen: What are you especially proud of?

Nico: To have survived so far. I often thought
that it was useless to go on living. As a child, I was very
sad, but looking back, I am grateful for my childhood. I
do not think that I can still make any bad experiences, I
I have them all behind me. I realize that one does not
die and then is dead. It continues, only in a
different form. There is no escape...

Her grave is impossible to find. It is in a forest, in Berlin,
obscured by ivy, trees, and leaves.

Danny Fields

Lutz Graf-Ulbrich took on the task of telling friends and family of Nico's passing, including her beloved Aunt Helma. She remembered, "Lutz brought us the news of her death. That was all terrible. I do not want to go through that time again." Graf-Ulbrich and Ari began to plan Nico's funeral. They decided to have her cremated, as she had written in her notebook specifically that she wanted "to be burned." This entry appeared next to a carefully handwritten copy of William Blake's poem "The Tyger," Nico's animal on the Chinese horoscope.

Even in death, Nico could not find a place to rest. It was not possible to get her cremated in Ibiza as her German nationality made her a "foreigner," so her body was placed in a crate and shipped to Barcelona, where friends and family had been told it would not be a problem to have the service performed. However, in an eerie echo of her hospital refusals, her body was barred from entry as there was a two-week backlog of funeral services. The crate was finally flown to Berlin, with the ever-supportive Helma and cousin Ulli paying for transportation. Nico finally got her wish and was cremated, her ashes being placed in an urn.

Alan Wise wanted the ashes to be sent to Manchester, saying that Nico had told him she wanted to be spread over the moors above the city. With this in mind, Wise and the Manchester contingent held a memorial service on August 6 at a Yorkshire church where Nico had supposedly once said she wanted to be buried.

Meanwhile, other plans were in motion for the final resting place of Nico's remains. Ari and Graf-Ulbrich decided that because of the close relationship between Grete and Nico, the two should be reunited at last. Nico's remains would be interred at Grunewald Forest Cemetery, a burial ground still known by many as "Suicide Cemetery." Located on the outskirts of Berlin, Suicide Cemetery got its name from the high number of people who took their lives in the nearby Havel river, only to have their bodies washed ashore and buried, often illegally, by their relatives in Grunewald Forest (in the past, suicide victims were not allowed to be buried on sacred soil, leaving few other options for the bereaved). It was here, amidst the green, overgrown foliage within the gated cemetery, that Nico's ashes were buried, alongside her mother's, on August 16, 1988.

Many of Nico's friends from Manchester attended the funeral, among them James Young, Alan Wise, Eric Random, Graham Dowdall, Phil Rainford, and Victor Brox, as well as Barbara Wilkin's parents and sister. Wilkin was preparing to get married when she heard the news. "When I found out, I thought, 'I have to fly out, get my flight, because Ari is alone there.' Lutz flew out, so that was okay. Alan couldn't fly; he didn't go onto airplanes. I missed most of it [the funeral] because I was in transit. I was flying over [it] and I could see them down there in the middle of a forest at a beautiful lake."

"I remember being really, really sad," says Faction drummer Graham Dowdall. "The most distinct memory: as we lowered her into the hole, a little shrew came out of the hole and ran away. It was a beautiful moment. We all saw it as it scampered away. The whole thing was so sad. There's this famous star and singer—a human being—and the only people who were there to commemorate her life were a handful of friends. That was it. It was like, 'Wow, so that's how it ends.' That was horrible. It's sad to lose your friend, and particularly to lose her at a time when she was about to burst into a new vein of post-heroin creativity."

Phil Rainford was especially disturbed by the absence of the East Coast community. "Alan informed all of those New York people that there was the funeral going on, and we didn't get an answer off any of them," Rainford recalls. "Not even, 'She passed away? Sorry to hear [that].' Nothing. There were not that many people at her funeral; there were about twenty, maybe a few more. It was all people who had either known her as a child or as a teenager or as a young woman, or the people from Manchester. I think that they were her friends. They were the people that cared about her. We all really liked her and had great affection for her. I loved her as a friend and felt very protective of her. All of these people that had nothing to do with her for the last ten, fifteen years of her life, they were never there." Wilkin concurs about the glaring absence of those from Nico's Factory days, saying, "None of those big names were there—none from New York." However, like Rainford, Wilkin affirms that "quite a few" people from Nico's adopted home town of Manchester made the journey to say their last goodbyes to the singer. Danny Fields tells me that he was never made aware of Nico's funeral, as he would have made it a priority to go if he would have known. Fields makes it a point to visit Nico's grave at every opportunity; he has been there at least five times to pay his respects to his dear friend since her passing.

One person from Nico's past who did show up on his own was

her long-time lover and collaborator Philippe Garrel, making the trip from Paris to Berlin. Described by Young as "a shy, rumpled little guy in a borrowed suit and tie," Garrel was one of the only attendees representing Nico's post-youth/pre-Manchester existence that day.

"It is convenient now for them to be friends with somebody that is mythologized," says Rainford. "They have a connection with her in some way. When Nico was alive, it was convenient for her to have that connection with Bob Dylan and the Velvet Underground and Andy Warhol, because that was a selling point for her as well. But in actual fact, they weren't her friends in the sense that they actually cared about her. The one she had a bit more connection with was the Welsh guy, John Cale, out of the Velvet Underground. He produced a couple of her records, but once he was done, he would disappear. Maybe he'd call her once a year to say, 'How are you, Nico?' and that'd be about it. None of the other ones ever did. And even he didn't turn up at her funeral."

After the ceremony, the attendees got together at a lakeside café for a few drinks, bought by Aunt Helma, and shared their favorite Nico stories. In an effort to offset the funeral costs, Graf-Ulbrich had set up a memorial concert that evening at the same Berlin planetarium where Nico had performed just months before. The recording of Nico's last performance, at "Fata Morgana," was played, as the visual effects of the lights, stars, and planets swirled by.

———

"Everyone was concerned about the unstable Ari," Graf-Ulbrich recalled of the period right after Nico's death. "To me, he seemed more or less okay, but he was obviously taking tranquilizers." According to James Young, a deeply distressed Ari tried to sell the last of Nico's methadone to interested buyers, his own dependency on drugs increasing in the months following the funeral. Alan Wise set up Nico's only child to inherit any money from sales or publishing that would have been due to his mother. "When I got my mum's royalties for the first time, I spent the money on smack," Ari confided. "I was hooked. I was taking a gram a day... I called my psychiatric doctor in Paris and I spent two weeks in the hospital. I got off heroin. Then I got a check from the Velvet Underground and bought a ticket for Raroia, Tahiti. I was taking Valium, pot, and beer and I got beaten up, then arrested, and someone tried to kill me."

Ari returned to the East Coast of the U.S. in the hope of recapturing some of the magic from his younger years. Yet things did not improve for the lost son. "Back in New York, I went out of my mind," he writes. "I spent winter out on the street; rescuers found me in the River Hudson. I had no money, no passport, nothing. Someone told the cops, who took me to a psychiatric hospital. They gave me five brain electric shocks. A friend got me out and took me back to Paris. I had two months of treatment in psychiatric hospitals there and then in the south of France. Now I'm trying to get back into myself. I'm not yet strong enough, but one day, when I am, I will confront my father and I will do it for the sake of my mother."

As he had haunted Nico, Alain Delon is a dark, unpleasant ghost who still torments Ari. Nico never stopped trying to get the actor to recognize her son, but sadly she died without achieving any resolution. "My mother was accused of 'poisoning' the life of the star and his family," Ari asserted. "It was not so. Certainly, she was obsessed, all her life, by Delon, to the point of writing letters to him that she never sent. Shortly before her death, she had written him a letter of reproach for not having reached out to me. She would have so desired that something bring peace to our three minds."

"For me, she was a very good mother," Ari said in a 2018 interview. "She gave me everything, even the drugs. I lived it with her without it being a problem. In the end, we shared the drug, the same syringe, it was a way of being together. Until the last moments of her life, she was flamboyant. She had a crazy, dry, acidic humor, with a great sense of derision, a rock'n'roll woman who seized the stage like a lioness.

"I have only good memories of my mother. She was a very funny character, she had a great sense of humor. She loved me very much, we had a special relationship. It was unique, almost like man and wife, although nothing incestuous, although people sometimes thought we were married. We had an artistic relationship. She was a great lady and I miss her very much. To me she was just my mother, a great woman who always tried to protect me.

"There was something that never was broken between us... although we've been separated by these bloody bureaucrats and laws. My mother was an artist. Is an artist. She was there for me.

"She was what she was," he concludes, "living her life the way she wanted to. And she did it until the end."

EPILOGUE

In 1996, the Velvet Underground was inducted into the Rock & Roll Hall of Fame in the U.S. Nico was not included. "Not everyone bought their album, but everyone who did started a band," proclaims the website. It goes on to say, "The Velvet Underground was literary but down to earth, schooled in both highbrow culture and the streets. They wrote about life as they saw it—drugs and all—but they saw the beauty in bleakness." Just like during her time with the group, Nico was not seen as truly being part of the group and went unrecognized as the brave, trailblazing maverick she was, although all of her former bandmates—Lou Reed, John Cale, Maureen Tucker, and Sterling Morrison—received the accolade. Her absence was a glaring omission.

Ten years later, in 2006, local councilors in Nico's birthplace of Cologne, Germany, denied a proposal to call an unnamed square within the city "Christa-Päffgen-Platz." The reason given as to why they could not move forward with the idea was that it was because of her "drug career."

ACKNOWLEDGMENTS

It has taken more than the proverbial village—more like several galaxies of people—to put together what I hope is a compelling, thoughtful, and proper biography on the complicated, funny, talented, flawed, and inspiring Christa Päffgen. It has been an honor to dedicate these last years trying to set the record straight and illustrate the very real woman behind the myth. It would never have happened without the generous, unending support of so, so many people.

The biggest thanks has to go to my husband James for being my world, and always encouraging me to go for the seemingly impossible. I love you with all of my heart. You inspire me every day to just give it a bit more.

I never thought in a zillion, million years I would have the opportunity to write a book for Faber or Hachette. It is beyond a bucket list accomplishment, and I am forever grateful and indebted to the all-round legend that is my agent Matthew Hamilton. Your belief in me means everything. Having you in my life makes it a better place to be.

The patience, generosity and support of my editors has blown my mind, and I am eternally grateful to the goddess that is Faber's Alexa von Hirschberg and Hachette's fabulous Ben Schafer. To somewhat quote Hall & Oates, you've made my dreams come true.

Another massive shout-out must go to the Faber team, Alex Bowler, Mo Hafeez, Hannah Marshall, Dan Papps and Josephine Salverda, as well as the beautiful Hachette crew Michael Barrs, Carrie

Napolitano, Michael Giarratano and of course Zachary Polendo. I am honored and grateful for all your work on this special project.

This book would never have been the comprehensive text it hopefully is without the friends, family, neighbors, colleagues, fans, and even random strangers, ranging from people I met at the British Library to the archivist at the Andy Warhol Museum, being so insanely generous with time, resources, emails, phone calls, contacts, cups of tea, and my constant fact-checking.

SO THANK YOU FROM THE BOTTOM OF MY HEART TO: Ian Bahrami, Actors Studio New York, Andy in Brixton, Joe Bidewell, Bruno Blum, Victor Bockris, Joe Boyd, Victor Brox, Budgie, Clive Crocker, David Croland, Jonathan Donahue, Marianne Enzensberger, Tammy Faye Starlight, Steve Finger of the Los Angeles Free Press / Los Angeles Free Press Archive, Ford Models New York, Christina Fulton, Lutz Graf-Ulbrich, Matt Gray at the Andy Warhol Museum, Stella Grundy, David J. Haskins, Peter Hook, Phil Jones, Robert King, "Spider" Mike King, Mark Lanegan, Mark the cab driver, Stephen Mallinder, Jonas Mekas, Gillian McCain, Kris Needs, Lucy O'Brien, Danny O'Sullivan, Andrew Loog Oldham, Ari Päffgen, Davey Payne, Henry Rollins, Peter Saville, Jerry Schatzberg, Aaron Sixx, Cosey Fanni Tutti, Jim Tisdall, Lol Tolhurst, John Torjusson, Michael Wadada and Guy Webster.

Thank you to Vincent Fremont for being my first interview and being so generous with thoughts and memories.

BIGGEST HUGE KISSES AND HUGS to the living legend that is Danny Fields. I love you. Thank you. You are amazing. I could not have asked for a more meticulous, loving, honest, funny, generous human to come into my life—you are a joy.

To Dave Navarro—of the hundreds of interviews I did for this book, yours was one of my favorites. Thank you from the bottom of my heart for sharing your time, your support and your thoughts with me and everyone who reads this book. You are a true gem. A big thank you to the fabulous human that is Peter Katsis for making it happen. You are brilliant.

To Mr. Iggy Pop—I can never thank you enough. From the first moment I found out I was going to have the honor of interviewing you to the kind words about the book, I am humbled. This undertaking would not have been complete without you, and I am ever so grateful. Thank you to Henry McGroggan for all of the encouragement and support—it means more than I can say.

Thank you to Robert and Ollie at Orbit Beer for being the fire starters to the Nico marketing campaign here in the UK. Huge love to my rad Northern pal Mal Campbell and the Trades Club in Hebden Bridge for all the support from the second news dropped of the book.

Huge thank yous to some other "behind the scenes" folks that made all of the interviews, transcribing, and research magic happen: Dave Anderson, Alice Atkinson, Kevin Banducci, Neil Bradshaw, Alice Cowling, Matthew Elblonk, Jenn Federici, Rafa Cervera, Steve Chibnall, Kunal Dole, Laura Dre, Kevin Gasser, Luke Griffiths, Constantin Grönert, Peter Hale, Ed Hamilton, Robert L. Heimall, Mike Heron, Emily Holley, Carrie Kania, Daniel Kellner, Becky Knight, Betsy Lerner, Beth Lopez-Barron, Joel McIver, Alexandra Mills, Alicia Morton, Jeremy Nagle, Jean Petrovic, Marie-Hélène Raby, Maggie Rodford, Gaynell Rogers, Corrina Seddon, Fran Shepard, Lisa Silverstein, Kirsty Swift, Barry Taylor, Taylor Thompson, Brendan Toller, Dave Tomberlin, Ayşegül Üldeş, Cyndi Villano, Jon "Webbo" Webster, and Leone Webster.

Thank you Christian Biadacz for sharing your incredible interview with Helma Wolff.

I would not get through without my family of friends—love you to the Milky Way and back: Lucy & Shaks Ahmed, Carissa Ainley, Nina Butkovich Budden, Calyx Clagg, Kristen Carranza, Emma Curley, Terry Currier, Bill Frith, Janeen Rundle and the Oregon Music Hall of Fame, Cyn Dillane, Audrey Faine, Julie Foxen, Peasy Gordon,

Stacy Horne, Alex Hurst, Jessica Jones, Ian Luke, The Mandell family, Kym Martindale, Rebecca McGrellis, Rich McGonigal, Ian Scott McGregor, Becky McGrellis, Pat McGrellis, Christina Meloche, Roisin O'Connor, Megan Page, Kelly Paschal-Hunter, Tim Piumarta, Marci Prolo, Will Sergeant, Francesca Shepard, Sheri Siegfried, Ben Smith, Long Sun, Jo Whitty, and my beloved BIMMers, Hayley Jordan, Nic Ledger and Laurence Tritton. Thank you to my guru and mentor David O'Connor for being the best boss ever.

Thank you to my best friend of over two decades, the infallible, inspiring Lynne Collins. I love you so much and am honored to have you in my life.

My UK family of besties—do not know what I would do without you. Thank you for being my backbone Andrea Fincham, Alix Brodie-Wray, Niamh Downing, Margareth Ainley, Julia Ruzicka, Julie Weir.

Special thank you to my idol and all around badass Barney Hoskyns. I am also hugely grateful to Jeffrey Smith and Nicole Raney at Discogs for believing in my writing and helping me to stay positive during the plague lockdown.

Thank you to Rich Novak for believing in me and being an amazing mentor.

Thank you to my tireless research assistants—this book would not be here without you. Big love Cameron Black and Roisin Downing.

Thank you to Andrea Halter and Philip Steger for tirelessly and generously sharing your resources and work with me.

The folks who were close to Nico during her Manchester years— Una Baines, Graham Dowdall, Jane Goldstraw, Phil Rainford, Barbara Wilkin—you have given so much to this story and I am honored and thankful. You are all such special people.

To James Young, who wrote one of the best books ever about rock 'n' roll—thank you for being a sounding board, for making me laugh and always inspiring me to write better.

THANK YOU to my Santa Cruz family, for always cheering me

on and reminding me of what is important: my forever VP Tami Cady, Tori Kistler (lady bugs rock!), Bruce and Mary McPherson, my brother from another mother Steve Palopoli, and my adopted big sister Celeste Faraola Perie.

A big hug and a kiss to my Aunt Janet Pucci for being the best role model of how to be a strong, beautiful woman, and to my Uncle Ray Santana for teaching me patience, acceptance, and how to eat a sawdust taco.

If I stupidly forgot you, thank you too.

Lastly, a huge thank you to Christa Päffgen. It has been a pleasure and a privilege to spend the last four years with you. I hope I have done you justice.

NOTES

1. Thank you, Philip Stegers, for all of the help in tracking down the information about the orphanage, the factory, and the *Meldekarte*.
2. During the war, the factory operated under the name of Klöckner Humboldt Deutz AG (KHD).
3. In her diary, Nico refers to her grandfather, Albert Schulz, as "Opa." In his interview with biographer Richard Witts, Ulli refers to Schulz as "Opi."
4. During World War II, the Silesia region was the site for both the Auschwitz and the Gross-Rosen concentration camps.
5. One account, written by an anonymous female journalist between April 20 and June 16, 1945, notes how people were gradually returning to the habits of cavemen, a lack of modern necessities—electricity, running water, transport, shops—bringing out the most primal of behaviors. For example, she recalls seeing a horse die in the street; instantly "penknives are straight out, hacking it to bits for meat; people fight over their portions."
6. In 1966, she shot a series of Warhol "Screen Tests," holding the very same kind of chocolate.
7. Tatjana Gsovsky was an internationally renowned ballerina, choreographer, and ballet mistress at a variety of well-respected institutions, including the Berlin State Opera House and the Deutsche Oper Berlin.
8. Famous shopping and leisure destination in Berlin.
9. In one 1956 shot, Nico poses outdoors, against a stone wall, a fountain and ivy directly behind her. Wearing a floral cocktail dress, pearls looped around both her neck and her wrists, hair pulled neatly back, she appears incredibly young and vulnerable, as if she is playing dress-up in an adult's wardrobe. In another set of images, taken by Tobias for *Vogue*, the teen morphs repeatedly: in one frame, she is hidden partially by a black veil, a cigarette holder seductively placed between parted lips, the

portrait of elegant sophistication; in the other, an off-the-shoulder white lace dress is accessorized with black gloves and a flowered fan, Nico staring directly down the lens. In a fourth Tobias image shot from the same year, a fresh-faced, tanned, pixie-haired Nico dons a striped shirt and straw hat, the photo one of the few in which the model is smiling.

10. The photographer was a survivor. Like Nico's father, the aspiring artist had been conscripted into the *Wehrmacht*—the unified armed forces of Nazi Germany—and was sent to the Russian Front. There he began documenting the war through the camera lens, a skill he had taught himself from the age of ten. Shortly before the war ended, he deserted, only to be captured by U.S. troops and thrown into an American prisoner of war camp, where he stayed until being released in 1945. After the war, Tobias began a relationship with another man, an American civilian named Dick, who worked for the occupation government. Such liaisons were illegal in Germany under Paragraph 175, a part of the German criminal code of the time that made homosexual acts between men a crime. Both Tobias and his lover were forced to flee in order to avoid arrest, ending up in Paris. It was here, using a camera that had been a gift to him from Dick, that Tobias began pursuing photography as a possible profession. His pictures first appeared in a 1953 issue of *Vogue*; however, this triumph was quickly followed by Tobias being thrown out of his adopted country for resisting arrest during a police raid on a gay club. He found himself deported back to his native Germany, moving first to Frankfurt in search of yet another new beginning. Having been labeled a sex offender after his previous breach of Paragraph 175, the photographer needed a cash injection to sustain himself. He entered and won a competition worth 3,000 Deutsche Marks. The prize also included his photo being featured as the November 1953 cover shot for *Frankfurter Illustrierte*, positioning Tobias as one of the most sought-after fashion photographers of the post-war generation. Though he found success in Frankfurt, Tobias was intrigued by Berlin, where he hoped to find the embers of the swinging 1920s scene. It was there that he first locked eyes on a young Christa Päffgen.

11. A set of images, taken in Paris at the studio of French photographer Jeanloup Sieff, illustrates the emerging identity of the model. With Nico blonde and short-haired throughout, each image showcased a different possibility for the Nico identity. In one, the model is bathed in shadow,

wearing a long-sleeved black shirt and pants. Glancing to the side, the light falls perfectly on her defined cheekbones and the spiraling smoke emanating from the cigarette held between her fingers. In another shot, Nico is naked from the waist up, wearing only what appears to be a pair of black-footed tights. Her body is twisted around so that her back is to the lens, her emaciated figure highlighting every rib wrapping around her back to her chest. Eyes directly to camera, she looks defiant, scowling, mad, while still holding the cigarette. In a final picture, Nico appears nude, her body carefully positioned to preserve her modesty.

12. There has also long been a rumor that Nico makes a guest appearance in a Hemingway classic. A scene in the opening chapter of 1964's *A Moveable Feast* arguably could be based on the singer but is not specific enough to verify conclusively.

13. It makes sense that Nico would want to align herself with Chanel in any way possible. The two shared a similarly dysfunctional upbringing. Chanel was raised by nuns in an Aubazine orphanage, becoming a ward of the state after the death of her mother and abandonment of her father. The sisters helped secure the girl a job as a seamstress, which she left at the age of seventeen to pursue a career as a cabaret singer, which proved unsuccessful. Having to find a way to stay financially afloat, Chanel become a mistress to wealthy socialite Etienne Balsan. Balsan helped the ambitious young woman relocate to Paris and open her first boutique. He also introduced her to his upper-class circle of friends, providing her entrée to the elite of France.

Chanel, like Nico forty years later, dared to transcend the expected parameters for behavior and style. As her legend grew in the 1920s, the designer began experimenting with materials, styles, and accessories that had solely been the reserves of men. Her success, as well as her work methods, were unheard of, especially for a woman. At other fashion houses, garments were sketched out then cut from the patterns, before being stitched together. "A sketch, that's not a body," she said. "Here, we don't sell slips of paper. For a dress to be pretty, the woman who's wearing it must look as if she were nude underneath." Chanel's approach of needing "to touch and feel a woman's body," her habit of tactically handling "her models in ways that she would never touch a man" were unconventional; but they allowed her to stitch together designs on a live person, creating her distinctive style. As it was mainly women that Chanel worked with, it was mainly women who observed the designer's creative processes. This led to Chanel feeling repeatedly let down by colleagues and collaborators alike, as a sense of female solidarity seemed impossible.

14. By the time of Nico's arrival in Paris in 1956, attitudes had shifted, with the city being internationally known as a sanctuary for the LGBT community, and often referred to by some as "Paris-Lesbos" thanks to its reputation as the world capital of lesbianism. Yet even those with money, power, and status had to be discreet. Regardless of the city's tolerant attitudes, "normalcy"—i.e. straight, heterosexual relationships—had to be maintained at all costs. If Chanel was bisexual or gay, it is unlikely she would have publicly confirmed and announced it.

15. Crocker's description of Ibiza in the 1950s sounds incredibly appealing. "I came here and I went to live on the beach," he recalls. "It's now a crowded tourist beach, but it was nothing. There were three little houses, and I rented one of them. It was all sand and sunshine. I decided to go into town from Port d'es Torrent, which is on the Sant Antoni side. It was deserted and wonderful. There weren't any roads. Tarmac roads to the airport didn't come until way in the 1960s. People were very easy. I didn't lock my car, for instance. I didn't lock the house. There wasn't any stealing."

16. Another liaison with a famous icon is said to have taken place during the run-up to the making of the 1967 Warhol film *I, a Man*, starring Nico. According to biographer Richard Witts, Nico divulged to actress Tina Aumont "at the time," but "never mentioned again," that she had had sex with none other than fellow Factory Superstar Edie Sedgwick. When asked about this supposed romance, music manager Danny Fields told me, "I can't even *imagine* such a thing without chortling." He dismisses this story, because if it had actually happened, "it would have been known to us... They may have cuddled one night at the Castle [in LA]; it was scary for the two of them being alone there," Fields postulated. He continued, "Nico asked me to come up and stay because, you know, I'm so strong and always armed to the teeth. But Edie had a boyfriend who was leaving when I got there, and neither of them ever liked *any* girls very much. I don't think [Nico] had many girlfriends. She was like so many of them are: a man's woman... The girls around then were so nuts, anyhow... the two of them [Nico and Edie] chasing after

404

whatever drugs were around. I can't imagine they sat and had a girlie talk, though. Well, maybe they did. You know, it's one of those things. Like Jane Austen can't picture a conversation between men, so she never has two men alone talking to each other; you will never find that in her books. I can't picture a conversation between women like Nico and Edie Sedgwick. And I won't even try."

17. Like Nico, as a teenager Mangano had supported herself by modeling, going on to win the Miss Rome beauty pageant in 1946, before becoming a contestant in the Miss Italia contest a year later. She parlayed this success into a film contract, simultaneously marrying film producer Dino De Laurentiis.

18. Cover features included the Italian publication *Tempo*, where she is named as "Nico Otzak," with the foreboding tagline under her image proclaiming, "*Una debutante senza batticuore*"—a debutante without heartbeat. Another Italian periodical from the same year features a fresh-faced Nico on the front, this time billing her as "Nico Otzaak, the very blond Berliner model, very well known in Italian high fashion ateliers. Also Nico Otzaak, very new demonstration of intercommunicability between the two environments, fashion and cinema, had some time ago a part in the film *La Tempesta*, directed by Alberto Lattuada." The May 1959 edition of *Elle* has a multiple-page spread of Nico, this time looking extremely slim, at the beach in a variety of modest swimwear, including one photo where she is in a checked bathing costume, and another where she is posed by a large beach ball. A series of covers followed in 1959, ranging from German magazine *Der Stern*—in which Nico, credited as "Krista Päffgen," has a wide-eyed, schoolgirl head shot, complete with a bow holding back her blonde tresses—to a set of shots by Frank Horvat for *Jours de France*. Photographed for the latter in the Bois de Boulogne, a large public park in Paris, wearing a full-length ice-blue Nina Ricci gown, Nico—here named as "Nico Otzack"—looks otherworldly, as if she has just emerged from a fairy tale. The images are beautiful, haunting, and dark, as Nico peeks out from a sea of desolate trees.

19. Started in 1946 by married couple Eileen and Jerry Ford, Ford Models was New York's aspirational, elite agency, and the first to establish an international presence, representing women from around the globe. Some Ford models from the 1960s became household names, including Jean

Shrimpton, Ali MacGraw and Candice Bergen. In 1968, Ford put out a book, *Eileen Ford's Book of Model Beauty*, which was filled with makeup and health advice. The book also included images of Ford's most successful protégées from the 1950s and '60s. Nico is not among them.

20. The Actors Studio is best known for working to refine dramatic arts skills in its student body of playwrights, thespians, and other artistic professionals, and for teaching the "method acting" mode of performance, an approach which requires an actor to have complete emotional identification with a role.

21. The largest film studio in Europe, located in Rome. Considered the center of Italian cinema.

22. This cinematic tour de force spawned terminology that is still used decades after its release. "Paparazzi" comes from Marcello Rubini's wingman, the photographer Paparazzo, who attempts to snap the notable and the sensational, while the polo-neck sweater donned by Nico became known in Italy as a "Dolce Vita." Even the title itself has passed into popular vernacular around the globe, connoting "mindless hedonism" in the U.S. and Britain, and a contrasting "sense of physical well-being" in Italy.

23. To this day, only twenty-six foreign-language films have ever grossed more than $10 million in the U.S.

24. Having already won an Oscar for best foreign film with 1952's *Forbidden Games*, a movie about two children who create a graveyard for deceased animals, Clément was well known for his attention to detail and for reveling in the difficulties of nontraditional shoots.

25. The January 24, 1961, issue of the Italian magazine *Mascotte Spettacolo* features a stunning portrait of the model, taken by Enrico Sarsini. Nico looks sweetly into the camera in a modest long red shirt dress. Here she is billed as "Nico Otzack." The bold print on the front includes the cryptic caption "On the Cover: the beautiful model-actress [*sic*] Nico Otzack collects all... the difficult people who live between Via Veneto and Via Margutta among the second-rate characters who are stirring in the cinema waiting for the right opportunity. Suspended between filmmakers and painters, the beautiful, very elegant Nico shows no excessive haste. She feels, with her innate optimism, that sooner or later they will notice her: once upon a time Fellini was attracted by her 'type' and included her in the interminable cast of 'La Dolce Vita.' There is no reason why others do not follow the example of the popular director:

our cover has, this time, the function of a reminder for filmmakers who are distracted by other matters."

Just four months later, the image taken by photographer Jeanloup Sieff for the cover of Swiss magazine *Camera No. 5* once again illustrates Nico's chameleon-like ability to radically change appearance. Still noted as "Nico Otzack," she is platinum blonde, appears barely made up and wears a sea-foam-green cardigan, buttoned conservatively all the way to her chin. She looks similarly demure on the front of the September issue of U.S. magazine *Esquire*, in a picture taken by Robert Denton and Dan Wynn. She still has a surname in the credits, but has dropped the "c," here being referred to as "Our Cover girl, Nico Otzak."

26. Nico appeared in an array of wacky ads, including a *Harper's Bazaar* spread for Neocol cold cream and another within the pages of *Elle* magazine, in which she poses in a dowdy pink-tinged dress next to a dishwasher, the bold print proclaiming, "Everything clean… The washing up of five people clean in six minutes!"

27. The film is famous for having a fluid narrative structure, the characters referred to throughout as simply "the man" and "the woman."

28. The male Nico was working on the groundbreaking movie on race and class, *Shadows*, directed by John Cassavetes. Cassavetes was an early pioneer and advocate of independent films in America.

29. One advertising campaign for Lanvin perfume, shot by Willy Maywald, has the dark, mysterious bottle in the foreground, with Nico's head, resting on a pillow, hovering and slightly blurred behind it.

30. It would be more than twenty years before Brox next heard from his former lover and protégée. "I had not spoken to her in a very long time… it was totally out of the blue," he told me, referring to a 1985 phone call he received from the singer. "'Victor? It's Nico. Do you have any heroin?'"

31. The image became the cover for the January 1963 edition of *Elle* magazine, with the uplifting cover caption: "Hello 1963! Happy New Year 1963! But first, happy first week! This brand-new issue brings you our warm wishes by the radiant grace of this brand-new mother."

32. As an adult writing his autobiography, Ari uses the word "abandoned" to describe him leaving Grete on her own, though he was just two when he left Ibiza with Boulogne.

33. Dylan decided to go to Paris for a few days to meet the man who had

been translating his songs into French, Hugues Aufray. Aufray made the 1965 LP *Aufray Chante Dylan*, one of the first albums made up entirely of Dylan covers, and very likely the first such record to be performed by a non-English speaker.

34. The friend was Ben Carruthers. Carruthers was already well known in his own right, having had a role in John Cassavetes's pioneering movie *Shadows*. Nico may have met him through Nikos Papatakis, the producer of *Shadows*.

35. Judy Collins released a version of the song in 1965, saying that Dylan wrote it for her, but also noting that he said the same thing to Joan Baez. The liner notes for Dylan's 1985 *Biograph* box set confirm that a version of the song was taped for Collins on January 14, 1965, but do not specify who the song was about or for.

36. Upon returning to New York, Nico encouraged photographer Jerry Schatzberg to get hold of Dylan's records. During one of our interviews for this book, he told me, "She was one of the few people that kept talking to me about Bob Dylan." Schatzberg was not sure about the affair between the two, but says of the time, "The thing is, everybody dated Bob Dylan! Everybody would say, 'Oh yeah, I dated him.' He probably went out with a lot of people. He was always in the company of a lot of people." However, it was Dylan's music that Nico was most keen for Schatzberg to check out. "She'd be like, 'Jerrrry, have you listened to Bob Dylan?' in that voice of hers!" Schatzberg laughs. "I'd say, 'No, not yet, Nico. I will, I will, don't worry.' If she'd hear that I was in Paris, she'd come to my hotel and call me up from downstairs and say the same thing. Nico was just sort of funny. I love the idea that she would just find out where I was and call me up just to ask me if I'd heard Bob Dylan yet.

37. It may have been on this visit that Nico shot a series of Spanish television commercials and print ads for Fernando de Terry brandy. She is in full Swinging Sixties mode throughout the campaign, with thick, thick eyelashes, tanned skin, and heavy eye makeup. The ads are great examples of *Mad Men*-era cheese, from clichéd scenarios—Nico sitting by a crackling fire with a handsome gent; Nico leaning against a potted plant, glancing at the guy in the foreground, who is holding a snifter of booze—to the simply "Huh"?—Nico in a polo-neck sweater, holding a volleyball in one hand and a bottle of Terry in the other, surrounded by

men holding up newspapers; this is *after* the opening scene of a white stallion dashing through breaking waves on a beach. In yet another ad, she is shown in a tuxedo, posing and pouting with a bottle of the grog, the other hand leading the same large horse by a rein. Though originally filmed in 1964, the campaign ran for at least three years. In his 1999 autobiography *What's Welsh for Zen*, John Cale remarks on seeing one such ad while on vacation in the Canary Islands in 1967, with his then fiancée Betsey Johnson. In it, Nico is donning the same white pantsuit that became her trademark during her Velvet Underground tenure.

38. Stage name of actress, model and sometime singer Danièle Ciarlet. Like Nico, Ciarlet had many famous beaus during the 1960s and '70s, including Brian Jones and actor Jack Nicholson. She and Nico also shared the commonality of heroin addiction while they made *Le Bleu des origines*.

39. Two years after his affair with Nico, Jones found himself on trial for drug possession. A psychiatric report on the guitarist came back with findings that may have explained his sexual appetite, saying, "Mr. Jones' sexual problems are closely interrelated to his difficulties of aggression… He is still very involved with Oedipal fixations. He is very confused about the maternal and paternal role in these. Part of his confusion would seem to be the very strong resentment he experiences toward his dominant and controlling mother, who rejected him and blatantly favored his sister."

40. It was Warhol's second visit to the French capital in just over a year. He'd made his debut there in 1964, when he introduced himself to Europe via his pop art screen print renderings of electric chairs. The new show was filled with large, bright, neon flowers, representing the burgeoning hippie movement in the U.S. and the return of spring to the city.

41. In her autobiography, another member of Warhol's clique, Ultra Violet, describes the Factory, saying, "The one thing that unites us all at the Factory is our urgent, overwhelming need to be noticed. Fame is the goal, rebellion the style, narcissism the aura for the superstars, demi-stars, half-stars, bad-stars, no-stars, men, women, crossovers, over-sexed, desexed, switch-sexed, decadent, satanic denizens of Warhol's new utopia."

42. A letter from Nico to Dylan was auctioned off at Christie's on April 30, 2002. Sent to Dylan, care of the Savoy Hotel, in late May 1965, it

shows Nico's acute understanding of how important her connection to the emerging icon could be for her career, as she writes, "Please, please, you promised to write me songs & I want to sing your songs… They are the only ones that make sense for me & my life depends on them."

43. Page went on to be the guitarist and founder of Led Zeppelin.

44. Oldham now pins what he considers the failure of "I'm Not Sayin' " on the fact that he was trying to copy a hit Bob Lind record of the time, "Elusive Butterfly." Still determined to make something happen, Oldham soldiered on, though he later said of the experience, "It's not working, she can't sing it." However, "A lot of people like the record ['I'm Not Sayin"]. I don't because I know what's wrong with it, and it wasn't a hit," he concludes.

45. The filming was most likely done on May 8, 1965, when Nico visited Dylan at the Savoy Hotel in London.

46. Nico featured in a random assortment of advertisements, including one for sweater company Bernhard Altmann, in which she waxed lyrical about the product's "cable stitches of baby-sized braids on rich-as-whipped-cream cashmere."

47. Warhol Superstar Ultra Violet described Morrissey's role at the Factory as being "father to the rest of the group. He is pleasant, sensible, the most normal of the crew and takes care of business. He sees that bills are paid, papers signed, supplies delivered. He has the soul of a social worker—which he was, with a degree from Fordham College, until he became keeper of the menagerie. His uncombed frizzy hair covers his forehead. He has light eyes that constantly dart about. He is thin, tall, dressed in black jeans and a black turtleneck."

48. Between 1964 and 1966, Warhol made more than five hundred of these short treatments, though few were ever publicly screened.

49. "If there exists beauty so universal as to be unquestionable," Malanga once wrote, "Nico possesses it."

50. Panna Grady was an American heiress who, in the 1960s, was known for hosting parties that brought together artists and the literary elite, as well as for being a generous patron to writers, primarily poets.

51. The two share a sandwich and a cigarette, as the camera zooms in and out, panning up and down. Discussion moves from Nico trying to discern if there is any sexual spark between the two to her being motherly and urging Borscheidt to relax. The overriding narrative, if

there is one, relates to the comfort and established parameters that the closet provides, with freedom and the unknown lurking beyond its walls.

52. Though a reel from it was included as an opener at some of the first premieres of *Chelsea Girls*.

53. $80,000 in 1964 is the equivalent of around $620,000 today.

54. In the same passage from *Please Kill Me*, Aronowitz goes on to complain that Nico refused to sleep with him, which brings doubt to the validity of his tale, casting it instead as possibly just a case of bitterness and disappointment in failing to bed the German beauty.

55. There also exists a set of films taken by a young cinematographer, Danny Williams, and Warhol insider Barbara Rubin. Shot on January 27 and 28, 1966, the tapes include an appearance by the Velvet Underground on New York talk show host David Susskind's television program. The reels also show the group traveling on a bus and cameos by other Factory associates and New York artists, including Tuli Kupferberg and Ed Sanders of the Fugs, Angus MacLise, Gerard Malanga and Paul Morrissey. They do not have any sound, are often out of focus, and Nico is absent throughout. Williams went on to become an important part of the Warhol/Factory circle, both personally and professionally. Soon after meeting Warhol, he moved into the artist's Manhattan town house. Williams was charged with creating the wiring for much of the Velvets' light show and shooting other "experimental" footage, using Warhol's own Bolex 16 mm camera. He mysteriously disappeared, aged twenty-seven, after visiting his family in Massachusetts. The car he borrowed was found next to the ocean, but his body was never recovered.

56. Using the word "big" instead of "tall" in this context seems a bit of a knock, as "big" comes across as meaning oversized and unappealing, in contrast to "tall," which is more aspirational. Even these basic adjectives create a context of belittling Nico and chipping away at what little she had created in her seemingly glamourous modeling career.

57. Before subletting the Jane Street apartment, Nico lived at the Chelsea Hotel.

58. Two of Reed's other former girlfriends claim the track was inspired by them. Shelley Albin asserted that the song came from a conversation that she and Reed had during their college years, while Barbara Hodes argued that the tune's origin came from being "about the sign Pisces, and about its liquidity and duality."

59. This was the first Warhol film to feature sound. Shot in 1964, Gerard Malanga is shown wearing a tuxedo, while off-screen discussion can be heard between several others, including Billy Name.

60. Filmed in 1964, the silent black-and-white Warhol film *Henry Geldzahler* features the art curator, Henry Geldzahler himself, smoking a cigar and becoming increasingly uncomfortable over ninety-seven minutes.

61. Part of the footage from that night was later used in Mekas's avant-garde movie *Scenes from the Life of Andy Warhol*.

62. The plot centers around the last night of Mexican Hollywood star Lupe Velez. She has planned the perfect suicide, setting the stage with lit candles and donning decadent attire, before ingesting a large dose of barbiturates. Instead of making a glamourous exit, Velez is depicted dragging herself to the bathroom, nauseous from the drugs. The final scene shows the starlet drowning in the toilet bowl's water—a chilling parallel to Edie's own trajectory.

63. Sedgwick saw Dylan as her opportunity to build on the acting career she had started with Warhol. But she also had romantic inclinations. "She said, 'They're going to make a film and I'm supposed to star in it with Bobby.' Suddenly it was Bobby this and Bobby that, and they realized that she had a crush on him," says Malanga in 2009's *Uptight: The Velvet Underground Story*.

64. Edie left the Factory and Warhol aged twenty-two, returning for sporadic visits. Addicted to heroin, she took to always wearing long sleeves to hide her track marks from the probing eyes of former friends. She passed away from an overdose at the age of twenty-eight.

65. Another Warhol protégé, who appeared in several of the artist's films, including *Chelsea Girls*.

66. Warhol was especially appreciative of their stylish attire, writing in *POPism*, "The kids at the Dom looked really great, glittering and reflecting in vinyl, suede, and feathers, in skirts and boots and bright-colored mesh tights, and patent leather shoes, and silver and gold hip-riding miniskirts, and the Paco Rabanne thin plastic look with the linked plastic disks in the dresses, and lots of bell-bottoms and poor boy sweaters, and short, short dresses that flared out at the shoulders and ended way above the knee. Some of the kids at the Dom looked so young that I wondered where they got the money for all those fashionable clothes."

67. Though Cale recalls this as being the studio where the initial tracks were

recorded, other sources say it was at Scepter Records Studio on West 54th Street in New York.

68. Dolph said of the artist's participation during the sessions, "Warhol was there on occasion. He had his little tape recorder, which he carried all the time. I seem to remember him there probably for about two hours in the aggregate over maybe three occasions. But he was totally fascinated by what was going on, and I don't think he made any aesthetic judgment whatsoever. 'Gee, that sounds good' might have been it. He was a spectator.

69. On both, the chanteuse signed her name as "Nico" and "Christa Päffgen."

70. Gerard Malanga later claimed that Morrison "adopted his look" of trademark skintight leather pants after seeing Malanga dance on stage at the Trip with the EPI.

71. Sessions took place at TTG Studios in Hollywood.

72. Though no known footage exists of the eight-week series, an interview with Paul Morrissey in 1967 recorded that Nico's appearance had a price tag of $500 attached (Warhol charged $1,500). A script from one episode survives, and it seems farcical that Nico would be involved. In this particular show, Nico was to talk about the 1947 movie thriller *Dick Tracy Meets Gruesome*. The pages read: "Hi luvs. I'm Nico. It's just super-marvelous being Miss Pop Art of 1966. It's something I've always dreamed of, but never thought would happen to little me. Imagine! Andy Warhol, the famous pop artist, Campbell Soup Cans, underground movies, the Plastic Inevitable, picking me! But, I'm not here to talk about little me, I mean, what I'm here to talk about is so super-fabulous, these movies that Channel 7 is going to show for the next eight weeks, they are REALLY what's happening." The lines are completely improbable and show again a complete disconnect between the woman striving to be taken seriously as an artist and any other good-looking generic presenter.

73. Another cause for stress was the loss of their stronghold at the Dom. Upon returning from California, they were greeted with a nasty surprise: in their absence, Bob Dylan's manager had swooped in on the growing following the EPI had built and renamed the venue the Balloon Farm. This led to the band refusing to play any New York shows, as they were annoyed and worried that any additional scenes they started would also be snatched from under them. "There was a lot of backbiting going

on in the band," John Cale later recalled of the time. To top it all off, Warhol was noticeably absent from EPI gigs, his attention and interest clearly pulled somewhere else. A short tour of the Midwest in October and November, with shows sometimes paying less than $1,000 each for the entire group to split between them and de facto tour manager Paul Morrissey having to use a Greyhound bus as transport, did not help sweeten an already dour atmosphere. "It wasn't very good when Andy started losing interest in the whole project," said Cale, as "For one thing, traveling with thirteen people and a light show is a kind of mania if you don't get enough money. And the only reason we got a lot of money... was because Andy was with us." Nico echoes this frustration in her diary, writing, "Touring with The Velvets and Ari was fun but no money was to be made, we used to get five dollars each to live on per day, it just reminds me, what the Papers said about the fabulous amounts of money we were supposed to have made, sometimes we did not have a bed at night and had to spend the night in the car with little Ari, as he was. There were too many people involved and traveling with us, even when they had nothing to do, they all wanted to be part of it...'The Plastic Exploding Inevitable.'

74. Such statements, though not made by Nico, arguably have impacted on her legacy, and help to underpin the myth of her being racist.

75. The ceremony included Warhol painting one of the paper dresses from Abraham & Straus—this time worn by a model—with ketchup, as he "thought they were so great" he "couldn't help doing something with one at that wedding." Wedding presents included "an inflatable Baby Ruth bar" from Warhol.

76. Though advertised to appear with the band for a February 17 performance in Massachusetts, the chanteuse was absent, with many of those attending saying that her failure to appear negatively impacted the show—another indication that, more than a year after joining the band, she was still considered the star attraction.

77. Nico did not return the singer's affections, which may have led to a later altercation. Friend and former lover Lutz Graf-Ulbrich remembered Nico showing him, "...a scar on her wrist, there was a little fight with Leonard Cohen or something, he tried to hold her somehow...I don't know what really happened." Nico herself told *Twen* magazine in 1969 that she was "afraid" of Cohen, confiding, "Every time I see him, I

have to make it clear to him that this is not what he wants. He always imagines I'm the ideal girlfriend for him, as if I should become his wife or something. I should not say that, but he does not make any secret of it, and that's why I can tell you. I like him as a person as long as he does not make any applications." Regardless, Cohen always had respect for Nico, being one of the few men—one of the few people, in general—to recognize her artistic talent as an individual. These feelings are obvious in a 1974 interview, as he openly praised Nico, saying, "She's incredible. She's a great singer and a great songwriter. Completely disregarded from what I can see. I don't think she sells 50 records, but she's one of the really original talents in the whole racket."

78. *The Velvet Underground & Nico* eventually went gold, selling over 500,000 copies.

79. Emerson went on to feature in Andy Warhol's *Lonesome Cowboys* and Paul Morrissey's *Heat*, before being found dead on a New York street in 1975 after a rumored drug overdose.

80. "These Days" was originally called "I've Been Out Walking" on the masters filed with Verve on May 17, 1967 (it also had that name when Browne recorded it as a publishing demo for Elektra on January 7, 1967).

81. The meeting took place at the apartment of Robert Fraser, Warhol's art dealer in Britain, who was already making a name for himself in London's underground scene. Several months earlier, he had been arrested with the Rolling Stones in a much-publicized drug bust and was about to go on trial. David Croland was at the meeting, recalling, "We went to his [Fraser's] house, and sitting on the bed was this cute guy he was talking to—that was Paul McCartney. I didn't really know who a lot of these people were. I knew who Paul was, but in the context where it's just eight people and one of them is Paul McCartney, I didn't really piece it together. And then I realized, 'Oh that's him.' He was so nice!

82. Nico never spoke negatively about the drummer in the press, even referring to Tucker as the "best drummer ever" in one interview.

83. The documentary, called *Monterey Pop*, was directed by D. A. Pennebaker, and it captures the live performances of many of the bands who graced the events stage, including Jefferson Airplane, the Who, and the Mamas and the Papas. A quick glimpse of Nico can be seen at the 35 minute, 15 second mark.

84. Journalist Bruno Blum talked about the same story, having heard it from the same source, the Doors' manager Bill Siddons.
85. The song was also featured on *The Marble Index*, the first album featuring songs written by Nico.
86. Warhol had just had a successful run with his newest film, *My Hustler*, which showed at the Hudson Theater in New York. Hudson owner Maury Maura wanted Warhol to give her a movie similar to the risqué Swedish film from earlier in the year, *I, a Woman*. He conceded to her wishes, titling the new film *I, a Man*, and planned to pack in a lot of scintillating scenes with the gorgeous duo of Morrison and Nico.
87. An MGM royalty statement revealed that a mere 459 copies were sold between September 1, 1968, and February 14, 1969.
88. There is also a fourth section of *Four Star*, which was only screened once, when the complete twenty-five-hour marathon was shown in its entirety. Referred to as *Nico—Katrina*, it was publicly viewed only at the New Cinema Playhouse on December 15–16.
89. There is one additional film, shot in 1967, that included Nico. In *Sunset*, the viewer can hear a disembodied Nico reciting a poem while images of a sunset float across the screen. The thirty-three-minute film was shot in Houston instead of Warhol's usual location of New York.
90. The book included a pop-up castle; a paper accordion (with sound); a multicolored pop-up airplane; a folded geodesic dome and paper disk with "The Chelsea Girls" printed on it suspended on a wire spring between two unopened pages; a 45 rpm flexi-disk with a portrait of Lou Reed, which plays a supposedly unreleased song by Nico and the Velvet Underground; an illustration of a nose with two colored overlays on a double-folded page; a Hunt's Tomato Paste can; a sheet of stamps to be placed in water; and a melted gold balloon that fuses two pages together.
91. Many of the traits that friends, collaborators and especially journalists described in Nico from 1968 onwards are attributable to the long-term effects of heroin use, including poor dental hygiene and a failure to address basic needs, like eating or washing. Other more serious issues also arise with addicts, such as brain damage similar to that associated with the early stages of Alzheimer's. The accusations that Nico "lied," created completely fictitious stories and would stare into the ether do not take into account that opiate abuse impairs many mental functions, including memory. Other problems include poor reasoning, impaired

decision-making, emotional processing and behavior regulation, and a weakened ability to imagine future events and interactions, which can have a strong effect on a person's goal-directed action. Nico's seemingly spaced-out replies in interviews, detachment from those around her, and inability to look beyond scoring her next fix—before she got into methadone—are also in line with the well-known impacts of heroin.

92. Mohawk's real name was Barry Friedman.

93. Morrissey once described Nico's "Innocent and Vain," taken from her 1973 album *The End*, as "my youth in one piece of music." From the mid-1990s until 2002, "Innocent and Vain" was also the last song on Morrissey's concert interval tape prior to his stage entrance music.

94. Clémenti had already gained notoriety as a questionable admirer of Catherine Deneuve in 1967's *Belle de Jour*.

95. Townsend's piece was called, "A Normal Day for Brian, A Man Who Died Every Day," and was printed in *The Times*; Morrison's work was titled, "Ode to L. A. While Thinking of Brian Jones, Deceased."

96. Garrel forbid subtitles, a problem for anyone who did not speak French or German, the two languages that are used in the movie. In 2005, a Japanese version popped up on DVD that did, at last, supply a translation for the rest of the audience.

97. Nico also made a movie called *Cleopatra* with Michel Auder in 1970. The cast was made up almost entirely of Warhol prodigies, including Viva, Ultra Violet, Ondine, and Gerard Malanga. It is extremely rare and hard to find.

98. French singer and actress.

99. Record label where Fields was working at the time.

100. This is a dig at Cale about his new role as producer.

101. Iggy Pop's real name.

102. This is probably a reference to Fields sending Nico to his Uncle Herman for some much-needed dental work. "I was never crazy about him, but still he was a really good dentist," says Fields. "The bill was around $400...Andy said, 'See if he'll take a painting,' for payment. Herman was so offended! He said, 'I'd rather not be paid at all than take that garbage.' He was offered some cans or flowers or Liz Taylors or something—ha ha."

103. Dallesandro was the star of three Warhol/Morrissey films, including cult classics *Flesh* and *Trash*.

104. Nico harbored distrust and dislike for the Panthers after the passing

of her friend, actress Jean Seberg, in 1979. Seberg had died of probable suicide after a mental breakdown. It was rumored to have been caused by a false story that the FBI planted about Seberg becoming pregnant with a Black Panther's child in 1970. Nico blamed the political organization for her friend's death.

105. Not that this is an excuse for her horrendous actions. It does, however, illustrate that it was not a premeditated attack.

106. Fan tributes marked Morrison's grave for the first couple of years after his death, until a concrete grave curb was installed. It wasn't until 1981, on the tenth anniversary of his death, that he got a proper headstone and bust, created and installed by Croatian artist Mladen Mikulin. Less than seven years later, by March 1988, the bust had been stolen.

107. A bootlegged tape, featuring twenty minutes of Reed and Cale fiddling around, eventually surfaced. While Nico does not sing or play on the recording, she can be heard in the background.

108. Nico's mention of doing press and interviews is another indication that she was trying to be as proactive as she could without formal support.

109. This is a strange inclusion, as the movie is documented as coming out in February 1972.

110. Perhaps she felt burned after being called out by a music journalist in New York for having her hand firmly down the front of Iggy Pop's trousers several years before.

111. Which was Andy Warhol's favorite Velvets song.

112. The controversial lyrics referred to territories ceded at Versailles and eventually seized back by Hitler.

113. Vicious and Nico had met when Spungen moved from New York to London to pursue Jerry Nolan of the New York Dolls. Nothing happened with Nolan; however, Spungen did meet the Sex Pistols, and immediately took up with the band's bassist, Vicious.

114. Charles Pierre Baudelaire, French poet.

115. Translated as "Flowers of Evil," this controversial book of poetry, first published in 1847 by Baudelaire, deals with topics of modernity, eroticism, and decadence.

116. Images of Nico are rare after *The Marble Index*, as it appears she did few photo shoots once she was no longer a part of the Velvet Underground. This makes the Giacomoni set of pictures that much more important in tracing Nico's visual history.

117. The initials stand for the club's full official name, Country, Bluegrass, and Blues.

118. Located in the New York neighborhood of TriBeCa, the Mudd Club was a venue for emerging music and underground events.

119. Post-punk band fronted by singer Neneh Cherry.

120. Founder of Factory Records.

121. When asked if Nico had mentioned Jimi Hendrix as one of her conquests, J said that his name was not included on the list of luminaries.

122. Toman also played with the Durutti Column and Primal Scream.

123. His main subject would have been Romantic literature, specifically William Blake.

124. This would have been in either 1979 or 1982, when Nico performed at the venue.

125. Iconic Manchester producer who was a partner at Factory Records. Also produced Joy Division.

126. Alphonse Mucha was an artist who was heralded as the "master of the art nouveau poster," thanks to the popularity of his designs

127. In a 1985 *Melody Maker* article, Nico talks about her vegetarian diet. "I'm a vegetarian for now about 20 years, and I like to wear leather. It shows that animals are precious. One is never stuck anywhere if you have a pair of boots on and leather pants and your car breaks down in the middle of the desert. I can wear very warm clothes in the desert and it doesn't bother me."

128. An orgy.

129. Post-punk band from Manchester who were on Factory Records.

130. According to Alan Wise, around this time Nico received a marriage proposal from a Jewish neighbor. "He was about 110. He owned the house she lived in. What she used to do was light the fires for him on a Saturday. Jewish law states that one shouldn't do any work on a Saturday, so they invite non-Jewish people in. Incredible as it sounds, she volunteered to light the fires for him and put the oven on. She'd done this as a child. But he asked her to marry him. She seemed to think it was serious."

131. Another bizarre twist was later revealed in an interview with Alan Wise. "We went back to her hold out with a BBC camera crew, this was a few months ago [in 2018]. We returned to the house on Prestwich Park South, 'Moresby' it's called. It's a big Victorian house; Nico lived

in the upper part of the house, the new owner restored into one about 20 years ago. When she saw the BBC crew, the owner came down. She said, 'You must have come about Nico; she left her room in a mess.' I said to her 'Do you mean to tell me you haven't tidied it up in all that time?' 'No, I left it the same but I found a letter.' Unfortunately, the BBC crew nicked it but it was written by Nico to Alain Delon asking him to look after Ari. It was never sent.

132. Blood poisoning.

133. It's unclear if the capitalization of 'Superstar' is also a reference to Warhol's Factory intimates.

134. Nico often uses an upper-case "E" when writing the word "End" in her diary. Again, this may be a reference to the song of that name and/or death—or neither.

135. There is a photograph on the internet of the two of them playing pool together.

136. Illustrating the slight changes in "truth" that can occur, manager Alan Wise said in an interview that "they saw her at a café and waved and she waved back."

137. Nico's notebook was eventually turned into a book, which has been used as source material throughout this biography.

138. Wilde and Nico share a birthday: October 16.

139. Saturn return is an astrological transit that occurs when the planet Saturn returns to the same place in the sky that it occupied at the moment of a person's birth. While the planet may not reach that exact spot until the person is twenty-nine or thirty years old, the influence of the Saturn return is considered to start in the person's late twenties— notably, at the age of twenty-seven.

SOURCES

Books

Ambrose, J. (2013) *Chelsea Hotel Manhattan: A Raw Eulogy to a New York Icon*. London: Headpress.

Ambrose, J. (2009) *Gimme Danger: The Story of Iggy Pop*. London: Music Sales. Kindle edition.

Angell, C. (2006) *Andy Warhol Screen Tests: The Films of Andy Warhol, Catalogue Raisonné*. New York, London: Harry N. Abrams.

Angell, C. (1994) *The Films of Andy Warhol: Part II*. New York: Whitney Museum of American Art.

Ari (2001) *L'Amour n'oublie jamais* ("Love Never Forgets"). Pauvert: Departemente de la Librairie Artheme Fayard. Translated for this project into English.

Baddeley, G. (2006) *Goth Chic: A Connoisseur's Guide to Dark Culture*. London: Plexus.

Bangs, L. (2003) *Mainlines, Blood Feasts and Bad Taste: A Lester Bangs Reader*. London: Serpent's Tail.

Bangs, L. (2013) *Psychotic Reactions and Carburetor Dung*. London: Serpent's Tail.

Barker, D. (2006) *33 1/3 Greatest Hits, Volume 1*. London: Continuum. Kindle edition.

Baxter, J. (2013) *Fellini*. London: CB Creative Books. Kindle edition.

Baxter, J. (1993) *Fellini: The Biography*. New York: St. Martin's Press.

Blake, M. (2006) *Punk: The Whole Story*. London: Dorling Kindersley.

Bockris, V. (1989) *The Life and Death of Andy Warhol*. London: Bantam.

Bockris, V. (1994) *Lou Reed: The Biography—Fully Revised Edition*. London: Random House.

Bockris, V. (2014) *Transformer: The Complete Lou Reed Story*. London: HarperCollins.

Bockris, V. (1989) *Warhol*. London: Penguin.

Bockris, V. (2003) *Warhol: The Biography*. Cambridge: Da Capo Press.

Bockris, V. and Cale, J. (1990) *What's Welsh for Zen: The Autobiography of John Cale*. London: Bloomsbury.

Bowman, M. (2015) *Fellini: The Sixties* (Turner Classic Movies). Philadelphia: Running Press. Kindle edition.

Boyd, J. (2010) *White Bicycles: Making Music in the 1960s*. London: Serpent's Tail. Main edition, Kindle edition.

Browne, D. (2001) *Dream Brother: The Lives and Music of Jeff and Tim Buckley*. London: Fourth Estate.

Butler, P. (2010) *Angels Dance and Angels Die: The Tragic Romance of Pamela and Jim Morrison*. London: Omnibus.

Carrera, A. (2018) *Fellini's Eternal Rome: Paganism and Christianity in the Films of Federico Fellini (Classical Receptions in Twentieth-Century Writing*. London: Bloomsbury Academic. First edition, Kindle edition.

Carson, D.A. (2011) *Grit, Noise, and Revolution: The Birth of Detroit Rock 'n' Roll*. Ann Arbor: University of Michigan. Kindle edition.

Chaney, L. (2011) *Chanel*. London: Penguin.

Cherry, J. (2013) *The Doors Examined*. Stoke-on-Trent: Bennion Kearny. Kindle edition.

City of Cologne (2013) *From Cologne Orphanage to Kids: History(s) of the Sülzer Children's Home, 1917–2012*.

Clapton, D. (2012) *Lou Reed and the Velvet Underground*. London: Music Sales. Kindle edition.

Clayson, A. (2004) *Brian Jones*. London: Music Sales. Kindle edition.

Clooney, R. (2011) *Mr. Mojo Risin' (Ain't Dead)*. Leicester: Matador. Kindle edition.

Cohen, L. (2014) *Leonard Cohen on Leonard Cohen*. London: Omnibus Press.

Coplans, J. (1971) *Andy Warhol*. London: Weidenfeld & Nicolson.

Cosgrave, B. (2012) Vogue *on Coco Chanel (*Vogue *on Designers)*. London: Quadrille. Kindle edition.

Dalton, D. and Scherman, T. (2009) *Pop: The Genius of Andy Warhol*. New York: HarperCollins.

Danto, A. C. (2009) *Andy Warhol (Icons of America)*. London: Yale University Press. Kindle edition.

Davis, S. (2011) *Jim Morrison: Life, Death, Legend*. London: Ebury Publishing. Kindle edition.

DeCurtis, A. (2017) *Lou Reed: A Life*. London: John Murray.

Dimery, R. and MacDonald, B. (2007) *Rock & Roll Heaven: A Fascinating Guide to Musical Icons Who Have Joined the Great Gig in the Sky*. New York: Barron's Educational Series Inc., U.S.

Doggett, P. (2013) *Lou Reed: The Defining Years*. London: Omnibus Press. Kindle edition.

Doggett, P. (2007) *There's a Riot Going On: Revolutionaries, Rock Stars, and the Rise and Fall of '60s Counter-Culture*. London: Canongate. Kindle edition.

Doggett, P. (1991) *Lou Reed: Growing Up in Public*. London: Omnibus.

Donlon, H. (2017) *Shadows Across the Moon: Outlaws, Freaks, Shamans and the Making of Ibiza Clubland*. London: Jawbone Press.

Eisen, J. (1970) *The Age of Rock 2*. New York: Random House.

Enzensberger, M. (1987) *Hymne an eine Schlampe*. Berlin: Satz.

Evans, J. V. (2012) "The Long 1950s as Radical In-Between: The Photography of Herbert Tobias," in Bauer, H. and Cook, M. (Eds), *Queer 1950s: Rethinking Sexuality in the Postwar Years (Genders and Sexualities in History)*. London: Palgrave Macmillan UK. Kindle edition.

Faithfull, M. (1994) *Faithfull*. London: Michael Joseph.

Fowlie, W. (1994) *Rimbaud and Jim Morrison: The Rebel as Poet*. London: Souvenir.

Frith, S. and Horne, H. (1987) *Art into Pop*. London, New York: Methuen.

Gaar, G. G. (1992). *She's a Rebel: The History of Women in Rock & Roll*. New York: Seal Press.

Gidal, P. (1971) *Andy Warhol: Films and Paintings*. London: Studio Vista.

Gilmore, M. (2012) *Night Beat: A Shadow History of Rock & Roll*. London: Picador. Kindle edition.

Goddard, S. (2009) *Mozipedia: The Encyclopaedia of Morrissey and the Smiths*. Cornwall: Random House.

Gold, J. (2016) *Total Chaos: The Story of the Stooges as Told by Iggy Pop*. Nashville: Third Man Publishing.

Goldsmith, K. (2009) *I'll Be Your Mirror: The Selected Andy Warhol Interviews*. New York: Da Capo Press. Kindle edition.

Gorman, P. (2001) *In Their Own Write: Adventures in the Music Press*. London: Sanctuary.

Graf-Ulbrich, L. (2015) *Nico—In the Shadow of the Moon Goddess*. Luxembourg: CreateSpace Independent Publishing Platform.

Graham, A. R. (2009) *I Remember Jim Morrison*. Crucibulum Publishing. Kindle edition.

Handhardt, J. G. (1988) *The Films of Andy Warhol*. New York: Whitney Museum of American Art.

Harvard, J. (2004) *The Velvet Underground's* The Velvet Underground and Nico *(33 1/3)*. London: Bloomsbury Publishing. Kindle edition.

Haskins, D. J. (2014) *Who Killed Mister Moonlight? Bauhaus, Black Magick, and Benediction*. London: Jawbone.

Hemingway, E. (1964) *A Moveable Feast*. New York: Charles Scribner's Sons. Kindle edition.

Hepworth, D. (2017) *Uncommon People: The Rise and Fall of the Rock Stars 1955–1994*. London: Transworld. Kindle edition.

Hesthamar, K. (2014) *So Long, Marianne* (translated by H. V. Goldman). Toronto: ECW Press.

Heylin, C. (2009) *All Yesterdays' Parties: The Velvet Underground in Print, 1966–1971*. New York: Da Capo Press. Kindle edition.

Heylin, C. (2008) *Babylon's Burning: From Punk to Grunge*. London: Penguin.

Heylin, C. (2011) *Behind the Shades: The 20th Anniversary Edition*. London: Faber & Faber. Kindle edition.

Heylin, C. (1996) *Bob Dylan: A Life in Stolen Moments Day by Day 1941– 1995*. London: Exclusive Distributors.

Heylin, C. (1988) *Bob Dylan: Stolen Moments*. Romford: Wanted Man.

Heylin, C. (1996) *Dylan: Behind Closed Doors—The Recording Sessions (1960–1994)*. London: Penguin.

Heylin, C. (1993) *From the Velvets to the Voidoids: A Pre-Punk History for a Post-Punk World*. London: Penguin.

Hogan, P. (1997) *The Complete Guide to the Music of the Velvet Underground*. London: Omnibus Press.

Hogan, P. (2017) *The Dead Straight Guide to the Velvet Underground*. Huntingdon: This Day in Music.

Hogan, P. (2007) *The Rough Guide to the Velvet Underground*. London: Rough Guides.

Holzman, J. (2014) *Follow the Music: The Life and High Times of Elektra Records in the Great Years of American Pop Culture*. New York: FirstMedia Books. Kindle edition.

Hopkins, J. (2013) *Behind Closed Doors*. Baltimore: Hopkins Publishing. Kindle edition.

Hopkins, J. (2014) *The Lizard King: The Essential Jim Morrison*. London: Plexus Publishing Ltd. Kindle edition.

Howard, D. N. (2004) *Sonic Alchemy: Visionary Music Producers and Their Maverick Recordings*. Milwaukee: Hal Leonard Corporation.

Huddleston, J. (2013) *Love Him Madly: An Intimate Memoir of Jim Morrison*. Chicago: Chicago Review Press. Kindle edition.

in60Learning (2018) *Coco Chanel: The Lady Behind the Little Black Dress*. in60Learning.com.

Jackson, L. (2011) *Brian Jones: The Untold Life and Mysterious Death of a Rock Legend*. London: Piatkus. Kindle edition.

James, D. and Rygle, A. (2014) *Billy Name: The Silver Age*. London: Reel Art Press.

Johnstone, N. (2012) *Patti Smith: A Biography*. London: Omnibus. Kindle edition.

Jones, D. (2015) *Mr. Mojo: A Biography of Jim Morrison*. London: Bloomsbury Publishing.

Koch, S. (2015) *Stargazer: The Life, World and Films of Andy Warhol*, third edition. New York: Open Media Publishers. Kindle edition.

Koestenbaum, W. (2015) *Andy Warhol*. New York: Open Road Media.

Kostak, M. C. (1992) *The Velvet Underground Handbook*. London: Black Spring Press Ltd.

Kronstad, B. (2016) *Perfect Day: An Intimate Portrait of Life with Lou Reed*. London: Jawbone Press.

Kubernik, H. and Kubernik, K. (2011) *A Perfect Haze: The Illustrated History of the Monterey International Pop Festival*. Santa Monica: Santa Monica Press. Kindle edition.

Kugelberg, J. (2009) *The Velvet Underground: New York Art*. New York: Rizzoli International.

Larkin, C. (2011) *The Encyclopedia of Popular Music*. London: Music Sales. Kindle edition.

Larsson, B. E. (n.d.) *Hotel Chelsea: A Legend in Sex, Drugs and Rock'n'Roll*. Amazon Media EU S.à r.l.

Leibovitz, L. (2014) *A Broken Hallelujah: Rock and Roll, Redemption, and the Life of Leonard Cohen*. New York: W. W. Norton.

Leigh, M. (1991) *The Velvet Underground*. London: Velvet.

Levy, A. (2015) *Dirty Blvd.: The Life and Music of Lou Reed*. Chicago: Chicago Review Press.

Levy, S. (2016) *Dolce Vita Confidential: Fellini, Loren, Pucci, Paparazzi and the Swinging High Life of 1950s*. Rome: Orion. Kindle edition.

Lough, J. (2013) *This Ain't No Holiday Inn: Down and Out at the Chelsea Hotel 1980–1995*. Tucson: Schaffner Press. Kindle edition.

McCain, G. and McNeil, L. (1997) *Please Kill Me: The Uncensored Oral History of Punk*. London: Abacus.

McKenna, K. (2001) *Book of Changes: A Collection of Interviews*. Seattle: Fantagraphics.

Madsen, A. (2015) *Chanel: A Woman of Her Own*. New York: Open Road Distribution. Kindle edition.

Malanga, G. (2002) *Archiving Warhol: An Illustrated History by Gerard Malanga*. London: Creation Books.

Malanga, G. (1967) *Screen Tests: A Diary*. New York: Kulchur.

Malanga, G. (2009) *Uptight: The Velvet Underground Story*. London: Music Sales. Kindle edition.

Manzarek, R. (1999) *Light My Fire: My Life with the Doors*. London: Penguin. Kindle edition.

Maywald, W. (1990) *The Splinters of the Mirror. An Illustrated Autobiography*. Munich: Schirmer/Mosel Verlag Gm.

Morrison, J. and Strete, C. (2016) *Dark Journey*. ReAnimus Press. Kindle edition.

Mother Clara Fey and Your Work of Love (1967) Booklet 1. May 8, 12th year. Cologne: Sülzgürtel.

Murciello, L. (2012) *Coco Chanel: Biography of the World's Most Elegant Woman—A Short Guide to the Life of Coco Chanel*. Hyperink. Kindle edition.

Nadel, I. B. (2010) *Various Positions: A Life of Leonard Cohen*. Toronto: Random House of Canada. Kindle edition.

Nico (2001) *Cible mouvante. Chansons, poèmes, journal*. Annecy: Pauvert.

Painter, M. and Weisman, D. (2007) *Edie: Girl on Fire*. San Francisco: Chronicle Books.

Picardie, J. (2010) *Coco Chanel: The Legend and the Life*. London: HarperCollins.

Plimpton, J. and Stein, G. (2010) *Edie: An American Biography*. London: Random House. Kindle edition.

Prochnicky, J. and Riordan, J. (2014) *Break on Through: The Life and Death of Jim Morrison*. Image Workshop Press.

Rawlings, T. (2016) *Brian Jones—The Final Truth: The Murder of a Rolling Stone*. Kindle edition.

Record Retailer Yearbook (1969) London: England.

Reed, J. (2014) *Waiting for the Man: The Life and Music of Lou Reed*. London: Omnibus.

Reed, L. (1993) *Between Thought and Expression: Selected Lyrics of Lou Reed*. Westport: Hyperion.

Rees-Roberts, N. and Waldron, D. (2015) *Alain Delon: Style, Stardom and Masculinity*, first edition. London: Bloomsbury Academic. Kindle edition.

Reynolds, S. (1995) *The Sex Revolts: Gender, Rebellion, and Rock 'n' Roll*. Cambridge, MA: Harvard University Press.

Riordan, J. (2014) *Break on Through: The Life and Death of Jim Morrison*. Image Workshop Press. Kindle edition.

Rips, N. (2016) *Trying to Float: Chronicles of a Girl in the Chelsea Hotel*. London: Simon & Schuster. Kindle edition.

Roxon, L. (1971) *Lillian Roxon's Rock Encyclopedia*. New York: Grosset & Dunlap.

Rubin, S. G. (2018) *Coco Chanel: Pearls, Perfume, and the Little Black Dress*. New York: Abrams Books for Young Readers. Kindle edition.

Schinder, S. (2007) *Icons of Rock: An Encyclopedia of the Legends Who Changed Music Forever*. Westport: Greenwood Publishing.

Sewall-Ruskin, Y. (2016) *High on Rebellion: Inside the Underground at Max's Kansas City*. New York: Open Road Media.

Seymore, B. (2012) *The End: The Death of Jim Morrison*. London: Omnibus. Kindle edition.

Sharp, C. (2007) *Who Killed Martin Hannett?: The Story of Factory Records' Musical Magician*. London: Aurum Press.

Shaw, G. (1997) *The Doors on the Road*. London: Omnibus Press.

Sheppard, D. (2008) *On Some Faraway Beach: The Life and Times of Brian Eno*. London: Orion. Kindle edition.

Shorr, C. O. (2015) *Speeding into the Future: The Amphetamine-Fuelled Generation*. New York: Open Road Media.

Shorr, C. O. (2015) *Your Fifteen Minutes Are Up (Andy Warhol's Factory People Book 3)*. New York: Open Road Media.

Simmons, S. (2015) *Serge Gainsbourg: A Fistful of Gitanes*. United for Opportunity. Kindle edition.

Simmons, S. (2011) *I'm Your Man: The Life of Leonard Cohen*. New York: Ecco.

Simon, L. (2012) *Coco Chanel (Critical Lives)*. London: Reaktion Books. Kindle edition.

Smith, P. S. (1981) *Andy Warhol's Art and Films*. Ann Arbor: UMI Research Press.

Somma, R. (Ed.) (1971) *No One Waved Good-bye: A Casualty Report on Rock and Roll*. New York: Outerbridge & Dienstfrey.

Sounes, H. (2015) *Notes from the Velvet Underground*. London: Transworld. Kindle edition.

Spitz, B. (1991) *Dylan: A Biography*. London: W. W. Norton & Company. Kindle edition.

Stevens, J. (2017) *Coco Chanel*.

Strodder, C. (2007) *The Encyclopedia of Sixties Cool: A Celebration of the Grooviest People, Events, and Artifacts of the 1960s*. Solana Beach: Santa Monica Press.

Talevski, N. (2010) *Rock Obituaries: Knocking on Heaven's Door*. London: Music Sales.

Thompson, D. (1999) *Better to Burn Out: The Cult of Death in Rock'n'Roll*. New York: Thunder's Mouth Press 1999.

Thompson, D. (1989) *Beyond the "Velvet Underground."* London: Omnibus.

Thompson, D. (2011) *Dancing Barefoot: The Patti Smith Story*. Chicago: Chicago Review Press. Kindle edition.

Thompson, D. (2002) *The Dark Reign of Gothic Rock: In the Reptile House with the Sisters of Mercy, Bauhaus and the Cure*. London: Helter Skelter.

Thompson, D. (2012) *Hearts of Darkness: James Taylor, Jackson Browne, Cat Stevens, and the Unlikely Rise of the Singer-Songwriter*. Perth: Backbeat Books. Kindle edition.

Thompson, D. (2009) *Your Pretty Face Is Going to Hell: The Dangerous Glitter of David Bowie, Iggy Pop, and Lou Reed*. Backbeat. Kindle edition.

Tillman, L. (2016) *Factory—Andy Warhol/Stephen Shore*. London: Phaidon Press Limited.

Tippins, S. (2014) *Inside the Dream Palace: The Life and Times of New York's Legendary Chelsea Hotel*. New York: Simon and Schuster.

Trynka, P. (2009) *Iggy Pop: Open Up and Bleed—The Biography*. London: Little, Brown. Kindle edition.

Trynka, P. (2014) *Sympathy for the Devil: The Birth of the Rolling Stones and the Death of Brian Jones*. London: Transworld. Kindle edition.

Unterberger, R. (2009) *White Light/White Heat: The Velvet Underground Day-by-Day*, revised and expanded e-book edition. London: Jawbone Press.

Various (2007) *The* Mojo *Collection: 4th Edition*. London: Canongate. Kindle edition.

Vaughan, H. (2011) *Sleeping with the Enemy: Coco Chanel, Nazi Agent*. New York: Random House.

Violet, U. (1988) *Famous for 15 Minutes: My Years with Andy Warhol*.

Viva (2015) *Superstar: A Novel*. New York: Open Media Publishers. Kindle edition.

Wade, C. (2015) *The Music of the Velvet Underground*. Wisdom Twins Books. Kindle edition.

Wallach, J. (1999) *Chanel: Her Style and Her Life*. London: Mitchell Beazley.

Warhol, A. (1968) *A, a Novel*. New York: Grove Press.

Warhol, A. (2014) *The Andy Warhol Diaries*, edited by Pat Hackett. Hachette: New York.

Warhol, A. (1991) *Andy Warhol: In His Own Words*. London: Omnibus.

Warhol, A. (1967) *Andy Warhol's Index* (book), with the assistance of Stephen Shore, Paul Morrissey, Ondine, Nico, Christopher Cerf, Alan Rinzler, Gerald Harrison, Akihito Shirakawa, and particularly David Paul; several photographs by Nat Finkelstein; factory photos by Billy Name. New York: Random House.

Warhol, A. (2018) *Fame*. London: Penguin.

Warhol, A. (1979) *The Philosophy of Andy Warhol: From A to B and Back Again*. London: Pan Books.

Warhol, A. (2007) *POPism*. London: Penguin. Kindle edition.

Watson, S. (2003) *Factory Made: Warhol and the Sixties*. New York: Pantheon Books.

West, L. (2015) *Open Doors: A Rock and Roll Romance about Love, Soulmates and Jim Morrison*. morningmayan publishing. Kindle edition.

Wilcock, J. (1971) *The Autobiography and Sex Life of Andy Warhol*. New York: Other Scenes.

Wiseman R. (1982) *Jackson Browne, the Story of a Hold Out*. Garden City, NY: Doubleday.

Witts, R. (1993) *Nico: The Life and Lies of an Icon*. London: Virgin Books.

Woronov, M. (2013) *Swimming Underground: My Time at Andy Warhol's Factory*. Los Angeles: Montaldo Publishing.

Wrenn, M. (1991) *Andy Warhol in His Own Words*. New York: Omnibus Press.

Young, J. (2018) *The End*. Paris: Éditions Séguier.

Young, J. (1992) *Nico: Songs They Never Play on the Radio*. London: Bloomsbury.

Zak, A. (2000) *The Velvet Underground Companion: Four Decades of Commentary*. New York: Schirmer Books.

Journals

Attias, B. A. (2016) "Authenticity and Artifice in Rock and Roll: 'And I Guess That I Just Don't Care,'" *Rock Music Studies*, vol. 3, no. 2, pp. 131–47.

Bannister, M. (2010) "'I'm Set Free…': The Velvet Underground, 1960s Counterculture, and Michel Foucault," *Popular Music and Society*, vol. 33, no. 2, pp. 163–78.

Bazin, Y. and Riot, E. (2013) "Woman in Love, Artist or Entrepreneur? The Edifying, Mystifying Life of Coco Chanel," *Society and Business Review*, vol. 8, no. 3, pp. 281–313.

Bertolino, A. and Holm-Hadulla, R. M. (2013) "Creativity, Alcohol and Drug Abuse: The Pop Icon Jim Morrison," *Psychopathology*, September 18.

Colombo, E., Michelangeli, A. and Stanca, L. (2014) "La Dolce Vita: Hedonic Estimates of Quality of Life in Italian Cities," *Regional Studies*, vol. 48, no. 8, pp. 1404–18.

de Almeida, A. F. (2016) "Shooting 'Sublime Blondes in Tight Dresses': The Paparazzi in Fiction Film and Television from *La Dolce Vita* to *Dirt*," *Celebrity Studies*, vol. 7, no. 1, pp. 34–44.

Incognito (2013) "Velvet Underground," *Science and Culture: A Monthly Journal of Natural and Cultural Sciences*, vol. 79, no. 3/4.

Leung, G. (2015) "The Factory: Photography and the Warhol Community. Billy Name: The Silver Age; Black and White Photographs from Andy Warhol's Factory," *afterimage* (Visual Studies Workshop), vol. 42, part 6, pp. 39–40.

Littlejohn, J. (2017) "Rock, Counterculture and the Avant-Garde, 1966–1970: How the Beatles, Frank Zappa and the Velvet Underground Defined an Era," *Rock Music Studies*, vol. 4, no. 1, pp. 72–3.

Loydell, R. (2017) "Post-Punk Poet: An Interview with Dick Witts of the

Passage," *Punk & Post-Punk*, vol. 6, no. 3, pp. 415–22.

Majstorović, D. (2017) "A Young Lion, the Lizard King, and Erotic Politician: Tracing the Roots of Jim Morrison's Mythical Image," *Journal of Communication Inquiry*, vol. 41, no. 2, April, pp. 157–73.

Marshall, K. and Loydell, R. (2017) "Thinking Inside the Box: Brian Eno, Music, Movement and Light," *Journal of Visual Art Practice*, vol. 16, no. 2, pp. 104–18.

McFadzean, E. (2000) "What Can We Learn from Creative People? The Story of Brian Eno," *Management Decision*, vol. 38, part1/2, pp. 51–7.

Needham, G. (2016) "Warhol and Nico: Negotiating Europe from *Strip-Tease* to *Screen Test*," *Journal of European Popular Culture*, vol. 7, no. 2, pp. 123–42.

Ortiz, R. L. (1998) "L. A. Women: Jim Morrison with John Rechy," *Literature and Psychology*, vol. 44, no. 3, pp. 41–77.

Rosenberg, S. (1995) "Fowlie, Wallace. Rimbaud and Jim Morrison: The Rebel as Poet," *Nineteenth-Century French Studies*, vol. 23, no. 3/4.

Television

Pop 2 (1972) Ina.fr.

Newspapers and Magazines

Saeptem (2018) "Le Fils illégitime d'Alain Delon révèle comment sa mère Nico l'a initié à la drogue." *Gala*, April 16.

Altham, K. (1966) "Rolling Stone Oldham: Talented, Insulting, Outrageous," *New Musical Express*, August 5, 1966.

Andrews, C. (1975) "Nico: *The End* (Island)," *Creem*, May.

Aronowitz, A. (1971) "Over His Dead Body: Memories of Jim Morrison," *New York Post*.

Bangs, L. (1971) "Nico: A Kind of Frozen Purity," *Fusion*, November 12.

Banks, R. (1978) "Subway Sect: An Eiffel of the Subways in Paris," *ZigZag*, April.

Barnes, M. (2002) "Kevin Ayers: Invisible Jukebox," *The Wire*, December.

Barrios, G. (1970) "Velvet Underground: An Interview with Sterling Morrison," *Fusion Magazine*, March 6.

Bartlett, K. (1968) "Superstars Pop Out at Warhol's Party," publication unknown. Taken from Danny Fields's personal archive.

Bell, M. (1975) "The Doors Consumers' Guide, Part 2," *New Musical Express*, October 11.

Bell, M. (1975) "The Doors: *Strange Days*," *New Musical Express*, January 4.

Bell, M. (1992) "Reissues: Nico Drama of Exile, Chelsea Live," *Vox* (archive: 1990–1999), no. 24, September 1, p. 86.

Bell, M. (1993) "The Velvet Underground: 'We Will Confront the Myth…'" *Vox*, July.

Bergan, R. (2011) "Obituary: Nikos Papatakis—Charismatic Nightclub Owner and Subversive Film Director," *Guardian*, March 9.

Bernède, S. (2001) "Ari: The Whole Portrait of Alain Delon," *La Dépêche*.

Biasotti, D. (2004) "The Rise and Fall of the Neoprene Lizards: The Kaleidoscope Story." Available at http://www.pulsatingdream.com. Accessed July 16, 2020.

Black, J. (1994) "The Fugs: F*** Art, Let's Levitate the Pentagon," *Q*, March.

"Blue Is the Warmest Colour" (2015) *Mint*, September 11.

Bockris, V. (2004) "Heart of Darkness: The Velvet Underground," *Mojo*, March.

Bohn, C. (1981) "In Nico Time," *New Musical Express*, spring.

"Book Reviews: The Many Lives of Coco Chanel; Martin Amis Returns in Fine Form" (2014) *Maclean's*, vol. 127, no. 40, pp. 68–72.

Brown, M. (1975) "John Cale: *Fear* (Island); Nico: *The End* (Island)," *Crawdaddy!*, May.

Cannon, G. (1968) "Andy Warhol: A Mirror of American Death," *New Society*, June 13.

Cannon, G. (1968) "1968: The Shaken City Walls," *Guardian*, December 24.

Charlesworth, C. (1973) "Jackson's Song for Everyman," *Melody Maker*, November 17.

Childs, A. (1974) "A Happy Sad Starsailor from Washington D.C.," *ZigZag*, October.

Cohen, S. (1986) "Lou Reed Don't Live Here No More," *Spin* (archive: 1985–2000), vol. 2, no. 4, Jul 1, pp. 50–2, 54.

Coley, B. (1989) "Lou Reed and John Cale: Déjà Vu," *Spin*, April.

Colman, D. (2015) "The Velvet Underground as *Peanuts* Characters: Snoopy Morphs into Lou Reed, Charlie Brown into Andy Warhol," *Open Culture*, July 1.

Condon, J. (n.d.) *What Goes On*, no. 3.

Connolly, C. (2005) "She Screamed for Help but Her Neighbours Barricaded the Door." *Daily Telegraph*, July 4.

"Critics' Choice: Top Artists" (1978) *Billboard* (archive: 1963–2000), vol. 90, no. 48, December 2, p. R61–2.

Cromelin, R. (1975) "Flo & Eddie: *Illegal, Immoral & Fattening*," *Phonograph Record*, September.

Cromelin, R. (1974) "Kevin Ayers, John Cale, Nico & Eno: *June 1, 1974* (Island)," *Creem*, December 1974.

Dadomo, G. (1977) "Danny Fields: The Fields Connection," *Sounds*, July 9, 1977.

Dadomo, G. (1978) "Nico," *Sounds*, April 28.

Dalton, D. (1999) "John Cale: What's Welsh for Zen?" *Gadfly*, January.

Dalton, D. (2002) "Marianne Faithfull: The Curse of the Multiplying Mariannes," *Gadfly*, March 18.

Dalton, D. (2002) "Nico and *The Marble Index*: A Conversation with Danny Fields," *Gadfly*.

Dalton, D. and Kaye, L. (1977) "The Velvet Underground," *Rock 100*.

de Rabaudy, M. (2001) "Ari, Son of No One," *L'Express*.

Demorest, S. (1975) "Eno: The Monkey Wrench of Rock Creates Happy Accidents on *Tiger Mt.*" In *Circus*, April.

Diehl, D. (1968) "The Jefferson Airplane, Bob Dylan, The Doors, The Who, The Grateful Dead, Nico, and Yes, The Beatles Slept Here," *Eye Magazine*. From the personal archive of Danny Fields.

Doyle, T. (2000) "Lou Reed—Cash for Question," *Q*, no. 164.

Edmonds, B. (1970) "Nico: *The Marble Index*," *Fusion*, June 12.

Fabian, J. (1998) "Soul in Exile," *Uncut* (archive: 1997–2000), no. 17, October 1, pp. 68–70.

Gagne, C. (1996) "Buying & Booking Guide: Nico Icon," *Film Journal International* (archive: 1996–2000), vol. 99, no. 3, March 1, pp. 116–17.

Gascoigne, L. (2014) "The Years of *La Dolce Vita*," *The Spectator*, no. 9,690, p. 49.

Gill, A. (1997) "Jackson Browne: *The Next Voice You Hear—The Best of…*(Elektra)," *Mojo*, November.

Gold, M. (1974) "The Mysterious Journey of John Cale," *Creem*, October.

Goldstein, R. (1967) "The Billy James Underground," *The Village Voice*, August 3.

Goldstein, R. (1967) "The Velvet Underground: *The Velvet Underground & Nico* (Verve)," *The Village Voice*, April 13.

Greenfield, R. (1971) "Shards of Velvet Afloat in London: Nico and John Cale," *Rolling Stone*, February.

Greenspun, R. (1972) "'Inner Scar' by Talented Young Frenchman Shown," *New York Times*, October 7.

Gundle, S. (2000) "*La Dolce Vita*," *History Today*, vol. 50, no. 1, January 1, pp. 29–35.

Halliday, A. (2014) "The Crazy, Iconic Life of Nico; Andy Warhol Muse, Velvet Underground Vocalist, Enigma in Amber," *Open Music*, November 24.

Harrison, F. (1995) "Velvet Underground," *National Magazine Co. Ltd.*, part 113.

Harrison, I. (2018) "Nico's Last Decade," *Mojo*, September.

Harron, M. (1981) "The Lost History of the Velvet Underground: An Interview with Sterling Morrison," *New Musical Express*, April 25.

Harron, M. (1980) "Pop Art/Art Pop: The Warhol Connection," *Melody Maker*, February.

Hasted, N. (1997) "John Cale: Remembrance of Things Past," *Independent*, June 28.

Hasted, N. (2010) "Mystery Jets: From Songs of Innocence to Grown-up Experience," *Independent*, July 16.

Hellenthal, K. G. (2009) "Mother Clara Fey and Her Work of Love," *German Provincial Motherhouse of the Sisters of the Poor Child Jesus*, no. 1, May 8, 1967.

Hogan, P. (1997) "Nico: *The End*" (Island IMCD 174).

Hoskyns, B. (2001) "The Backpages Interview: Marianne Faithfull," *Rock's Backpages*, July 28.

Hoskyns, B. (2016) "'Danger: Depressing': John Cale's *Music for a New Society*," *Domino Records*, January.

Hoskyns, B. (1983) "A Stronger Music to Die In: John Cale's New Society," *New Musical Express*, February 19.

Hoskyns, B. (2002) "Tears Gone By: The Rebirth of Marianne Faithfull," *Rock's Backpages*, February 16.

Hull, R. A. (1981) "Velvet Underground: White Light/Dark Shadows," *Creem*, July.

Huxley, P. (2000) "Lost Boys and Fallen Angels: Nico," *Uncut*, no. 39, August 1, p. 44.

Hynde, C. (1974) "The Velvet Underground: *1969 Live*," *New Musical Express*, April 27.

Jaffee, L. (2011) "*Chelsea Mädchen*: The Funny Side of Nico," *Rock's Backpages*, November.

Jobey, L. (1996) "I'll Be Your Mirror Crack'd: The Decline and Fall of Nico," *New Statesman*, October 25, p. 41.

Jones, J. (2016) "Patti Smith's New Haunting Tribute to Nico: Hear Three Tracks," *Open Music*, September 7.

Kaye, L. (1976) "Lou Reed," *New Musical Express*, January 24.

Kemp, M. (1990) "John Cale/Lou Reed: 15 Minutes with You," *Option*, July.

Kent, N. (1979) "Dr. Iggy and Mr. Pop," *New Musical Express*, March 24.

Kent, N. (1975) "Joni Mitchell," *New Musical Express*, January 11.

Kent, N. (1974) "Last Drongo in Paris," *New Musical Express*, May 4.

Kent, N. (1974) "Lou Reed: A Stumble on the Wild Side," *New Musical Express*, March 9.

Kent, N. (1974) "New York Dolls: Dead End Kids on the Champs-Elysées," *New Musical Express*, January 26.

Kent, N. (1974) "Phil Manzanera: Snake-Eyed Latin Lothario Goes Pan-Tonic," *New Musical Express*, August 24.

Kent, N. (1973) "A Walk on the Wild Side of Lou Reed," *New Music Express*, June 9.

Kreikebaum, U. (2014) "Missbraucht im Kölner Kinderheim" ("Abused in Cologne Children's Home"). *Kölner Stadt-Anzeiger*, October 20.

Kubernik, H. (2008) "Leonard Cohen," *Rock's Backpages*, February.

Lake, S. (1974) "I'm Not a Beggar Woman—Nico Talks to Steve Lake," *Melody Maker*, June.

Lake, S. (1974) "Rock Goes to Church," *Melody Maker*, December 1974.

Lazell, B. (1993) "Black Angels & Death Songs," *Vox* (archive: 1990–1999), no. 34, July 1, pp. a4–6.

Levy, E. (1994) "Santa Barbara—The Velvet Underground & Nico," *Variety* (archive: 1905–2000), vol. 354, no. 6, March 14, p. 57.

Malins, S. (1994) "Into the Black," *Vox* (archive: 1990–1999), no. 44, May 1, p. 132.

Malins, S. (1994) "James Young," *Vox* (archive: 1990–1999), no. 41, February 1, p. 60.

Mechling, L. (2018) "7 Musicians Reflect on Nico's Enduring Influence," *New York Times*, August 1.

Mills, F. (2005) "The Stooges: Raw Power Revisited," *Detroit Metro Times*, August 10.

Mills, F. (2005) "The Stooges: Real Cool Time," *Harp*, September.

Moreland, Q. (2017) "Review: *Chelsea Girl*," *Pitchfork*, November 12.

Morley, P. (1978) "The Pop Group/Nico/Linton Kwesi Johnson/Cabaret Voltaire: An Appraisal of 'Next Year's Thing,'" *New Music Express*, October 21.

Needs, K. (1978) "Nico in London: Rare 1978 Interview," *Zigzag*, June.

New Yorker, The (2013) "The Talk of the Town: George Packer on the Eternal Shutdown; Chelsea Hotel Rooms; Calling Andrew Jackson; a Dream Archive; Brooklyn Scroll," *The New Yorker*, October 28, pp. 21–5.

"Nico" (1974) *Melody Maker*, November 16.

"Nico: Shrink Rap" (1985) *Melody Maker*, July.

Nolan, T. (1967) "Groupies: A Story of Our Times," *Cheetah*, December.

O'Brien, G. (1982) "Bop Art," *Artforum*, February.

O'Grady, A. (1980) "Leonard Cohen: Incurable Romantic," *RAM*, April.

Pareles, J. (n.d.) "Pop: Nico Sings at Danceteria," n.p.

Patterson, A. (2012) "*Nico Icon*: Directed by Susanne Ofteringer," *Rock's Backpages*, December.

"Patti Smith Celebrates the Dead" (2012) *Maclean's*, vol. 125, no. 23, p. 78.

Penman, I. (1978) "The Fall," *New Musical Express*, August 19.

Penman, I. (1994) "John Cale: Music for the Last Day." *Wire*, July.

Penman, I. (2016) "Patti Smith: *M Train*," *London Review of Books*, May 5.

Peregrine, A. (2015) "France: The Birthplace of Binge-Drinking," *Daily Telegraph*, January 27.

Perrignon, J. (2001) "Portrait of Ari Päffgen-Boulogne: The Errant Son," *Libération*.

Pouncey, E. (1991) "Album Reviews: Nico—*The Marble Index*," *Vox* (archive: 1990–1999), no. 10, July 1, 1991, p. a18.

Pouncey, E. (1999) "Iggy Pop: Coming Through Slaughter," *Wire*, November.

"Record Review: Candymen, Dick Smothers, Nabors, Lana Cantrell, Jimmy Smith, Nico, Jobim, Roselli, N&F Top New LPs" (1967) *Variety* (archive: 1905–2000), vol. 248, no. 7, October 4, p. 44.

"Record Review: Monkees, 'Maggie Flynn,' Mothers, Terry Reid, Mathis, 'Zebra,' Nico, Mandel, Woody Allen Top New LPs" (1968) *Variety* (archive: 1905–2000), vol. 253, no. 2, November 27, p. 52.

Reynolds, S. (2007) "Kevin Ayers and Robert Wyatt," *Guardian*, October 24.

Reynolds, S. (2007) "From the Velvets to the Void," *Guardian*, March 16.

Riegel, R. (1980) "Nico: Bogart's, Cincinnati," *Creem*, September.

Robert, R. (1982) "Nico: *Do or Die* (Roir)," *Sounds*, December 25.

Robertson, S. (1981) "Nico: *Drama of Exile* (Aura)," *Sounds*, February 4.

Robertson, S. (1979) "A Sandy Robertson's Hollywood Confidential," *Sounds*, September 1.

Rose, C. (1983) "Nico: When the Peroxide Fades," *New Music Express*, January 29.

Rosenbaum, J. (2006) "Confessions of an Opium Eater: Philippe Garrel," *Sight and Sound*, vol. 16, no. 8, August, pp. 24, 26–7.

Rowland, M. (1989) "Life Lessons: Bonnie Raitt and Jackson Browne," *Musician*, August.

Runtagh, J. (2017) "*The Velvet Underground & Nico* at 50: John Cale Goes Track by Track Through the Debut That Changed Music," *People Magazine*, March 31.

Salewicz, C. (1975) "Nico/Mike Heron: Imperial College, London," *New Musical Express*, February 8.

Sanders, E. (1969) "Nico, the Cologne Girl in the U.S. Underground," *Twen*, August.

Sanjek, D. (1996) "Nico Icon," *Popular Music and Society*, vol. 20, no. 3, pp. 1,712.

Schulps, D. (1977) "Kevin Ayers," *Trouser Press*, September.

Severin, S. (1996) "Style: I'll Be Your Mirror—Steve Severin, Founder Member of Siouxsie & the Banshees, Recalls with Affection His Brief Acquaintance with Nico, the Ice-Cool Icon of the Velvet Underground," *Guardian*, October 23, p. 12.

Simpson, D. (2019) "Nico in Manchester: 'She Loved the Architecture—and the Heroin,'" *Guardian*, July 5.

Sinker, M. (1996) "Nico Icon," *Sight and Sound*, vol. 6, no. 11, November 1, p. 56.

Sischy, I. (1998) "Coco Chanel," *Time*, vol. 151, no. 22, June 8, p. 98.

"Sister Ray Says" (1993) *Vox* (archive: 1990–1999), no. 34, July 1, p. 23.

Snow, M. (1983) "Nico/1919: Brixton Ace, London," *New Musical Express*, June.

Snow, M. (1993) "The Velvet Underground: Party on, Dudes!," *Q*, July.

Springer, M. (2013) "Nico, Lou Reed & John Cale Sing the Classic Velvet Underground Song 'Femme Fatale' (Paris, 1972)," *Open Culture*, September 9.

Stratton, J. (2005) "Jews, Punk and the Holocaust: From the Velvet Underground to the Ramones—the Jewish–American story," *Popular Music*, vol. 24, no. 1, pp. 79–106.

Strauss, N. (1996) "Film View; A Siren Who Sang of Herself," *New York Times*, January 14.

Suck, J. (1977) "The Weirdest John Cale Interview You've Ever Read…," *Sounds*, September 3.

Sullivan, J. (2013) "Lou Reed: On the Wild Side," *Rock's Backpages*, October.

Sullivan, J. (1996) "The Needle and the Damage Done," *Boston Globe*, August 10.

Sullivan, J. (1979) "Strange Interlude with Nico," *Trouser Press*, July.

Sweeting, A. (1988) "Nico: A Baleful Dark Brown Voice," *Guardian*. July 23.

Sweeting, A. (1988) "Tom Tom Club: The Byrne Issue," *Guardian*, October 14.

Talu, Y. (2017) "Nikos Papatakis," *Film Comment*, vol. 53, no. 5, pp. 62–5.

Thompson, D. (2007) "The Doors in 1967: From Zeroes to Heroes in Six Months Flat," *Goldmine*, August.

Thompson, D. (2001) "Jim Morrison: Death on the Instalment Plan," *Mojo*, September.

Toms, K. (2008) "Italian Cinema's Sweet Success: Wetsuits and Bolsheviks 10 Facts about *La Dolce Vita*," *Guardian*, February 17.

"Too Dead to Care: Ian Curtis 1957–1980" (1998) *Uncut* (archive: 1997–2000), no. 12, pp. 57–9, 61, 63–7.

Trynka, P. (2007) "John Cale: The *Mojo* Interview," *Mojo*, February.

Turner, L. (2012) "Interview: Marc Almond on *Desertshore*," *The Quietus*, November 19.

Turner, S. (1976) "Jackson Browne," unpublished, for *NME*.

"UK Discography" (1993) *Vox* (archive: 1990–1999), no. 34, July 1, p. a7.

"Velvet Underground" (1974) *Melody Maker*, November 2.

Verdot-Belaval, A. (2018) "Ari Boulogne, the Sad Story of the Illegitimate Son of Alain Delon." *Gala*, November 8.

Walker, C. (1986) "The Girl with the Faraway Eyes," *The Age*, February 21.

Watson, D. (1985) "Nico: 'Watch Out, the World's Behind You,'" *New Musical Express*, August 3.

Watts, M. (1979) "Who's Afraid of Amanda Lear?" *Melody Maker*, February 10.

Welch, C. (1974) "Nico," *Melody Maker*, July 4.

Wiener, T. (1993) "Performing Arts—Nico: The End by James Young," *Library Journal*, vol. 118, no. 12, p. 84.

Williams, R. (1970) "Nico: *Desertshore* (Reprise)," *Melody Maker*, January 31.

Williams, R. (1970) "Nico, the Lonely Chanteuse," *Melody Maker*, March 21.

Williams, R. (1978) "The Pop Group/LKJ/Nico/Cab Voltaire," *Melody Maker*, October 21.

Williams, R. (1969) "The Velvet Underground: It's a Shame that Nobody Listens," *Melody Maker*, October 25.

Wray, D. D. (2018) "Nico: The Manchester Years—Life After the Velvet Underground," *Loud and Quiet*, June 21.

Websites

"Antoine Muraccioli in the USA" (2014) Available at https://heroculte. wordpress.com/2014/08/05/antoine-muraccioli-in-the-usa/. Accessed June 29, 2018.

Antonia, N. (2018) "Nico & the Last Testament of Doctor Demetrius." Available at https://ninaantoniaauthor.com/tag/alan-wise/. Accessed July 15, 2020.

Ash, L. (2015) "The Rape of Berlin." Available at https://www.bbc.co.uk/news/magazine-32529679. Accessed March 19, 2019.

"*Athanor*." Available at https://letterboxd.com/film/athanor. Accessed July 29, 2019.

"*Athanor*: A Short Synopsis." Available at https://en.unifrance.org/movie/34122/athanor. Accessed July 29, 2019.

Batson, C. B. (2012) "Nico: *The End* [Reissue]," *Trebuchet* magazine, September 29. Available at http://www.trebuchet-magazine.com/nico-the-end-reissue/. Accessed April 9, 2019.

BBC Inside Out (2008) *Nico Icon Play*. Available at https://www.youtube.com/watch?v=T_Kr9wjTUmc&t=169s. Accessed July 15, 2020.

"Berlin at the End of the War, 1945" (2014) Available at https://rarehistoricalphotos.com/berlin-end-was-1945. Accessed March 20, 2019.

"Black Photograph." Available at https://erenow.net/biographies/various-positions-a-life-of-leonard-cohen/8.php. Accessed June 22, 2019.

Bos, C. (2017) "Cologne Has No Place for Nico." Available at https://www.ksta.de/kultur/kolumne-ueber-den-plattenrand-koeln-hat-fuer-nico-keinen-platz-29289296. Accessed July 15, 2020.

Brine, J. and Marnell, C. (2017) "Niconomicon: A Conversation with Lutz Graf-Ulbrich." Available at https://www.3ammagazine.com/3am/nico nomicon-conversation-lutz-graf-ulbrich-nico. Accessed August 21, 2020.

Cale, J. and Nico (1988) TV broadcast, March 24. Available at https://www.youtube.com/watch?v=6lPJEE8MSj8. Accessed September 3, 2019.

Cronin, F. (2012) "Nazi Legacy: The Troubled Descendants," *BBC News*. Available at http://www.bbc.co.uk/news/magazine-18120890. Accessed December 19, 2016.

desertshore (2009) "Nico Discusses Lou Reed & Velvet Underground." Available at https://www.youtube.com/watch?v=BM6WxweVyds. Accessed July 6, 2019.

Enault, R. (2013) "Serge Kruger: The True Hero of a Party Is Never the One Who Pays." Available at https://translate.google.com/translate?hl=en&sl=fr&u=http://roadsmag.com/serge-kruger-le-vrai-heros-dune-fete-est-toujours-celui-qui-paie944756558009/&prev=search/. Accessed April 29, 2019.

"German Singer Nico Dies in Spain" (1988) Available at https://www.upi.com/Archives/1988/07/23/German-singer-Nico-dies-in-Spain/2653585633600/. Accessed December 17, 2020.

"How Does It Feel to Be High on Heroin?" (n.d.) Available at https://www.quora.com/How-does-it-feel-to-be-high-on-heroin#. Accessed December 19, 2016.

John Peel Wiki: "Nico." Available at https://peel.fandom.com/wiki/Nico. Accessed June 30, 2020.

"June 3, 1968—The Shooting of Andy Warhol" (n.d.) Available at https://www.warholstars.org/chron/andydies68n33.html. Accessed September 23, 2020.

Landemaine, O. (n.d.) "The Velvet Underground: Live Performances and Rehearsals, 1965–66." Available at http://olivier.landemaine.free.fr/vu/live/1965–66/perf6566.html. Accessed June 18, 2019.

"*Le Bleu des origines*." Available at https://letterboxd.com/film/le-bleu-des-origines. Accessed August 13, 2019.

"*Le Bleu des origines*" synopsis. Available at https://mubi.com/films/le-bleu-des-origines. Accessed August 12, 2019.

"*Le Bleu des origines*—User Reviews: Hypnotic Study of Nico and Zouzou" (n.d.) Available at https://www.imdb.com/title/tt0077242. Accessed August 12, 2019.

"*Les Hautes* Solitudes" (1974) Available at https://www.imdb.com/title/tt0071600/. Accessed August 8, 2019.

"Let's Kiss and Say Goodbye" (1988) Available at https://www.imdb.com/title/tt0133397/?ref_=nm_flmg_act_1. Accessed December 17, 2020.

"Life for Young People in Nazi Germany" (n.d.) Available at https://www.bbc.com/bitesize/guides/z897pbk/revision/2. Accessed March 18, 2019.

"Long-Term Effects of Heroin" (n.d.) Available at http://www.drugfreeworld.org/drugfacts/heroin/long-term-effects.html. Accessed December 19, 2016.

Metzger, R. (2015) "'The Inner Scar': Velvet Underground Singer Nico Stars in Obscure, Pretentious French Art Film, 1972." Available at https://dangerousminds.net/comments/the_inner_scar_velvet_underground_singer_nico. Accessed July 26, 2019.

Metzger, R. (2012) "True Goth: When Nico Sang with Bauhaus." Available at https://dangerousminds.net/comments/true_goth_when_nico_sang_with_bauhaus_1981. Accessed August 25, 2019.

Mirkin, G. (2016) "Nico Died Senseless Death After Falling from Bicycle Without Helmet." Available at https://villages-news.com/nico-died-senseless-death-falling-bicycle-without-helmet/. Accessed October 25, 2019.

Mironneau, S. (2011) "Nico: Fashion Model." Available at http://smironne.free.fr/NICO/MODE/mode15.html. Accessed April 17, 2019.

Morrison, S. (1990) Interview. Available at http://olivier.landemaine.free.fr/vu/live/1965–66/perf6566.html. Accessed May 23, 2019.

Nam, S. (2015) "Film Comment Selects 2015: *Un Ange Passe*," *Slant Magazine*, February 23. Available at https://www.slantmagazine.com/film/film-comment-selects-2015--un-ange-passe. Accessed August 8, 2019.

Nico (1985) Interview. Available at https://www.youtube.com/watch?v=MOeU-BF78gM&t=96s. Accessed July 11, 2019.

Nico (2009) Nico in Manchester. Available at https://www.youtube.com/watch?v=4ORa382rBXM. Accessed June 3, 2019.

Nico Discusses Lou Reed and the Velvet Underground. Available at https://www.youtube.com/watch?v=BM6WxweVyds. Accessed October 24, 2019.

Nico Icon Play—BBC *Inside Out*. Available at https://www.youtube.com/ watch?v=T_Kr9wjTUmc&t=246s. Accessed October 24, 2019.

"Philippe Garrel—*Un Ange Passe* (1975)." Available at https://worldscinema. org/2019/02/philippe-garrel-un-ange-passe-1975. Accessed August 8, 2019.

Poe, E. A. (1847) Excerpt from "To———. Ulalume: A Ballad." Available at https://www.poetryfoundation.org/poems/44889/to-ulalume-a-ballad. Accessed November 5, 2019.

Pruitt, W. (2018) "Andy Warhol Was Shot by Valerie Solanas. It Killed Him 19 Years Later." Available at https://www.history.com/news/andy-warhol-shot-valerie-solanas-the-factory. Accessed September 23, 2020.

Sisson, J. (2016) "Mysticism in Film: "The Inner Scar" ("La Cicatrice Intérieure," 1972) Part 3. Available at http://wearecult.rocks/mysticism-in-film-the-inner-scar-la-cicatrice-interieure-1972-part-3. Accessed January 27, 2021.

Un ange passe (1975): Plot. Available at https://www.imdb.com/title/ tt0073838/plotsummary. Accessed August 8, 2019.

The Velvet Underground: Rock and Roll Hall of Fame Induction. Available at https://www.rockhall.com/inductees/velvet-underground. Accessed November 6, 2019.

Walker, C. (1986) "The Girl with the Faraway Eyes." Available at http:// www.clintonwalker.com.au/nico.html. Accessed October 25, 2019.

"What Are the Long-Term Effects of Heroin Use?" (n.d.) The National Institute on Drug Abuse. Available at https://www.drugabuse.gov. Accessed December 19, 2016.

"When Leonard Cohen Met Nico" (2016) Available at http://graham-russell. blogspot.com/2016/11/when-leonard-cohen-met-nico.html. Accessed June 24, 2019.

Wordsworth, W. (1850) "The Prelude, or Growth of a Poet's Mind." Available at http://metaphors.iath.virginia.edu/metaphors/16743. Accessed July 17, 2019.

Yarwood, S. (2004) "An Interview with James Young, March 2004." Available at https://web.archive.org/web/20110811205904/http://www.btinternet. com/~stephen.yarwood/JY_int.htm. Accessed October 24, 2019.

Radio Shows

Being Nico (2018) WDR 3 Westdeutscher Rundfunk, October 14.

Browne, J. (2005) Interviewed by Jody Denberg of KGSR radio. October.

Walker, S. (1986) Nico, interview 3RRR FM, August 2. Available at http://smironne.free.fr/NICO/rrr.html. Accessed July 17, 2019.

Ward, E. (2005) "Nico, the Voice of Disaffected Youth." On *Fresh Air*. Available at https://www.npr.org/templates/story/story.php?storyId=5044641&t=1553091869911. Accessed March 19, 2019.

Archives

Danny Fields personal archive.

Marble Index invitation: Warhol archive.

Art Show

McCain, G. and McNeill, L. (2019) Too *Fast to Live, Too Young to Die*. Museum of Art and Design, New York, April 9–August 18.

Album

Ayers, K. (1973) *Bananamour*. Sire.

Liner Notes

Gilbert, P. (1985) *Heroin*.

Hogan, P. (2012) Nico, *The End* (Island IMCD 174).

Houghton, M. (2007) *Frozen Borderline*.

Williams, R. (1990) *Marble Index* CD.

Films

**** (1967) Directed by Andy Warhol.

65 Revisited (2007) Directed by D. A. Pennebaker.

Ari and Mario (1966) Directed by Andy Warhol. Distributed by the Factory, U.S.

Athanor (1972) Directed by Philippe Garrel.

Beautiful Darling (2010) Directed by James Rasin.

Chelsea Girls (1966) Directed by Paul Morrissey and Andy Warhol. Available on Amazon Prime Video. Viewed July 6, 2019.

Cleopatra (1970) Directed by Michel Auder.

Curious: The Velvet Underground in Europe (1993) Directed by Declan Lowney.

Danny Says (2015) Directed by Brendan Toller. Magnolia Pictures. Available on Netflix. Viewed March 13, 2018.

Diaries Notes and Sketches (1969) Directed by Jonas Mekas.

Don't Look Back (1967) Directed by D. A. Pennebaker.

Exploding Plastic Inevitable (1967) Directed by Ronald Nameth.

For the First Time (1959) Directed by Rudolph Maté.

Gimme Danger (2016) Directed by Jim Jarmusch.

Harlot (1964) Directed by Andy Warhol. Distributed by the Factory, U.S.

Henry Geldzahler (1964) Directed by Andy Warhol. Distributed by the Factory, U.S.

I, a Man (1967) Directed by Andy Warhol. Distributed by the Factory, U.S.

Imitation of Christ (1967) Directed by Andy Warhol. Distributed by the Factory, U.S.

John Cale (1998) Directed by James Marsh.

La Deuxième Femme (1978) Directed by Pierre Clémenti.

La Dolce Vita (1960) Directed by Federico Fellini. Italy: Riama Film, Cinecittà, Pathé Consortium Cinéma. Available on Amazon Prime Video. Viewed June 10, 2019.

La Vraie Histoire de Gérard Lechômeur (1982) Directed by Joaquín Lledó.

Le Berceau de cristal (1976) Directed by Philippe Garrel.

Le Bleu des origines (1979) Directed by Philippe Garrel.

Les Hautes Solitudes (1974). Directed by Philippe Garrel.

L'Interview (1986) Directed by Sylvain Roumette.

Lou Reed: Rock & Roll Heart (1998) Directed by T. Greenfield-Sanders. American Masters, Eagle Rock Entertainment, WNET Channel 13 New York.

Lou Reed: Transformer (2001) Directed by B. Smeaton. Isis Productions.

Lupe (1966) Directed by Andy Warhol. Distributed by the Factory, U.S.

Man Called Rocco (1961) Directed by Jean Becker.

Monterey Pop (1968). Directed by D. A. Pennebaker.

Nico, 1988 (2017) Directed by Susanna Nicchiarelli.

Nico: An Underground Experience + Heroin (1985) Directed by Malcolm Whitehead.

Nico: Evening of Light (1969) Directed by François de Menil.

Nico/Antoine (1966) Directed by Andy Warhol. Distributed by the Factory, U.S.

Nico: Icon (1995) Directed by Susanne Ofteringer. Available on youtube. com. Viewed November 10, 2018.

Positano (1969) Directed by Pierre Clémenti.

Salvador Dalí (1966) Directed by Andy Warhol.

Sausalito (1967) Directed by Andy Warhol.

Scenes from the Life of Andy Warhol (1990) Directed by Jonas Mekas.

Strip-Tease/Sweet Skin (1963) Directed by Jacques Poitrenaud. Available on Amazon Prime Video. Viewed January 5, 2019.

Sunset (1967) Directed by Andy Warhol. Distributed by the Factory, U.S.

Tempest (1958) Directed by Alberto Lattuada.

The Closet (1966) Directed by Andy Warhol. Distributed by the Factory, U.S.

The Inner Scar (1972) Directed by Philippe Garrel.

The Sandpiper (1965) Directed by Vincente Minnelli.

The Velvet Underground and Nico: A Symphony of Sound (1966) Directed by Andy Warhol. Distributed by the Factory, U.S. Available on youtube. com. Viewed March 31, 2019.

The Velvet Underground: Psychiatrist's Convention, NYC, 1966 (1966) Directed by Andy Warhol.

The Velvet Underground Tarot Cards (1966) Directed by Andy Warhol.

The Velvet Underground at Bataclan '72 (1972) Directed by Claude Ventura.

Un ange passe (1975) Directed by Philippe Garrel.

Velvet Underground: Under Review (2006) Directed by Tom Barbor-Might.

Vinyl (1965) Directed by Andy Warhol. Distributed by the Factory, U.S.

Voyage au jardin des morts (1978) Directed by Philippe Garrel.

TV

"Chelsea Hotel" (1981) *Arena*, season 6, episode 3. Directed by Nigel Finch.

Disco 2 (1971) Episode #2.21.

The Merv Griffin Show, season 6, episode 85. December 27, 1968.

The Old Grey Whistle Test (1975) Episode #4.18.

"Philippe Garrel—Portrait d'un artiste" (documentary) (1999) *Cinéma, de notre temps*. Directed by Françoise Etchegaray.

"The Velvet Underground" (1986) *The South Bank Show.* Directed by Kim Evans.

SOURCE NOTES

Introduction

"What I have in common with Nico" Hoskyns, B. (2001), "The Backpages Interview: Marianne Faithfull," *Rock's Backpages*.

Chapter 2

"My sister was notified by the *Wehrmacht*" Interview of Helma Wolff by Christian Biadacz.

"We assume they killed him" / "He was an adventurer" Wolff / Biadacz interview.

"My mother came to see me" Nico (2001) *Cible mouvante. Chansons, poèmes, journal.* Annecy: Pauvert.

"something about a factory in Berlin" Interview of Graham Dowdall by Jennifer Otter Bickerdike.

Chapter 3

"The air attacks grew stronger" Witts, R. (1993) *Nico: The Life and Lies of an Icon.* London: Virgin Books.

"We spent a lot of time together" Interview of Helma Wolff by Christian Biadacz.

"He was wonderful" / "She spent so much time in there" Witts (1993).

"In 1942, the train passed by our house" Nico (2001) *Cible mouvante. Chansons, poèmes, journal.* Annecy: Pauvert.

Chapter 4

"better a Russky on top" Ash, L. (2015) "The Rape of Berlin." Available at https://www.bbc.co.uk/news/magazine-32529679. Accessed March 19, 2019.

"the first English word I learned" / "in these schools" / "overcome mental hang-ups" Nico (2001) *Cible mouvante. Chansons, poèmes, journal.* Annecy: Pauvert.

"Christa was a very strange girl" / "At the age of twelve" / "Christa wanted to move on" Interview of Helma Wolff by Christian Biadacz.

Chapter 5

"It started about the age of twelve" Interview of Helma Wolff by Christian Biadacz.

"When I was young in Berlin" Nico (2001) *Cible mouvante. Chansons, poèmes, journal.* Annecy: Pauvert.

"She took walks on the Kurfürstendamm" / "Christa was always noticed" Wolff / Biadacz interview.

"an alternative school" / "Paris was the center of the fashion world" Witts, R. (1993) *Nico: The Life and Lies of an Icon.* London: Virgin Books.

"My sister said" Wolff / Biadacz interview.

"At 16, I became a photo model" / "I have not thought long" Sanders, E. (1969) "Nico, the Cologne Girl in the U.S. Underground," *Twen*, August.

"Models have one name" / "When Tobias took the first fashion photos" Witts (1993).

"almost broke her heart" / "started to suffer" Wolff / Biadacz interview.

"I was retouching photographs" Maywald, W. (1990) *The Splinters of the Mirror. An Illustrated Autobiography.* Munich: Schirmer/Mosel Verlag Gm.

"You could say I looked the same" / "I reserved all my energy in Berlin" / "I could not admit that I was out of my depth" Witts (1993).

Chapter 6

"would all be wonderful" / "the practical problems" / "I think my sister made friends" / "coughing and coughing" / "It was a wild music" Witts, R. (1993) *Nico: The Life and Lies of an Icon.* London: Virgin Books.

"wrote a Novel" Nico (2001) *Cible mouvante. Chansons, poèmes, journal.* Annecy: Pauvert.

"We were like a gang" Witts (1993).

"Chanel was simply lonely" Wallach, J. (1999) *Chanel: Her Style and Her Life.* London: Mitchell Beazley.

"this crazy idea" Interview of Clive Crocker by Jennifer Otter Bickerdike.
"I wonder if you can tell" / "She was not a typical woman" / "Nico had these romances" Witts (1993).

Chapter 7

"I was tall, I was blonde" Witts, R. (1993) *Nico: The Life and Lies of an Icon*. London: Virgin Books.
"ornamental, useless" Young, J. (1992) *Nico: Songs They Never Play on the Radio*. London: Bloomsbury.
"It is never easy to eat" Witts (1993).
"Nico was like the Kelippot" Strauss, N. (1996) "Film View; A Siren Who Sang of Herself," *New York Times*, January 14.
"She was observant" / "She was very, very curious" Interview of David Croland by Jennifer Otter Bickerdike.
"Your name is Nico?" *Nico: Icon* (1995) Directed by Susanne Ofteringer. Available on youtube.com. Viewed November 10, 2018.
"From that moment" / "I liked the name Christa" / "I had spent a lot of time" / "I got to the point" / "She hadn't thought about it" Witts (1993).

Chapter 8

"I was with my friends" Witts, R. (1993) *Nico: The Life and Lies of an Icon*. London: Virgin Books.
"the most dangerous man" / "He was like a gypsy" Witts (1993).
"a good model, very professional" Witts (1993).

Chapter 9

"Although she [Nico] knew" / "It couldn't have been" Interview of Helma Wolff by Christian Biadacz.
"I was just leaving for Paris" Witts, R. (1993) *Nico: The Life and Lies of an Icon*. London: Virgin Books.
"[Nico] had rented a very nice house" Wolff / Biadacz interview and Witts (1993).
"I am the most happy girl" / "Alain Delon!" / "You can imagine the silence" / "I didn't want anything" / It was like a fairy tale" Witts (1993).

"One day she called me" *Nico: Icon* (1995) Directed by Susanne Ofteringer. Available on youtube.com. Viewed November 10, 2018.

"It seems that Alain Delon does not answer" Ari (2001).

"We had to separate" / "It was frightening to see her mother" / "[M]entally the mother relied entirely" / "The mother started to howl" Witts (1993).

"beside himself with fury" / "I was angry with this arrogance" Witts (1993).

"[Taking French nationality] was not possible" / "As a German citizen" Witts (1993).

"a romantic liaison" / "Papatakis was a decent chap" Witts (1993).

"She was simply breathtaking" / "She wanted to know everything" / "There was a rule for entry" Interview of Victor Brox by Jennifer Otter Bickerdike.

Chapter 10

"Once your chance goes by" *Strip-Tease/Sweet Skin* (1963) Directed by Jacques Poitrenaud. Available on Amazon Prime Video. Viewed January 5, 2019.

"One should certainly raise objections" / "The road to hell is paved" Witts, R. (1993) *Nico: The Life and Lies of an Icon*. London: Virgin Books.

"We went to see the premier" / "This apartment was filled with bottles" / "We would always sit in the back" / "She brought this young kid" / "I remember being in England" Interview of Clive Crocker by Jennifer Otter Bickerdike.

Chapter 11

"I was paralyzed" / "Everyone was down from Harvard" / "The only thing we had to drink" / "In the middle of the evening" / "A lovely, beautiful, nineteen-year-old" Interview of Danny Fields by Jennifer Otter Bickerdike.

"Our party was held in due course" Letter from Danny Fields personal archive with permission.

"Parkinson's disease and solitude" / "We were alone, Omi and me" Ari (2001) *L'Amour n'oublie jamais* ("Love Never Forgets"). Pauvert: Departemente de la Librairie Artheme Fayard. Translated for this project into English.

"I learned of Ari's existence" Ari (2001).

"I arrived and I was shocked" / "With these papers I went to the French Consul" Witts, R. (1993) *Nico: The Life and Lies of an Icon*. London:

Virgin Books.

"He was christened Ari" Interview of Helma Wolff by Christian Biadacz.

"Before we took him" *Nico: Icon* (1995) Directed by Susanne Ofteringer. Available on youtube.com. Viewed November 10, 2018.

"She took over the kid" Interview of Clive Crocker by Jennifer Otter Bickerdike.

"She [Edith] said to Christa" Wolff / Biadacz interview.

"When he heard about it, two years after" *Nico: Icon* (1995).

Chapter 12

"I was traveling with one of his friends" Sanders, E. (1969) "Nico, the Cologne Girl in the U.S. Underground," *Twen*, August.

"for an evening and a week" Witts, R. (1993) *Nico: The Life and Lies of an Icon*. London: Virgin Books.

"His music fascinated me" Sanders, *Twen* (1969).

"As I was from Berlin" / "He was so charming" / "about me and my little baby" Witts (1993).

"he...changed the idea that I had" / "[Dylan] didn't like it when I tried" Witts (1993).

"To be a model in that period" / "a bit of a hustler" / "You felt she was trying" Witts (1993).

"terrifying" / "She had nothing to do..." Interview of Helma Wolff by Christian Biadacz.

"It's really very simple..." / "Brian was the kind of man" / "It was fascinating and frightening" / "he was really too stoned" / "He was scared of her" Witts (1993).

Chapter 13

"One evening we were together in a nightclub" Maywald, W. (1990) *The Splinters of the Mirror. An Illustrated Autobiography*. Munich: Schirmer/ Mosel Verlag Gm.

"Gerard Malanga told me about the studio" McCain, G. and McNeil, L. (1997) *Please Kill Me: The Uncensored Oral History of Punk*. London: Abacus.

"Pundits seem to have it Brian played" / "I obviously heard the result" / "He [Page] didn't have anything" Interview of A.L.Oldham by Jennifer Otter Bickerdike. May 23, 2019.

"I was acting a role that I had to do" Witts, R. (1993) *Nico: The Life and Lies of an Icon*. London: Virgin Books.

"We were all so wonderfully stoned" / "I didn't socialize with her" Interview of A.L.Oldham by Jennifer Otter Bickerdike. May 23, 2019.

"She was one of a new breed of woman" Thompson, D. (2009) *Your Pretty Face Is Going to Hell: The Dangerous Glitter of David Bowie, Iggy Pop, and Lou Reed*. Backbeat. Kindle edition.

"good instincts" / "heart is in the right place" *Don't Look Back* (1967) Directed by D. A. Pennebaker.

"She called us from a Mexican restaurant" / "tilted her head to the side" / "Paul said that we should use Nico" Warhol, A. (2007) *POPism*. London: Penguin. Kindle edition.

"I first heard of Nico, one day" / "It was perilous to be there" / "Most people at The Factory" / "Nico was spectacular" *Nico: Icon* (1995) Directed by Susanne Ofteringer. Available on youtube.com. Viewed November 10, 2018.

"The way they did movies" Unterberger, R. (2009) *White Light/White Heat: The Velvet Underground Day-by-Day*, revised and expanded e-book edition. London: Jawbone Press.

Chapter 14

"He withdrew from the art world" / "An hour's worth" / "These films were truly experimental" Witts, R. (1993) *Nico: The Life and Lies of an Icon*. London: Virgin Books.

"quickie underground movies" Violet, U. (1988) *Famous for 15 Minutes: My Years with Andy Warhol*.

"I really became his manager" Witts (1993).

"handed down" / "Our crowd was photographed a lot" Interview of David Croland by Jennifer Otter Bickerdike. October 15, 2018.

"Andy was very good at launching people" Interview of Vincent Fremont by Jennifer Otter Bickerdike. October 23, 2017.

"He liked to possess them" Interview of Jerry Schatzberg by Jennifer Otter Bickerdike. December 10, 2017.

"A girl always looks more beautiful" Wrenn, M. (1991) *Andy Warhol in His Own Words*. New York: Omnibus Press.

"I could see that she had more problems" / "Ooh, that's great" Wilcock, J.

(1971) *The Autobiography and Sex Life of Andy Warhol*. New York: Other Scenes.

"The first thing that registered to me" Malanga, G. (2009) *Uptight: The Velvet Underground Story*. London: Music Sales. Kindle edition.

"The first thing I realized about the Velvet Underground" McCain, G. and McNeil, L. (1997) *Please Kill Me: The Uncensored Oral History of Punk*. London: Abacus.

"We have to think of something to do with the Velvets" Wilcock (1971).

"the most beautiful moment of my life" Unterberger, R. (2009) *White Light/White Heat: The Velvet Underground Day-by-Day*, revised and expanded e-book edition. London: Jawbone Press.

"Nico never had any taste" McCain and McNeil (1997).

"One night we went to the Café Bizarre" Nico (2001) *Cible mouvante. Chansons, poèmes, journal*. Annecy: Pauvert.

"I felt that the one thing the Velvets didn't have" Bockris, V. (1994) *Lou Reed: The Biography—Fully Revised Edition*. London: Random House.

"like she could have made the trip over" / "very mod and spiffy" / "She had straight shoulder-length" / "She had this very strange way" Warhol, A. (2007) *POPism*. London: Penguin. Kindle edition.

"Andy always liked to have" / "Andy's persona" Interview of Vincent Fremont by Jennifer Otter Bickerdike.

"only wanted to be with the underground people" Nico (2009) Nico in Manchester. Available at https://www.youtube.com/watch?v=4ORa382rBXM. Accessed June 3, 2019.

"I have always been in the wrong place" Nico (2009).

"After we met them" / "We wanted her to have" Malanga (2009)

"They're supposed to work" McCain, G. and McNeill, L. (2019) *Too Fast to Live, Too Young to Die*. Museum of Art and Design, New York, April 9–August 18.

"The idea of having her in the band" *Nico: Icon* (1995) Directed by Susanne Ofteringer. Available on youtube.com. Viewed November 10, 2018.

"Andy suggested we use Nico as a vocalist" Bockris (1994).

"We said fine, she looks great" Thompson, D. (2009) *Your Pretty Face Is Going to Hell: The Dangerous Glitter of David Bowie, Iggy Pop, and Lou Reed*. Backbeat. Kindle edition.

"there were problems from the very beginning" Bockris (1994).

"was a schmuck, from the first" / "was hostile to Nico" Thompson (2009).

"Of course, Lou Reed almost gagged" McCain and McNeil (1997).

"I didn't want to say they needed somebody" / "Lou was very reluctant" McCain and McNeil (1997).

"Andy Warhol persuaded Lou Reed" Interview of Victor Bockris by Jennifer Otter Bickerdike. October 18, 2018.

"No one knew what to make of her" Thompson (2009).

"She was much more ready" Goddard, S. (2009) *Mozipedia: The Encyclopaedia of Morrissey and the Smiths*. Cornwall: Random House.

"Nico was sort of the bigger of the two" Watson, S. (2003) *Factory Made: Warhol and the Sixties*. New York: Pantheon Books.

"the most ethereal and lovely" Thompson (2009).

"Nico's the kind of person" / "Lou loved the fact that Nico was big" Bockris (1994).

"If you get into Nico" Gibbs, V. (1971) in the *Metropolitan Review*. Accessed at the British Library, July 2019.

"I was this poor little rock and roller" Watson (2003).

"You could say that Lou was in love" / "Whoever seemed to be having undue influence" Hogan, P. (2017) *The Dead Straight Guide to the Velvet Underground*. Huntingdon: This Day in Music.

"very sweet and lovely" Watson (2003).

"quarreled a lot" Nico (2009).

"But he could be nice to me" / "One night Nico came up to me" Witts (1993).

"Lou must have been in love with Nico" Malanga (2009).

"Andy said I should write a song about Edie" Bockris (1994).

"Nico has a little time living with Lou" / "It's a rock world thing" Interview of Victor Bockris by Jennifer Otter Bickerdike.

"I have a couple of interviews of Nico" Interview of Bruno Blum by Jennifer Otter Bickerdike. September 20, 2018.

"both consummated and constipated" / "psychological love songs" McCain and McNeil (1997).

"Lou's affection for Nico quickly faded" / "Lou liked to manipulate women" / "I don't think anyone was impressed" / "Lou said hello to her" *Nico: Icon* (1995)

"absolutely torn up about it all" Thompson (2009).

"Lou wanted to be the queen bitch" *Nico: Icon* (1995)

"All the revisionist speculation about her" Thompson (2009).

Chapter 15

"I told him I'd be glad" Warhol, A. (2007) *POPism*. London: Penguin. Kindle edition.

"The psych convention started out as a con" McCain, G. and McNeil, L. (1997) *Please Kill Me: The Uncensored Oral History of Punk*. London: Abacus.

"The Velvets started to blast" Violet, U. (1988) *Famous for 15 Minutes: My Years with Andy Warhol*.

"what does her vagina feel like?" Violet (1988).

"Those people were flabbergasted" / "The press played it like it was" McCain and McNeil (1997).

"It was obvious she didn't have a voice" / "Gerard had noticed how lost Edie looked" Bockris, V. (1989) *Warhol*. London: Penguin.

"Mick Jagger of the Velvet Underground" / "She was a new type of female superstar" Warhol (2007)

"in Warhol's version of stardom" / "Divinity, star, what's the next" Watson, S. (2003) *Factory Made: Warhol and the Sixties*. New York: Pantheon Books.

"We're sponsoring a new band" Unterberger, R. (2009) *White Light/White Heat: The Velvet Underground Day-by-Day*, revised and expanded e-book edition. London: Jawbone Press.

"My name was somewhere near the bottom" McCain and McNeil (1997).

"When Nico kept insisting" Unterberger (2009).

"They played the record" McCain and McNeil (1997).

"not to care" / "only a rehearsal" Unterberger (2009).

"Edie Sedgwick tried to sing" McCain and McNeil (1997).

"Edie began asking Andy" / "She told Andy" / "Andy couldn't resist asking" / "She left and everybody was kind" Malanga, G. (2009) *Uptight: The Velvet Underground Story*. London: Music Sales. Kindle edition.

"It was Edie's farewell" McCain and McNeil (1997).

Chapter 16

"The students couldn't take their eyes off Nico" Warhol, A. (2007) *POPism*. London: Penguin. Kindle edition.

"Nico drove, and that was an experience" Warhol (2007).

"I still had my American license" / "Oh my God!" Witts, R. (1993) *Nico: The Life and Lies of an Icon*. London: Virgin Books.

"Ann Arbor [home to the University of Michigan]" Warhol (2007).

"While a beautiful blond girl sang" Unterberger, R. (2009) *White Light/White Heat: The Velvet Underground Day-by-Day*, revised and expanded e-book edition. London: Jawbone Press.

"I walked into that store" Interview of David Croland by Jennifer Otter Bickerdike.

"come blow [their] mind[s]" Unterberger (2009).

"When we opened the Dom" / "When we started moving around" Heylin, C. (1993) *From the Velvets to the Voidoids: A Pre-Punk History for a Post-Punk World*. London: Penguin.

"a cross-section of straights and gays" Bockris, V. (1989) *Warhol*. London: Penguin.

"When you go to the Dom" / "The amazing thing is" Violet, U. (1988) *Famous for 15 Minutes: My Years with Andy Warhol*.

"incredible... It was like Marilyn" Interview of David Croland by Jennifer Otter Bickerdike.

"Our actual salary from Paul Morrissey" / "We played music" / "A lot of people would come" Bockris, V. (1994) *Lou Reed: The Biography—Fully Revised Edition*. London: Random House.

"And with the Velvets come the blonde" / "a fashion model, answering only" / "Modeling is such a dull job" / "Nico sings terribly" Unterberger (2009).

"Everybody in the Velvet Underground" / "Everybody wanted to be the star" McCain, G. and McNeil, L. (1997) *Please Kill Me: The Uncensored Oral History of Punk*. London: Abacus.

"Nico took an age" / "Lou was always ill at ease" / "Nico walked out" / "Lou could not stand" Bockris (1994).

"He had a reputation for being mean" Bockris, V. (2014) *Transformer: The Complete Lou Reed Story*. London: HarperCollins.

"The floorboards were torn up" / "We set up the drums" Bockris (1994).

"What he did do is he made it all" *Lou Reed: Transformer* (2001) Directed by B. Smeaton. Isis Productions.

"Lou didn't want Nico to sing" Witts (1993)

"All I remember is suddenly" / "Lou didn't want her" Malanga, G. (2009)

Uptight: The Velvet Underground Story. London: Music Sales. Kindle edition.
"The whole time the album" Warhol (2007).

Chapter 17

"build up an LP operation" / "[Wilson] told us to wait" / "I sent it [the demo]" / "That girl is fantastic" / "When I went back" Unterberger, R. (2009) *White Light/White Heat: The Velvet Underground Day-by-Day*, revised and expanded e-book edition. London: Jawbone Press.

"On tour, Nico was the one" Woronov, M. (2013) *Swimming Underground: My Time at Andy Warhol's Factory*. Los Angeles: Montaldo Publishing.

"I love LA" Bockris, V. (1989) *Warhol*. London: Penguin.

"Nico could probably make it" Malanga, G. (2009) *Uptight: The Velvet Underground Story*. London: Music Sales. Kindle edition.

"From the moment we landed" Watson, S. (2003) *Factory Made: Warhol and the Sixties*. New York: Pantheon Books.

"probably the single most untalented" Bockris (1989)

"will replace nothing" / "the long-haired, deep-voiced" / "Nico, the chanteuse" / "It's nice that the Trip" / "neither art nor order" / "The audience was fine" / "They saw this as" Unterberger (2009).

"We used to tape our rehearsals" / "You've got to get another song" / "terribly insipid" / "He sang it!" Witts, R. (1993) *Nico: The Life and Lies of an Icon*. London: Virgin Books.

"Everyone [from New York] was on drugs" Interview of Bruno Blum by Jennifer Otter Bickerdike.

"very bland and low" / "the sound of an amplified" / "If there exists a beauty" / "just a very, very beautiful" / "Nico would be most effectively" Malanga (2009).

"perfect as a cadaver" Unterberger (2009).

"Nico was not a phoney" Interview of David Croland by Jennifer Otter Bickerdike.

"everyone was feeling" / "Amphetamine was the big drug" Warhol, A. (2007) *POPism*. London: Penguin. Kindle edition.

"knocking unannounced" / "She would just turn up" Watson (2003).

"She was a Francophile" / "pride that she'd had a son" Interview of Iggy Pop by Jennifer Otter Bickerdike.

Chapter 18

"beautiful," "impactful" and "schizophrenic" Bockris, V. (1989) *Warhol*. London: Penguin.

"Tell the story of your life" Wrenn, M. (1991) *Andy Warhol in His Own Words*. New York: Omnibus Press.

"already playing the role of Nico" / "For my scenes, Paul and Andy" Witts, R. (1993) *Nico: The Life and Lies of an Icon*. London: Virgin Books.

"a passive-aggressive signal" Bockris, V. (1994) *Lou Reed: The Biography— Fully Revised Edition*. London: Random House.

"a hip place where Harlem met bohemia" http://www.furious.com/perfect/ tinpalace.html

"almost 100 percent black clientele" / "get some white people in" Unterberger, R. (2009) *White Light/White Heat: The Velvet Underground Day-by-Day*, revised and expanded e-book edition. London: Jawbone Press.

"it was pathetic to see" Warhol, A. (2007) *POPism*. London: Penguin. Kindle edition.

"she sort of spun off out of the band" *Nico: Icon* (1995) Directed by Susanne Ofteringer. Available on youtube.com. Viewed November 10, 2018.

"Nico and Lou had a fight" Warhol (2007).

"They threw me out" Sanders, E. (1969) "Nico, the Cologne Girl in the U.S. Underground," *Twen*, August.

"Too many scenes of jealousy" *Being Nico* (2018) WDR 3 Westdeutscher Rundfunk, October 14.

"I was glad to see Nico go" Sanders, *Twen* (1969).

"a very good group" *Being Nico* (2018).

"They do not like women at all" Sanders, *Twen* (1969).

"regret a minute of it!" Nico Discusses Lou Reed and the Velvet Underground. Available at https://www.youtube.com/ watch?v=BM6WxweVyds. Accessed October 24, 2019.

"whitest white twill" Warhol (2007).

"barely audible against" / "Nico is the first psychedelic singer" Violet, U. (1988) *Famous for 15 Minutes: My Years with Andy Warhol*.

"artist" and "unemployed go-go dancer" / "a white minidress" Warhol (2007).

"This is not exactly the wedding" Unterberger (2009).

"I do not like to perform" Sanders, *Twen* (1969).

"He was one of the most beautiful children" Interview of David Croland by
   Jennifer Otter Bickerdike.
"swallowed anything" / "For a little boy of four" Ari (2001) *L'Amour n'oublie
   jamais* ("Love Never Forgets"). Pauvert: Departemente de la Librairie
   Artheme Fayard. Translated for this project into English.
"That was one of the saddest" Croland interview.
"It was only on the plane" / "I slept in the bed" / "The TV seemed" Ari (2001).
"She came to see him once" *Nico: Icon* (1995).
"He was christened Ari" / "She couldn't take care of herself" Interview of
   Helma Wolff by Christian Biadacz.
"she was angry about" / "He [Delon] made out" / "I was calling him"
   Interview of Robert King by Jennifer Otter Bickerdike.

Chapter 19

"He didn't like this place" Holzman, J. (2014) *Follow the Music: The Life and
   High Times of Elektra Records in the Great Years of American Pop Culture.*
   New York: FirstMedia Books. Kindle edition.
"He was doing this gig with Nico" Browne, J. (2005) Interviewed by Jody
   Denberg of KGSR radio. October.
"We didn't play every night" / "There were loops" Witts, R. (1993) *Nico:
   The Life and Lies of an Icon.* London: Virgin Books.
"never noticed the crowd" Meltzer, R (1971) in *Screw Magazine.* Accessed at
   the British Library, July 2018.
"smoky [and] noisy" / "The camaraderie which had been part" Unterberger,
   R. (2009) *White Light/White Heat: The Velvet Underground Day-by-Day,*
   revised and expanded e-book edition. London: Jawbone Press.
"They originally wanted Nico" Witts (1993).
"Leonard Cohen the Canadian poet" Warhol, A. (2007) *POPism.* London:
   Penguin. Kindle edition.
"I didn't know any of these people" Thompson, D. (2009) *Your Pretty Face
   Is Going to Hell: The Dangerous Glitter of David Bowie, Iggy Pop, and Lou
   Reed.* Backbeat. Kindle edition.
"I was madly in love with her" / "The years went by" "When Leonard
   Cohen Met Nico" (2016) Available at http://graham-russell.blogspot.
   com/2016/11/when-leonard-cohen-met-nico.html. Accessed June 24, 2019.
"He came to see me" Warhol (2007).

"She was physically like a goddess" / "Gee, I'm barely eighteen" Witts (1993).
"It wasn't done in any kind of malicious way" / "much to my" Unterberger (2009).

Chapter 20

"I didn't go for the arrangements" Unterberger, R. (2009) *White Light/White Heat: The Velvet Underground Day-by-Day*, revised and expanded e-book edition. London: Jawbone Press.

"loosely put together" Wiseman R. (1982) *Jackson Browne, the Story of a Hold Out*. Garden City, NY: Doubleday.

"This record was basically" Browne, J. (2005) Interviewed by Jody Denberg of KGSR radio. October.

"None of us had any patience" Unterberger (2009).

"If they'd just have allowed" Bockris, V. (2014) *Transformer: The Complete Lou Reed Story*. London: HarperCollins.

"She just turned up on the doorstep" Witts, R. (1993) *Nico: The Life and Lies of an Icon*. London: Virgin Books.

"arrival on short notice from London" Unterberger (2009).

"Nico really was never a member" *Lou Reed: Rock & Roll Heart* (1998) Directed by T. Greenfield-Sanders. American Masters, Eagle Rock Entertainment, WNET Channel 13 New York.

"It was time for her to leave" Interview of Lou Reed by Georgia Straight 1968. Accessed at the British Library, July 2019.

"What she was doing was just a part" / "It was never meant to be" / "Her leaving was" / "Nico set the tone" /"I was never totally" Unterberger (2009).

"At the time there weren't a lot" Interview of Dave Navarro by Jennifer Otter Bickerdike.

"was so unhappy" Unterberger (2009).

"When I was a teenager" / "It was pretty much a redneck" Interview of Mark Lanegan by Jennifer Otter Bickerdike.

"It's kinda hard to be a fan" Dave Navarro interview.

"my favorite female album" Interview of Peter Hook by Jennifer Otter Bickerdike.

"The material she sang" Unterberger (2009).

"People more want to talk" Interview of Una Baines by Jennifer Otter Bickerdike.

"That's all she faced" Interview of JD by Jennifer Otter Bickerdike.

"I was not in good nick" Interview of Andrew Loog Oldham by Jennifer Otter Bickerdike.

"last time I saw Brian Jones" Unterberger (2009).

"bragged of her fling" / "her attraction to Hendrix" Witts (1993).

Chapter 21

"We were staying at the dumpy" Witts, R. (1993) *Nico: The Life and Lies of an Icon*. London: Virgin Books.

"I once heard a story from Bill" Interview of Aaron Sixx by Jennifer Otter Bickerdike.

"gaga" / "at every opportunity" / "I'm going to take another von" Manzarek, R. (1999) *Light My Fire: My Life with the Doors*. London: Penguin. Kindle ed.

"It just wasn't that sort of vibe" Interview of Danny Fields by Jennifer Otter Bickerdike.

"Evidently, she gave great head" Manzarek (1999).

"I saw them [the Doors] perform" *Danny Says* (2015) Directed by Brendan Toller. Magnolia Pictures. Available on Netflix. Viewed March 13, 2018. Quote modified in an interview of Danny Fields by Jennifer Otter Bickerdike, March 30, 2021.

"Jim Morrison was a callous" McCain, G. and McNeil, L. (1997) *Please Kill Me: The Uncensored Oral History of Punk*. London: Abacus.

"strange haunted house" Gorman, P. (2001) *In Their Own Write: Adventures in the Music Press*. London: Sanctuary.

"It was this two-story house" McCain McNeil (1997).

"quite a cast" Unterberger, R. (2009) *White Light/White Heat: The Velvet Underground Day-by-Day*, revised and expanded e-book edition. London: Jawbone Press.

"We finally got up to the house" *Danny Says* (2015).

"Nico and Edie fled to their bedrooms" Gorman (2001).

"We started smoking" / "He would just open his palm" *Danny Says* (2015).

"Jim and Nico standing" Gorman (2001). Quote modified based on interview of Danny Fields by Jennifer Otter Bickerdike, March 31, 2021.

"He said to me one day" / "He was the first man" Batson (2012).

"That's what I think" Unterberger (2009).

"Peyote was a spiritual drug" / "We had visions in the desert" / "Everything was open" / "We had a too-big appetite" Batson (2012).

"You could say that Jim" / "I like my relations" / "Jim Morrison had the best" Witts (1993).

"She [Nico] was obsessed with Jim" *Nico: Icon* (1995) Directed by Susanne Ofteringer. Available on youtube.com. Viewed November 10, 2018.

Chapter 22

"In San Francisco, we're a smash" Violet, U. (1988) *Famous for 15 Minutes: My Years with Andy Warhol.*

"I say to Andy" Violet (1988).

"She would practice it" / "thought she was the Queen" Witts, R. (1993) *Nico: The Life and Lies of an Icon.* London: Virgin Books.

"The moon goddess Nico" Unterberger, R. (2009) *White Light/White Heat: The Velvet Underground Day-by-Day*, revised and expanded e-book edition. London: Jawbone Press.

"Chic crowds turned up at Nico's opening" / "people were starting to file out" Interview of Danny Fields by Jennifer Otter Bickerdike.

"Opening night was very crowded" Eisen, J. (1970) *The Age of Rock 2.* New York: Random House.

"She had a big crush on him" / "a series of scenes" Warhol, A. (2007) *POPism.* London: Penguin. Kindle edition.

"Most pop music to me is noise" Walker, S. (1986) Nico, interview 3RRR FM, August 2. Available at http://smironne.free.fr/NICO/rrr.html. Accessed July 17, 2019.

"[*smoking a cigarette, starts playing*" Nico (1985) Interview. Available at https://www.youtube.com/watch?v=MOeU-BF78gM&t=96s. Accessed July 11, 2019.

"I like the [cover] picture" / "They call her the Dietrich" / "Nico is beautiful" Unterberger (2009).

"I've never much cared for [the Warhol films]" McKenna, K. (2001) *Book of Changes: A Collection of Interviews.* Seattle: Fantagraphics.

"Elektra's Danny Fields" Unterberger (2009).

Chapter 23

"She used to say how there used to be" Interview of James Young by Jennifer Otter Bickerdike.

"looked good" Nico (2001) *Cible mouvante. Chansons, poèmes, journal.*

Annecy: Pauvert.

"They'd pretend, these agencies" James Young interview.

"Nico was into drugs way back" / "Lou knew that" Interview of Victor Bokris by Jennifer Otter Bickerdike.

"Most people self-medicate" Interview of Vincent Fremont by Jennifer Otter Bickerdike.

"Show me one person" *Nico: Icon* (1995) Directed by Susanne Ofteringer. Available on youtube.com. Viewed November 10, 2018.

"I guess artists have always" / "As there is in our society" Danny Fields personal archive.

"Some of the most well-known jazz musicians" Victor Bokris interview.

"She [Nico] just fits into those fears" Interview of Una Baines by Jennifer Otter Bickerdike.

"People tend to look at male musicians" Interview of Cosey Fanni Tutti by Jennifer Otter Bickerdike.

"Nico's slide into heroin" Victor Bokris interview.

"it was the Velvet Underground" Interview of Robert King by Jennifer Otter Bickerdike.

"I remember she used to come back" Interview of Clive Crocker by Jennifer Otter Bickerdike.

"She started to take more drugs" *Nico: Icon* (1995).

"obscured for years" Victor Bokris interview.

"It was almost a burden" Dalton, D. (2002) "Nico and *The Marble Index*: A Conversation with Danny Fields," *Gadfly*. Available at http://www.rock sbackpages.com/Library/Article/nico-and-the-marble-index-a-conversation -with-danny-fields. Accessed July 16, 2019. Quote slightly modified based on interview of Danny Fields by Jennifer Otter Bickerdike, March 31, 2021.

"Everything was turbulent about her" Reynolds, S. (2007) "From the Velvets to the Void," *Guardian*, March 16. Available at https://www.theguardian .com/music/2007/mar/16/popandrock3. Accessed July 16, 2019.

"In her photographs" Dalton (2002). Quote modified based on interview of Danny Fields by Jennifer Otter Bickerdike, March 31, 2021.

"Nico arrived in the Factory" *Being Nico* (2018) WDR 3 Westdeutscher Rundfunk, October 14.

"Fred doted on eccentrics" / "liked to lie in the bathtub" / "Nico was a true specimen" Warhol, A. (2007) *POPism*. London: Penguin. Kindle edition.

"Nico sleeps or stays sequestered" Unterberger, R. (2009) *White Light/White Heat: The Velvet Underground Day-by-Day*, revised and expanded e-book edition. London: Jawbone Press.

"The next phase of Nico" Dalton (2002).

"It has to do with my going to Berlin" Thompson, D. (1989) *Beyond the "Velvet Underground."* London: Omnibus.

"In the '60s, in the Velvet Underground" Victor Bokris interview.

"I write the music independently" Sanders, E. (1969) "Nico, the Cologne Girl in the U.S. Underground," *Twen*, August.

"She was so afraid" Dalton (2002).

"Danny was close to the whole Warhol crowd" *Danny Says* (2015) Directed by Brendan Toller. Magnolia Pictures. Available on Netflix. Viewed March 13, 2018.

"At that time, I think I had established" Dalton (2002).

"Even though it wasn't technically" *Being Nico* (2018).

Chapter 24

"She sat and read books of poetry" / "I don't know how much Wordsworth" Dalton, D. (2002) "Nico and *The Marble Index*: A Conversation with Danny Fields," *Gadfly*. Available at http://www.rocksbackpages.com/ Library/Article/nico-and-the-marble-index-a-conversation-with-danny-fields. Accessed July 16, 2019.

"She was sent to me by Elektra" / "She was absolutely beautiful" / "For the actual shoot" / "In the early 1970s" Interview of Guy Webster by Jennifer Otter Bickerdike.

Chapter 25

"Frazier Mohawk is the producer of the record" Dalton, D. (2002) "Nico and *The Marble Index*: A Conversation with Danny Fields," *Gadfly*. Available at http://www.rocksbackpages.com/Library/Article/nico-and-the-marble-index-a-conversation-with-danny-fields. Accessed July 16, 2019.

"The songs were already in Nico's head" Houghton, M. (2007) *Frozen Borderline*. Liner notes.

"Before I did *Index*" Thompson, D. (1989) *Beyond the "Velvet Underground."* London: Omnibus.

"every opportunity" Thompson (1989)

"You've got to remember" Unterberger, R. (2009) *White Light/White Heat: The Velvet Underground Day-by-Day*, revised and expanded e-book edition. London: Jawbone Press.

"I was enormously comforted" Goddard, S. (2009) *Mozipedia: The Encyclopaedia of Morrissey and the Smiths*. Cornwall: Random House.

"that's all I could listen to" Houghton (2007)

Chapter 26

"It hurt so much, I wished I was dead" "June 3, 1968—The Shooting of Andy Warhol" (n.d.) Available at https://www.warholstars.org/chron/andydies68n33.html. Accessed September 23, 2020.

"Please don't make me laugh" Thompson, D. (2009) *Your Pretty Face Is Going to Hell: The Dangerous Glitter of David Bowie, Iggy Pop, and Lou Reed*. Backbeat. Kindle edition.

"I was with Nico and Susan" Interview of David Croland by Jennifer Otter Bickerdike.

"playing of the album" *Marble Index* invitation: Warhol archive.

"an ear-piercing 16 minutes" / "Nico spent the whole summer" / "a tall redhead who refuses" Bartlett, K. (1968) "Superstars Pop Out at Warhol's Party," publication unknown. Taken from Danny Fields's personal archive.

"Of course. There's very little good music" Unterberger, R. (2009) *White Light/White Heat: The Velvet Underground Day-by-Day*, revised and expanded e-book edition. London: Jawbone Press.

"They won't let me back past the frozen borderline" Danny Fields archive.

"guided tour" / "of the legendary Rock Castle" Diehl, D. (1968) "The Jefferson Airplane, Bob Dylan, The Doors, The Who, The Grateful Dead, Nico, and Yes, The Beatles Slept Here," *Eye Magazine*. From the personal archive of Danny Fields.

"The list of tenants" / "She speaks in her tentative manner" /"a goldfish pond in the garden" / "A twenty-two room castle" Diehl (1968)

Chapter 27

"I can't make out a single real word" Unterberger, R. (2009) *White Light/ White Heat: The Velvet Underground Day-by-Day*, revised and expanded e-book edition. London: Jawbone Press.

"She'd call up and, in her low moan" Holzman, J. (2014) *Follow the Music: The Life and High Times of Elektra Records in the Great Years of American Pop Culture*. New York: FirstMedia Books. Kindle edition.

"Restricted sales but a beautiful album" Unterberger (2009).

"When I think of what I did at Elektra" McCain, G. and McNeil, L. (1997) *Please Kill Me: The Uncensored Oral History of Punk*. London: Abacus.

"It's an artifact" Unterberger (2009).

Chapter 28

"that album allowed a lot of European angst" Witts, R. (1993) *Nico: The Life and Lies of an Icon*. London: Virgin Books.

"I like the Velvet Underground" Unterberger, R. (2009) *White Light/White Heat: The Velvet Underground Day-by-Day*, revised and expanded e-book edition. London: Jawbone Press.

"I was meeting a lot of people" / "A lot of people who were interesting" / "I don't remember the specific first time" Interview of Iggy Pop by Jennifer Otter Bickerdike.

"The next night or so" McCain, G. and McNeil, L. (1997) *Please Kill Me: The Uncensored Oral History of Punk*. London: Abacus.

"You kind of expected that Iggy" McCain and McNeil (1997).

"keeping company with her from time to time" / "She was nine or ten years older" / "I was really thrilled" / "She didn't want to be cuddled" / "You know, [I was] a young, smart-ass rock singer" / "She had all the accoutrements" Interview of Iggy Pop by Jennifer Otter Bickerdike.

"When Nico moved into the Fun House" / "The Stooges didn't want" McCain and McNeil (1997).

"She would come to our rehearsals" / "She'd be very opinionated" / "She'd try to cook" Iggy Pop interview.

"She'd make these great curry dishes" / "The first time I ever had a Beaujolais" McCain and McNeil (1997).

"She'd feed me red wines" / "She had a mix of so many things" Iggy Pop interview.

"Nico would call me all the time" McCain and McNeil (1997).

"The more we were together" / "In retrospect" / "It was getting colder" / "It's not a long period" Iggy Pop interview.

"Nico stayed a long time" McCain and McNeil (1997).

"I had a toy piano" Thompson, D. (1989) *Beyond the "Velvet Underground."* London: Omnibus.

"I think it really pissed off de Menil" / "There are a lot of farms" / "It was very physical"/ "She probably wanted that imagery" / "What a great song" Iggy Pop interview.

"We all went out to this farm" / "I remember after she left" McCain and McNeil (1997).

"In my way, I loved her" Iggy Pop interview.

Chapter 29

"Laurence Olivier doing Richard the Third" / "You thought he should" / "There was nothing to see" Witts, R. (1993) *Nico: The Life and Lies of an Icon.* London: Virgin Books.

"misadventure" "Brian Jones: Sympathy for the Devil," *Rolling Stone,* August 9, 1969. https://www.rollingstone.com/music/music-news/brian-jones-sympathy-for-the-devil-182761/

"This new one is very important" Williams, R. (1970) "Nico, the Lonely Chanteuse," *Melody Maker,* March 21. Available at https://www.rocksbackpages.com/Library/Article/nico-the-lonely-chanteuse. Accessed July 27, 2019.

"Dear Danny, I am getting nostalgic" Danny Fields personal archive.

"The beginning of the school year" Ari (2001) *L'Amour n'oublie jamais* ("Love Never Forgets"). Pauvert: Departemente de la Librairie Artheme Fayard. Translated for this project into English.

"Clémenti speaks French" Greenspun, R. (1972) "'Inner Scar' by Talented Young Frenchman Shown," *New York Times,* October 7. Available at https://www.nytimes.com/1972/10/07/archives/inner-scar-by-talented-young-frenchman-shown.html. Accessed July 26, 2019.

"You need a bloody big spliff" Metzger, R. (2015) "'The Inner Scar': Velvet Underground Singer Nico Stars in Obscure, Pretentious French Art Film, 1972." Available at https://dangerousminds.net/comments/the_inner_scar_velvet_underground_singer_nico. Accessed July 26, 2019.

"it started out with Philippe" *Nico: Icon* (1995) Directed by Susanne Ofteringer. Available on youtube.com. Viewed November 10, 2018.

"Garrel was Nico's...nightmare" Interview of Robert King by Jennifer Otter Bickerdike.

"It was extraordinary" / "She came back to New York" Witts (1993).

"She didn't seem to help herself" / "If she hadn't been jonesing" Dalton, D. (2002) "Nico and *The Marble Index*: A Conversation with Danny Fields," *Gadfly*.

Chapter 30

"old people's home" / "From then on" / "She never visited her mother" Interview of Helma Wolff by Christian Biadacz.

"There were dead pigeons" / "The most sensational feature" Witts, R. (1993) *Nico: The Life and Lies of an Icon*. London: Virgin Books.

"All three of us went to visit" Ari (2001) *L'Amour n'oublie jamais* ("Love Never Forgets"). Pauvert: Departement de la Librairie Artheme Fayard. Translated for this project into English.

"I would go in their [Elektra's] office" / "On one of those visits" / "Some months later" / "I still hadn't met either" / "When Moe gave me a cautious" / "Whatever had gone on" / "We met in New York" / "wasn't super-friendly" / "I don't think she had the ability" / "I'd gotten to know Nico" / "was a kind of naive painter" Interview of Joe Boyd by Jennifer Otter Bickerdike.

"Her singing was more confident" Witts (1993).

"a chilling little chanson" Unterberger, R. (2009) *White Light/White Heat: The Velvet Underground Day-by-Day*, revised and expanded e-book edition. London: Jawbone Press.

"She'd play me her new records" Witts (1993).

"A favorite New York memory" Interview of Iggy Pop by Jennifer Otter Bickerdike.

"What's so strong about Nico" Interview of Cosey Fanni Tutti by Jennifer Otter Bickerdike.

"I met Nico in 1970" / "She would cry"/ "I had a big crush"/ "there were a lot of facets"/ "She used to play that harmonium" Interview of Vincent Fremont by Jennifer Otter Bickerdike.

Chapter 31

"still best friends"/ "if he wants to work"/ "a movie director who gets killed"/ "I would really like to write" Unterberger, R. (2009) *White Light/White*

Heat: The Velvet Underground Day-by-Day, revised and expanded e-book edition. London: Jawbone Press.

"stunningly rude" John Peel Wiki: "Nico." Available at https://peel.fandom.com/wiki/Nico. Accessed June 30, 2020.

(*Reed begins to play guitar* / Nico (*animated*) / Fields: You wanna do / Nico: What do you want / Fields: Are [you?] in touch with Joe / Nico: Tell me / Nico: I'd like to play. Danny Fields personal archive.

"The woman [Marks] was apparently saying" / "She was black, she was white" Witts, R. (1993) *Nico: The Life and Lies of an Icon*. London: Virgin Books.

"We interviewed a lot of girls" Interview of Joe Boyd by Jennifer Otter Bickerdike.

"One night she came home with Joe" Interview of Vincent Fremont by Jennifer Otter Bickerdike.

"Nico was, I dunno" Reynolds, S. (2007) "From the Velvets to the Void," *Guardian*, March 16. Available at https://www.theguardian.com/music/2007/mar/16/popandrock3. Accessed March 3, 2019.

"hated black people" Personal email to Dr. Jennifer Otter Bickerdike from Danny Fields, July 30, 2019.

"When you come from Germany" / "insufficient, and kind of comical" Interview of Danny Fields by Jennifer Otter Bickerdike.

"She was so far from being a Nazi" Dalton, D. (2002) "Nico and *The Marble Index*: A Conversation with Danny Fields," *Gadfly*.

"I remember one afternoon" Interview of Iggy Pop by Jennifer Otter Bickerdike.

"a fit of madness" / "I mentioned it in one song" *Being Nico* (2018) WDR 3 Westdeutscher Rundfunk, October 14.

"I'm a little afraid of them" "Nico: Shrink Rap" (1985) *Melody Maker*, July. Available at https://www.rocksbackpages.com/Library/Article/nico-shrink-rap. Accessed July 26, 2019.

"Jim's grave did not resemble" / "Can you give me some information" Danny Fields personal archive.

Chapter 32

"It annoyed me so much" Witts, R. (1993) *Nico: The Life and Lies of an Icon*. London: Virgin Books.

469

"just how ambivalent Reed felt" / "so moved by the experience" / "At the time" Interview of Victor Bockris by Jennifer Otter Bickerdike October 18, 2018.

"London March 13th, Dear Dany" Danny Fields personal archive.

"Wait until you smell her!" Interview of Danny Fields by Jennifer Otter Bickerdike.

"Athanor (Nico) is searching for fire" "*Les Hautes* Solitudes" (1974) Available at https://www.imdb.com/title/tt0071600/. Accessed August 8, 2019.

"I never kiss and tell" Reynolds, S. (2007) "From the Velvets to the Void," *Guardian*, March 16. Available at https://www.theguardian.com/music/2007/mar/16/popandrock3. Accessed March 3, 2019.

"Those albums are so incredible" Thompson, D. (1989) *Beyond the "Velvet Underground."* London: Omnibus.

"Nobody knew who she really was" Graf-Ulbrich, L. (2015) *Nico—In the Shadow of the Moon Goddess.* Luxembourg: CreateSpace Independent Publishing Platform.

"When she performed" Interview of Lutz Graf-Ulbrich by Jennifer Otter Bickerdike July 4, 2017.

"I went to her room and said bye" Brine, J. and Marnell, C. (2017) "Niconomicon: A Conversation with Lutz Graf-Ulbrich." Available at https://www.3ammagazine.com/3am/niconomicon-conversation-lutz-graf-ulbrich-nico. Accessed August 21, 2020.

"She invited me to her home" Graf-Ulbrich (2015).

"I worshipped her" / "My years with Nico" *Nico: Icon* (1995) Directed by Susanne Ofteringer. Available on youtube.com. Viewed November 10, 2018.

"Nico generally liked philosophers" Lutz Graf-Ulbrich interview.

"She didn't hold hands" Brine and Marnell (2017).

"so hard to follow as a person" *Nico: Icon* (1995).

"When she was taking heroin" / "After a while" Brine and Marnell (2017).

"I was addicted" / "sitting around hallucinating" *Being Nico* (2018) WDR 3 Westdeutscher Rundfunk, October 14.

"I remember she once said" Brine and Marnell (2017).

"She wasn't working on songs" Unterberger, R. (2009) *White Light/White Heat: The Velvet Underground Day-by-Day*, revised and expanded e-book edition. London: Jawbone Press.

"We were always looking for it" / "We bought some heroin" *Nico: Icon* (1995).

"He was angry and jealous" Brine and Marnell (2017).

"Andy [Warhol] was uncomfortable" / "I remember realizing" Interview of Vincent Fremont by Jennifer Otter Bickerdike.

"One night I go to his [Reed's] place" / "You see him do this to Nico" / "The reason that what Lou did" Interview of Victor Bockris by Jennifer Otter Bickerdike.

"The Nico episode [was] a bone of contention" Bockris, V. (1994) *Lou Reed: The Biography—Fully Revised Edition*. London: Random House.

"The way she has been treated" Victor Bockris interview.

"I think that John [Cale] was probably" Interview of Jonathan Donohue by Jennifer Otter Bickerdike.

"Lou Reed is a very loyal Person" / "One time in Berlin" Nico (2001) *Cible mouvante. Chansons, poèmes, journal.* Annecy: Pauvert.

"She only had a limited command" Reynolds (2007).

"far scarier than The Doors' original" Hogan, P. (2012) Nico, *The End* (Island IMCD 174). Liner notes.

"It's her interpretation" Phil Jones (1974) in *Melody Maker*, May 18, 1974. Accessed at the British Library, August 2018.

"If Morrison sang it as a lizard" Reynolds (2007).

"*The End* is full of these confused" Lake, S. (1974) "Rock Goes to Church," *Melody Maker*, December 1974.

"truly chilling" Hogan (2012).

"[Brian] Eno making air-raid noises" Reynolds (2007).

"The very high priestess of Weird" Lake, S. (1974) "Rock Goes to Church," *Melody Maker*, December 1974.

"They don't come much more Gothic" Hogan (2012).

"fascinating to watch" / "attempting to actually communicate" / "I thought it [the LP]" Lake, S. (1974) "I'm Not a Beggar Woman—Nico Talks to Steve Lake," *Melody Maker*, June 1974.

"When I sang on that song" Thompson (1989).

"very taken with what I'm doing" / "Nico is a woman you can only use"/ "Oh yes…a lot" / "Much of Nico's time of late" Lake, S. (1974) "I'm Not a Beggar Woman—Nico Talks to Steve Lake," *Melody Maker*, June 1974.

"I don't want to be anybody's Talisman" Nico (2001) *Cible mouvante. Chansons, poèmes, journal.* Annecy: Pauvert.

Chapter 33

"to show love to my father" "Philippe Garrel—*Un Ange Passe* (1975)."
Available at https://worldscinema.org/2019/02/philippe-garrel-un-ange-passe-1975. Accessed August 8, 2019.

"A woman sitting on a bench" *Un ange passe* (1975): Plot. Available at https://www.imdb.com/title/tt0073838/plotsummary. Accessed August 8, 2019.

"Nico had no management" *Being Nico* (2018) WDR 3 Westdeutscher Rundfunk, October 14.

"Money which we earned from Nico" Graf-Ulbrich, L. (2015) *Nico—In the Shadow of the Moon Goddess.* Luxembourg: CreateSpace Independent Publishing Platform.

"I was invited to parties still" Nico (2001) *Cible mouvante. Chansons, poèmes, journal.* Annecy: Pauvert.

"She always wore this big, black robe" Interview of Lutz Graf-Ulbrich by Jennifer Otter Bickerdike July 4, 2017.

"Dear Danny, when will we see" Danny Field personal archive.

"hang[ing] out in and around the pool" *Being Nico* (2018).

"sealed with a handshake"/ "never saw a penny" Graf-Ulbrich (2015).

"When I invited Nico" Graf-Ulbrich interview.

"The winter was cold" Graf-Ulbrich (2015).

"Staying at the Chelsea Hotel" Nico (2001).

"I went down to the Chelsea" Interview of Joe Bidewell by Jennifer Otter Bickerdike.

"I didn't know Lutz" / "I remember her style of dress" Interview of Jim Tisdall by Jennifer Otter Bickerdike.

"After we had filled out the immigration papers" Graf-Ulbrich (2015).

"Nico's physical appearance" Dadomo, G. (1978) "Nico," *Sounds*, April 28. Available at https://www.rocksbackpages.com/Library/Article/nico. Accessed August 12, 2019.

"It's true. She could be insecure" Brine, J. and Marnell, C. (2017) "Niconomicon: A Conversation with Lutz Graf-Ulbrich." Available at https://www.3ammagazine.com/3am/niconomicon-conversation-lutz-graf-ulbrich-nico. Accessed August 21, 2020.

"In the end, she wanted to be as ugly" / "She wanted to destroy herself" "She was a bit out of shape" / "Snark sells" Jim Tisdall interview.

"Does time passing make you sad?" Dadomo (1978).

"She's dressed in black cape" Needs, K. (1978) "Nico in London: Rare 1978 Interview," *Zigzag*, June.

"Dear Lutz, I was here" / "Dear Lutz, I'll go back" Graf-Ulbrich (2015).

Chapter 34

"I am a pagan" / "I was in fashion too long" Thompson, D. (1989) *Beyond the "Velvet Underground."* London: Omnibus.

"Nico had an otherworldly character" Thompson, D. (2002) *The Dark Reign of Gothic Rock: In the Reptile House with the Sisters of Mercy, Bauhaus and the Cure.* London: Helter Skelter.

"I know Siouxsie was a huge Nico fan" / "She [Nico] opened the door" Interview of Dave Navarro by Jennifer Otter Bickerdike.

"the way she presented herself" Interview of Mark Lanegan by Jennifer Otter Bickerdike.

"Amidst those awed by her" Interview of Peter Clarke by Jennifer Otter Bickerdike.

"They threw glasses at Nico" / "The annoying thing" / "No one else could have" Needs, K. (1978) "Nico in London: Rare 1978 Interview," *Zigzag*, June.

"who had never been to a Punk concert" / "If I had a machine gun" Thompson (2002).

"I stood on the stage at Hemel Hempstead" Peter Clarke interview.

"It was probably one of the best line-ups" Interview of Stephen Mallinder by Jennifer Otter Bickerdike.

"We went to meet her at the Marquee" Interview of Cosey Fanni Tutti by Jennifer Otter Bickerdike.

"I winced because that meant I'd have to pay" / "She was really shocked" Graf-Ulbrich, L. (2015) *Nico—In the Shadow of the Moon Goddess.* Luxembourg: CreateSpace Independent Publishing Platform.

"we got backstage there was Nico!" Wrenn, M. (1991) *Andy Warhol in His Own Words.* New York: Omnibus Press.

"The area around the CBGB was not the finest" / "She tried with both hands" / "No one has told me about two shows" / "The audience welcomed her" / "She screamed" Graf-Ulbrich (2015).

"A memorable gig" Interview of Joe Bidewell by Jennifer Otter Bickerdike.

"She asked me why I had not" / "In addition to accompanying" / "The whole thing was on a budget" / "Drinking was one of her addictions" / "The hard part [of the tour]" Interview of Jim Tisdall by Jennifer Otter Bickerdike.

"I was at the Mabuhay Gardens" McCain, G. and McNeil, L. (1997) *Please Kill Me: The Uncensored Oral History of Punk*. London: Abacus.

"This film is very special" Needs, K. (1978) "Nico in London: Rare 1978 Interview," *Zigzag*, June.

"At the top of a neo-classical building" "*Le Bleu des origines*—User Reviews: Hypnotic Study of Nico and Zouzou" (n.d.) Available at https://www. imdb.com/title/tt0077242. Accessed August 12, 2019.

"He's being very good to himself" Dadomo, G. (1978) "Nico," *Sounds*, April 28. Available at https://www.rocksbackpages.com/Library/Article/ nico. Accessed August 12, 2019.

"I was busy doing my homework" / "I was beginning to be frightened" / "This bewitchment helped" / "I do not remember the sequences" Ari (2001) *L'Amour n'oublie jamais* ("Love Never Forgets"). Pauvert: Departemente de la Librairie Artheme Fayard. Translated for this project into English.

"She gave him heroin" / "Nico had told me that she got Ari hooked" *Nico: Icon* (1995) Directed by Susanne Ofteringer. Available on youtube.com. Viewed November 10, 2018.

Chapter 35

"The heroin was the reveler" / "We were a magical" Ari (2001) *L'Amour n'oublie jamais* ("Love Never Forgets"). Pauvert: Departemente de la Librairie Artheme Fayard. Translated for this project into English.

"I'm only going by what Nico said" / "She was a very...playful person"/ "I was sitting in the kitchen" / "When I knew her" / "The real Nico?" / "She didn't ever use her own name"/ "Every day in Ladbroke Grove" / "Her English was good" / "One time, Lou Reed came to stay" Interview of Robert King by Jennifer Otter Bickerdike.

"rarely showed her emotions" Ari (2001).

"Of course I have new songs" / "I've been waiting to put new songs" Dadomo, G. (1978) "Nico," *Sounds*, April 28. Available at https://www. rocksbackpages.com/Library/Article/nico. Accessed August 12, 2019.

"I have just enough for an album" Needs, K. (1978) "Nico in London: Rare 1978 Interview," *Zigzag*, June.

"I've been sort of disappearing" Thompson, D. (1989) *Beyond the "Velvet Underground."* London: Omnibus.

"I've signed it in my head" Dadomo (1978).

"It was really boring" / "I always wanted to sing" / "Lou was the boss" / "as a tribute to Lou" / "not quite so destructive" / "Cale and a few other people" Thompson (1989).

"My mother showed some distrust" Ari (2001).

"was the capital of music" / "There was quite a lot of heroin" / "Nico, who was in her forties" / "I remember Nico being very friendly"/ "was such a mess" / "You never knew what Nico" / "secretive" / "Nico did her vocals" / "Sixx had released an album" / "It was all junkie business" / "Nico didn't like it" / "it had already been out" / "career was broken" / "It was all pretty heavy"/ "I went backstage" Interview of Bruno Blum by Jennifer Otter Bickerdike.

"If you harken back" / "There was a tall woman" / "She was forever telling stories"/ "She came with a French/Vietnamese woman" / "I said that I would pay" / "Nico was very overweight"/ "She kept giving excuses" / Quilichini started putting together"/ "I made it totally clear" / "The £2,000 sounds right" / "I picked the album cover shot" / "Aaron, I need some money" / "From Nico's standpoint" / "They stitched together" Interview of Aaron Sixx by Jennifer Otter Bickerdike.

"Duget and Quilichini were driving" Aaron Sixx interview.

Chapter 36

"Rip were based in Ladbroke Grove" Interview of Phil Jones by Jennifer Otter Bickerdike.

"I think Alan is written out" / "Alan was one of the founders" Interview of Phil Rainford by Jennifer Otter Bickerdike.

"Alan was one of the guys" Interview of Aaron Sixx by Jennifer Otter Bickerdike.

"He was like your cartoon" Phil Rainford interview.

"The Rough Trade agency" Interview of James Young by Jennifer Otter Bickerdike.

"We were booking artists" Interview of Nigel Bagley by Jennifer Otter Bickerdike.

"her arms were horrible" Phil Jones interview.

"She had this chap in tow" Phil Rainford interview.

"I thought she was quite charming" *Nico: Icon* (1995) Directed by Susanne Ofteringer. Available on youtube.com. Viewed November 10, 2018.

"At that first Rafters gig" Phil Jones interview.

"I met her for the first time" Interview of Michel Wadada by Jennifer Otter Bickerdike.

"I was about sixteen when I met Mark" / "We went into Rafters" Interview of Una Baines by Jennifer Otter Bickerdike.

"Nico was really down and out" James Young interview.

"Everybody had heard of her" Phil Jones interview.

"I took them [Nico and King] back to the hotel" / "By this time, Nico'd moved" Phil Rainford interview.

"I found her somewhere to live" Interview of Alan Wise by Jennifer Otter Bickerdike.

"She had no money" Phil Rainford interview.

"the past: Berlin, the war" *Nico: Icon* (1995) Directed by Susanne Ofteringer. Available on youtube.com. Viewed November 10, 2018.

"I spoke to Andrew Loog Oldham" Brine, J. and Marnell, C. (2017) "Niconomicon: A Conversation with Lutz Graf-Ulbrich." Available at https://www.3ammagazine.com/3am/niconomicon-conversation-lutz-graf-ulbrich-nico. Accessed August 21, 2020.

"She needed to perform" Phil Jones interview.

"He was absolutely besotted" James Young interview.

Chapter 37

"The first time I heard the Velvet Underground" / "I thought she was stunningly beautiful" / "She'd previously met Peter" / "She comes in with her black robes" / "She looked somewhat haggard" / "When we did that first gig in Manchester" / "She once gave me a list" / "The lasting legacy is her music" Interview of David J. Haskins by Jennifer Otter Bickerdike.

Chapter 38

"Alan gave me a call" / "I would speak to Alan" Interview of Aaron Sixx by Jennifer Otter Bickerdike.

"We hooked her up with musicians" Interview of Phil Jones by Jennifer Otter Bickerdike.

"period of perceived disintegration" Young, J. (1992) *Nico: Songs They Never Play on the Radio*. London: Bloomsbury.

"She was a very modest person" / "I lived in Holland at the time" Interview of Barbara Wilkin by Jennifer Otter Bickerdike.

"beautiful, powerful and dark" / "I was enraptured" / "someone had stolen her diary" Interview of Stella Grundy by Jennifer Otter Bickerdike.

"I was enormously comforted" / "a tumbler half-filled with brandy" / "When you sing a high note" Goddard, S. (2009) *Mozipedia: The Encyclopaedia of Morrissey and the Smiths*. Cornwall: Random House.

"We realized what an icon she was" Phil Jones interview.

"I think a lot of the people" Interview of Una Baines by Jennifer Otter Bickerdike.

"She used to say all the time" / "She was a bit of a leech" Phil Jones interview.

"She met a few people" Barbara Wilkin interview.

"I saw her being searched by police" Interview of Richard Hector-Jones by Jennifer Otter Bickerdike.

"People just accept you for who you are" / "If they [people approaching her] or at interviews" Interview of James Young by Jennifer Otter Bickerdike.

"I'd always been a fan of the Velvet Underground" / "When I was doing the solo gig" Interview of "Spider" Mike King by Jennifer Otter Bickerdike.

"I went up to a rehearsal" Interview of Graham Dowdall by Jennifer Otter Bickerdike.

"I think she was aware that there was a scene" Interview of Martin Bramah by Jennifer Otter Bickerdike.

Chapter 39

"There was a knock at my door" / "Nico, yeah" *Nico: Icon* (1995) Directed by Susanne Ofteringer. Available on youtube.com. Viewed November 10, 2018.

"I said, 'What's going on?'" / "It was the end of my academic life" *Nico: Icon* (1995).

"a swing jazz bebop drummer" Young, J. (1992) *Nico: Songs They Never Play on the Radio*. London: Bloomsbury.

"You did have to force her to be creative" Interview of Phil Rainford by Jennifer Otter Bickerdike.

"[I decided to write the book about Nico] for money" *Nico: Icon* (1995).

"The thing about myths" Phil Rainford interview.

"There was a sense of a really solid identity" Interview of James Young by Jennifer Otter Bickerdike.

"very funny...You could have a real laugh" Interview of Phil Jones by Jennifer Otter Bickerdike.

"She had few clothes" Phil Rainford interview.

"Everything was in a big leather holdall" Interview of Spider Mike King by Jennifer Otter Bickerdike.

"As I got to know her over the years" / "You had to force her to go and socialize" Phil Rainford interview.

"We went to her house" / "She never wore heels" Phil Jones interview.

"She was almost proud that her teeth were rotten" James Young interview.

"shocked to see Nico's teeth" Woronov, M. (2013) *Swimming Underground: My Time at Andy Warhol's Factory*. Los Angeles: Montaldo Publishing.

"I don't think she'd have labeled herself a feminist" Interview of Una Baines by Jennifer Otter Bickerdike.

"She concluded that taking heroin" / "She was not a sexual being" James Young interview.

"All the time I knew her" / "We got a certain amount of heroin" / "She'd forget the words" / "In the afternoon before we played" Spider Mike King interview.

"When we were on the road" Interview of Martin Bramah by Jennifer Otter Bickerdike.

"I'd been thrown in the deep end" Phil Rainford interview.

"We had an experience going through customs" Una Baines interview.

"She'd write bits of poems on a fag packet" Phil Rainford interview.

Chapter 40

"Alan Wise did a pretty good job" *Being Nico* (2018) WDR 3 Westdeutscher Rundfunk, October 14.

"She understood she was doing something" Interview of Phil Jones by Jennifer Otter Bickerdike.

"We'd become her backing band" "When it come [KB came?] to the music" Interview of Una Baines by Jennifer Otter Bickerdike.

"To become emotionally close" / "I had no real understanding" Interview of James Young by Jennifer Otter Bickerdike.

"Her gigs were very unusual" / "She used to use it as an ashtray" Interview of Michael Wadada by Jennifer Otter Bickerdike.

"Could I trust Nico?" / "The van was parked near a tree" James Young interview.

"We were very poor" Ari (2001) *L'Amour n'oublie jamais* ("Love Never Forgets"). Pauvert: Departemente de la Librairie Artheme Fayard. Translated for this project into English.

"We went to London" Una Baines interview.

"When I joined, it was like being recruited" James Young interview.

"People would go to the gigs" / "There was a time when Nico was in the back" Interview of Spider Mike King by Jennifer Otter Bickerdike.

"Sometimes I used to try and gauge the temperature" Interview of Phil Rainford by Jennifer Otter Bickerdike.

"The fascists were throwing coins" Spider Mike King interview.

"She was at one end of this room" / "We used to sing together quite a lot" Phil Rainford interview.

"In Naples I was drinking late" Spider Mike King interview.

"The regret is that she didn't make more music" Simpson, D. (2019) "Nico in Manchester: 'She Loved the Architecture—and the Heroin,'" *Guardian*, July 5. Available at https://www.theguardian.com/music/2019/jul/05/nico-in-manchester-she-loved-the-architecture-and-the-heroin. Accessed August 26, 2019.

"She was perceived as a strong female artist" / "She could never work with" Interview of Stephen Mallinder by Jennifer Otter Bickerdike.

"Had I more money, I would have more power" Nico (2001) *Cible mouvante. Chansons, poèmes, journal.* Annecy: Pauvert.

"Nico was in a man's world" Interview of Barbara Wilkin by Jennifer Otter Bickerdike.

"People see Nico, the ice queen" Interview of Graham Dowdall by Jennifer Otter Bickerdike.

"She had a pool of musicians" Barbara Wilkin interview.

"I mean that there was something unbearably pathetic" / "One by one, the motley company" Rose, C. (1983) "Nico: When the Peroxide Fades," *New Music Express*, January 29. Available at https://www.rocksbackpages.com/Library/Article/nico-when-the-peroxide-fades/. Accessed August 29, 2019.

"There were many gigs we were at" Barbara Wilkin interview.

"I think she felt that her conspicuous addiction" / "It is incorrect to say"
/ "She would embellish the truth" / "I can think of lots of examples"
Graham Dowdall interview.

Chapter 41

"I was living in St. Paul's Road" / "At the time, my children's father"/ "Over
the next few weeks" / "She didn't like women" / "I think she liked me
because she knew"/ "I went into Manchester city center" / "I remember
how badly treated she was too" / "I think sometimes she just craved"
Interview of Jane Goldstraw by Jennifer Otter Bickerdike.

"Alan had a very, very serious turn" / "We tried, Nico and me, to see them"
Interview of Barbara Wilkin by Jennifer Otter Bickerdike.

Chapter 42

"If I was writing my book" / "I think Alan got the flat here" / "A room was
rented to us" / "In those days, it was showing" / "I remember the bloody
bedsheets" / "She'd never show any skin" Interview of John Torjusson by
Jennifer Otter Bickerdike.

"She didn't like to bathe too often" Interview of Barbara Wilkin by Jennifer
Otter Bickerdike.

"I think that her appearance was a way" Interview of James Young by
Jennifer Otter Bickerdike.

"Her relationship to her own beauty is so conflicted" Interview of Danny
Fields by Jennifer Otter Bickerdike.

"Nico looked bad at times" / "would always turn up" / "Alan [Wise] lived
downstairs" Barbara Wilkin interview.

"Whenever you went to her room" James Young interview.

"We sometimes used to go to the pub" Barbara Wilkin interview.

"I don't think she had a big racist philosophy" John Torjusson interview.

"I think it's become part of the legend" Interview of Graham Dowdall by
Jennifer Otter Bickerdike.

"She would go to the separate Greek shop" / "Slimming pills, which are
basically speed"/"She would always say" Barbara Wilkin interview.

"I think the people around her amused her" James Young interview.

"I think she was a bit contemptuous" John Torjusson interview.

"used to complain about Al's smells" James Young interview.

"Al worshipped Nico" Graham Dowdall interview.

"I remember him coming up the stairs" John Torjusson interview.

"very affectionate" James Young interview.

"two-fifths of the Velvet Underground" Interview of John Cooper Clarke by Jennifer Otter Bickerdike.

"She was so proud of having Ari" Barbara Wilkin interview.

"I think Ari was a very lost kind of person" John Torjusson interview.

"She had a strong sense of self" James Young interview.

"I think she really had the measure of people" Interview of Una Baines by Jennifer Otter Bickerdike.

"She was an intelligent woman" James Young interview.

"Nico used to hang around the Peace Eye" Interview of Ed Sanders by Jennifer Otter Bickerdike.

"not a very nice time" Barbara Wilkin interview.

"I played music all the time" John Torjusson interview.

"So Nico wasn't having sex" Graham Dowdall interview.

"There was no big ceremony" Interview of Phil Rainford by Jennifer Otter Bickerdike.

"She didn't really socialize with the Manchester glitterati" Simpson, D. (2019) "Nico in Manchester: 'She Loved the Architecture—and the Heroin,'" *Guardian*, July 5. Available at https://www.theguardian.com/music/2019/jul/05/nico-in-manchester-she-loved-the-architecture-and-the-heroin. Accessed August 26, 2019.

"I used to do the sound for the Stockholm Monsters" / "As a musician, to watch Nico" / "I remember she did a tour of eastern Europe" / "She couldn't pay for a session once" Interview of Peter Hook by Jennifer Otter Bickerdike.

Chapter 43

"didn't really want to be involved" / "Alan told me that Beggars wanted to do something" Interview of Aaron Sixx by Jennifer Otter Bickerdike.

"John Cale was actually worse than Nico" / "She was in a much better place" / "He had this production genius" / "The core Faction was me and Jim" Interview of Graham Dowdall by Jennifer Otter Bickerdike.

"It was quite a thrill to unexpectedly" Interview of Peter Saville by Jennifer

Otter Bickerdike.

"She might be pushing 50" "Nico: Shrink Rap" (1985) *Melody Maker*, July.

"I think Cale just appreciated her art" Interview of Mark Lanegan by Jennifer Otter Bickerdike.

"She raises a hand to her face" Watson, D. (1985) "Nico: 'Watch Out, the World's Behind You,'" *New Musical Express*, August 3.

"I've not quite arrived yet"/ "Where I live right now reminds me of Berlin" NZ Interview with Nico (1985). Available at https://www.youtube.com/watch?v=MOeUBF78gM&list=RDQMyDcbQVPSxg8&start_radio=1. Accessed August 30, 2019.

"The real reason for my Residence here" Nico (2001) *Cible mouvante. Chansons, poèmes, journal*. Annecy: Pauvert.

"She ended up in squalor" BBC Inside Out (2008) *Nico Icon Play*. Available at https://www.youtube.com/watch?v=T_Kr9wjTUmc&t=169s. Accessed July 15, 2020.

"It was a different time" Interview of Phil Jones by Jennifer Otter Bickerdike.

"I remember talking to Alan" Interview of Aaron Sixx by Jennifer Otter Bickerdike.

"She decided to stop, and to get on the methadone" *Nico: Icon* (1995). Directed by Susanne Ofteringer. Available on youtube.com. Viewed November 10, 2018.

"She just said she'd had enough" Interview of Jane Goldstraw by Jennifer Otter Bickerdike.

"Methadone is a horrible drug" / "Nico clean? You kidding?" Interview of James Young by Jennifer Otter Bickerdike.

"She preferred to smoke hashish" Interview of Barbara Wilkin by Jennifer Otter Bickerdike.

"They're cutting the trees down in the Garden" / "As sure as it had to be today" / "Starting Monday, I will get my medication" / "Opening a new Bank account" / "Tuesday morning, afternoon" / "When a man from the council" / "My superstition being justified" / "What the hell am I going to sit on" / "Oh yes, I feel very privileged" / "A Newspaperman doesn't" / "Human nature is clumsy" / "Somehow I never managed" Nico (2001).

"We were talking about death" Young, J. (1992) *Nico: Songs They Never Play on the Radio*. London: Bloomsbury.

"The moment is mine" Nico (2001).

Chapter 44

"It frightens me how much we are alike" / "Monday morning, today" Nico (2001) *Cible mouvante. Chansons, poèmes, journal.* Annecy: Pauvert.

"She never ceased writing letters" Ari (2001) *L'Amour n'oublie jamais* ("Love Never Forgets"). Pauvert: Departemente de la Librairie Artheme Fayard. Translated for this project into English.

"Possibly the only rumor about Nico" *Being Nico* (2018) WDR 3 Westdeutscher Rundfunk, October 14.

"My Management doesn't do me justice" / "When they say, that it's time" Nico (2001).

"Bondi 17 February 1986" Graf-Ulbrich, L. (2015) *Nico—In the Shadow of the Moon Goddess.* Luxembourg: CreateSpace Independent Publishing Platform.

"The End of the month" / "But nothing can give me a bad reputation" Nico (2001).

"At the end of 1986, I left [the Faction]" Interview of James Young by Jennifer Otter Bickerdike.

"everything just looks right" Warhol, A. (2014) *The Andy Warhol Diaries*, edited by Pat Hackett. Hachette: New York.

"I'd hardly seen her" Young, J. (1992) *Nico: Songs They Never Play on the Radio.* London: Bloomsbury.

"In exactly three months and four days" / "It's late and I find it hard to write" / "Writing this book" / "All those young Musicians" / "Tour is starting in ten days" Nico (2001).

"She was tired of the endless tours" James Young interview.

"There weren't many people there" Interview of Andy by Jennifer Otter Bickerdike.

"Code of Honor" / "The sound of the life-support machines" / "I can feel my nerves" / "Today is my third day here" / "In the morning Ari's Psychiatrist" / "At this place in Paris" / "Wherever I may wind up" Nico (2001).

Chapter 45

"A study of the alienated people" "Let's Kiss and Say Goodbye" (1988) Available at https://www.imdb.com/title/tt0133397/?ref_=nm_flmg_

act_1. Accessed December 17, 2020.

"Nico was a mysterious figure" / "I was so nervous to contact her" Turner, L. (2012) "Interview: Marc Almond on *Desertshore*," *The Quietus*, November 19. Available at https://thequietus.com/articles/10721-marc-almond-desertshore-interview. Accessed September 3, 2019.

"The last time I put her on" Harrison, I. (2018) "Nico's Last Decade," *Mojo*, September.

"Nico didn't like the idea" Young, J. (1992) *Nico: Songs They Never Play on the Radio*. London: Bloomsbury.

"Looking back, I think it was" Interview of James Young by Jennifer Otter Bickerdike.

"Compared with her last tour of Japan" Young (1992).

"the Moon" / "When I met her in her last years" / "There was a little stage" Graf-Ulbrich, L. (2015) *Nico—In the Shadow of the Moon Goddess*. Luxembourg: CreateSpace Independent Publishing Platform.

"Nico's new positivism" Young (1992).

"The gig in Berlin was fantastic!" Interview of Graham Dowdall by Jennifer Otter Bickerdike.

"really fired up" / "At the last concert, Nico kept saying" James Young interview.

"She counted the money and was happy" Graf-Ulbrich (2015).

"She really flipped out" https://www.3ammagazine.com/3am/niconomicon-conversation-lutz-graf-ulbrich-nico. Accessed August 21, 2020.

"I still think that I am rather apt" Nico (2001) *Cible mouvante. Chansons, poèmes, journal*. Annecy: Pauvert.

"She was actually looking really well" Interview of Jane Goldstraw by Jennifer Otter Bickerdike.

"We finally got her royalties for her" Interview of Phil Jones by Jennifer Otter Bickerdike.

"I think Ibiza meant for Nico a refuge" / "[She] was definitely not a party animal" Donlon, H. (2017) *Shadows Across the Moon: Outlaws, Freaks, Shamans and the Making of Ibiza Clubland*.

Chapter 46

"I'm flying to Ibiza" Witts, R. (1993) *Nico: The Life and Lies of an Icon*. London: Virgin Books.

"Yes. Death for example" *Being Nico* (2018) WDR 3 Westdeutscher Rundfunk, October 14.

"One is only once in a lifetime" Nico (2001) *Cible mouvante. Chansons, poèmes, journal.* Annecy: Pauvert.

"Warm, naive again" Ari (2001) *L'Amour n'oublie jamais* ("Love Never Forgets"). Pauvert: Departemente de la Librairie Artheme Fayard. Translated for this project into English.

"Toward the end, she wanted to work" https://ninaantoniaauthor.com/tag/alan-wise/. Accessed March 31, 2021.

"She wanted to focus on writing" / "I had salmonella and she took care of me" Ari (2001).

"We'd heard Nico was on the island" Interview of Peter Hook by Jennifer Otter Bickerdike.

"See you later, darling" / "The night of the 18th, as she wasn't back yet" / "The next morning, no Nico" Ari (2001).

"'Has someone been brought in?'" Interview of Clive Crocker by Jennifer Otter Bickerdike.

"Once there, the doctor" Ari (2001).

"They said, 'She was in here.'" Clive Crocker interview.

"Manolo entered the room" Ari (2001).

"It was a terrible sight" Clive Crocker interview.

"headlines of the newspapers everywhere" / "When I entered, I felt strange" / "The terrible look on her face" Graf-Ulbrich, L. (2015) *Nico—In the Shadow of the Moon Goddess.* Luxembourg: CreateSpace Independent Publishing Platform.

"We walked on past the giant elevated clock" Donlon, H. (2017) *Shadows Across the Moon: Outlaws, Freaks, Shamans and the Making of Ibiza Clubland.*

"refused to deal with her" Young, J. (1992) *Nico: Songs They Never Play on the Radio.* London: Bloomsbury.

"The sun. And that was what killed her" https://www.3ammagazine.com/3am/niconomicon-conversation-lutz-graf-ulbrich-nico. Accessed August 21, 2020.

"She was 49, but it was more a miracle" Harrison, I. (2018) "Nico's Last Decade," *Mojo*, September.

"Nico died from not having health insurance" McCain, G. and McNeil, L. (1997) *Please Kill Me: The Uncensored Oral History of Punk.* London: Abacus.

"She didn't even reach this thing" Interview of Andrew Loog Oldham by

Jennifer Otter Bickerdike. August 10, 2018.

"It's ironic, given her inclination" / "To survive all those years" Witts, R. (1993) *Nico: The Life and Lies of an Icon*. London: Virgin Books.

"I always regret that" Peter Hook interview.

"I feel sure it could have been prevented" Interview of James Young by Jennifer Otter Bickerdike.

"A fortnight before her death" Ari (2001).

"She was going through her memories" /"It's the sun," *Nico: Icon* (1995) Directed by Susanne Ofteringer. Available on youtube.com. Viewed November 10, 2018.

"Last year I was talking to Ari" Donlon (2017).

Chapter 47

"Twen: What are you especially proud of?" Sanders, E. (1969) "Nico, the Cologne Girl in the U.S. Underground," *Twen*, August.

"Her grave is impossible to find" Interview of Danny Fields by Jennifer Otter Bickerdike.

"Lutz brought us the news of her death" Interview of Helma Wolff by Christian Biadacz.

"When I found out, I thought" Interview of Barbara Wilkin by Jennifer Otter Bickerdike.

"I remember being really, really sad" Interview of Graham Dowdall by Jennifer Otter Bickerdike.

"Alan informed all of those New York people" Interview of Phil Rainford by Jennifer Otter Bickerdike.

"None of those big names were there" Barbara Wilkin interview.

"a shy, rumpled little guy" Young, J. (1992) *Nico: Songs They Never Play on the Radio*. London: Bloomsbury.

"It is convenient now for them to be friends" Phil Rainford interview.

"Everyone was concerned about the unstable Ari" Graf-Ulbrich, L. (2015) *Nico—In the Shadow of the Moon Goddess*. Luxembourg: CreateSpace Independent Publishing Platform.

"When I got my mum's royalties" / Back in New York, I went out of my mind" / "My mother was accused of 'poisoning' the life" Ari (2001) *L'Amour n'oublie jamais* ("Love Never Forgets"). Pauvert: Departemente de la Librairie Artheme Fayard. Translated for this project into English.

"For me, she was a very good mother" Bernède, S. (2001) "Ari: The Whole Portrait of Alain Delon," *La Dépêche.* Available at https://translate.googleusercontent.com/ translate_c?depth=1&hl=en&prev=search&pto=aue&rurl=translate. google.com&sl=fr&sp=nmt4&u=https://www.ladepeche.fr/ article/2001/04/22/224369-ari-tout-le-portrait-d-alain-

Epilogue

"Not everyone bought their album" The Velvet Underground: Rock and Roll Hall of Fame Induction. Available at https://www.rockhall.com/ inductees/velvet-underground. Accessed November 6, 2019.

"drug career" Bos, C. (2017) "Cologne Has No Place for Nico." Available at https://www.ksta.de/kultur/kolumne-ueber-den-plattenrand-koeln-hat-fuer-nico-keinen-platz-29289296. Accessed July 15, 2020.

LIST OF PLATES

Plate section 1

Page 1: Nico's birth details as registered on her mother's registration card, or *Meldekarte*. Image courtesy of the author.

Page 2 (top): The Kinderheim Sülz orphanage. Image courtesy of the author.

Page 2 (bottom): A child walking through the rubble in Berlin, 1945. Photograph by ullstein bild via Getty Images.

Page 3: Nico posing in 1956. Photograph by ullstein bild via Getty Images.

Page 4 (top): Andy Warhol kneels on the ground with Ari, New York, 1966. Photograph by Fred W. McDarrah/Getty Images.

Page 4 (bottom): Nico with Irving Blum and Andy Warhol in Los Angeles, 1966. Photograph by Steve Schapiro/Corbis via Getty Images.

Page 5: Typewritten notes for a television performance of "No One Is There," 1968. Image courtesy of Danny Fields's personal archive.

Pages 6–7: Contact sheet taken in the London Docklands in summer 1965. Image courtesy of the Peter Whitehead archive.

Page 8 (top): Nico with members of the Velvet Underground in Los Angeles, 1966. Photograph by Steve Schapiro/Corbis via Getty Images.

Page 8 (bottom): Nico performs at Steve Paul's nightclub in New York, 1967. Photograph by Fred W. McDarrah/Getty Images.

Plate section 2

Page 1 (top): Nico appears on *Ready, Steady, Go!* in 1965. Photograph by Michael Ochs Archives/Getty Images.

Page 1 (bottom): Nico with Brian Jones at the Monterey International Pop Festival, 1967. Photograph by Fotos International/Getty Images.

Page 2 (top): Nico with Tom Wilson at ABC studios in New York, 1967. Photograph by PoPsie Randolph/Michael Ochs Archives/Getty Images.

Page 2 (bottom): Nico poses for a portrait session, around 1967. Photograph by Michael Ochs Archives/Getty Images.

Page 3 (top): Nico at the Dom in New York, 1967. Photograph by Fred W. McDarrah/Getty Images.

Page 3 (bottom): Nico in the garden behind the Portobello Hotel in London, 1974. Photograph courtesy of Danny Fields's personal archive.

Page 4 (top): Nico performing at the Mabuhay Gardens in San Francisco, 1977. Photograph by Ruby Ray/Getty Images.

Page 4 (bottom): The house on Effra Road where Nico lived in the 1980s. Image courtesy of the author.

Page 5: Nico in 1985. Photograph by Peter Noble/Redferns.

Page 6 (top): The Foresters pub in Manchester. Image courtesy of the author.

Page 6 (bottom): Nico's grave marked on the cemetery map where she is buried in Berlin. Image courtesy of Danny Fields.

Page 7: Two photographs of Nico's grave in the Grunewald Forest cemetery in Berlin. Images courtesy of Danny Fields.

Page 8: Mural of Nico near Piccadilly Station in Manchester. Image courtesy of the author.